MOUNT UP!

One Cavalryman's World War II Diary:
Europe & Beyond

J. F. Gough

Copyright © 2012 Jerome F. Gough
All rights reserved.
ISBN: 9781693380372

DEDICATION

To his grandchildren:
Judith, Trey, Conor, Joel, Katie, Tyler, Merril, and Spencer

Table of Contents

INTRODUCTION 7
PROLOGUE 9
1. THE EARLY YEARS 18
2. ALL FOR ONE, ONE FOR ALL 31
3. GOT LEAVE, GOT MARRIED, GOT BUSTED 55
4. OFF TO WAR: FIRST STOP, BRITAIN 64
5. ORGANIZATION & EQUIPMENT OF 71
THE 15TH CAVALRY GROUP 71
6. EARLY NORMANDY HEROICS 82
7. FINAL PRE-COMBAT PREPARATION 91
8. U.S. ARMY TANKS, GERMAN PANZERS: EQUIPMENT, ORGANIZATION & MORE 99
9. ON THE CONTINENT AT LAST 114
10. COMBAT ON THE BRITTANY PENINSULA 129
11. FIGHTING ON THE CROZON PENINSULA 159
12. DEFENSIVE SCREENING IN HOLLAND 175
13. THE SIEGFRIED LINE & ROER PLAIN 192
14. TROUBLE IN THE ARDENNES 217
15. INTO THE RHINELAND 229
16. ACROSS THE RHINE & INTO GERMANY'S RUHR VALLEY 251
17. THE WAR ENDS IN EUROPE 269
18. WORLD WAR II COMES TO AN END 287
19. HOMEWARD BOUND 295
20. THE POSTWAR YEARS 303
EPILOGUE 309
    AUTHOR'S NOTE 321
APPENDIX 322
    SELECT BIBLIOGRAPHY 326

PUBLISHED WORKS 327
NEWSPAPERS 338
PERIODICALS 339
WEBSITES OF INTEREST 341
LIST OF MAPS 342
ACKNOWLEDGEMENTS 343
ABOUT THE AUTHOR 345

INTRODUCTION

Only a few months before his death in 1996, it occurred to me how little I knew of my father's past. On that occasion, we came to an understanding of sorts as he approached me with a surprising request.

We were alone at his home one hot South Carolina afternoon with the air conditioning off at his insistence. It was so humid inside that the wallpaper was peeling from the walls. I had taken time off from work to check on him and we were sorting his mail, separating bills and other important items from the unsolicited matter that had accumulated over time. That was no easy task since as he had abundant physical problems and his mental status had begun to wane due to significant memory loss. On his dining room table was a mountain of unopened envelopes and other neglected junk mail. The pile was so high that much of it had cascaded onto the floor into several heaps.

At one point during that arduous process, he went to his bedroom, supposedly to lie down and take a rest, but he soon reemerged with a cardboard shoebox tucked under his arm. He asked me to open it and I discovered a cache of personal papers and documents, including a trove of several numbered, hand-written, pocketsize notebooks. I was taken aback immediately, as it was extremely unusual to see him teary eyed. After he handed the material over to me, I noticed that it related mostly to his military service, before, during, and after the Second World War. To the best of my knowledge, he had never shown it to anyone else. For both of us, it was a rare emotional moment, as we knew he had little time left on this Earth, and he wanted that information preserved for posterity.

In writing this biographical narrative, my goal was to use Dad's notes and World War II pocket diary entries to gain a better understanding of the man behind the mask he showed us in life. In the process, I came to appreciate the depth of the challenges he and his peers experienced, as they grew to adulthood in a very tumultuous America.

As I begin, let me assert that this work is in no way meant to disparage my late father, neither is it hagiography. Rather, it was my intent to come to an understanding of the man and to record his earnest efforts to become a productive American citizen who rose above the modest circumstances of his birth. With the assistance of our kind and unselfish mother, he did so and went on to provide a relatively pleasant life for my siblings and me. For that gift, we are eternally grateful.

Both parents are gone now, and I am acutely aware that superannuation is upon me. Therefore, I put aside my golf sticks temporarily and forsake all further procrastination so that I may get on with the task to follow his written path, appended with subjective analysis and memories of my own. I do this because I believe it is important for my family now, and for the enlightenment of kindred generations. Also, duty calls, Dad asked me to do this and I promised him I would.

PROLOGUE

For as long as I can remember, my father was something of a puzzle. In the emotional desert that was our home, he could be pleasant on occasion, but most of the time he would amuse himself by verbally provoking one or more members of our household. My reaction was to walk away or undertake a self-defeating strategy of passive-aggressive protest; on occasion, I did a little bit of both. On the other hand, Mom had to endure his antics, as it was simply not in her nature to be confrontational. Instead, to the end of her days she maintained that he was "her cross to bear."

While socializing outside our household, he was gregarious and friendly, but at home the surface charm evaporated. There he was generally short-tempered and inflexible. To make matters worse, he was most often inaccessible, and his attitude around the family was mainly that of detachment.

Growing older, my connection with him became much more complicated. We quarreled over the years until finally, around the time of my mother's agonizing fight with terminal cancer, our relationship cratered due to his apparent indifference to her emotional needs. Consequently, after her death I moved on with my life, and he did likewise.

As time went on, I entertained the thought that his eleven-month military service during World War II on the European continent may have had something to do with his frame of mind. By no means was he a combat hero, but like so many others of his generation, he played a role in the global conflagration. It is also quite possible that other significant factors entered into the mix, as he suffered the loss of his mother at an early age and his family endured hardship in the Great Depression, the worldwide, economic decline of the 1930s. Also, highly germane to this discussion is the fact that shortly after returning from war he obtained employment with the federal government and worked for three decades at a secret U.S. signals intelligence–gathering agency, the National Security Agency (NSA). In that line of work, he became acquainted with many disturbing global developments that occurred during the uneasy post–World War II era.

Many Americans in Dad's generation knew of the famous 1946 "Iron Curtain" speech by Sir Winston S. Churchill. By then, he was no longer Britain's first minister to the King of England[1] yet he warned of the danger of totalitarianism and expressed the view that no one knew "what Soviet Russia and its Communist international organization" intended with "their proselytizing tendencies." In his famous address, delivered at Westminster College in Fulton, Missouri, he stated: "From Stettin in the Baltic to Trieste in the Adriatic, an iron curtain has descended across" the European Continent.[2]

Similarly, George Orwell, author of the novel *1984*, spent the immediate postwar period explaining the "great dangers" that remained following victory over Fascism. To this day, it is believed that Orwell's warning of "the curtain's shadow lengthening westward" provided the name for what we have come to know as the "Cold War."[3]

As it turned out, within only a few days after the Japanese surrender in 1945, Soviet Premier Joseph Stalin secretly ordered the development of a nuclear weapons program. Global tensions continued in early 1948, as homegrown communists, assisted by the Soviet Army, took over Czechoslovakia.

Shortly thereafter, in 1949, the Soviet Union acquired its first atomic weapon. By the mid-to-late 1950s, they gained possession of thermonuclear technology[4] and intercontinental ballistic missiles. By then the U.S. and its Western Allies were in deadlock with the Soviets over promises made at the Yalta Conference concerning Eastern Europe. Relations deteriorated

---

[1] In an election held only a few days before the Allies gained final victory over Japan, Clement Attlee became Britain's new prime minister.
[2] William Manchester and Paul Reid, *The Last Lion, Winston Spencer Churchill: Defender of the Realm, 1940-1965* (New York: Little, Brown and Co., 2012), 960.
[3] Thomas E. Ricks, *Churchill & Orwell: The Fight for Freedom* (New York: Penguin Press, 2017), 222-223, 236.
[4] The U.S. exploded its first hydrogen bomb in November 1952 on Eniwetok Atoll in the Pacific Ocean; it was 500 times more powerful than the bomb dropped on Hiroshima. William I. Hitchcock, *The Age of Eisenhower: America and the World in the 1950s* (New York: Simon & Schuster, 2018), 94 and 114.

further, as the Soviets continued their expansionist policies by gobbling up satellite states and preventing democratic national elections.

Matters worsened when Mao Zedong's communist forces defeated the Chinese Nationalists in late 1949, creating the People's Republic of China (PRC). After that, the communists began to exploit other parts of the world, and the U.S. and Great Britain found themselves cold war adversaries with the Soviets and the newly created PRC.[1]

Within a few months, tensions escalated sharply when fighting erupted in June 1950 on the Korean Peninsula. There United Nations (UN) and U.S. military forces battled Soviet-supported North Korean and PRC troops[2] to prevent a takeover of noncommunist South Korea. That event produced the first live-fire action of the Cold War, prompting fear of a third world war.[3] Unease concerning a broadening of that armed conflict lessened after President Harry S. Truman relieved Gen. Douglas MacArthur of command of all U.S. and UN military forces in early April 1951.[4]

Following Stalin's death in 1953, it was hoped that global unrest might lessen, but that proved illusory, as in 1956 Soviet Army troops brutally crushed the Hungarian uprising, causing thousands of civilian deaths.[5] Within days, matters intensified when the Suez Crisis erupted in the Sinai Peninsula of Egypt.[6] According to one author, that dangerous dilemma

---

[1] John Lewis Gaddis, *The Cold War: A New History* (New York: Penguin Press, 2005), 35-36, 68 and 122.
[2] Those Chinese People's Volunteer Army troops were regular army soldiers, not volunteers. Hampton Sides, *On Desperate Ground: The Marines at the Reservoir, the Korean War's Greatest Battle* (New York: Doubleday, 2018), 63.
[3] Forrest C. Pogue, *George C. Marshall: Statesman 1945-1959* (New York: Viking, 1987), 486-487.
[4] MacArthur was relieved from command, as he was unable to support the policies of the U.S. and the UN. Ibid., 483.
[5] Similar Soviet military suppression produced many deaths in Czechoslovakia in 1968, following the "Prague Spring" reform movement against Russian domination.
[6] The British, French, and Israeli plot to retake the Suez Canal signaled a potential Soviet response to nuclear weapons, but skillful U.S. diplomacy ended "the most dangerous moment of the cold war until the Cuban missile crisis." Michael Korda, *Journey to a Revolution: A Personal Memoir and History of the Hungarian Revolution of 1956* (New York: HarperCollins, 2006) 105, 106.

sparked "the first direct threat of nuclear war between the Soviet Union and the West."¹ Thankfully, by November 1956, U.S. President Dwight Eisenhower managed a situation that nearly became a "far more deadly conflagration".²

By early 1961, Nikita Khrushchev (Stalin's successor) declared publicly that the Soviets were "on the side of 'wars of national liberation.'"³ Not long afterward, the Cuban Bay of Pigs fiasco⁴ caused relations to intensify with Moscow. Desperation set in as the socialist, utopian ideology of communism continued to misfire and the Soviets ordered construction of a massive wall to divide Berlin; they called it the "anti-Fascist defense barrier."⁵ In point of fact, it was erected solely to impede the flight of East Germans to West Germany, as armed border guards were ordered to shoot anyone trying to flee the communist "workers' paradise."⁶

Subsequently, the Cuban Missile Crisis⁷ erupted in the fall of 1962, at which point President John F. Kennedy ordered a naval blockade imposed

---

¹ Evan Thomas, *Ike's Bluff: President Eisenhower's Secret Battle to Save the World* (New York: Little, Brown, 2012), 217.
² Hitchcock, *The Age of Eisenhower*, 323 and 330.
³ Khrushchev's wars of liberation were intended to be "wars of guerilla aggression" against former colonial masters. Robert Dallek, *An Unfinished Life: John F. Kennedy, 1917–1963* (Boston: Little, Brown, 2003), 448.
⁴ In April 1961, a Cuban exile force invaded Cuba, backed by the Central Intelligence Agency, attempted to overthrow Castro's communist regime. Nearly 1,500 anti-Castro, exile-invaders were defeated by Castro's much larger armed force at the Bay of Pigs. Ibid., 359-366.
⁵ Michael Dobbs, *One Minute to Midnight* (London: Arrow Books, 2009), 216; in 1952, Soviet troops helped the East Germans close their border with West Germany, leaving the Berlin route as the only means of escape.
⁶ Dallek, *An Unfinished Life: John F. Kennedy, 1917–1963*, 426. Even Khrushchev knew that "paradise" was a place where people want to be, not a place they run from. Jerrold L. Schecter et al., *The Spy Who Saved the World: How a Soviet Colonel Changed the Course of the Cold War* (New York: Charles Scribner's Sons, 1992), 421.
⁷ U.S. reconnaissance discovered the covert deployment of Soviet bombers and nuclear ballistic missiles in Cuba. By mid-October 1962, U.S. intelligence estimated those Soviet missiles would be operational in a week and within only "a few minutes of being fired eighty million Americans

around the island.[1] That action by the Soviets to secretly deploy nuclear ballistic missiles less than 100 miles from America's southern border caused huge concern, as when fully installed, each Soviet missile had a one-megaton warhead with the destructive force of many Hiroshima-type atomic bombs.[2] Thus, the task of intercepting the shipment of more missiles at sea created enormous fear that imminent nuclear confrontation was imminent.[3]

Despite the U.S. Navy's overall advantage in weaponry at that time, great danger lurked in Cuban waters as four Soviet Foxtrot submarines with nuclear-tipped torpedoes in their launch tubes prepared for action.[4] According to actual participants on both sides, that dangerous activity "brought the world to the edge of nuclear winter."[5] To make matters worse, officials in Washington were totally unaware of the presence in Cuba of Soviet tactical nuclear weapons: short-range cruise missiles[6] and Luna rockets. (That Kremlin secret, along with the nuclear targeting of the Guantanamo naval base, lasted for several decades.) Had GITMO been destroyed with tactical nuclear cruise missiles, JFK would have been under tremendous pressure to respond in kind, and the thought of confining war to Cuba would have been next to impossible. Thus, many experts agree that

---

would be dead." Robert F. Kennedy, *Thirteen Days* (NY: W.W. Norton, 1969), 23, 35-36.

[1] Dobbs, *One Minute to Midnight*, 39.
[2] Ibid., 43.
[3] Sherry Sontag et al., *Blind Man's Bluff* (New York: Public Affairs, 1998), 45.
[4] Each Soviet nuclear-tipped torpedo was equal to 10 kilotons, i.e., 10,000 tons of TNT. Dobbs, *One Minute to Midnight*, 58, 94.
[5] W. Craig Reed, *Red November* (NY, William Morrow, 2010), 178. That 1962 showdown brought the U.S. and the Soviets "as close as they ever would to global nuclear war." Peter A. Huchthausen, *October Fury* (Hoboken, NJ: John Wiley, 2002), 1.
[6] The Soviet short-range nuclear missile had roughly the power of the bomb dropped on Hiroshima. Dobbs, *One Minute to Midnight*, 125; that nuclear cruise missile could destroy a U.S. aircraft carrier group or major military base. Unaware that tactical nuclear weapons had been deployed to within fifteen miles of GITMO in October 1962, the incineration of nearly 6,000 U.S. Marines would have taken only two minutes following orders from Moscow. Ibid., 121, 124-125, 179, 206-208, 249 and 352.

it would have taken only one false step at the time to produce a full-scale nuclear exchange.[1]

Fortunately, adroit diplomacy averted a thermonuclear disaster as Premier Khrushchev ordered his soldiers to dismantle, crate up, and withdraw all Soviet nuclear weapons from Cuba and destroy their launch sites.[2] To accomplish that feat, JFK pledged that Cuba would not be invaded in the future by American military forces, and he discreetly promised to remove U.S. Jupiter missile bases from Turkey.[3]

Two years later, Khrushchev was deposed as Soviet Premier and Alexei Kosygin replaced him. By then, the PRC had joined the world's nuclear club after conducting their first successful atomic test in late 1964, and within three years they detonated their first hydrogen bomb.[4]

As bitter fighting continued to run its course in Vietnam during the decade of the 1960s (between ARVN[5] and U.S. military forces opposing Vietcong and the North Vietnamese Army), a more perilous threat for America arose. Beginning in 1967, U.S. Navy warrant officer, John A. Walker, Jr., began to spy for the Soviets. He stole and sold them highly sensitive U.S. cryptographic material, technical manuals, and key lists to the KW-7 encryption machine, our military's most widely used encoding and deciphering device at the time. Later, he and his treasonous followers provided other vital secrets, including the Pentagon's full-scale war plan

---

[1] Gen. John E. Hyten of the U.S. Strategic Command noted recently that once an enemy employs a "small-yield" nuclear weapon on a battlefield for tactical effect, the 1945 threshold is crossed and "the United States will respond strategically, not tactically." *Washington Post,* September 19, 2017, A7.

[2] All tactical nuclear warheads were removed from Cuba by December 1, 1962. (National Security Archive Electronic Briefing Book No. 449) http://www.nsarchive2.gwu.edu

[3] The obsolete U.S. Jupiter medium-range ballistic missiles based in Turkey were withdrawn in 1963, and replaced with Polaris submarine missiles in the Mediterranean Sea that provided a greater defense shield against the Soviet nuclear threat. Sorensen, *Kennedy,* 696, and Dobbs, *One Minute to Midnight,* 338.

[4] Schecter, *The Spy Who Saved the World,* 265.

[5] "ARVN" is the abbreviation for Army of the Republic of [South] Vietnam.

with the Soviets, the Single Integrated Operational Plan (SIOP), which listed and located all U.S. nuclear weapons on land and at sea, plus their intended targets and trajectories. Over time, other classified material was stolen, including the location of sensitive underwater hydrophones anchored in the Pacific and North Atlantic near Russian naval bases (the Sound Surveillance System or SOSUS) that tracked Soviet submarines as they approached the U.S.[1]

By early 1968, circumstances became far worse for America when North Korean naval forces seized the USS *Pueblo*, a signals intelligence-gathering ship in international waters.[2] Only upon release of the crew from captivity nearly a year later was U.S. intelligence made aware that a working KW-7 cryptographic machine on the *Pueblo* had been captured and given to the Soviets months earlier. That theft on the high seas enabled them to use the stolen operations manual and monthly key lists to decipher an estimated one million classified U.S. military messages. From that point on the Soviets "had access to the battle plans of the U.S. Atlantic Fleet."[3] To be clear, the Soviets then had the ability to read our nation's most sensitive "mail", and had we gone to war with them, we would have been at an enormous disadvantage.

Not until 1985, when the Walker espionage ring was finally unmasked did it become known that the Soviets had stolen America's entire defensive playbook for war. Clearly Walker's treachery made the decades that followed very hazardous by Cold War standards. Looking back, a former director of the Central Intelligence Agency remarked that 1968 "was one of

---

[1] Pete Earley, *Family of Spies: Inside the John Walker Spy Ring* (NY, Bantam, 1988), 11, 49-51. John Walker was "the most important" spy in Soviet history, as he supplied them "the equivalent of a seat inside" the Pentagon. Kenneth Sewell et al., *Red Star Rogue* (NY: Simon & Schuster, 2005), 153.

[2] The precursor to the *Pueblo* event was the June 1967 Israeli attack on another spy ship, the USS *Liberty*, in international waters off the Sinai Peninsula. Having observed the American Navy's failure to protect the *Liberty*, the Soviets concluded that our surveillance ships "were ripe for harvest" and the North Koreans snatched the *Pueblo*, an act that was likely the most productive intelligence coup of the twentieth century. James M. Ennes, Jr., *Assault on the Liberty* (NY: Random House, 1979), 192.

[3] Oleg Kalugin et al., *The First Directorate* (NY: St. Martin's Press, 1994), 84.

the worst years in modern American history."[1] Moreover, in a 1992 NSA report, classified until 2012, it was determined that while some sensitive documents from the *Pueblo* were burned before its capture, the loss of certain classified material (the KW-7, undoubtedly) to the Soviets dwarfed "anything in previous U.S. cryptologic history."[2]

The troubling events mentioned above extend well beyond the scope of this narrative, and they are certainly not all-inclusive. Yet, to the extent Dad knew of them, they surely had a significant impact on his state of mind in the years after World War II. It is also likely that he came to know of other national security threats that likewise endangered the survival of mankind during the latter half of the twentieth century. While there may be some who are unaware that the Cold War was a very fearful time, it should be understood that national security challenges pervaded the working life of all those, including my father, in the U.S. intelligence community during that era. And they undoubtedly continue today.

As discussed in the pages that follow, Dad's military experience involved wartime service in a mechanized U.S. Army cavalry reconnaissance squadron, deployed to England in early 1944. His unit came ashore at Utah Beach several weeks after the Allied landings on June 6, 1944. Within only a short time after arriving in France, he came to know the rigors and perils of combat with the enemy all too well.

Following the St.-Lo Breakout, his unit engaged in running firefights with the enemy while screening elements of Patton's Third Army on the Brittany Peninsula. As a tank crewman with the 17th Cavalry Reconnaissance ("Recce") Squadron of the 15th Cavalry Group, he fought to liberate Brittany and the port cities of St.-Malo and Brest. Later, his unit[3] was attached to the Ninth Army as it advanced through Holland, the Roer sector and across the Rhine, performing security and reconnoitering

---

[1] Robert M. Gates, *From the Shadows* (New York: Simon & Schuster, 1996), 23.
[2] Wall Street Journal, Wednesday, May 23, 2018, A13.
[3] The term "unit," when used in this narrative refers to the U.S. 15th Cavalry Group, of which Dad's "outfit," the 17th Cavalry Reconnaissance Squadron was a component part. That was simply the way he always expressed it.

missions during the encirclement and reduction of the Ruhr Pocket. His combat odyssey continued with the XIX Corps as Allied forces probed their way into Germany, and it ended in May 1945.

Later, Dad's cavalry unit became a military occupation force in Germany, and he was discharged from service in the fall of 1945, following war's end in the Pacific. Like all the other ecstatic soldiers, he came home, completed his education and put down roots in metropolitan Washington, D.C. It was there that he and Mom settled down and began raising a family of four "baby boomers"[1].

There is no doubt that his combat experiences, together with those inherent in his postwar federal career, played a role in his distant nature. Thus, in my view, the psychological equation is a complicated one. Absent consideration of other factors, including the misfortune he encountered in his formative years, the calculus is woefully incomplete.

The account that follows is intended to candidly chronicle his passage from child to man, at war and beyond. It is an effort to examine the complexity of his sphinxlike persona, to better understand him. As he was an enigmatic presence throughout our life together, his notes and war diary provided valuable insight, especially as they relate to his World War II service. They were the catalyst, which allowed me to see through his eyes into the past, making this quest of discovery possible. Thankfully, his written work supplied answers to many questions I never thought to ask while he was alive.

---

[1] Baby boomers are the generation born between 1946 and 1964 to parents who fought in the Second World War, or lived through that era.

1. THE EARLY YEARS

In September 1914, Joseph Vincent Gough (pronounced Goff) married his sweetheart, Katherine Mary McLaughlin, known as "Katie" to her family and friends. In marked contrast to that joyful event, the First World War, the so-called Great War,[1] had begun several weeks earlier in Europe.

Several years later, Francis Robert Gough was born in the borough of Ashland in east-central Pennsylvania. His birth in January 1919 occurred only a few months after Germany's defeat, the guns fell silent on the Western Front, and peace was restored in November 1918. Accordingly, it is quite possible that the Gough family considered my father's arrival as something of an omen, auguring better times ahead.

In any event, Dad was the third of six children born to that union. In order by age, his siblings were: Robert Edward, Joseph Vincent, Jr., Bernard Joseph, Mary Kathryn, and Adrian Jerome. They were a typical Irish-Catholic family, residing in a small town, tucked away from the rest of the world in the midst of the Allegheny Mountains: the anthracite, "hard" coal[2] region of Schuylkill County. Their home was located in one of the many row houses that still stand along Centre Street, the main roadway through the hilly town of Ashland.

While Dad's lineage was mainly of Scots-Irish origin, he was most proud of his forebears[3] who boldly emigrated from famine-ridden Ireland,

---

[1] According to one preeminent British historian, it would be, as H.G. Wells called it, "The War that will end all War." Martin Gilbert, *The Somme: Heroism and Horror in the First World War* (New York: Henry Holt and Co., 2006), xix.

[2] By 1900, eastern Pennsylvania produced nearly fifty-five million tons of anthracite (clean-burning) coal to run the factories and heat the homes of America. Gerard Helferich, *An Unlikely Trust: Theodore Roosevelt, J.P. Morgan, and the Improbable Partnership That Remade American Business* (Guilford, CT: Lyons Press, 2017), 70.

[3] My father was a third generation American by birth, as his paternal great grandparents came to America from the "Isle of St. Patrick" during the first half of the nineteenth century; his paternal grandparents, Michael and Mary Agnes (Kilroy) Gough were both born during the second half of that century: he in Pennsylvania and she in Lancashire, England.

more specifically rural County Mayo, north of Galway.[1] They were a part of the Irish diaspora, driven to America by the ravages of mass starvation, poverty, unemployment, and desperation so prevalent in Ireland during the first half of the nineteenth century. Along with many others, they would never again feel the warmth of a peat fire or enjoy the smell of its smoke. Instead, they risked a long, hazardous sea voyage, hoping that the new world would provide opportunities for social and economic advancement.[2] Once they arrived, however, they swiftly assimilated into the American way of life.

Dad's father, known by his many grandchildren as "Grand Pap", was born in Ashland in the late 1880s, and his mother was born several years later in Girardville, the adjoining small town situated only a few miles away in the shadow of Mahanoy Mountain.

The photograph on the next page is of my paternal grandparents, taken at a local landmark sometime following their marriage; it was known generally as "Teetering Rock". How my Grand Pap convinced his bride to hike up the side of that mountain in their Sunday best is a mystery to me; yet, on that occasion they may have been on a sort of honeymoon, an experience they could scarcely afford. In any event, this photo captures the rugged, mountainous terrain surrounding my father's hometown.

---

[1] County Mayo is located in the Province of Connaught on the rocky coastline of the Atlantic Ocean. It is a harsh place, as the soil is very unfriendly to agriculture.
[2] While discussing my family heritage, I am well aware that Dad's late sister, Mary Gough Woodward always insisted that our ancestors came to America in grand style, but I believe it much more likely that they were among the vast huddled masses, traveling in steerage.

In eastern Pennsylvania a bitter coal strike began in May 1902 when nearly 150,000 anthracite coal miners protested "low wages, harsh working conditions and long hours."[1] At some point in my youth, Dad informed me that Grand Pap began his working life as a child, laboring in the mines in order to help with the family's straitened financial circumstances. Initially, he likely began working a six day, ten-hour-a-day shift as a "breaker boy," earning less than a dollar a day, "separating out pieces of slate and other impurities from streams of coal speeding by on conveyor belts."[2] It was a time in our history when it was not uncommon to find youngsters working long hours in the mines. Child employment was endemic, and many years would go by before any child labor restrictions became settled law in America.

At any rate, the massive 1902 coal strike had been under way for months when President Theodore Roosevelt (hereinafter "TR"[3]) recognized the impending "terrible calamity" of a national fuel shortage in the upcoming winter months. Knowing that "a coal famine would starve the furnaces and fireplaces" that kept the public warm across America, the president threatened to send in the army to seize and operate the mines. He considered that action necessary to safeguard the public welfare, and described the situation in the coalfields as "more dangerous than anything since the Civil War."[4] TR's intervention and subsequent jawboning with union leaders and coal company owners eventually ended the coal strike in the fall of that year.[5]

As the strike lasted many months, it provided the stimulus for Grand Pap to redirect his life by returning to school and leaving dangerous mine work for good. Thereafter, through much effort and considerable good fortune, he learned the skills necessary to pursue employment in the field of woodworking, and ultimately, he became a professional finish carpenter.

---

[1] Doris Kearns Goodwin, *The Bully Pulpit* (NY: Simon & Schuster, 2013), 311.
[2] Goodwin, *The Bully Pulpit*, 311-319; Helferich, *An Unlikely Trust*, 66.
[3] By the twentieth century, the use of initials for presidents became popular, e.g., TR, FDR, DDE and LBJ. David McCullough, *The American Spirit* (New York: Simon & Schuster, 2017), 60.
[4] H.W. Brands, *T.R.: The Last Romantic* (New York: Basic Books, 1997), 458.
[5] Ibid., 450-462. See also, Edmund Morris, *Theodore Rex* (New York: Random House, 2001), 132-137, 150-169, as well as Nathan Miller, *Theodore Roosevelt: A Life* (New York: William Morrow, 1992), 370-378.

He became a craftsman in that trade and experienced a far less hazardous work environment compared to that encountered laboring underground in the mines.[1] Later, his diligence resulted in an expanded skill set, including proficiency in furniture repair and the upholstery trade.

More than once, my father told me stories of his childhood, when he and his brothers traveled far and wide to play among the slagheaps, spoil ponds, and mud puddles so common in that part of coal mining country. They learned to invent their own fun, as there was no extra money available for childlike amusements. Also, he informed me that while walking home they would carefully scan the railroad tracks in search of stray lumps of coal to bring home in their pockets. That practice was undoubtedly of great benefit to the family, since money was scarce, and like most other families, their home was heated solely by coal.

As potentially dangerous as it was for them to walk along the railroad tracks, activity of that sort to support the family's welfare was common for children during the depths of the Depression, as people had to watch every penny carefully. Similar to many others who lived through that era, Pop's family faced many economic challenges, and having survived, it explains his affinity for thrift and aversion toward waste. On occasion, he described another childhood chore he shared with his brothers: on cold, wintry nights they took turns tramping down to the cellar to shovel coal into a pot-bellied stove to keep their house warm. Such regular family tasks made them more responsible and likely added to their feelings of self-worth.

Following the untimely death of their mother from pneumonia in December 1924, the children were raised with the assistance of their Aunt "Mame"[2], my grandfather's eldest sister, a spinster whose given name was

---

[1] During the 1902 coal strike, the president of United Mine Workers called attention to the plight of a generation of children prematurely doomed to soot and the noise and blackness of the breaker. Morris, *Theodore Rex*, 153. The hazards mentioned included "ignitions of methane or coal dust, cave-ins, floods, and asphyxiation from carbon dioxide and carbon monoxide gas. Helferich, *An Unlikely Trust*, 66.
[2] Mame was a kind and intelligent woman, but she was also a formidable force, one not to be trifled with. She had the misfortune to have been born with a cleft palate; due to a lack of financial resources, that misfortune was never corrected. As a result, she went through life holding a handkerchief to the side of her mouth to shield her birth defect. The embarrassment she

Mary Agnes Gough. After that domestic tragedy, she became their surrogate mother and took up residence in the home, as my Grand Pap never remarried. She turned out to be a steady and able manager of the domestic needs of the family. For the remainder of their formative years, she got the children dressed, fed, and off to school on time, while my grandfather attended to his carpentry and upholstery business. Her ability to care for the children was the glue that kept them together and largely prevented them from being split up and parceled out among relatives, a common practice at that time after a parent's death.[1] Yet, as attentive and caring as Mame was, she could never replace the feelings and undying affection of a mother for her own children.

With as many as six to seven mouths to feed at any one time, the severely depressed economy hit the family hard. Money was scarce in the Gough household, and new clothes usually meant outgrown, hand-me-downs from Dad's older brothers. My father often mentioned that he learned early not to be late for meals, because to do so could result in going to school or bed hungry. Back then, if one was tardy to the table, unfortunate hunger might ensue, as the food supply was finite, and there were many hearty appetites around the table. But on the positive side, he and his siblings certainly came to understand the value of punctuality.

Another of his favorite stories related to Mame's unique method of enforcing proper manners at the kitchen table. She rarely raised her voice, but regularly draped a rolled-up dishtowel over her shoulder. If mischief were afoot, a snap of her wrist brought that device around to instantly chasten a targeted offender. Of course, that was a time when attitudes concerning child discipline were far different from today. It was also very fortunate for all concerned that her aim was superb, since the boys came away with little more than a temporary sting, which was naturally ameliorated by the mirth it brought to the others. Despite her belief in the merits of tough love, my father and his siblings always thought she was

---

felt was surely a by-product of unkind ridicule and derision encountered during her childhood, and it likely scarred her for life.

[1] In his teens, however, Dad's eldest brother Bob lived with his paternal aunt, Teresa "Tess" (Gough) Scott and her husband in Washington, D.C., and his baby sister Mary, at a very early age, resided with their maternal uncle, Dr. Robert McLaughlin and his family in Philadelphia.

caring and compassionate, but they also knew she was an exacting person for whom everything was black or white; there were no debates, excuses, or "gray areas."

Because she was my baptismal Godmother, I remember her as a reserved woman whose speech contained a hint of Irish brogue. Knowing her as I did, I am convinced that she would have made an outstanding nun, as she was quick-witted, had a sharp intellect, a keen eye, and the requisite lightning-fast reflexes. But apparently, she never received "the calling."

On a separate note, a favorite expression in the Gough family was: "Children should be seen and not heard." That peppery phrase came down to us from our stern Grand Pap, who doled out disapproval in first-rate fashion.[1] Dad, also a stranger to plaudits or praise, claimed that the sentiment was an old Irish expression. (As to that, I had my doubts and considered it nothing more than the usual malarkey.)

Other examples of old-school patriarchal concern, passed along to us at an early age included the essential theme that my father brooked no departure from his stated demands. Specifically, his admonishments included demands such as show others respect by removing your headwear (baseball caps) when going indoors, make your bed, hang up your bath towels, and keep your elbows off the supper table and your feet off the furniture. Whenever anything untoward happened at home, Dad would erupt and his stinging words were harsh and hurtful. To this day, I am still reminded of his hard-edged, tongue-lashings. Needless to say, avoiding the crosshairs of that censure mechanism became the main goal of my adolescence. Clearly, his criticism was nothing to look forward to, yet it may have been somewhat beneficial, as I learned valuable coping skills early

---

[1] One example of Grand Pap's prickly personality remains fresh in my mind. While visiting him as a youngster, he took me on a walk around Ashland, to include a tour of his beloved volunteer fire company. While there, we passed a colleague of his, leaning back in a folding chair. Obviously deep in his cups, he made a snide remark as we passed. I ignored him, but on returning home, granddad reported his disappointment, as I failed to respond to the inebriate. He had expected me to knock the guy out of his chair. Pop read me the riot act, and I felt bad about letting him down until my mother set me straight a little later. She told me my instinct to overlook the defenseless drunk was correct; anything else, she said, would have been wrong.

in life. Thankfully, instruction in proper etiquette and deportment in social situations came later through my mother's ever-patient guidance.

Looking back, Dad's grade school education began in 1925 at St. Joseph's Parochial School. Later, he attended St. Joseph's High School from 1934 until sometime in late 1936, at which point he said he "quit." His explanation: "The nuns were giving me trouble."[1] From that explanation, it seems that Pop in his youth was clearly bereft of direction and rather ambivalent about his future. Evidently, he had a problem with the notion of cause and effect, not to mention difficulty with the concept of personal accountability.

Beginning in the spring of 1937 until the end of summer in 1938, Dad worked in President Franklin D. Roosevelt's New Deal Civilian Conservation Corps (CCC). Congress had enacted that relief measure within the first one hundred days of FDR's initial term in office, putting thousands of unemployed men like my father to work maintaining natural resources within America's forests and national parks.[2]

While in the CCC, Pop wore a uniform and lived as if he were actually in the military: he began the workday with reveille at 6:00 a.m., ate his meals in a mess hall, lived under supervision and discipline, and after taps, he went to sleep on a bunk in a wooden barracks.[3] His base pay was $30 a month and the bulk of it (from $22 to $25) was sent home to his family by

---

[1] While Dad thought the nuns had it in for him, my lengthy experience in the penal network known as parochial school tells me otherwise. Nuns were none too fond of us kids; the key to survival was to avoid taking it personally.

[2] H. W. Brands, *Traitor to His Class: The Privileged Life and Radical Presidency of Franklin Delano Roosevelt* (New York: Doubleday, 2008), 332-334, 389-392.

[3] By May 1933, the CCC was placed under War Department control. Gen. Douglas MacArthur considered it a "military windfall," since use of army officers as CCC trainers inoculated the army against budget cuts and preserved the "seed corn of America's national security". Mark Perry, *The Most Dangerous Man in America: The Making of Douglas MacArthur* (New York, Basic Books, 2014), 7-10. Years later, General Marshall described his work with the CCC as "the most instructive service I ever had, and the most interesting." Forrest C. Pogue, *George C. Marshall: Education of a General* (New York: Viking Press, 1963), 311.

compulsory allotment check.[1] The labor he performed involved mostly reforestation work planting saplings. It also included other demanding outdoor tasks, such as chopping down dead and diseased trees, clearing brush, and cutting trails and firebreaks to prevent fires from spreading in the central Pennsylvania woods. Such strenuous toil with pickaxe and shovel caused Pop to reevaluate the benefit of further schooling. By then he had most certainly come to recognize that higher education could lift him out of a life of manual labor. As a consequence, he returned to high school and graduated in 1939, thereby gaining the dubious distinction as the sole sibling in the family to enroll at venerable "St. Joe's" only to graduate from a public high school.

---

[1] Brinkley, *Rightful Heritage: Franklin D. Roosevelt and the Land of America*, 174-175; Harvey Ferguson, *The Last Cavalryman: The Life of General Lucian K. Truscott, Jr.* (Norman: University of Oklahoma Press, 2015), 64.

This is a photograph of my father taken at the time of his Ashland High School graduation. He appears to have been in a rare, happy mood, as the decision to return to school to complete his secondary education as it certainly served him and our family well for the rest of his life.

Because the monetary wherewithal for higher education was unavailable following his high school graduation, Dad worked for several months in his hometown at a series of odd jobs, which included a short stint at a shoe store, employment as a delivery boy at a local meat market, and as a stock clerk in a neighborhood drugstore.

In early 1940, Dad left Pennsylvania for good and moved to the bustling city of Washington, D.C., intent on finding more remunerative and fulfilling employment. At that time, he and his oldest brother Bob[1] shared living expenses while rooming together in a boardinghouse downtown. Later that year, he landed a job in the U.S. Army's Office of the Quartermaster General, and he continued to work as a civilian until the fall of 1941, at which time he received a special "Greeting" in the mail from his local draft board, ordering him to report for induction into military service.

Due to the rapid collapse of Denmark, Norway, Luxembourg, Belgium, Holland, and France to the Nazis in 1940, along with the subsequent German invasion of the Soviet Union in late June 1941, my father was not surprised when he received his draft notice in the mail; he had every reason to believe his carefree civilian life was soon coming to an end. Thus, in keeping with the attitude of many of his peers, he was undismayed about being "called up"; instead, he welcomed it. He considered military service a right of passage to manhood and he had no intention of sitting on the sidelines. He was fully aware that tyranny had been on the march for nearly a decade and like others of his generation, he knew the challenge of the Wehrmacht (Armed Forces of Germany) had to be met.

The basis for his entry on active military duty was the Selective Training and Service Act of 1940, which authorized our nation's first peacetime draft of its citizens into the military.[2] Its passage was deemed necessary by Congress given the armed aggression occurring in Europe and the Far East in the late 1930s;[3] however, because that legislation was passed in an

---

[1] Robert E. Gough had scarlet fever as a child and was classified "4-F" (medically unsuited for military service); ironically, he outlived all of his male siblings.

[2] Richard Moe, *Roosevelt's Second Act: The Election of 1940 and the Politics of War* (Oxford University Press, 2013), 293. Dad and three of his brothers were among 16,000,000 men between the ages of twenty-one and thirty-five, who registered for the draft within weeks of enactment of the Selective Training and Service Act of 1940, as amended in 1941.

[3] At that time, the U.S. Army was a military mouse; its strength was "nineteenth in the world, with a meager 174,000 men [in uniform], ahead of

election year, it contained a "politician's compromise," a one-year limit on the draftees' period of active military service.[1] By the summer of 1941, there was the very real possibility that, barring further legislative action, the progress made in the army's buildup would come to a screeching halt.

Finally, in August 1941, the wrangling on Capitol Hill ended, and the Senate passed the required extension to the prior draft act for eighteen months. Yet, it was anything but a sure thing, as the bill squeaked through the U.S. House of Representatives by a single vote.[2] Shortly afterward, the U.S. Army proceeded with its military training and National Guard units were federalized in preparation for the war. Due to the foresight and leadership of the president, Speaker of the House Sam Rayburn,[3] and Army Chief of Staff Gen. George C. Marshall, the selective service system continued the draft and increased the military's size to more than eight million men in uniform by the end of the Second World War in 1945.[4]

Around the time Pop became ensnared in the draft, FDR had increased U.S. naval protection of supply shipments to Britain under the Lend-Lease program. In short order, the Germans signaled their hostile intentions by

---

Bulgaria but just behind Portugal." Eric Larrabee, *Commander in Chief* (New York: Harper & Row, 1987), 114. Our national leaders had retreated into a pattern of isolation following the First World War, deciding that our military forces were "to defend the Americas but would go no further." Niall Barr, *Eisenhower's Armies: The American-British Alliance during World War II* (New York: Pegasus Books, 2015), 77. By early 1941, the U.S. Army comprised around 300,000 men, "compared to Germany's 4 million and Britain's 1.6 million." Lynne Olson, *Citizens of London* (New York, Random House, 2010), 67. Yet by the end of November 1941, the U.S. Army totaled more than 1.5 million men. Edward M. Coffman, *The Regulars: The American Army, 1898-1941* (Cambridge: Belknap Press of Harvard University Press, 2004), 374.

[1] James MacGregor Burns, *Roosevelt: The Soldier of Freedom* (New York: Harcourt Brace Jovanovich, 1970), 120.
[2] Forrest C. Pogue, *George C. Marshall: Ordeal and Hope, 1939-1942* (New York: Viking Press, 1967), 145.
[3] For a superb discussion of U.S. House Speaker Sam Rayburn's adroit tactics in "freezing" that momentous vote, see John G. Leyden's article, "How Mr. Sam Saved the Draft". *Washington Post,* August 18, 1991, C5.
[4] Michael Fullilove, *Rendezvous with Destiny* (NY: Penguin Press, 2013), 98.

spilling American blood in the fall of 1941, when two U.S. Navy destroyers on convoy duty were torpedoed in the North Atlantic Ocean. The USS *Kearny* was the first vessel struck and eleven crewmen died in that attack. Only a few days later, the USS *Reuben James* became the first American ship to be sunk by one of Adm. Karl Doenitz's submarines, causing the loss of an entire crew.[1] Thus, anti-German resentment began to build in America, as there could be little or no doubt in anyone's mind that our country would soon join the global struggle against tyranny. Yet, by the early fall of 1941, the U.S. Army's preparedness for combat amounted to only one infantry division, two bomber squadrons, and three pursuit (or fighter) groups.[2]

---

[1] Burns, *Roosevelt: The Soldier of Freedom*, 147-148; Kenneth S. Davis, *FDR: The War President, 1940-1943* (New York: Random House, 2000), 323-324.
[2] Pogue, *George C. Marshall: Ordeal and Hope, 1939-1942*, 159.

2. ALL FOR ONE, ONE FOR ALL

Francis R. Gough reported for induction into the U.S. Army on October 14, 1941[1], and along with many others who were prepared to do their duty, he was loaded on a Greyhound bus headed south to a draftee reception center in Richmond, Virginia. After passing a rudimentary physical examination, he and his cohorts were transported by railroad to Camp Lee (later renamed Fort Lee) near Petersburg in Prince George County, Virginia. There he wound up in a single-file line, rolled up both sleeves, and dropped his pants to receive inoculations in both arms and both buttocks (eleven altogether) from army medics. Immediately afterward, saluting officers and the flagpole on post, not to mention sitting down, must have been a challenge. Immediately following that series of vaccinations, the new inductees lined up again for their obligatory military haircuts. After a quick scalping, they joined another line and stripped down to their skivvies, prior to receipt of their khaki uniforms and other necessary GI[2] equipment.

Since Pop arrived at Camp Lee a few weeks earlier than many of the other trainees, he was obliged to perform extra duty. What followed were several days of being shouted at, as well as some initial training in basic soldier skills, e.g., physical conditioning, running, marching, close-order drill, and other duties like kitchen patrol ("KP" in military jargon), which entailed scrubbing pots and pans and peeling potatoes. Other activities for the recruits included cleaning the latrine, mounting guard, and participating in that time-honored army ritual known as "police call", which involved picking up loose paper, gum wrappers, trash, and cigarette butts. Besides preserving tidiness in the company area, the latter long-established, new recruit task had little relevance to military duty, but it kept the men busy and out of trouble.

---

[1] By then, the Japanese had been at war with China for more than four years.
[2] The term "GI" (short for "Government Issue") is a useful reference to equipment and members of the U.S. armed forces, but it is mainly used to refer to an enlisted member of the U.S. Army.

As he was well into his twenties and had previously spent time in the paramilitary CCC, Dad adjusted to military life more readily than many of the other draftees. It is also quite conceivable that some of the recruits may have been underage,[1] striving to be soldier-adventurers at a time when war was on the horizon. In any event, such factors apparently worked to his advantage, and since he happened to be a platoon elder, he was designated "acting" corporal. That exalted status, unofficial and temporary as it was, pleased him very much, even though it entailed no extra pay.

Surprisingly, Dad's graduation from high school had the salutary effect of putting him in the top quartile among his fellow recruits since only about one in four had a high school diploma. Incredibly, a mere one in three GIs serving during the Second World War had as much as a grade school education, and slightly over one in ten had attended college for a semester.[2] Those statistics are a far cry from today's all-volunteer, professional army, which requires a high school diploma (or equivalent) for enlistment.[3] Nonetheless, those 1941 draftees were a representative cross-section of America; they were highly motivated, but untrained in the art of war.

Following a few days of routine military duty, he and his fellow recruits were rousted out of their tarpaper–covered barracks and ordered to "Fall In" for their usual early morning roll call. They formed up in several lines in the company street as usual, and stood at attention on hearing the command to do so. At that moment, an officer stepped forward and read from his clipboard an official list, specifically designating Dad and several others as new recruit cavalry "troopers." At first, he was perplexed and uncertain about that change of circumstance, but it took him only a short time to appreciate his stroke of good fortune. (He was surely pleased to have escaped the infantry; like most of his peers, his preference was to ride, rather than walk.)

---

[1] During World War II, the minimum age for American conscription was eighteen. Paul Fussell, *Wartime* (NY: Oxford University Press, 1989), 53.
[2] Rick Atkinson, *The Guns at Last Light: The War in Western Europe, 1944-1945* (New York: Henry Holt, 2013), 19.
[3] At the outset of the draft, the Army's enlistment standards were modest compared to today, requiring only a fourth-grade education and the ability to speak English. Lee Kennett, *G.I.: The American Soldier in World War II* (New York: Charles Scribner's, 1987), 18.

On the morning of October 18, 1941, he heaved his barracks bag aboard a fifteen-car troop train, and bid good-bye to the Commonwealth of Virginia along with about four hundred other raw recruits headed west to an old frontier army installation: Fort Riley, Kansas.[1] More specifically, their destination was the U.S. Army Cavalry Replacement Training Center (CRTC) in northeastern Kansas, situated on flat, sandy ground near the confluence of the muddy Republican and Kansas Rivers.

On his arrival, he was assigned to the third training increment, and reported to Troop D, Sixth Training Squadron, 3rd Training Regiment. At that moment, he and his fellow trainees were unaware that, when their thirteen-week cycle of basic cavalry training was complete, their nation would be squarely in the middle of a bloody world war.

The motto of CRTC was "Build Well" and the basic recruit training Dad received there was harsh, but fair. It was designed to build cavalry troopers at that critical time in our nation's history and the training included instruction in horsemanship, motor operations, motor maintenance, and cavalry weapons. Unfortunately, however, during the summer and fall of 1941, many new army recruits underwent individual combat training "with wooden rifles, mock-up tanks, and missing radios."[2] Dad's CRTC training, nevertheless, required that he gain proficiency with a variety of weapons: the M1903 Springfield rifle,[3] the semi-automatic M1 Garand[4] rifle and

---

[1] Fort Riley was established in 1852 to protect settlers from American Indian attack. Ferguson, *The Last Cavalryman*, 40. It later became the U.S. Cavalry's Mounted School. Geoffrey Perret, *Old Soldiers Never Die: The Life of Douglas MacArthur* (New York, Random House, 1996), 59.

[2] Matthew D. Morton, *Men on Iron Ponies* (DeKalb: Northern Illinois University Press, 2009), 73.

[3] The bolt-action Springfield rifle was such a close copy of Germany's early design that our government "was forced to pay the Mauser Company hundreds of thousands of dollars in royalties." Chris Kyle with William Doyle, *American Gun: A History of the U.S. in Ten Firearms* (New York: William Morrow, 2013), 124, 136; that nine-pound rifle was a throwback to World War I, but with an attached telescopic sight, it was used in World War II, mostly in a sniper role due to its accuracy. Coffman, *The Regulars: The American Army, 1898-1941*, 405.

[4] Canadian John C. Garand's gas operated, clip fed .30-caliber M1 was adopted by the U.S. as the world's first standardized, semi-automatic service rifle, but by early 1943, they were in such short supply that the troops

carbine, the .45-caliber pistol,[1] .30- and .50-caliber machine guns, 60-mm mortar, and the 37-mm cannon.

Fort Riley, back then and now, is a vast military post, which extends for many miles and lends itself well to varied training opportunities. Known locally as "The Rimrock" it can be "freezing cold in winter and unbearably hot and humid in the summer."[2] Numerous temporary structures at CRTC allowed the trainees to develop realistic combat problem-solving skills. A false hamlet was built so that cavalry recruits could learn street-to-street and house-to-house fighting techniques. It resembled a small town of around five hundred inhabitants, similar to the kind of village a cavalry reconnaissance unit would be called on "to patrol and reconnoiter" in wartime.

Training of the nature described above certainly served the men well, as they fought their way across the European continent during World War II. To that point, CRTC successfully trained around 125,000 fully qualified cavalry replacements from 1941 to 1945.[3]

---

trained with old bolt-action Springfield rifles. Yet, more than five million M1 rifles were used in World War II. Bruce N. Canfield, *The M1 Garand Rifle* (Woonsocket, RI: Andrew Mowbray, 2013), 109, 142, 592-595. As late as May 1943, there were so few M1s available that they were issued only to men about to be shipped overseas. Geoffrey Perret, *There's a War to be Won* (New York: Ballantine, 2013), 84. The M1's advantage was its milder recoil after firing, as it didn't pound the shoulders of the infantrymen as severely as the 1903 Springfield. Coffman, *The Regulars: The American Army, 1898-1941*, 405.

[1] One U.S. war veteran observed that the .45-caliber semi-automatic pistol was "a weapon of little use in any arena larger than an elevator." James R. McDonough, *Platoon Leader: A Memoir of Command in Combat* (New York, Ballantine, 1985), 158.

[2] Carlo D'Este, *Patton: A Genius for War* (NY: HarperCollins, 1995), 143.

[3] Sgt. David F. Woods, "The C.R.T.C. in World War II," *Cavalry Journal*, Vol. 54, no. 6, (November-December 1945), 61-62.

The grainy photograph above shows my father with a cavalry mount, which had been assigned him at CRTC. There, he underwent horsemanship training and learned an important lesson: to be a successful cavalryman, the rider must form a special bond with his mount. (I may be wrong, but the horse in question seems somewhat tense, apprehensive and unsure concerning the competence of his designated rider.)

When Dad underwent basic cavalry training in late 1941, approximately 60 percent of the men in each training increment became horseman and the rest were placed in motor units and provided mechanized instruction. Back then, it was believed that CRTC was establishing two types of cavalry credentials: those who were "horsey" and others termed "greasy." Among the equipment available for training purposes were saddles, spurs, and bridles for the horses and "iron ponies" i.e., Willys jeeps, Harley-Davidson motorcycles,[1] scout cars, armored cars, half-tracks, light tanks, and combat cars.[2]

Dad apparently showed some mechanical aptitude, as he was designated a member of the greasy category, handed a wrench, and sent to the motor pool; immediately following completion of basic training, he was assigned to a motorized unit. Thus, on completion of CRTC training, his mounted cavalry experience came to an end, as the only horsepower available thereafter was of the armored/mechanized variety. (Yet, while assigned to mechanized, tracked vehicles, the terminology: "mount up" and "dismount" remain the same.)

Later, it is likely that he was disappointed to witness the demise of the "Boots-and-Saddle" bugle calls and horse-cavalry charges, since he seemed to enjoy wearing his cavalry attire: a flat-brimmed, Stetson campaign hat with yellow hat cord and tassels, cavalry boots and flared, jodhpur riding breeches.[3] However, something tells me he didn't regret the lost opportunity to perform "stable duty", i.e., watering, feeding, and grooming his mount, nor did he miss getting kicked by one of those equine creatures or having to muck out the horse manure in the stalls at the end of each day.

---

[1] The motorcycle rider wore a .45-caliber semi-automatic pistol strapped to his hip and a .45-caliber Thompson submachine gun in a front-mounted holster. Jeeps replaced motorcycles ultimately, as they handled poorly on rough terrain, mud, ice and snow, and were deemed too noisy for reconnaissance duty. Gordon L. Rottman, *World War II US Cavalry Groups: European Theater* (Oxford, UK: Osprey, 2012), 4.
[2] *Historical and Pictorial Review*, Cavalry Replacement Training Center, 3rd Regiment, Fort Riley (Army and Navy Publishing, 1941), 7-8.
[3] Prior to World War II, U.S. cavalrymen were a tight-knit group, known as "the most glamorous, preening, strutting soldiers the Army possessed." Perret, *Old Soldiers Never Die*, 59.

In the photograph below, Pop is seen resting atop a 17-ton U.S. Army M5 Stuart light tank: it appears to be an improved model of the earlier Stuart tank lineage as the engine deck is noticeably bulged at the rear. Nearly 9,000 M5 and M5A1 Stuart tanks were produced during World War II.[1]

As the Stuart underwent redesign, modifications included an extended turret to the rear of the tank to accommodate a radio set, an improved gun mount allowing installation of a gun telescope, a more rugged drive sprocket, and an emergency escape hatch in the belly of the tank's hull.[2] The rubber-block track pads above were subject to alteration with steel tracks and grousers when necessary to gain better traction on slippery terrain once they encountered the wet, wintery weather of Northern Europe.

---

[1] Michael E. Haskew, *Tank: 100 Years of the World's Most Important Armored Military Vehicle* (Minneapolis, MN: Zenith Press, 2015), 128.
[2] Steven J. Zaloga, *Stuart U.S. Light Tanks in Action* (Warren, MI: Squadron/Signal, 1979), 22. The M5 light tank was named after the American Civil War cavalryman Maj. Gen. James Ewell Brown "Jeb" Stuart, C.S.A.

The emphasis on mechanization at CRTC was undoubtedly a direct American response to the specter of Germany's rout of the Polish horse cavalry in 1939 and the collapse of the French forces during the early summer of 1940.[1] In the words of a prominent journalist and historian while driving back to Berlin in September 1939: "The roads [are] full of motorized columns of German troops returning from Poland. In the woods [there is] the sickening smell of dead horses . . . Here, the Germans say, a whole division of Polish cavalry charged against hundreds of German tanks and was annihilated."[2]

Although the U.S. cavalry branch fought long and hard to retain a combat role for its horses, by 1942 the Army Ground Forces had eliminated the equestrian force as an element of its ground reconnaissance structure. As a logical consequence, army veterinarians and farriers had to make way for vast numbers of newly trained mechanics.

As World War II progressed the Allies became fully mechanized while the German army, which was committed to the operational concept of *Blitzkrieg* (meaning lightning war in German), continued to lag behind due to its reliance on horses. Every German infantry division in France in 1944 relied heavily on horse-drawn vehicles. German horses were necessary to convey to the field rations, ammunition, and weaponry, such as field artillery, anti-tank guns, and almost every other supply imaginable.

In Normandy, German horse-drawn transportation exceeded that of their mechanized vehicles by a factor of two to one in the summer of 1944.[3]

---

[1] In May 1940, the future of horse cavalry was clarified in favor of a separate American mechanized force as German panzers attacked handily through Belgium, Holland, and Luxembourg to the French border. Lee F. Kichen, "The Death of the Horse Cavalry and the Birth of the Armored Force", *On Point: Journal of Army History,* Army Historical Foundation, Vol. 23 no. 3 (Winter 2018), 12.

[2] William L. Shirer, *Berlin Diary: The Journal of a Foreign Correspondent, 1934-1941* (New York: Galahad Books, 1995), 212. Stories of Polish cavalry squadrons attacking German tanks were for the most part apocryphal, but undeniable due to the relative imbalance of mechanized equipment and resources. Richard J. Evans, *The Third Reich at War* (New York, Penguin Press, 2009), 4.

[3] Richard Hargreaves, *The Germans in Normandy* (Barnsley, South Yorkshire, UK: Pen & Sword, 2006), 26.

According to one military author, the German Army used nearly 2.7 million horses during World War II, nearly twice as many as they had used during the First World War.[1] That proposition seems counterintuitive, but the fact remains that fewer horses were needed during the earlier war due to its more static nature, which involved miles of zigzagged trench works, underground dugouts and vast networks of barbed-wire entanglements.

The picture below depicts German soldiers astride their four-legged, nineteenth-century mode of transportation, providing vivid evidence of the lack of full mechanization within the German army during World War II.

As a consequence, the vast majority of German infantrymen in the *Wehrmacht* marched into battle on foot with supplies and supporting artillery hauled to the front by horses. One former U.S. combat infantry officer observed that the German's reliance on horsepower to pull its war supplies

---

[1] George Forty, *German Infantryman at War, 1939-1945* (Surrey, UK: Ian Allen Publishing, 2002), 6.

across Europe in the mid-twentieth century was akin to "replaying the techniques of the Napoleonic Wars."[1]

Full Allied mechanization during the war was the product of the readily available resources of manpower, raw materials, and manufacturing capability of America. At the same time, an ever-decreasing resource base, coupled with American daylight and Royal Air Force (RAF) nighttime bombing, greatly diminished Germany's industrial capacity.[2] The enemy's lack of mobility became quite evident following the collapse of the Falaise Pocket in mid-August 1944, when many bloated horse carcasses and overturned horse-drawn supply wagons were found strewn along the German line of retreat. After that battle, the body of a dead enemy soldier was found sitting atop an artillery caisson with the reins of four dead horses still in his hands. Following that rout of the enemy, it took three months for bulldozers to clear the bones and decaying remains of some eight thousand horses from that portion of France.[3]

By the time my father completed his basic cavalry training in late January 1942, world circumstances had changed dramatically: we were at war with Imperial Japan, Fascist Italy, and Germany's National Socialists (the Nazis).[4] War with the Japanese began soon afterward on December 7, 1941; war with the latter two nations resulted from the declarations of war against the United States on December 11, 1941, by the German *Führer*[5] Adolf Hitler,[6] and the Italian *Duce* Benito Mussolini, in compliance with the

---

[1] Paul Fussell, *The Boys' Crusade: The American Infantry in Northwestern Europe, 1944-1945* (New York: Modern Library, 2003), xiii.
[2] By 1938, the Germans realized their shortage of domestic fuel and petroleum products limited their mechanized development. Yet, they knew their animal-based agricultural economy offered "a total of 3,400,000 horses" for military use. Morton, *Men on Iron Ponies*, 59-60.
[3] Atkinson, *The Guns at Last Light*, 166-170.
[4] Fullilove, *Rendezvous with Destiny*, 346.
[5] In German, the term *Der Führer* means "the leader"; *Il Duce* has the same meaning in the Italian language.
[6] Hitler's declaration of war on the U.S. was "perhaps the greatest error, and certainly the single most decisive act" of World War II. Martin Gilbert, *The Second World War: A Complete History* (New York: Henry Holt, 1989), 277.

1940 Tripartite Pact (the "Pact of Steel").[1] During the halcyon days prior to 1942, members of the Rome-Berlin-Tokyo Axis bound themselves to assist one another in the event any of the signatories was attacked by "an external power not involved in the European or Sino-Japanese conflicts". That agreement left no doubt that it was aimed directly at the U.S.[2]

Below is a copy of a German propaganda postcard image[3] depicting the odious, egomaniacal Adolf Hitler, creator of the so-called Thousand-Year Reich.

Most of us know that Hitler's narcissism and hubris caused unimaginable death and destruction from 1933 until his self-inflicted demise

---

[1] Clearly, Hitler had "grossly overestimated Japanese military power." Ian Kershaw, *To Hell and Back: Europe 1914-1949* (New York: Viking, 2015), 352.
[2] Ian Kershaw, *Hitler, 1936-1945: Nemesis* (NY: W.W. Norton, 2000), 326.
[3] Dad gained possession of the postcards somewhere in Germany in 1945.

in 1945. What many may not know is that he was a strict vegetarian, who avoided nicotine and imbibed little to no alcohol. Yet by late 1944, he suffered chronic indigestion and had the appearance of a haggard, debilitated old man: his right eye often drooped, his left arm and hand shook uncontrollably, and he walked with a shuffled gait.[1]

As he rarely traveled abroad, Hitler was clueless about life in America, and he had no clear concept of life in other nations. He had a low regard for our art and culture, especially jazz, ragtime and swing music, and he had the mistaken opinion that America was little more than a mongrel country of Negroes and Jews.[2]

While the Führer's appreciation for the music of composer Richard Wagner was well known, it was not publicly acknowledged that he also was a great fan of Hollywood films during the 1930s. Nightly, he watched movies in the Reich Chancellery, and while on vacation he viewed them in the great hall of his alpine mountain retreat (the *Berghof*) near Berchtesgaden, overlooking his native Austria.[4] A few of Hitler's favorite U.S. motion pictures were *King Kong* and *Gone with the Wind*.[5] He also

---

[1] David Stafford, *Ten Days to D-Day: Countdown to the Liberation of Europe* (London: Little, Brown, 2003), 21; Peter Caddick-Adams, *Snow & Steel: The Battle of the Bulge, 1944-45* (New York: Oxford University Press, 2015), 55.
[2] Max Hastings, *Inferno: The World at War, 1939-1945* (NY: Alfred A. Knopf, 2011), 193; Caddick-Adams, *Snow & Steel: The Battle of the Bulge*, 1944-45, 122-123; Kershaw, *To Hell and Back: Europe 1914-1949*, 464-465.
[3] Hitler purchased *Haus Wachenfeld*, as the *Berghof* was known originally in June 1933, using royalties from the sale of his book, *Mein Kampf* (My Struggle). As it was compulsory reading in the Third Reich, he became a very wealthy man. James Wilson. *Hitler's Alpine Retreat* (Hanovertown, PA: Casemate, 2005), 8. Hitler became a millionaire from his book sales, which sold roughly ten million copies by 1945. Ian Kershaw, *Hitler, 1889-1936: Hubris* (New York: W.W. Norton, 1999), 242-43, 536.
[4] Apparently, the prior owner of Haus Wachenfeld was given a choice at the time of sale of that house in the Bavarian Alps: either allow the purchase to go forward or become a resident in a Nazi concentration camp. Rochus Misch, *Hitler's Last Witness: The Memoirs of Hitler's Bodyguard* (London: Frontline Books, 2014), 66.
[5] William L. Shirer, *Berlin Diary*, 587-588; Misch, *Hitler's Last Witness*, 70-71.

enjoyed watching Walt Disney cartoons, and was described as "delighted" when his propaganda minister Josef Goebbels presented him with "eighteen Mickey Mouse films at Christmas in 1937."[1]

Equally unusual is the fact that Hitler liked to bowl and had an alley installed for his personal use in the basement of the *Berghof*. However, he kept his interest in bowling private, thinking it an unfitting avocation for a great world leader.[2]

He fiercely maintained great distance between himself and the German public, believing that the "masses needed an idol" to lead them.[3] His egotism and self-conceit led him to believe that being unmarried gave him a powerful sexual allure with German women. He thought he would lose his sparkle if he married, as then the ladies would no longer idolize him.[4]

The postcard image, on the next page, was issued to commemorate the Nazi *Anschluss*, the annexation of Austria into the German Reich. That event and the subsequent 1938 Munich Agreement led to Germany's acquisition of the Sudetenland and the later takeover of Czechoslovakia through Hitler's cunning deceit.

---

[1] Kershaw, *To Hell and Back: Europe 1914-1949*, 464-465.
[2] Misch, *Hitler's Last Witness*, 65.
[3] Kershaw, *Hitler, 1936-1945: Nemesis*, 30.
[4] Albert Speer, *Inside the Third Reich* (New York: MacMillan, 1970), 92.

13·MÄRZ 1938
EIN VOLK EIN REICH
EIN FÜHRER

    Following closely on the heels of such treachery came the subsequent Nazi invasion of Poland in September 1939, and the beginning of war with Great Britain and France. Then, the unthinkable occurred when the Nazis attacked Russia by surprise in June 1941,[1] as the Führer ordered his Drive to the East to achieve *Lebensraum* (living space) in Eastern Europe.[2] The slogan at the bottom of the postcard reads, "One People, One Empire, One Leader" in English. Hitler used that slogan as propaganda in posters and at the end of his political speeches to arouse the German masses.

---

[1] In spite of the August 1939 German-Soviet Non-Aggression Pact, Hitler double crossed Stalin by renouncing the mutual neutrality agreement when he felt it was no longer useful.

[2] Andrew Nagorski, *Hitlerland: American Eyewitnesses to the Nazi Rise to Power* (New York: Simon & Schuster, 2012), 225.

When the U.S. entered the war in late December 1941, Great Britain had been at war with the Axis powers for more than two years. By that time, the British "had almost reached the limits of manpower and matériel reserves."[1] If the war was to be won the American high command realized that success in Europe was first on the agenda together with a furious expansion of its armed forces.

Consistent with the patriotic zeal of the time, my father applied for Officer Candidate School (OCS) following his completion of basic training, but he was unsuccessful, as it was determined that he did not possess "enough military background". To be sure, he was much chagrined by that negative turn of events, but his prior erratic academic record most likely had much to do with that outcome.

In any event, Private First Class Gough's downcast spirits improved somewhat in March 1942, when he and many other troopers were loaded on trucks and transported three miles to Camp Funston[2], Kansas. There the 15th Cavalry Regiment was reactivated as a mechanized regiment under the command of Col. Frank J. Richmond, and assigned motorized mounts (four-wheel-drive jeeps, M3 half-tracks, armored self-propelled artillery vehicles, and light tanks).

Depicted on the next page is the 15th Cavalry's distinctive regimental crest, which includes the image of a golden raging lion at the top and at the bottom the motto: *"Tous Pour Un, Un Pour Tous"* (meaning **All For One, One For All** in French). The central shield of that crest includes a crossed black dagger and Kris sword (traditional Moro bladed weapons) in the center to honor the 15th Cavalry Regiment's participation in the fighting

---

[1] Unger and Hirshson, *George* Marshall: *A Biography* (New York: HarperCollins, 2014), 139-140.

[2] Camp Funston was a training camp located on the grounds of Fort Riley; it was named after Maj. Gen. "Fighting Fred" Funston, who fought in the Philippines in 1898. He was responsible for capturing Emilio Aguinaldo (the Filipino nationalist leader) and earned the Medal of Honor. Coffman, *The Regulars: The American Army, 1898-1941*, 53; Andrew Carroll, *My Fellow Soldiers: General John Pershing and the Americans Who Helped Win the Great War*, (New York: Penguin Press, 2017), 59-60.

waged against guerrilla forces in the early 1900s during the so-called Philippine Insurrection.[1]

Reactivation of the 15th Cavalry Regiment was necessary during the Second World War, as it had been deactivated after returning from France at the end of the First World War.[2] Following its release from military occupation duty in Germany after World War II, it was reorganized as the 15th Constabulary Regiment in May 1946.[3] (Today, several Troops of the 5th Squadron, 15th Cavalry Regiment, continue to train modern cavalry scouts within the 194th Armored Brigade, stationed at Fort Benning, Georgia.)

---

[1] Shelby L. Stanton, *World War II Order of Battle*, U.S. Army (Ground Force Units), (Novato, CA: Galahad Books, 1984), 309.
[2] The Lion Rampant: A Brief History of Combat Operations in the European Theater during 1944-45 of the 15th Cavalry Group, Mechanized (1945), 5 (hereinafter "TLR"); CAVG-15-0, entry 427, Record Group 407, National Archives II, College Park, MD.
[3] Rottman, World War II US Cavalry Groups: European Theater, 37.

Dad's first assignment in the 15th Cavalry Regiment was to the motor pool of Troop E in May 1942, commanded by Lt. Thomas J. Fiori. He remained there for around six months until he was transferred to the supply room and promoted to the rank of corporal, assistant to the supply sergeant.

The photograph above shows Pop standing to the left of some tumbleweed while pointing to a metal, red-over-white, swallow-tailed cavalry guidon, which designated the location of Troop E of the 15th

Cavalry Regiment in 1942. He is shown wearing the distinctive khaki cavalry breeches and calf-high cavalry boots, while proudly displaying his corporal stripes. His regiment was then encamped in the rolling, dusty hill country of northeastern Kansas, where they continued the hard work of getting organized, gearing up and preparing for the challenges that lay ahead. By that point, he seems to have found that military discipline and army life suited him well.

As Dad's training continued, the cadence and reality of war came ever closer for all Americans. In June 1942, a German U-boat landed a small party of saboteurs on Long Island, New York, but fortunately, they turned out to be inept and were soon captured by the authorities. By August 1942, six of them were tried, convicted, and electrocuted in Washington, D.C. Since their remains went unclaimed, they were buried on the grounds of the city's Blue Plains wastewater treatment plant. The other two German spies cooperated with American investigators and spent the rest of the war behind bars.[1]

In Europe, Czech resistance fighters assassinated Hitler's main Holocaust[2] planner, *SS-Gruppenführer* Reinhard Heydrich, in Prague. As a result, the Nazis burned the village of Lidice to the ground; the men were rounded up and shot, the women were sent to a concentration camp, and the children were led away for racial cataloguing. All told, some 5,000 Czech civilians perished in that 'orgy' of German revenge.[3] By mid-1942, 1.5 million European Jews had been liquidated to further Hitler's "final solution".[4]

While still in garrison, Corporal Gough was granted a furlough in September 1942, his first after more than eleven months in the army.

---

[1] Michael Dobbs, *Saboteurs: The Nazi Raid on America* (New York: Alfred A. Knopf, 2004), 253-254, and 264-265.
[2] The Holocaust was Hitler's deranged plan to totally annihilate the European Jewish population. The Nazis and their allies killed at least 5.5 million Jews, but "the probable total" amounts to around six million. Evans, *The Third Reich at War*, 318.
[3] Ibid., 275-278.
[4] Jay Winik, *1944: FDR and the Year That Changed History* (New York: Simon & Schuster, 2015), 264-265, 305.

Naturally, he was happy to return home to see his father, eldest brother Bob, and Aunt Mame, all of whom knew he was coming home, but he reportedly surprised his sister Mary and their neighbors. He indicated that he missed seeing his brothers Joe and Bernard, who had been inducted into military service only two weeks earlier. He said his family was very glad to see him, but guessed he was the happiest, as "it sure was swell to see my family again."

On returning to duty, Pop learned that his unit had been relocated to the Pawnee Flats area (between Fort Riley and Camp Funston). To his complete satisfaction, the new camp was described as being equipped with "modern utilities." (No doubt Pop was referring to indoor plumbing with running water and flush toilets in lieu of the outdoor latrines and open-air slit trenches.)

By October 1942, Troop E received a number of new men (known as "fillers") to round out their roster. Dad expressed displeasure with that development, since their presence caused "extra [administrative] duty for the old hands" in the troop. Nevertheless, he soon became aware of the utility of "newbies", who relieved the more experienced soldiers from the drudgery of disagreeable duty in and around the barracks.

At the same time the 15th Cavalry Regiment continued to organize and train for combat in Kansas, U.S. military forces overseas accomplished much to stem the advancing tide of the Axis. Specifically, then-Lt. Col. Jimmy Doolittle led sixteen B-25 "Mitchell" twin-engine bombers off the flight deck of the USS *Hornet* on a bombing raid of Tokyo in April 1942. That surprise attack, boosted the morale of all Americans at home and announced to the Japanese people that serious payback for Pearl Harbor was coming its way.

Indeed, American naval forces won two enormous victories in 1942: the first was in the Coral Sea in May, followed one month later at Midway.[1] By

---

[1] The U.S. victory in the Coral Sea was the first great naval action between aircraft carriers; it was the first battle in which no ship on either side sighted the other. Samuel Eliot Morison, *The Two-Ocean War: A Short History of the U.S. Navy in the Second World War* (Boston: Little, Brown & Co., 1963), 142. At Midway, U.S. naval aviators sank four of the six Japanese aircraft carriers used in the December 1941 Pearl Harbor attack; it became known as the

early August, a land offensive got underway when men of the U.S. 1st Marine Division ("The Old Breed") splashed ashore at Guadalcanal to contest Japanese occupation of the Solomon Islands. (Those accomplishments shifted the momentum away from the Japanese military.)

Later, in November 1942, Anglo-American forces focused their attention on the Germans by launching a successful amphibious invasion of French North Africa (Morocco and Algeria) code-named, Operation Torch. By then, Hitler's military had reached its high-water mark, as the Germans occupied nearly one-third of Europe and controlled half its population. Nazi conquest spanned an area from the Channel Islands in the west to the northern Caucasus in the east, and from northern Norway to the Sahara Desert. As one historian put it: "Not since Napoleon had a single figure held such absolute sway" across the European landmass.[1] However, as the war progressed the Axis experienced a steady downward slide, as the Grand Alliance[2] gained momentum.

By late January 1943, the 15th Cavalry Regiment (Mechanized) was situated at Camp Maxey, Texas, northeast of Dallas, near the Red River border with Oklahoma. There they deployed to continue their pre-combat preparation in more remote terrain; later they participated in large-scale army maneuvers in Louisiana from June to August 21, 1943.

On completion of their tactical training, they returned to Camp Maxey, and in early September 1943, they redeployed to the barren environment of Camp Coxcomb at the Desert Training Center in the Mojave Desert of

---

turning point of the Pacific War. Gordon W. Prange, *Miracle at Midway* (New York: McGraw-Hill, 1982), 395. It was "the most complete naval victory since Horatio Nelson's near annihilation of the Spanish and French fleets at Trafalgar in 1805." From that point on, the Japanese never gained the strategic initiative. Craig L. Symonds, *The Battle of Midway* (New York: Oxford University Press, 2011), 358.

1 Mark Mazower, Hitler's Empire: How the Nazis Ruled Europe (New York: Penguin Press, 2008), 223.
2 The combined military forces of the U.S., Great Britain, and the Soviet Union were commonly referred to as the "Grand Alliance" in World War II.

southern California.[1] They remained there until early February 1944, encamped under harsh, arid conditions for the purpose of gaining much-needed seasoning; in the process, they learned to fight in large unit formations under the mental and physical rigors of actual combat.

In the photograph below, Pop is seen mounted on a hot, dusty Stuart light tank with one of his crewmen, whom he identified as Corporal (Cpl.) W. J. Scott. They appear to be a tired and sweaty duo, ready for some needed rest and good old army chow.

In the staged photograph on the next page, Pop is seen standing in the California desert wearing a holstered pistol, posing like a gunslinger, with a M1928 Thompson submachine gun, known as a "Tommy Gun". That formidable weapon could fire twenty .45-caliber rounds in quick succession from its stick magazine, making it a very popular piece of ordnance. In

---

1 Conditions at the Desert Training Center were routinely disagreeable: the equipment failed and the men undergoing training "fell from heat exhaustion and rattlesnakes." D'Este, Patton: A Genius for War, 408, 411.

some quarters, it was said that arming a soldier with such a weapon turned him into a one-man army.[1]

What concerns me about the picture above is the pistol on Pop's right hip, worn "cowboy" style. That seems to violate the manner in which tank crewmen wore their personal protection during World War II.

---

[1] The Tommy Gun proved to be very popular with the criminal element in America during the 1930s; they referred to that lethal weapon as the "Chicago Typewriter" when augmented with a 50 or 100-round drum magazine. Around 1.5 million Thompson submachine guns were manufactured for the U.S. military during World War II. See Chris Kyle with William Doyle, *American Gun*, 168 and 277.

My understanding is that pistols were worn in shoulder holsters, tucked under the armpit, allowing the crew to exit a knocked-out, burning tank rapidly without getting stuck in a hatch. (Nevertheless, I surmise these photos were sent home to the family in 1943 mainly to show off his fledgling mustache.)

In the photograph above, my father stands in front of his thinly armored and under-gunned M5A1 Stuart light tank, featuring a "half-donut bulge" above the slender 37-mm main gun tube.[1] He appears wearing a tanker's Knute Rockne-style leather helmet that included goggles, a throat microphone, and headphones sewn into the leather earflaps. By contrast, most M8 armored car reconnaissance crewmen wore a standard steel helmet since they operated more often in dismounted fashion.[2]

One may observe above the minimal sloping of the Stuart tank's armor and the removable steel grousers attached to the turret, which provided some extra protection for its occupants in combat. American tank crews

---

[1] Zaloga, *Stuart U.S. Light Tanks in Action*, 29.
[2] Rottman, *World War II US Cavalry Groups: European Theater*, 12.

were known to mount all sorts of odds and ends (bedrolls, bags, spare track segments, an extra bogie wheel or two, sandbags,[1] even logs) to the outside of their tank to prematurely trigger the explosion of an enemy anti-tank warhead before it penetrated the turret or armored hull.[2] Note also the 30-caliber coaxial machine gun barrel protruding from the turret and the periscope on the underside of the open driver's hatch. The latter greatly aided the driver's ability to maneuver the tank when it was under enemy fire and the hatch was closed or "buttoned up".

---

[1] General Patton took great exception to sandbag "armor", thinking sandbags were ineffective. He believed the extra weight put excessive strain on the tank's suspension and powertrain. Thus, he ordered all units in his Third Army to discontinue that practice. Steven J. Zaloga, *M4 (76mm) Sherman Medium Tank 1943-65*, (Botley, UK: Osprey Publishing, 2003), 24.
[2] Caddick-Adams, *Snow & Steel*, 428.

3. GOT LEAVE, GOT MARRIED, GOT BUSTED

Family lore has it that Dad first met Christine Rose Hula in February 1942. She had gone to Manhattan, Kansas, to attend an evening dance with two of her girlfriends, Anna Mae and Lucille. On their arrival, however, they encountered a slight problem gaining admission to the United Service Organizations (USO) Center, as they had failed to secure cards of admittance in advance. Consequently, they were required to present identification at the door to convince the USO hostesses that they were in fact wholesome, upstanding young ladies, and that their moral character was beyond reproach. As they happened to be teachers at the high school in Delia, Kansas, that requirement was settled in a matter of minutes, and they were admitted graciously to the dance and invited to secure admittance cards for future use.

Shortly after Christine and her friends entered the dance hall, my father glanced her way and decided to linger a little while longer. He was smitten soon thereafter and mustered up the courage to ask her to dance. As it happened, the couple spent the remainder of the evening together, dancing, chatting, and enjoying each other's company.

Following that first meeting, they corresponded back and forth and subsequently arranged to meet and spend time together over several weekends, whenever he could obtain a forty-eight-hour pass; their usual rendezvous was the Walgreens drugstore in Topeka. From that time on, their relationship gradually blossomed into romance.

Dad's romantic pursuit of Christine was certainly the best decision he ever made, as her pleasant personality enriched his life and lightened his temperament somewhat. She had earned a bachelor's degree in music from Marymount College in Salina, Kansas.[1] Following her graduation from college in 1941, she began a short career teaching music and English at

---

[1] The "programme" from her senior piano recital reveals that she played a number of classical works *"andante non troppe e molto maestro"* as follows: two pieces by J.S. Bach (*Prelude and Fugue in B flat major* and *Toccato in D minor*); *Sonata in A major* by Domenico Scarlatti; *The Hungarian Rhapsody No.* 2 by Franz Liszt; *Ballade in G minor* by Frederic Chopin; and *Concerto No. 1 in B flat minor* by Pyotr Ilyich Tschiakovsky. *The Garland*, 1941.

various high schools in rural Kansas. From letters Dad wrote her while on maneuvers in Louisiana, it is clear that they became engaged during 1943.

This photograph, as well as that on the page that follows, were taken of Christine Rose Hula, while she attended Marymount College.

She was a poised and pretty, but reserved college graduate, who revered music, culture and the arts. On the other hand, Pop back then was quite rough around the edges, and could best be described as having a somewhat devil-may–care-attitude. Given their incongruous backgrounds and lack of shared interests, it was always a mystery to me how they came to marry one another. Yet, she was obviously in love with him, and likely as not, her higher education had opened her mind to experiencing life away from family and friends in Kansas. Also, she was no doubt intrigued about the possibility of greater cultural fulfillment and the enjoyment of big city life, in contrast to her years on the endless prairie.

Below is a photograph of Sergeant Gough without his mustache. (That circumstance was likely in keeping with Christine's preference.) His garrison cap with 15th Cavalry regimental crest appears set at a jaunty angle, and he seems rather pleased with himself that he found his true love and she agreed to be his bride.

When the high school at which Christine worked let their students out for the summer, she routinely went home to the family farm in south-central Kansas to help with the harvest. Her parents, Louis Adolph and Frances Mary Hula, were both of Czech-American descent, and were wed in February 1914.[1] Together, that down-to-earth couple ran a farm and several grain elevators in tiny Blackstone, Kansas. There they raised chickens for home consumption and worked the land growing commercial crops: red winter wheat and animal fodder, such as alfalfa hay and grain sorghum. They were a hardy, industrious people, infused with the pioneer spirit of the American West, who augmented their farm income by owning and operating a general merchandise store and a grain-buying business, both situated adjacent to the old homestead.

Blackstone was a miniscule place located roughly ten miles west of Caldwell, Kansas, in Sumner County; one would have to pass through it on the way to the bustling metropolis of Bluff City, Kansas. On that Great Plains site stood a quaint collection of wooden buildings surrounded by a few large, wind-blown shade trees. Adjacent to the farmhouse was a vegetable garden, garage, windmill, chicken coup and a tornado-proof storm shelter.[2] Also, situated there were several steel bins next to a single spur line of railroad track. Nearby was a small, one-room white schoolhouse where my grandmother taught Christine, her older brother (Louis) and several other children from neighboring farms their lessons through the elementary grades. She was their schoolteacher simply by virtue of the fact that, for many miles around, she alone had a high school diploma.[3]

---

[1] Two children were born of that marriage: Louis John Hula in July 1916, and Christine Rose Hula in December 1918.
[2] That cyclone-proof cellar near our grandparent's vegetable garden provided us much enjoyment as children; we had fun running down there whenever the wind picked up and the sky grew dark. Along with the imagined intrigue of that underground structure were the ubiquitous spider webs that frightened my sisters, and the many vegetables our grandmother canned, her Mason jars filled with pickled cucumbers and an assortment of fruit preserves.
[3] Frances Mary (nee Lovci) Hula graduated from Caldwell High School in 1911. *The Jayhawker 1912*, 39.

Later, when our maternal grandparents grew too old to operate the farm, they made "the move to town" in the early 1950s. Now it exists only as an intersection of two lonely dirt roads, except for the pleasant memories of those who had the good fortune to have experienced it. (Sadly, the "home place" was sold and the buildings were either moved or torn down, but I'm happy to report that that ground remains today in productive cultivation.)

By early summer of 1943, Dad encouraged Christine by letter to be careful around farm machinery and wrote that he regretted having to leave her and go overseas to fight the war. In the very same letter, however, he wrote that he looked forward to the "swell adventure awaiting him in new lands" and mentioned that it would be great to be in a position to tell his "children and grandchildren all about" World War II, when he returned. Dad's conflicted message to her on that occasion calls to mind Gen. George Patton's inspirational words to his soldiers: "When it's all over and you're home once more, you can thank God that twenty years from now, when you're sitting around the fireside with your grandson on your knee and he asks you what you did in the war, you won't have to shift him to the other knee, cough, and say, 'I shoveled shit in Louisiana.'"[1]

At about that time, Christine apparently had in mind quitting her job as a teacher in order to follow him from one army camp to another. But in subsequent correspondence, Dad did his best to squelch that idea. He said he would welcome having her near, but explained that the hardships involved were extreme, and that all she could find for off-post housing were "run down places." That, he said, "was no life for a sweet thing like you."

Regarding his experience in Louisiana during summer maneuvers, Dad complained to her by letter in mid-July 1943 that they were the "Red Army"[2], which always withdrew, never went on the attack, and were always the "losers of this [mock] war." He also griped about the ever-present heat

---

[1] Quoted in Martin Blumenson, *Patton: The Man behind the Legend, 1885-1945* (New York: William Morrow, 1985), 223.
[2] For war-gaming purposes, the American military ordinarily designates the friendly force as the "Blue Army" and the enemy force assumes the title of "Red Army."

and ubiquitous flies, chiggers, mosquitoes, and venomous snakes he encountered in the Louisiana swamps.

Months later, after a rather lengthy courtship for those times (nearly two full years), Francis and Christine were married before a small group of family and friends on a cold, blustery Christmas Eve in 1943 at Our Lady of Sorrows Catholic Church in Bluff City, Kansas.

The formal wedding photograph on the next page shows the newly married couple, looking quite happy at a time when the rest of the world was coming apart at the seams. She wore a flowing white veil and bridal gown, accented by a decorative prayer book. Dad had on his army dress-A uniform, enhanced by several marksmanship badges, service ribbons, and a blue-over-white, X Corps patch on his left shoulder sleeve.[1]

---

[1] Pop's X Corps assignment was apparently brief, perhaps covering the Louisiana swamp maneuvers and/or during pre-deployment training in the California desert, as the X Corps was shipped off to fight Japanese forces in the Pacific during 1944.

By the time he obtained a two-week furlough to get married in December 1943, Pop had successfully climbed the enlisted ladder to "buck" sergeant, which equated to three stripes or chevrons on both of his sleeves. However, shortly thereafter his military rank underwent a drastic alteration.

Following their brief honeymoon in Wichita and Kansas City, it so happened that he miscalculated the time it would take him to travel by train back to his unit in the California desert. He thought he had passage straight through to his destination, but he was in error.[1] Since he was traveling by himself during a time of war, he discovered to his dismay that all military supply and troop trains had absolute priority.

By the time his passenger train got underway, he realized his misfortune; thereafter, he was forced to change trains several times, as precedence in wartime was afforded to all competing military rail traffic. Naturally, that circumstance caused his progress to be delayed and he returned from leave late.

For his military tardiness, he was placed on report for AWOL[2] disciplinary action, which ultimately brought about his demotion to buck private. That reduction in rank significantly reduced his monthly service pay,[3] and he was transferred from Troop E to Troop F within the 15th Cavalry Regiment.

> Sometime later, Pop informed his diary, quite succinctly:
> "GOT LEAVE, GOT MARRIED, GOT BUSTED."
> Afterward, Christine continued with her high school teaching career, but by mid-1945 she was back on the farm, living with her parents, assisting them with the chores, and helping out to the best of her ability.

---

[1] Prior to their wedding, Pop was unaware that railroad unions were in turmoil and threatened to strike over wage concerns in the autumn of 1943; matters came to a head just two days after Christmas 1943, when FDR directed his secretary of war to seize and operate the railroads to insure that critical supplies were shipped to the nation's fighting men in wartime. Burns, *Roosevelt: The Soldier of Freedom*, 338, and Brands, *Traitor to His Class*, 757-758.

[2] The military acronym "AWOL" stands for Absent Without Official Leave.

[3] In 1943, U.S. Army pay amounted to little more than a $1.60 a day, totaling less than $50 per month for a private soldier. George W. Neill, *Infantry Soldier: Holding the Line at the Battle of the Bulge* (Norman: University of Oklahoma Press, 2000), 6.

4. OFF TO WAR: FIRST STOP, BRITAIN

Within a few weeks after their wedding, military matters became far more urgent for Dad, as his regiment increased its field training readiness and prepared for their overseas deployment. Like all of the other troopers at Camp Coxcomb, California, the end of January 1944 found him getting his personal affairs in order by executing his last will and testament and signing a general power of attorney in favor of his wife, Christine. At that time he also designated an allotment of his pay to her and made her the beneficiary of a standard government life insurance policy provided to all GIs.

Then, on February 6, 1944, the U.S. 15th Cavalry Regiment (Mechanized), totaling roughly 1,600 officers and enlisted men, boarded troop trains in Freda, California, which transported them across the continent to New York where they were to embark for the European Theater of Operations (ETO). On arrival, Dad's unit staged at Camp Shanks, New York, some thirty miles north of New York City. It was there they remained until railroad cars were dispatched to carry the regiment south to the New York Port of Embarkation for their trans-oceanic trip overseas.

On the last day of February 1944, they were ferried across the Hudson River to board the RMS *Queen Mary*, leaving from Pier 68 in lower Manhattan. The troops queued up, forming long lines and boarded "by the numbers", i.e., when their last name was called, they answered loudly with their first name and middle initial.[1] Among them was my father, who completed his long climb up the gangway with all the other olive green-clad soldiers, carrying full duffle bags on their shoulders. Sadly, due to the military need for operational security, there were no bands, relatives, friends, or waving crowds dockside to wish them well on their dangerous journey.

That huge troopship, the RMS *Queen Mary*, had the capacity to carry an entire army division (up to 15,000 soldiers) in one ocean crossing.[2] During

---

[1] Alex Kershaw, *The Bedford Boys: One American Town's Ultimate D-Day Sacrifice* (Cambridge, MA: Da Capo Press, 2003), 38.
[2] Burns, *Roosevelt: The Soldier of Freedom*, 368.

its conversion from luxury passenger liner to Allied troop transport, her exterior was painted navy gray. As a consequence, she was nicknamed the "Gray Ghost" due to her new, deceptive color scheme and excellent cruising speed.[1]

While essentially unarmed, the *Queen Mary* transited the Atlantic Ocean alone, without the impediment of a convoy or escort vessels. Other ships that required transit via the convoy system were at a greater disadvantage, because their transatlantic crossing could proceed only as fast as the slowest ship in the convoy. Her sister ship, the RMS *Queen Elizabeth* was also converted to troopship status during World War II, as they were the largest and fastest ships then afloat. Their great speed allowed them to cross the North Atlantic in five to seven days, depending on the weather.[2]

That ocean passage to Europe began after a full complement of American soldiers came aboard, and the mooring lines securing her to the pier were cast off. After several tugboats came alongside and pushed her out into a crowded New York Harbor her ship's horn sounded a loud blast as she gently eased into the Hudson River. While she maneuvered cautiously down the Upper New York Bay, slower vessels adjusted their courses to make way for her departure. The pilot on the bridge likewise made delicate course adjustments, providing the men an impressive skyline view to the left or port side of the ship.

Dad had a good look at the Empire State Building and the rest of the Manhattan skyline in the distance. Shortly afterward, many others on the right (or starboard) side of the ship saw Ellis Island and the Statue of Liberty on her pedestal, holding high the torch of freedom. As she gradually increased speed, that powerful three-funneled racehorse of the sea

---

[1] The RMS *Queen Mary* could accelerate up to a maximum speed of thirty-two knots, while the German U-boat had a top speed of only twelve knots on the surface, dropping to seven knots when submerged. She was so elusive that Hitler offered a $250,000 prize "to the first Nazi submariner who sank her." Kershaw, *The Bedford Boys: One American Town's Ultimate D-Day Sacrifice*, 42-43.

[2] By contrast, British soldiers and Hessian mercenaries spent roughly a month or more at sea in 1776, sailing in the opposite direction to crush American independence by force of arms. Joseph J. Ellis, *Revolutionary Summer* (New York: Alfred A. Knopf, 2013), 68.

slid gracefully through the Narrows, passing Staten Island to starboard and Long Island off to port.

On clearing the continental shelf, she turned to the open ocean and swung out into the cold, choppy waters of the North Atlantic, her engines steadily accelerating to full speed. Next, the captain set a course and the helmsman steered east by northeast to minimize the possibility of a German submarine encounter. At that moment, Dad and his cavalry regiment were on their way to war, not to return to America for nearly two years. As they began that voyage, many men aboard that troopship likely sensed that some among them might not return alive.

By the second day at sea, Dad wrote that he was only slightly sick from a mild headache, as the pitch and roll of the ship caused him only minimal disturbance. He mentioned that he tried to spend as much time as possible on deck, looking out on the horizon to avoid seasickness. On the next day, the ocean quieted down, and by the fourth and fifth day, he reported having a fine time, since the wind and weather had become slightly calmer.

Although the soldiers had been cautioned to stay out of the way of the ship's crew, he mentioned that he fought the monotony of long days at sea by walking the decks during daylight hours. He reported covering the entire ship on foot, except for the top deck (designated "officers only"), the bridge and engine rooms, which he described as "off limits." By the sixth day of their voyage, he reported the weather had become more turbulent, and he mentioned being ordered to report to the galley for two hours of KP duty. In his diary he wrote that he was not at all upset about that assignment as it relieved the tedium somewhat, and got him the opportunity for extra chow.

Since Pop was just an ordinary GI, his berthing arrangement was less than ideal, located deep within the foul-smelling bowels of the ship. Needless to say, it was not what he had anticipated. Like all the other enlisted men, he was assigned a canvas and metal-frame bunk, measuring about six feet long and two feet wide. To make matters worse, the bunks were stacked in tiers, one on top of the other, rising up many levels. As they had no more than around two feet of headroom between bunks, getting in and out of them required some dexterity; he also complained that sitting upright in his bunk was virtually impossible. Since the ship's ventilation system was poor, he described it as constantly humid and unpleasant; thus, there is slight wonder he spent much of his time at sea roaming around above deck.[1]

Despite his less than favorable review of life at sea, the trip was uneventful, and the *Queen Mary* successfully completed her mission in seven days. She rounded the northern tip of Ireland (the North Channel route), entered the Irish Sea and brought her important cargo safely to shore. That voyage to the United Kingdom covered a distance of some 3,300 miles.[2]

Dad wrote that he stood by the ship's rail and sighted the coastline early on the morning of March 7th 1944. He mentioned further that the weather was blustery as their ship crept into the Firth of Clyde, the estuary of Glasgow. There he saw the verdant backdrop of Argyll and observed loud, squawking sea gulls swooping overhead. On nearing their destination, the vibration of the ship's engines diminished and the choppy waves gradually changed from white caps on a slate-blue canvas to a calmer, murky green, as they entered protected waters and drew near the Scottish coastline.

After the mighty ocean vessel finally came to a stop, she stood at anchor all day. He and his mates thereafter responded to the order to "Lay below" and they remained crowded together in their foul-smelling shipboard quarters awaiting instructions for disembarkation. On the following day, they grabbed their gear, and as their ship stood offshore, they loaded onto an old, dilapidated channel ferry, the *King George*, (presumably the TS *King George V*) for transfer ashore.

There was no welcoming ceremony, but the men were pleased to have escaped their shipboard entombment and completed the ocean crossing safely to Greenock, Scotland, at the western mouth of the River Clyde.[3]

---

[1] Kennett, *G.I.: The American Soldier in World War II*, 115; to make matters worse, enlisted soldiers were not allowed to take showers. Only officers had that privilege at sea; thus, the "stench of unwashed thousands quickly filled every deck." They learned it was better to sleep in a lower bunk to avoid having to clamber down over several men, but when the sea got rough, the top bunk was the place to be, as there at least, no one would be "puking his guts out" mere inches above his head. Kershaw, *The Bedford Boys*, 42-43.

[2] John R. Slaughter, *Omaha Beach and Beyond* (St. Paul, MN: Zenith Press, 2007), 47.

[3] As a destination for supplies and millions of U.S. troops, the Clyde (Glasgow) harbor was superb and played a major role during World War II.

After stepping off the quay and onto European soil, the men lined up and marched off in "route step" to board a troop train for their trek southward.

During their lengthy railroad trip, they skirted several large cities, i.e., Glasgow, Manchester, and Birmingham, and continued along the rolling British countryside. After many hours, they arrived at their destination, the small town of Trowbridge, Wiltshire, in the southwest of England. There they detrained for the short transit to their new encampment, the Trowbridge Royal Artillery Barracks, where they remained billeted until mid-1944. That location was considered choice, since the landscape was scenic and only a few miles southeast of the scenic city of Bath, near Stonehenge, the famous prehistoric monument on Britain's Salisbury Plain.

At that location, there was adequate port infrastructure, easy access to the Atlantic Ocean, and as the harbor was far from enemy bomber bases in France, it was immune from enemy air attack. Paul Kennedy, *Engineers of Victory* (New York: Random House, 2013), 236.

The photograph above was taken after Pop's arrival in England. His wavy, brown hair was noticeably longer and his face reflected a newfound determination: what one Pulitzer-prize winning author saw in another American soldier: an "economy of expression."[1] In the photo he appears

---

[1] The phrase "economy of expression" described Ulysses S. Grant whenever he sat for a photograph. Carl Sandburg, *Abraham Lincoln: The War Years* (vol. 1) (New York: Harcourt, Brace & World, 1939), 463.

rather glum, but his countenance suggests that he was nearly finished with the process of girding for war. His somber, thoughtful expression reveals an understanding of his proximity to combat, as well as a newfound appreciation for his own mortality and the deadly seriousness of the job ahead.

The dark wool shirt under his single-breasted tunic provides clear evidence that he and his mates had encountered much colder weather. That dress-A uniform (including shirt and tie) was worn only when he was on leave or off duty. While training or on duty in the field, American GIs wore the usual, operational attire: loose fitting, olive drab fatigues, otherwise known as battle dress.

Out of view, Pop had on a Saint Christopher medallion, dangling from a chain around his neck, which also held his metal army identification dog tags. (His bride, Christine, had given him that religious medal shortly after their wedding in hopes that it would protect him from harm while he was away at war.)

His uniform in the photograph above bore witness to his then-recent demotion to private soldier (*sans* chevrons), and his lack of expression revealed a sense of chagrin and unhappiness as to that matter.

5. ORGANIZATION & EQUIPMENT OF THE 15th CAVALRY GROUP

In mid-March 1944, the 15th Cavalry Regiment underwent reorganization and was designated the 15th Cavalry Group (Mechanized). That restructuring resulted from the demise of the old horse cavalry as a U.S. Army combat force during the Second World War. The new cavalry group was envisioned to be an armored/mechanized, combined-arms reconnaissance force with added punch, as it was intended to go into battle with its own organic (permanently assigned) light tanks and artillery.

Between 1943 and 1944, sixteen U.S. cavalry regiments were similarly reorganized. In most cases, the regiment's 1st Squadron took the group's number, and the 2nd Squadron was assigned "an unrelated (usually higher) number in no discernable sequence."[1] Hence, the 1st Squadron of the old 15th Cavalry Regiment became the 15th Cavalry Squadron, and the 2nd Squadron became the 17th Cavalry Squadron. As restructured, the new U.S. Army mechanized cavalry **group**, rather than regiment, became the controlling headquarters, having only one organic element, the Headquarters and Headquarters Troop (HHT). It became strictly a command and control element without any service or logistical capabilities to support its attached squadrons, and its function was solely to direct and command the squadrons.

The two cavalry reconnaissance squadrons were the main fighting elements of the cavalry group, and were about "20 percent smaller" than a standard infantry battalion.[2] Each squadron was administratively self-sufficient, as to service support functions (administration, supply, mess and maintenance sections). Normally, the squadrons stayed attached to the parent group on a more or less permanent basis throughout their wartime service.[3]

During World War II, each U.S. Army cavalry squadron was organized, as follows: a Headquarters and Headquarters & Service Troop (HH&ST);

---

[1] Rottman, *World War II US Cavalry Groups: European Theater*, 8.
[2] Joseph Balkoski, *From Brittany to the Reich: The 29th Infantry Division in Germany, September-November 1944* (Mechanicsburg, PA: Stackpole, 2012), 126.
[3] Harry Yeide, *Steeds of Steel* (Minneapolis, MN: Zenith Press, 2008), 30.

three cavalry reconnaissance troops (each equating to an infantry company, but smaller, lettered Troop A, B, or C); an assault gun troop (Troop E); a light tank company (Company F); and a small medical detachment.[1]

The mechanized cavalry reconnaissance troop had a 56-man troop headquarters (HQ), which included its headquarters, administration, mess, supply & service and maintenance sections. That 140-man reconnaissance troop consisted of three platoons, each equipped with three M8 armored cars (the armored car section) and two scout sections, comprising three squads with two, four-man quarter-ton jeeps per scout squad. Three of the jeeps mounted .30 caliber, air-cooled machine guns and the other three carried 60-mm mortars and ammunition in quarter-ton trailers.

The 94-man light tank company (Company F) of the cavalry squadron had a 34-man HQ, consisting of two M5A1 Stuart tanks, an M3A1 halftrack personnel carrier (maintenance section), a tank-recovery vehicle, two quarter-ton jeeps with cargo trailers, a 2.5-ton cargo truck (known as the "deuce-and-a-half") and a one-ton ammunition trailer. Each of its three tank platoons had five Stuart light tanks, crewed by four men. In addition to the intrinsic weapons of the M5A1 tank, the tank company's small arms included 24 M1 carbines, 70 submachine guns (three per tank), as well as two bazookas and one 81-mm mortar on an armored recovery vehicle. (This weapons inventory was identical to a light tank company organic to a medium tank battalion.)[2]

U.S. Army doctrine at that time held that the three reconnaissance troops were the principal scouting and maneuver elements of the cavalry squadron;[3] the assault gun troop provided limited indirect artillery support to the squadron's maneuver elements; and the light tank company furnished direct fire support to overcome the enemy and accomplish the mission.

Although the cavalry squadron contained an array of short-range firepower, its weakness was its heavy dependence on thin-skinned vehicles, especially the workhorse, quarter-ton jeeps, which were essential to its highly mobile reconnaissance mission. Even with its predominance of

---

[1] Rottman, *World War II US Cavalry Groups: European Theater*, 9.
[2] The prior two paragraphs rely on Rottman, *World War II US Cavalry Groups*, 10-12.
[3] Only armored divisions in World War II included a fourth reconnaissance troop, Troop D. Yeide, *Steeds of Steel*, 28.

automatic weapons, 37-mm guns, light mortars, and self-propelled artillery, the organic weaponry of a mechanized cavalry unit was intended mainly for self-defense purposes and reconnaissance by fire.[1] That said, Dad's 17th Cavalry Recce Squadron's total strength was around 755 men of all ranks[2], including seventeen light tanks, numerous trucks, jeeps and several halftracks, forty M8 light armored cars and six self-propelled M8 75-mm HMC (howitzer motor carriages).

As to the M8 armored car, it was essentially a six-wheeled armored truck with three wheels mounted on each side. The front axle was used for steering and the rear two axles were fixed. Nicknamed the "Greyhound" by the British, it mounted a 37-mm cannon, a .30-caliber coaxial machine gun, and a .50-caliber M2 heavy machine gun attached to a circular steel ring on an open-topped, fully rotating turret for use mainly against enemy aircraft. While the M8 had its shortcomings, including poor cross-country mobility and minimal armored protection for its four-man crew, it provided a safe platform for the radios that were essential for requesting fire support and passing along reconnaissance information to higher command. Of particular note was the M8's road speed (up to 55 miles per hour) and good fuel economy, allowing cavalry groups to move more rapidly and farther than heavier U.S. armored divisions.

With respect to the assault gun troop (Troop E), its HQ numbered some 30 men, and its three 21-man assault gun platoons was comprised of two gun sections, each of which consisted of one M8 self-propelled HMC that replaced the earlier, more vulnerable halftrack assault gun. It was fitted with a short-barreled, "snub-nosed" 75-mm pack howitzer, mounted on a Stuart chassis.

---

[1] Rottman, *World War II US Cavalry Groups: European Theater*, 13.
[2] By comparison, an infantry battalion's strength was 825 men in 1945. *Ibid.,* 23.

Below is a 1942 image[1] of an M8 self-propelled howitzer motor carriage on a M5A1 chassis.

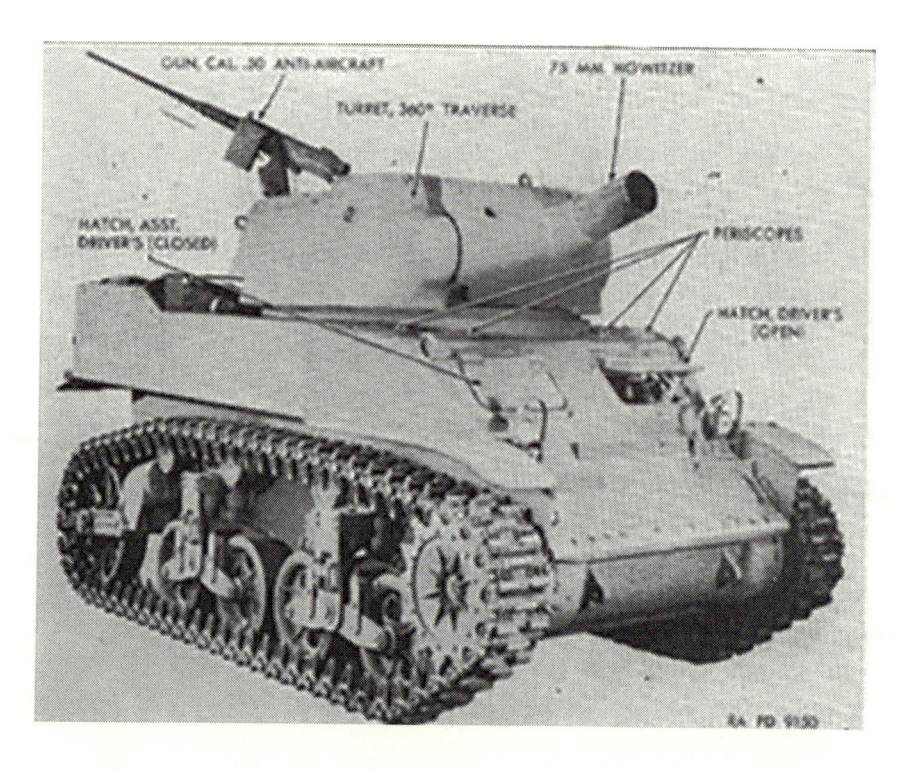

Each HMC assault gun had a five-man crew and towed an ammunition trailer, and each platoon's four-man ammunition section had a M3A1 halftrack and another towed ammunition trailer. In addition to its main gun, the HMC was armed with a .50-caliber M2 machine gun on a circular ring on the turret, allowing for 360 degrees of traverse. With its open-topped turret and light armor, the M8 HMC assault gun was not intended for use in the close support mode, but was more normally used to shoot indirect fire from protected, hull-defilade positions. The cavalry assault guns had a maximum range out to 9,600 yards, and the motor carriage held a combat load of forty-six rounds of high explosive (HE), armor piercing (AP), white phosphorus (WP or "Willie Pete") and smoke. The small arms

---

[1] Driving Instructions, *Light Tank, M5, M5A1, Motor Carriage, M8* (Detroit, Michigan: Cadillac Motor Car Division, General Motors Corporation, December 14, 1942), 14.

weapon inventory of Troop E also included 78 M1 carbines, 16 M1 rifles, 22 submachine guns, six .30 caliber machine guns, nine bazookas, and one 81-mm mortar.[1]

The use of HE or WP ammunition caused devastation to enemy infantrymen; even when fired short of the target, the shells exploded and sent splintered steel fragments, ricocheting for yards beyond the point of impact; such plunging fire had a devastating effect on enemy personnel, even when dug into shallow foxholes. On the other hand, armor-piercing (AP) ammunition was used mostly against armored vehicles, as the projectile would burst after penetrating an armor-clad vehicle. However, AP munitions were considered useless against enemy tanks when fired by 37-mm guns at ranges beyond 500 yards, but they were useful against enemy concrete bunkers and fortifications that were reinforced with steel rods. Smoke shells, by contrast, were put to good use to designate targets and screen friendly forces from enemy view.[2]

The embroidered shoulder patch, displayed on the left on the next page, was that of Dad's outfit, the 17th Cavalry Reconnaissance Squadron. Given its bright, colorful scheme, it was likely worn on the dress uniform only and never in combat, for very obvious reasons.[3]

---

[1] Rottman, *World War II US Cavalry Groups: European Theater*, 15. Howitzers are comparatively short-barreled artillery pieces that generally fire their rounds in battery on high-angled trajectories at relatively low velocities.
[2] War Department Armored Force Field Manual, FM 17-12, *Tank Gunnery* (Washington, D.C.: U.S. Government Printing Office, 1943), 18-21.
[3] Subdued shoulder sleeve insignia (brown or black patches on an olive drab sleeve) are a more recent development for use by U.S. Army soldiers.

17th Cavalry Recce Squadron

15th Cavalry Group and the 15th Cavalry Recce Squadron

The shoulder patch above on the right represents both the 15th Cavalry Group **and** the 15th Cavalry Reconnaissance Squadron; it was based on the original insignia of the 15th Cavalry Regiment.

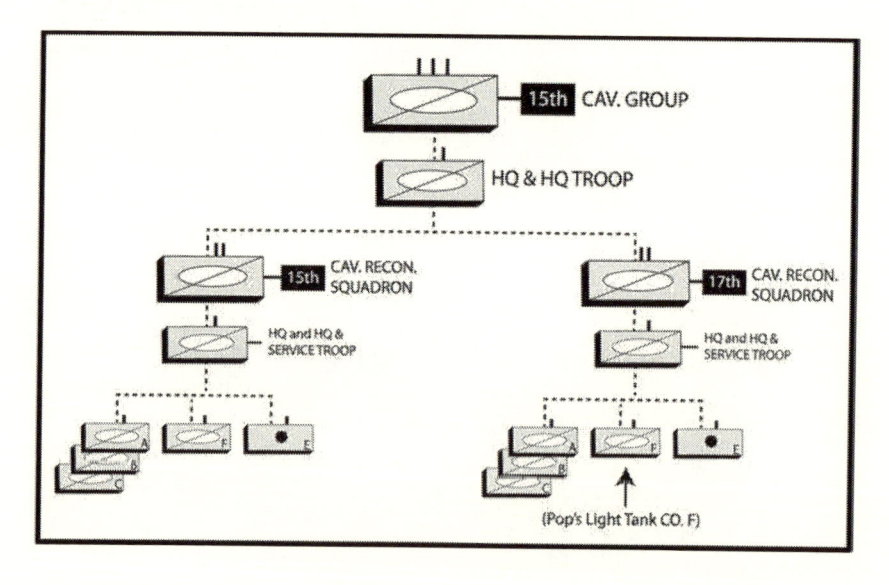

The chart above illustrates the organization of the 15th Cavalry Group during World War II, showing its two identical cavalry reconnaissance squadrons.

After the war ended, official analysis showed that U.S. Army cavalry units rarely performed their primary duty, as reconnaissance missions accounted for only 3 percent of their activity during World War II. Defensive operations accounted for 33 percent; "special" operations (i.e., acting as a mobile reserve, providing security and control in rear areas) made up 29 percent of their activity; "security" missions (i.e., blocking, screening, flank protection, filling gaps, and maintaining contact between widespread corps or divisions) accounted for 25 percent; and, offensive operations (i.e., exploitation, pursuit, and mop-up missions, looking out for infiltration or other scattered enemy forces) amounted to 10 percent.[1] Equally curious is the fact that "security and reconnaissance" cavalry missions often involved offensive combat, and that dismounted action was twice as frequent as mounted action.[2]

To sum up, after the 15th Cavalry Group's reorganization, Dad was assigned to Company F of the 17th Cavalry Recce Squadron as a light tank crewman. By early 1944, the two squadrons of the 15th Cavalry Group had settled into their new location and continued their pre-combat training. They drew more equipment and supplies, and made all preparations necessary to play an essential role in the invasion of France. Along with many other military units, they were but a small portion of a huge buildup of Allied ground forces that were assembling for the inevitable cross-Channel assault.

With its March 1944 reorganization, the 15th Cavalry Group was assigned to the Third U.S. Army and attached to Maj. Gen. Walton Walker's XX Corps. Shortly thereafter they joined the Advance Section of the U.S. Army's Communications Zone.[3] (Known as the COM-Z, it encompassed the rear area behind the actual zone of combat.)

Pop's diary reveals that from March 9 to May 18, 1944, the 15th Cavalry Group remained billeted in the vicinity of Trowbridge Barracks. Then on Friday, May 19, they were given an important security mission, that amounted to guarding an assortment of temporary camps housing the

---

[1] Trevor N. Dupuy, D. L. Bongard, and Richard C. Anderson, *Hitler's Last Gamble: The Battle of the Bulge, December 1944-January 1945* (New York: HarperCollins, 1994), 386.
[2] Yeide, *Steeds of Steel*, 271-272.
[3] TLR, 5.

invasion troops in the pre–D-Day[1] marshaling areas, arrayed along the southern coast of England near Dorchester and Southampton. For several months, British civilians had been evacuated from that area for obvious security reasons.

The 17th Cavalry Squadron was redeployed to the vicinity of Weymouth, Dorset, England, to surround and sequester the marshaling areas, embarkation points, and roads used by the troops in order to safeguard the secrecy of Operation Overlord, the Allied invasion of German occupied France. In the words of the Supreme Allied Commander, Gen. Dwight D. Eisenhower: "All southern England was one vast military camp." The area was cut off from the rest of England . . . The mighty host was tense as a coiled spring, a great human spring, coiled for the moment when it's energy could be released so that it could "vault the English Channel in the greatest amphibious assault ever attempted."[2]

By then nearly everyone in Europe was aware of the inevitable, as a massive Allied invasion of the continent from Britain was in the offing. Thus, the D-Day invasion force had to be confined, essentially incarcerated behind barbed wire barriers, military police, and security personnel to preserve the element of surprise for the Normandy landings. Most of the south coast of England had been "sealed off from the outside world," as had a strip of the shoreline north and south of Scotland's Firth of Forth, which flows into the North Sea.[3]

Dad's 17th Cavalry Recce Squadron was deployed to secure a bivouac area of the renowned 1st ("Big Red One") Infantry Division, commanded by Maj. Gen. Charles Huebner. Their orders were to shoot anyone who failed to respond to warning commands.[4] A "deadline" was established, "across which no unauthorized person was allowed to go in either

---

[1] "D-Day" in military terminology is the day a military force invades another country; the exact time it "hits the beach" is described as "H-Hour." Ernie Pyle, *Brave Men*, (New York: Henry Holt, 1944), 24.
[2] Dwight D. Eisenhower, *Crusade in Europe* (NY: Doubleday, 1948), 248-249.
[3] Stafford, *Ten Days to D-Day: Countdown to the Liberation of Europe*, 13.
[4] Lawrence Meyers, *Teacher of the Year: The Mystery and Legacy of Edwin Barlow* (Franklin, TN: H. H. & Sons, 2009), 194.

direction."[1] They were to keep out potential Nazi spies, and prevent the GIs from making any last minute pub trips or clandestine visits to see their lady friends. As Pop explained in his diary: "Our job is to keep the enemy <u>out</u> and our own forces <u>in</u>." (Emphasis in the original.)

He described his company bivouac area (Camp D-5) as situated very close to an airfield where twice daily numerous U.S. P-38 "Lightning" fighter aircraft skimmed over "the tops of [their] tents, coming and going." In the early morning hours of May 28 and 29, 1944, he reported experiencing two enemy air attacks near their security outposts. He mentioned they were not allowed to engage the enemy with anti-aircraft fire because "our own fighter planes were up there with them." He also wrote that an enemy bomb had landed and failed to explode near their security position (Post #4). After that close call, a move was considered prudent, and they marked the location of the German "dud" and left it for disposal by an ordnance team. Thereafter, in the interest of safety, they redeployed to a second security outpost to enable the engineer "bomb squad" to defuse it.

By May 1944, the Third Reich could reasonably be considered living on borrowed time. The military forces of the Grand Alliance had effectively surrounded them, but they still maintained control of a huge swath of Europe. In the north, the German Reich stretched to the Arctic regions of Norway, and to the south, it extended from Northern Italy to Rome. From east to west, it spanned an enormous distance from the Black Sea to the Atlantic seaports of France.[2] Despite the clearly deteriorating military situation at that time, the monstrous work of Hitler's regime continued unabated, as the first trainload of Jews arrived in Auschwitz that month. By July 1944, no fewer than 394,000 of those individuals became victims of the Nazi's round-the-clock gas chambers.[3]

---

[1] Eisenhower, *Crusade in Europe*, 248-249.
[2] Nicholas Stargardt, *The German War: A Nation Under Arms, 1939-1945* (New York, Basic Books, 2015), 419.
[3] Evans, *The Third Reich at War*, 617-618.

On Sunday, June 4, 1944, my father mentioned in his diary that he went to St. Peters Church[1] in the village of West Knighton, Dorchester, to pray, as he thought it was a Roman Catholic Church. In true ecumenical fashion, however, he wrote that he "stayed anyway" after discovering it was not a Catholic Church after all; he then put the time to good use by saying a few prayers and making his peace with the Almighty.

In early June, the U.S. 101st ("Screaming Eagles") and 82nd ("All-American") Airborne Divisions had finished their move to closed airfields in central and southern England, and Gen. Dwight "Ike" Eisenhower had established his advance command post at the seaport, southern coast city of Portsmouth. The weather on June 5 was severely inclement (cold, rainy and foggy), and everyone was on edge. But to ease his concerns that evening, Ike decided to inspect the men of the 101st Airborne Division at an airfield forty miles north of Portsmouth, and wished them well.[2]

During the evening of June 5th, at around 2345 hours[3] (11:45 p.m.), Dad reported hearing the loud roar of many engines filling the nighttime air; he described looking up to see many aircraft with three white identification stripes painted on their wings and the sky "filled with red and green [wingtip] lights" strung out in V-shaped formations. He wrote there were so many airplanes flying overhead that it looked "just like Christmas." He noted the heavily laden, twin-engine aircraft C-47 troop carriers that seemed to be coming from a northeast direction, and he counted "39 waves" passing over before being relieved from his duty post. He wrote, "Each wave had 40 or more planes," exclaiming further, "All night long, wave after wave of planes went over" some with gliders attached and filled with troops.

---

[1] St. Peters Church in Dorset belongs to the Church of England and the Diocese of Salisbury, and Thomas Hardy, the English author of novels such as *The Return of the Native* and *Tess of the d'Urbervilles* lived nearby and was a congregant.
http://www.opcdorset.org/WestKnightonFiles/WKnighton.htm
[2] Clay Blair, *Ridgway's Paratroopers: The American Airborne in World War II* (Garden City, New York: Dial Press, 1985), 216.
[3] The military uses a twenty-four-hour clock, i.e. 2400 hours is midnight, and it becomes 0001, as a new day begins.

On Tuesday, the sixth of June 1944, he wrote that he had heard a news flash over the radio that Allied ground forces had attacked early in the morning. (By that point in the war, the French were entering their 1,453rd day of occupation and oppression at the hands of German forces. For them, the concept of liberation was finally at hand.[1])

From 0730 to 1100 that morning, Pop described the sky as completely "filled with large aircraft . . . some were pretty well shot up . . . returning from an all-night raid . . . must have been thousands of them."

---

[1] Carlo D'Este, *Eisenhower: A Soldier's Life* (New York: Henry Holt, 2002), 532.

6. EARLY NORMANDY HEROICS

The landing on Omaha Beach was a very dangerous enterprise for American soldiers because it was such a "highly defensible piece of terrain."[1] Proof of that observation is the fact that U.S. soldiers incurred more than 8,000 casualties on the first day, D-Day, June 6, 1944.

The casualties from Omaha Beach, including the first-wave V Corps soldiers in the Big Red One and the 29th ("Blue-Gray")[2] Infantry Divisions, ran to about 4,700 men. At Utah Beach, the initial wave of VII Corps troops, the 4th ("Ivy") Infantry Division,[3] together with the supporting parachute infantry of the 101st Screaming Eagles and the 82nd All-American Divisions, sustained casualties of around 3,450 men on the Cotentin Peninsula.

To begin with, Omaha Beach near the town of Vierville-sur-Mer is essentially crescent-shaped (i.e., curved inward), which allowed the enemy to mass their gunfire and sweep the beach from both sides. The landing area was quite imposing, as it was nearly 7,000 yards wide, and flanked by cliffs and bluffs that rose to more than one hundred feet above sea level. To make matters worse, it was "honeycombed" with machine-gun nests and dug-in bunkers and embrasures.[4]

The higher casualty figure on Omaha resulted from the fact that the enemy occupied well-prepared defensive firing positions on high ground, directly overlooking the beach. Also, among the five beaches stormed by

---

[1] Joseph Balkoski, *Omaha Beach: D-Day, June 6, 1944* (Mechanicsburg, PA: Stackpole Books, 2004), 40.

[2] The 29th Blue-Gray Division was an Army National Guard outfit that included men from Virginia, the District of Columbia and Maryland, comprising regiments with lineage dating back to Union and Confederate service during the American Civil War. D'Este, *Patton: A Genius for War*, 584.

[3] The 4th Infantry Division was nicknamed the "Ivy" Division as a play on words from the Roman numerals "IV". Charles Whiting, *Papa Goes to War: Ernest Hemingway in Europe, 1944-45* (Wiltshire, UK: Crowood Press, 1990), 61.

[4] Harry Yeide, *The Infantry's Armor* (Mechanicsburg, PA: Stackpole, 2010), 137.

the Allies on D-Day, Omaha was unique in that it allowed mutually supportive plunging enemy fire from the cliffs above, as well as grazing fire.[1] The Germans had carefully laid down fields of fire that "could shoot parallel with the shore and cover every square foot of it for miles with artillery," reported one eyewitness.[2] Flanking embrasures were mounted directly on the beach in concrete-reinforced casemates, angled obliquely (sideways) to shield the enfilading enemy gunfire from observation on the seaward side. Those emplacements were well camouflaged and nearly unassailable from the sea, as Allied ship borne gun spotters could not see them to direct return fire. That allowed the Germans a highly destructive convergence of gunfire that swept the beach from end to end. Those near perfect, interlocking fields of fire were a significant force multiplier for the Germans.[3] Proof comes from the fact that, as they came ashore into that cauldron of enemy gunfire, the leading waves of the U.S. 1st and 29th Divisions suffered 90 per cent casualties.[4]

Situated nearly thirty miles west of Omaha beachhead, the terrain on Utah Beach was far less intimidating, since it was essentially flat and linear. Because of a floodplain located immediately behind the beach, enemy defensive works had to be positioned farther back from the landing area. Thus, the enemy defenders at Utah had relatively limited visibility of the American invasion force as they crossed that beach and advanced up the windblown sand dunes.

Nonetheless, both amphibious landings produced a near equal number of American combat soldiers on the soil of France by the end of D-Day, around 35,000 on each beachhead. While American losses were greater than those of the enemy, that outcome was not unexpected as an attacking force normally suffers greater losses than a defender. But by the end of D-

---

[1] Atkinson, *The Guns at Last Light*, 65.
[2] Pyle, Brave Men, 361.
[3] Adrian R. Lewis, *Omaha Beach: A Flawed Victory* (Chapel Hill: University of North Carolina Press, 2001), 275.
[4] Barr, *Eisenhower's Armies*, 365.

Day, the American landing forces and their Allies had gained full ownership of the Normandy beaches.[1]

Coincident with the American invasion, our British Allies made simultaneous attacks on D-Day, landing to the east of Omaha Beach at Gold and Sword Beaches, and Canadian forces landed successfully between the British at Juno Beach. The total number of Allied casualties on D-Day amounted to roughly 3,000 killed, missing, and wounded.[2]

Beyond the stark casualty numbers mentioned above, there were many examples of personal courage and valor displayed during the Normandy landings. As there were so many heroes on June 6, it would be unwieldy to try and enumerate them all, but I believe it useful to mention three particular instances of extraordinary bravery, as follows:

Landing with the assault wave at Omaha Beach First Lt. Jimmie W. Montieth, Jr., a former member of the Virginia Polytechnic Institute[3] Corps of Cadets, commanded a platoon in Company L, 3rd Battalion, 16th Regiment of the Big Red One. Under heavy enemy mortar and machine-gun fire, he led his platoon across Fox Red Beach, several hundred yards to the east of their intended landing area on Fox Green Beach.[4] Through withering fire and a tangle of obstacles, he organized his men and moved them off the beach, across a stone-laden shingle bank to the base of a bluff. From there, Monteith left the cover of his position and retraced his steps to retrieve some tanks on the beach in order to obtain their support. As their hatches were closed, the tank crewmen inside were unable to see much through their periscopes; consequently, he stood in the open and banged on the sides of the tanks, directing them to lay down supporting fire for his

---

[1] The previous two paragraphs draw on Balkoski, *Omaha Beach*, 343, and Joseph Balkoski, *Utah Beach* (Mechanicsburg, PA: Stackpole, 2005), 301, 325.
[2] Anthony Beevor, *D-Day: The Battle for Normandy* (NY: Viking, 2009), 151.
[3] Virginia Polytechnic Institute (VPI), Virginia's land-grant institution at Blacksburg; it was originally Virginia Agricultural and Mechanical College; now it is Virginia Polytechnic Institute and State University, popularly known as Virginia Tech. Duncan Lyle Kinnear, *The First 100 Years: A History of Virginia Polytechnic Institute and State University* (Richmond: William Byrd Press, 1972), 43, 465.
[4] *Omaha Beachhead (6 June-13 June), American Forces in Action*, Historical Division, U.S. War Department, 20 September 1945, Map No. II.

platoon. "The danger in this act was considerable."[1] While braving full exposure to intense enemy gunfire, he led two M4 Sherman tanks on foot through a minefield and into good firing position up the Cabourg draw, at which point the tanks "unleashed 75-millimeter main gun rounds and machine-gun fire on the enemy machine-gun nests and pillbox."[2] As explained by D-Day historian Joseph Balkoski, Lieutenant Monteith "waged a one-man war" against fierce German resistance at close range.[3] Later, he organized his men to repel a desperate German counterattack, which attempted "to push the Americans off their hard-won perch at the crest of the F-1 [Cabourg] draw."[4] Leading by example, without regard for his personal safety, Monteith urged his men to defend that critical exit off the beach until he was killed several hours later.

In a handwritten note General Eisenhower later wrote simply, "This man was good," when he agreed to the posthumous award of the Medal of Honor (the nation's highest award for battlefield bravery) to Montieth for his fearless valor and leadership that day.[5]

Pictured on the next page are two proud alumni of the Virginia Tech Corps of Cadets: my good friend John C. Watkins on the left and myself on the right. On that visit to Normandy some years ago, we paid our respects to the many dead who perished at Omaha Beach and lie buried in hallowed ground at the Normandy American Cemetery and Memorial near Colleville-sur-Mer.

---

[1] John C. McManus, *The Dead and Those About to Die: D-Day: The Big Red One at Omaha Beach* (New York: NAL Caliber, 2014), 166-167.
[2] Ibid., 167. See also Yeide, *The Infantry's Armor*, 142.
[3] Balkoski, *Omaha Beach*, 292.
[4] McManus, *The Dead and Those About to Die*, 234-237.
[5] Balkoski, *Omaha Beach*, 289-293.

On that day, John and I found the final resting place of a fellow Virginia Tech alumnus First Lt. Jimmie W. Montieth, Jr., whose white marble headstone is inlaid with gold leafing, designating him the recipient of the Medal of Honor for leading his men heroically across the beach and up a heavily defended bluff at Omaha Beach. Our visit was particularly poignant since John's late father, B. Chewning Watkins, was a friend of Montieth when both were members of the VPI Corps of Cadets. (As a member of the VPI Class of 1941, cadet Montieth was assigned to Battery K, 3rd Battalion.)

As to Utah Beach, the only soldier awarded the Medal of Honor there was Brig. Gen. Theodore Roosevelt, Jr., (the eldest son of the twenty-sixth U.S. president) who served as assistant division commander of the Big Red One during the earlier North Africa and Sicily Campaigns. Much like his late father and namesake, General Roosevelt was a man of iron will and patriotic fervor.

At Utah, General Roosevelt was a supernumerary general officer with the first wave of Maj. Gen. Raymond Barton's 4th Ivy Division. After making numerous requests to accompany the leading elements of the invasion, General Barton finally gave in and awarded him the honor of landing with the assault force. As a result, he became the ranking officer ashore and functioned as *de facto* Ivy Division commander on Utah Beach.

On learning that his men had mistakenly come ashore nearly a mile south of the intended landing point (les Dunes de Varreville), the general made his own quick reconnaissance of the area beyond the beach. As bullets and shrapnel flew all around, he calmly took control of a chaotic situation, announcing to his subordinates, "We're going to start the war from here!"

What made General Roosevelt's actions on June 6th so impressive was the fact that he was an arthritic, semi-disabled man in his mid-fifties with "congenitally weak vaguely cross eyes."[1] Nonetheless, he hobbled[2] courageously up and down that sandy beach with the use of his walking stick and contributed tremendous inspiration to the men through his leadership under fire. Without regard for his own safety, he repeatedly directed various groups of confused soldiers through the smoke and dust of German mortar and artillery fire, encouraging them to attack straight inland off the beach toward the enemy. Under constant fire, he repeatedly went from one location to another, quelling the chaos and rallying the men around him. For the courage he displayed on that occasion, his Medal of Honor was conferred posthumously, as he had succumbed to a fatal heart attack roughly one month following the landing on D-Day.[3]

---

[1] Atkinson, *The Guns at Last Light*, 59.

[2] While commanding the Big Red One Division's 26th Infantry Regiment during World War I, then-Major Theodore Roosevelt, Jr., sustained a leg wound in action. Pogue, *George C. Marshall: Education of a General*, 187.

[3] The prior four paragraphs draw on Cornelius Ryan's historic work: *The Longest Day: June 6, 1944* (New York: Simon & Schuster, 1959), 231-233 and Joseph Balkoski's more recent study: *Utah Beach*, 177-181, 332-333; also of great importance was the narrative in *Utah Beach to Cherbourg (6 June-27 June 1944) American Forces in Action Series*, Department of the Army, Historical Division, 1 October 1947, 47.

Like Lt. Jimmie Monteith and many other brave American soldiers, the remains of General Roosevelt and his younger brother Quentin (a fatality from World War I aerial combat) lie side-by-side in their final resting place, the American Cemetery and Memorial overlooking Omaha Beach.[1] (See photo, which I took on a more recent trip to Normandy.)

Concerning U.S. naval support provided the troops on D-Day, there is another individual I cannot help but mention, as I became acquainted with him in my youth. He taught algebra and trigonometry in the early 1960s, but little did I know that on June 6, 1944, then-Lt. Cdr. George Dewey Hoffman, a godson of a Spanish-American War hero of the Battle of Manila Bay, had command of a destroyer, the USS *Corry* (DD-463). On that morning, the *Corry* participated in the essential duty of escorting troopships across the English Channel to Utah Beach. Under gray, cloudy skies she arrived at her designated firing position in relatively shallow water off the Cotentin Peninsula's east coast. Along with nearly five thousand other Allied ships providing fire support for the Normandy invasion

---

[1] Flint Whitlock, *The Fighting First: The Untold Story of the Big Red One on D-Day* (Cambridge, MA: Westview Press, 2004), 347.

(including the aging U.S. battleships *Arkansas, Texas,* and *Nevada*), the *Corry* began a gun duel with two German heavy coastal batteries positioned ashore near the small French village of St.-Marcouf.

One of those German batteries mounted four massive 210-mm guns, which were larger than any other piece of ordnance on the entire Normandy invasion front. Needless to say, they made the *Corry*'s 5-inch guns seemed puny by comparison.[1] Nevertheless, so many shells were fired inland from the deck of the *Corry* that her four guns soon became red-hot. Starting at 0545 hours, she traded outbound fire for almost an hour from each of her guns, belching fire from their gun barrels at a rate of "eight 5-inchers a minute." That rapid rate of fire required the sailors to stand on the turrets "playing hoses on the barrels" to keep them from overheating.[2] They succeeded in knocking out one of the German batteries, but the enemy's massive incoming shells continued to bracket them.

Skipper Hoffman ordered a series of abrupt evasive maneuvers in an attempt to avoid the enemy's salvos. That tactic worked for a short while, but as they eased out of shallow water their luck ran out, as they reportedly ran over a submerged naval pressure mine tethered to the sea off Utah Beach.[3] The ensuing explosion "cracked the destroyer like an eggshell,"[4] broke her keel and jammed the ship's rudder, "causing the ship to go in a circle."[5] At the time it was observed the ship "literally jumped out of the water" and sank.[6]

According to one war historian, the *Corry* was the U.S. Navy's only major loss that day, resulting in "more casualties than had been suffered in the Utah Beach landings" up to the time of its sinking.[7] In recognition of

---

[1] Balkoski, *Utah Beach*, 213.
[2] Ryan, *The Longest Day*, 233; Balkoski, *Utah Beach*, 213.
[3] Controversy swirled following the final official action report as to whether enemy gunfire or a submerged naval mine caused the *Corry*'s sinking; no definitive answer was ever deduced following careful official analysis. Balkoski, *Utah Beach*, 215-217.
[4] Atkinson, *The Guns at Last Light*, 58.
[5] Balkoski, *Utah Beach*, 214.
[6] Ambrose, *D-Day, June 6, 1944: The Climatic Battle of World War II*, 266.
[7] Cornelius Ryan, *The Longest Day*, 234-235; the loss of the *Corry* resulted in twenty-two deaths and thirty-three injured sailors, out of a 250-man crew. Balkoski, *Utah Beach*, 323.

his gallantry, Hoffman was awarded the Silver Star Medal (our nation's third-highest military decoration for valor).

Following his retirement, Captain Hoffman earned a graduate degree and pursued a second career as a mathematics teacher at James Madison High School in Fairfax County, Virginia. Using a method, he learned as a midshipman at the U.S. Naval Academy, he assigned daily problems for students to solve individually at the blackboard. While we struggled, he'd seat himself in the "crow's nest" (as he called it) and watch closely, but occasionally his excitement to correct an error got the better of him. On those occasions, he'd launch himself from the edge of his desk and jam one foot into a nearby wastebasket. Appearing totally unconcerned about anything else but the mission at hand, he'd clomp his way up to the blackboard. Needless to say, those comic moments always grabbed our attention, and without fail the class would erupt in good-natured laughter.

In addition to aiding our understanding of algebra and trigonometry, Captain Hoffman shared with us some pithy nautical phrases when our best efforts fell short, such as "Give it the Deep Six" or "Send her below to Davey Jones' locker".

We considered him a most intelligent and caring old salt, yet little did we know the history of his heroic naval service on D-Day. Today, the mortal remains of that fine and caring patriot lie buried at Arlington National Cemetery.

7. FINAL PRE-COMBAT PREPARATION

Following completion and relief from their security mission in support of the D-Day invasion, the detached 17th Cavalry Squadron reassembled with its parent entity, the 15th Cavalry Group at Trowbridge Barracks. There they continued their training, drew extra equipment and made final preparations for the impending cross-Channel movement, as they were a follow-on force soon to be committed to combat on the continent of Europe.[1]

Dad's diary indicates he pulled his last shift of "security guard" duty from midnight to 0400 on June 7, and after two days of deployment they returned to Trowbridge. He wrote with pride that the "Tommies" (slang for British soldiers) had turned out in force to greet them on their arrival back "home."

Finally, on June 10, he mentioned that at long last they "got [their] tanks . . . [they had] come while we were away." He wrote that they were soon hard at it, cleaning them up, as he described their vehicles were "in terrible shape," oily and greasy, having "just come across [the ocean from America]." As an aside, he also noted that day that he had been transferred from the 3rd Platoon of Fox Company to the company headquarters section, and was assigned the gunner position on the HQ section's first tank.

On Monday, June 12, 1944, Dad diarized that he had heard a radio report that a group of high-ranking American officers were visiting Normandy. His understanding was that Generals "Eisenhower, 'Stimpson,'[2] and [Henry 'Hap'] Arnold," as well as "an Admiral [Ernest J. King] were on the French coast today." Pop then recorded his unease concerning all those shiny, multi-starred officers traveling in one group, making a prime target for the enemy. Famous war correspondent Ernie Pyle noted that "being generals, they know they must appear to be brave in order to set an example" for the troops. Thus, they refused protection from

---

[1] TLR, 5.
[2] Dad's diary reference is in error here, as neither Secretary of War Henry L. Stimson nor Gen. William H. Simpson accompanied General Eisenhower to Normandy on that occasion.

snipers, insisting: "No, certainly not, no armored cars for us, we'll just go in open command cars like anybody else."[1]

Indeed, June 12 marked Ike's first visit to France, as he escorted "Marshall, King and Arnold on a tour of the American zone." It happened to be very special day for Gen. George C. Marshall as he was finally returning to that portion of the world where he had performed with stellar distinction and gained the early attention of Gen. John "Black Jack" Pershing during World War I. That VIP group was driven up the bluffs of Omaha Beach (near Pointe du Hoc) to First U.S. Army Headquarters where Generals Leonard Gerow and Omar N. Bradley briefed them, while they consumed a K ration lunch.[2] General Eisenhower knew the morale value of visits by the high command to inspire and hearten the troops. Their presence, roaming around the areas, gave the soldiers "keen satisfaction" and instilled in them confidence "on the theory that the area is a safe one or the rank [flag officers] wouldn't be there."[3]

In addition to the Normandy visit by that gaggle of brass hats, June 12, 1944 was significant as the date of the first V-1 flying bomb attack by the Germans. That and subsequent launchings produced a wave of terror over London and other English cities during the summer of 1944. Even though their speed was slow enough to allow for interception, the 8,000 V-1 "buzz bombs"[4] launched in the first eighty days greatly damaged the morale of the British civilian populace.[5] In his memoirs, Britain's prime minister remembered the awful anxiety and helplessness imposed on the English citizenry by the unpredictable, random nature of the German V-1 attacks. Churchill explained, "The man going home in the evening never knew what he would find; his wife, alone all day or with the children, could not be

---

[1] What the generals didn't know was that no chances were taken with that collection of talent. Like Dad, the military police were worried so they hid armored vehicles along the route, behind hedges and under bushes, out of sight so the generals couldn't see them; they were "ready for action just in case." Pyle, *Brave Men*, 380.
[2] David Eisenhower, *Eisenhower: At War, 1943-1945* (New York: Random House, 1986), 296-297.
[3] Eisenhower, *Crusade in Europe*, 254.
[4] They were named buzz bombs based on the noise they made going overhead, and were also known by Londoners as "doodle bugs".
[5] Ibid., 258; D'Este, *Eisenhower*, 540.

certain of his safe return. The blind impersonal nature of the missile made the individual on the ground feel helpless."[1]

Meanwhile back at Trowbridge Barracks, where the squadron had been billeted for several months, Captain Fiori issued a written order dated 15 June 1944, which promoted five enlisted men[2] from Company F, 17th Cavalry Squadron from private soldier to private first class, including my father.

While Dad and his squadron mates were busy girding themselves for war, Christine Gough received a warm letter on June 19, 1944, from one of my father's maternal uncles, Robert L. McLaughlin of Ashland, Pennsylvania. He wrote on behalf of Pop's Aunt Annie, saying that she was pleased to receive their December 24, 1943 wedding picture; "It arrived on 'D-Day'—and she knew it was a good omen for Francis' safety." He mentioned that Francis had spent "a lot of summers" with his Uncle Martin and Aunts Cassie and Annie, and indicated that there were five brothers and three sisters on Dad's maternal side. Also, in that letter to Christine, Dad's Uncle Bob described himself and his brothers Tom and Frank as veterans of the American Expeditionary Forces in the First World War; Bob also mentioned that he had served in the 42nd ("Rainbow") Infantry Division for twenty-three months in England and France.[3] He proudly informed Christine that the names of nine Goughs, including my father, his three brothers (Joe, Bernard, and Adrian), and "four boys and a girl in the Navy WAVES,"[4] (children of John Gough—a cousin of Francis' father,")

---

1 Winston S. Churchill, *The Second World War: Triumph and Tragedy* (Boston: Houghton Mifflin, 1953), 39.
2 In addition to Dad, the other private soldiers from Fox Company, 17th Cavalry Squadron, promoted to the rank of private first class (PFC) on that occasion, were: Cornelius Lyons, Edward F. Young, Kenneth L. Hanna and Wilbur E. Reiboldt. Order #4, 16 June 1944, Co. F, 17th CAV RCN SQ.
3 Other alumni of the famed Rainbow Division include Douglas MacArthur and Theodore Roosevelt, Jr. See Martin Gilbert, The First World War: A Complete History (New York: Henry Holt and Co., 1994), 446.
4 WAVES were Women Accepted for Voluntary Emergency Service in the U.S. Navy. My mother-in-law, Lois Kavanagh Swinson, was a WAVE during World War II; she conducted Link instrument training and flight simulation instruction to naval cadet pilots from 1945 to 1946. After 1943 it

would soon be enshrined in Ashland's "World War II Honor Roll." Nine Gough surnames were included in a total of nearly nine hundred names serving in World War II from a population of around 6,600 Ashland inhabitants. Uncle Bob concluded, "We all are praying—and especially Aunt Annie—for the early and safe return of all the boys and—she especially mentions Francis."

By the afternoon of Tuesday, June 20, 1944, Dad reported that his company had left the motor pool in Trowbridge with a half load of combat ammunition and began a road march south in their tanks. He indicated they traveled in a column of platoons, keeping fifteen-minute gaps between each five-tank platoon. By that evening, they had arrived at their destination near the English Channel, at which point they parked their vehicles fifty feet apart and made certain their weapons were cleared before dismounting.

The next day's duty reportedly included small arms live firing at a range on the southern coast of England. Pop wrote that they had zeroed[1] their weapons, and after the requisite target shooting, he and several buddies stood on the English cliffs for the rest of the morning and "open[ed] up" with their side arms at some birds as they flew by; he reported he failed to hit any as they were far too small and nimble in flight, but he noted playfully that they had sent "a lot of lead [flying] toward France that morning." Pop also mentioned having his first opportunity to fire a .30-caliber machine gun from the hip, "Hollywood style, just like in the movies." Based on that experience, he announced a discovery that should have been obvious: "the barrel gets hot after 250 rounds."

On the following day, they again motor marched their tanks by platoons to a 37-mm gun "moving" target range. Prior to engaging their targets, Pop bore sighted his direct-vision telescopic gun sight.[2] While on that range, he

---

was said that no aviator was sent to the Pacific who had not received part of his training from a Wave. "Reminiscences of Captain Hancock," No. 1, p. 54, cited in Spector, *At War at Sea: Sailors and Naval Combat in the Twentieth Century,* 274.

[1] "Zeroing" a weapon requires calibration of the gun sights, aligning the aiming point of the front and rear sights with the desired point of impact of the round.

[2] The purpose of a bore sight adjustment "is to parallel the line of sight passing through the telescope with the horizontal and vertical axes of [the]

mentioned that each tank fired their allotment of ten main gun rounds, as well as around eight hundred .30-caliber rounds from their coaxially mounted machine gun.[1]

Initially, as they proceeded through the moving target range, the tank commander rode with his head protruding from the turret hatch in order to spot targets. Having the best field of vision, the commander continued to aid the gunner by adjusting errant fire onto the desired target. That day, Pop claimed he made eight hits with the 37-mm cannon.

On the next day, the tanks returned to the gunnery range and fired off more ammunition at stationary targets, using the telescopic sight out to a distance of one thousand yards; he reported with delight that he had made hits with ten out of eleven rounds. Afterward, Dad mentioned matter-of-factly that he and the crew climbed down and put a torque wrench to use to tighten both tracks.

Looking back, it was clear that tanks had come a long way since their initial use in World War I. Called "land battleships" by Winston Churchill, they literally walked into battle at an average speed of around two miles an hour.[2]

When the British Army first used tanks in September 1916 at the Battle of the Somme, they deployed eighteen in the attack: ten were hit by German gunfire, nine broke down due to mechanical problems, and five failed to make any advance at all; yet, they achieved "by far the deepest penetration of the German lines" since the battle began in early July.[3]

As one might guess, there was no interphone system in those early noisy tanks; thus, the tank commander was required to communicate with

---

bore of the gun." War Department Field Manual, FM 23-80, *37-MM Gun, Tank, M5 (Mounted in Tanks)* (Washington, DC: U.S. Government Printing Office, 1942), 43.

[1] Tank gunners were cautioned to conserve their 37-mm ammunition and use their bow and turret machine guns against exposed targets, i.e., infantry in the open, unprotected crews of weapons, and personnel in unarmored vehicles. War Department Armored Force Field Manual, FM 17-12, *Tank Gunnery*, 18.

[2] Winston Groom, *A Storm in Flanders: The Ypres Salient, 1914-1918: Tragedy and Triumph on the Western Front* (NY: Atlantic Monthly Press, 2002), 185-186.

[3] Gilbert, *The Somme: Heroism and Horror in the First World War*, 183, 190.

the driver physically through the use of his foot. To signal a forward advance, the commander had to kick his driver once in the back; to turn the vehicle left or right, the driver was notified by a kick either to the left or right shoulder; to order stop, the driver would receive one kick to the head; and to back up the tank, the driver would receive multiple kicks to the head.[1] While striking an enlisted man was normally a court martial offense in the U.S. Army, the method described above was deemed necessary for tank operation back then.[2]

During World War II, the gunnery readiness drills that my father and other members of his cavalry squadron undertook were deemed to be extremely important. In the adrenaline rush of combat, the loud engine noise inside the tank together with the clamor of enemy fire crashing outside the hull must have been extremely disconcerting for the crew. Clearly, the turret was no place for panic, confusion or indecision. Neither was it a place for idle chitchat in battle. Hence, regular tank crew gunnery drill and a rapid firing sequence was an absolute necessity for survival on the battlefield. Every member of the crew had to respond instantly to orders and perform his assigned job flawlessly.

One very important skill to be mastered was the technique of adjusting the tank's gunfire in order to fix the correct range to the target. The tank commander was trained to observe all firing from the turret hatch, if enemy return fire permitted. However, if the gunner on the left side of the main gun observed his fire clearly, he made his own corrections. If he failed to observe his fire due to battlefield dust or smoke, he applied the necessary corrections indicated by the tank commander.

At ranges exceeding 1,000 yards, or even less with poor visibility, the desired technique was to bracket the target. For example, where the first round landed "over" with a range setting of 1,500 yards and the setting for the second round was 1,100 yards and fell "short" of the target, a bracket was obtained. The commander would then tell his gunner to perfect his aim by splitting the bracket, i.e., firing his next round at a range setting of

---

[1] Eric Anderson, "The Dawn of American Armor: The U.S. Army Tank Corps in World War II," *On Point: Journal of Army History,* Army Historical Foundation, Vol. 21 no. 4 (Spring 2016), 7.
[2] D'Este, *Patton: A Genius for War,* 223.

1,300 yards.[1] Clearly, close teamwork and understanding between the gunner and tank commander is an indispensable element in combat.[2]

A typical main gun-firing sequence for a tank crew back then might have commenced somewhat as follows:

1) On spotting an enemy target, the tank commander would bark through his headset interphone to the driver: "STOP TANK";

2) The tank commander would then identify the enemy target to the turret gunner (for example, "TANK" or "TROOPS IN THE OPEN") and select the type of ammunition for use (AP, canister or HE);

3) Next, the commander would instruct the gunner to "TRAVERSE (rotate the turret) left or right" a certain number of degrees, or he would shout "STEADY ON" to stop the traverse when the enemy was directly ahead; when the target was acquired in the gunner's gun telescopic sight, the gunner would bellow "IDENTIFIED", and the commander would specify a range to the target;[3]

---

[1] Examples of the way the tank commander would announce ranges are as follows: "nine five" for 95 yards, "four five five" for 455 yards, "one three hundred" for 1,300 yards, "two nine two five" for 2,925 yards, "three thousand" for 3,000 yards, and so forth. War Department Armored Force Field Manual, FM 17-12, *Tank Gunnery*, 17.

[2] Ibid., 41-43.

[3] Estimation by eye was the usual method of determining range. At ranges under 1,000 yards, the gunner often was able to strike the target with the use of the gun sight reticle. At short ranges individual tanks attack targets on their own; at long ranges firepower was most effective through a concentration of fire by several tanks on an individual target. When such a concentration of fire on a target was desired, the platoon commander might determine the range with one gun and then announce it to the rest of the platoon. War Department Armored Force Field Manual, FM 17-12, *Tank Gunnery*, **32-35.**

4) When the main gun was fully loaded and the breech closed, the gunner would shout "UP" or "READY" and the tank commander would give the command to "FIRE!"[1] By activating the trigger a kinetic message from the gunner was launched down range and most likely it would have been accompanied by the following enthusiastic shout: "ON THE WAAAY!" or simply "AWAAY!

---

[1] Steven J. Zaloga, *Sherman Medium Tank, 1942-1945* (London: Osprey Publishing, 1993), 13.

8. U.S. ARMY TANKS, GERMAN PANZERS: EQUIPMENT, ORGANIZATION & MORE

At this juncture in the narrative, a pause seems appropriate to explain the basic features of the tank my father manned at the beginning of his wartime service by comparing its performance and capabilities to the armor employed by the enemy. Other matters relating to land warfare in Europe during the Second World War are also discussed below.

To begin with, Dad's M5A1 Stuart light tank had a crew of four men: a tank commander/loader sat or stood in the right rear of the turret, the gunner sat on the turret's left side, the driver sat below in the left front position, and the co-driver/radio operator/bow machine gunner sat forward and below on the right.[1] Both the driver and the co-driver/bow gunner had their own set of driving controls, as well as forward hatches for entering and exiting the tank, and each had a periscope for viewing purposes whenever the tank's hatches were buttoned up.

Since my father's enlisted rank fluctuated during the course of his military service, he was familiar with each of the tank positions described previously. That fact, standing alone, was of no moment since the entire tank crew had to operate like a joint venture; they all knew their collective fate hinged on the proper performance of each of them. Thus, a cross-trained tank crew was very important because each crewmember had to know how to use the radio, drive the tank, maintain all the equipment, and fire every weapon, since they were fighting far from home under conditions that often precluded a rapid resupply of replacements in the likely event of casualties.[2]

By design, the Stuart tank was mainly intended for use in screening, security, pursuit, and reconnaissance roles. In addition to the 37-mm cannon, its secondary armament included three medium, air-cooled machine guns: a .30-caliber machine gun, mounted coaxially with the main gun; a front hull, ball mounted .30-caliber machine gun for use by the co-driver; and another on the outside of the turret on a pintle mounting that was intended mainly for anti-aircraft use. The 37-mm main gun

---

[1] Zaloga, *Stuart U.S. Light Tanks in Action*, 22.
[2] Yeide, *Steeds of Steel*, 32-33.

ammunition included AP rounds, but their use at ranges beyond 500 yards was highly discouraged.[1] As a consequence, HE and canister rounds were used mostly in battle, as the Stuart was not expected to engage the enemy in tank-on-tank combat. Indeed, to do so in a Stuart was considered suicidal.[2]

HE rounds were used to destroy enemy strong points in support of attacking infantry, and canister was used mainly in a defensive role. Tantamount to a tank-fired shotgun spraying buckshot, canister was a devastating, close-range anti-personnel round.[3] In World War II, the canister round consisted of a metal case filled with 123 steel balls, each of which was three-eighths of an inch in diameter;[4] when the round emerged from a cannon's muzzle, the metal case disintegrated and the metal balls flew forward in a devastating pattern on enemy infantry at close range.[5]

On the positive side, the M5A1 light tank was known for its relative speed and mobility, as twin 220-horsepower Cadillac V-8 gasoline engines powered it, allowing it to scoot through muddy fields where the heavier Sherman could not.[6] Additionally, the V-8 engines were much quieter than the early M4 Sherman aircraft engines, making the Stuart a much better fit for the role of stealthy reconnaissance.[7] Nevertheless, the Stuart was

---

[1] War Department Armored Force Field Manual FM 17-12, *Tank Gunnery*, 18.
[2] The 37-mm cannon was the same weapon used in American tanks in World War I in French-made Renault tanks. D'Este, *Patton: A Genius for War*, 222.
[3] Zaloga, *Stuart U.S. Light Tanks in Action*, 22, 49.
[4] War Department Basic Field Manual FM 23-80, *37-mm Gun, Tank, M5 (Mounted in Tanks)*, 49; a later development was the "beehive" round, filled with hundreds of tiny darts that cut a scythe-like swath in its path. McDonough, *Platoon Leader*, 110.
[5] They were highly effective in repulsing attacking enemy infantry out to a range of 200 yards, and could be fired effectively while a tank was in motion. Yeide, *The Infantry's Armor*, 13; canister was "useless at greater ranges." War Department Armored Force Field Manual FM 17-12, *Tank Gunnery*, 18.
[6] Rottman, *World War II US Cavalry Groups: European Theater*, 15.
[7] The aircraft engines were holdovers from the 1930, as a lack of funding caused the army to use surplus radial engines in the early version of the M4 Sherman tank. Their replacement, a 500-horsepower Ford V-8 tank engine, made them "about 25 percent more powerful than the radial engine."

known to have a number of serious handicaps: its high silhouette, "absurdly thin" 63-mm lower frontal hull armor, and the 27-mm armor on the upper front, sides, and rear of the hull, which was sloped a mere twenty degrees.[1]

Theoretically, the Stuart's vertical-axis gyrostabilizer allowed it to fire its main gun on the move; hydraulically operated, it was intended to prevent the gun from being moved out of a set vertical position by the tank's lurching motion. The electric-power turret traverse was also deemed a huge improvement over the old, manual turret traverse method.[2] Yet, in the run-up to war, the thin, minimally sloped armor and modest main gun caused many to think the Stuart a nonbattle-worthy tank. The 37-mm cannon was so woefully inadequate that the German Panzer IV and the even older, obsolete Panzer IIIs were invulnerable at ranges beyond five hundred yards. Yet, it was thought that a Stuart might damage a Panzer IV[3] with a well-aimed, point-blank shot (at a range of two hundred yards or less), but even at close range, the 37-mm round could cause little or no damage to the well-beveled, sloped armor[4] of a larger German Panther.[5] The M5A1 Stuart's best chance of stopping a Panzer IV or a Mark V Panther was to

---

Belton Y. Cooper, *Death Traps* (Novato, CA: Presidio Press, 1998), 37 and 79.
1 Charles B. MacDonald, *A Time for Trumpets* (New York: William Morrow, 1985), 82. See also Zaloga, *Stuart U.S. Light Tanks in Action*, 49.
2 Patrick Feng, "M3/M5 Stuart Light Tank," On Point: Journal of Army History, Army Historical Foundation, Vol. 20 no. 2 (Fall 2014), 16
3 The German reference for armored fighting vehicle was *PanzerKampfwagen*, abbreviated as PzKpfw, and their tanks were known as panzers; thus, the Germans referred to this tank as a PzKpfw or Panzer IV, while the Allies called it a Mark IV. It was the most numerous German tank of World War II, equipping half the German tank units in Normandy. Max Hastings, *Overlord: D-Day and the Battle for Normandy* (NY: Simon & Schuster, 1984), 112.
4 Sloped armor allows for the deflection of incoming, armored-piercing rounds, thereby preventing penetration of the armored vehicle. "The geometry of the sloped [armor] plate is such that its thickness when measured on the horizontal plane is greater than the perpendicular thickness of the plate itself." Michael and Gladys Green, *Panther*, (Oxford, UK: Osprey, 2012), 126; an inch of sloped frontal armor provides the ballistic protection of 2.5 inches. Yeide, Steeds of Steel, 40.
5 Zaloga, *Stuart U.S. Light Tanks in Action*, 18, 28.

immobilize it by maneuvering danger close in order to fire a round at the enemy tank's front drive sprocket, rear-mounted idler wheel, or some other vulnerable portion of the track mechanism.[1] (That was not recommended as a close range tactical solution for a Stuart tank, as it required a near suicidal and reckless frame of mind on the part of the crew.)

Obviously, the most frightening of all German tanks, the Mark VI Tiger and the even more imposing Mark VII King Tiger or *Konigstiger* (Royal Tiger).[2] Those beasts were way out of the Stuart's league, since they were massively armored and mounted a long-barreled, high muzzle velocity, 88-mm cannon. As explained by British author and historian Max Hastings: muzzle velocity is chiefly a function of barrel length, and Allied troops were always shocked by their first encounters with the Tiger's gun, which they thought was "as long as a telephone pole."[3] Fortunately, for the Allied cause, the Germans could not produce vast numbers of precision-engineered heavy tanks in the late stages of the war due to a scarcity of skilled manpower and vital raw material resources.

By the spring of 1944, the only Allied tank capable of taking on the German Mark V Panther on equal terms was a British modification of the U.S. M4 Sherman medium tank, the "Firefly," armed with a seventeen pounder (76.2-mm), long-barreled, high muzzle velocity main gun. Later in 1944, the up-gunned M4A3 Sherman[4] tank arrived in Europe, providing a much-needed improvement with the addition of a 76-mm main gun; it proved to be a relatively good match against the 45-ton Panther, but continued in many ways to be inferior to the 63-ton Tiger.[5] The M4A3

---

[1] Lewis Sorley, *Thunderbolt*, (New York: Simon & Schuster, 1992), 63.
[2] The German Mark VI and Mark VII tanks were true monsters, but their weaknesses, besides mechanical unreliability, were their high fuel consumption, ponderous speed and slow manual turret traverse. Michael Reynolds, *Men of Steel* (New York, Sarpedon, 1999), 23.
[3] Hastings, *Overlord: D-Day and the Battle for Normandy*, 193.
[4] Ibid., 191 and 193.
[5] Only at close range was the 76-mm gun able to penetrate the frontal armor of the Panther or Tiger; not until the tungsten-core, hyper-velocity armor-piercing (HVAP) round came along could the Sherman kill Panthers from the front at 300 yards. Yet, that new ammunition was extremely scarce for the entire war. Yeide, *The Infantry's Armor*, 178. HVAP ammunition was first distributed to tank units in the ETO in September

Sherman was made available only on a very limited basis before D-Day, and entered combat thereafter mostly as replacements for destroyed Sherman tanks. In any event, the M4 Sherman proved to be very reliable and was the standard American tank for the Allies in their drive through France and Germany; however, General Bradley once remarked disgustedly that its short-barreled 75-mm gun often merely "scuffed German armor rather than penetrating it."[1]

As an aside, the Sherman was allegedly nicknamed the "Tommy Cooker" or "Ronson" by the British.[2] The latter moniker derived from a popular brand of cigarette lighter,[3] due to its unfortunate ability to catch fire (or "brew up" in the British vernacular) when penetrated by an AP round on the battlefield. The early version of the Sherman tank had a fire-prone reputation as main gun ammunition was racked inside along the vulnerable sidewalls. Later models of the Sherman provided bin storage for shells in the hull floor and diesel engines, making them much safer than the earlier gasoline-powered models.[4] Nevertheless, the 33-ton M4 Sherman tank remained a solid match against the Panzer IV, which the Germans used in large numbers throughout the war. The best prospect for survival when engaging a German Mark V Panther required a penetrating shot to the flank

---

1944, and U.S. tankers were thrilled, but due to a scarcity of tungsten, adequate quantities were unavailable, fewer than one round per vehicle per month. Zaloga, *M4 (76mm) Sherman Medium Tank 1943-65*, 18-19.
[1] John Prados, *Normandy Crucible: The Decisive Battle That Shaped World War II in Europe* (New York: New American Library, 2011), 81-82.
[2] The British were very apprehensive about the height of the Sherman tank, as it presented too much of a target for the German gunners. Bill Close, *Tank Commander*. (South Yorkshire, England: Pen & Sword Books, 2013), 87.
[3] The manufacturer's catchy slogan was "Lights up first time, every time." See http://archives.library.illinois.edu/blog/poor-defense-sherman-tanks-ww2/
[4] Andrew Marks, "The M4 Sherman Medium Tank," On Point: Journal of Army History, Army Historical Foundation, Vol. 19 no. 3 (Winter 2014), 15; however, a former historian for the 14th Armored Division Association observed that "dry storage of main gun ammunition" was the culprit for the frequent fires from enemy shells, not gasoline in the M4. James Lankford, "M4 Sherman" in Mail Call, On Point: Journal of Army History, Vol. 19 no. 4 (Spring 2014), 3.

or rear where the enemy's armor protection was known to be much thinner.[1]

Despite the existence of the German Panther's powerful, long barreled 75-mm main gun and thicker armor, the advantages of range and armor protection were reduced somewhat when Sherman tanks were employed at close quarters in the hedgerows of northern France. There the opposing tanks operated often at ranges of 200 yards or less because the thick, centuries-old hedgerows concealed nearly everything farther away.[2] Thus, in the close-in, hedgerow country of Normandy, Sherman tanks were able to engage panzers with some success due to their superior maneuverability, but when they encountered more open terrain, it was an unfair fight, as the Panther's main gun could penetrate an American tank out to a range of 2,500 yards.[3]

The enemy's lumbering Mark VI Tiger tank with its 88-mm cannon was the Sherman's greatest nemesis. For all its virtues, however, the formidable German Tiger could be defeated if it happened to come upon a Sherman tank unexpectedly. The Tiger's Achilles' heel was the hand-cranked turret traverse, which was cumbersome and very slow in bringing its massive gun tube into firing position.[4] By contrast, the Sherman tank was far more nimble, and with its electric turret traverse through 360 degrees, it could fire several AP rounds before the Tiger could successfully rotate its manual turret and get off an accurate shot. One writer described the difference between the two tanks as analogous to an automobile with "automatic

---

[1] MacDonald, *A Time for Trumpets*, 82.
[2] *St-Lo (7 July-19 July 1944), American Forces in Action Series*, Historical Division, War Department, Washington, DC: Center of Military History, U.S. Army, facsimile reprint, 46 (1984).
[3] Martin Blumenson, *Breakout and Pursuit: U.S. Army in World War II, ETO.* (Washington, DC: Office of the Chief of Military History, 1961), 205.
[4] Eric Lefevre, *Panzers in Normandy, Then and Now* (London: Plaistow Press, 1990), 42. The "H" model of the Mark IV panzer was in fact equipped with an electric turret traverse, served by a small auxiliary engine mounted at the tank's rear, which was removed in March 1944 when the "J" model of the Mark IV went into production. By then, a two-speed hand wheel replaced the electric turret traverse and an extra fuel tank increased the Mark IV's operational range. Ibid., 21, 23.

steering, hydraulic shift, and push-button window control and a car with none of the modern conveniences."[1]

To summarize, it bears repeating, when the U.S. entered the war in Europe **any** German tank could knock out **any** Allied tank at a range out to one thousand yards and more.[2] Given that absolute German advantage, it was clear that Dad's Stuart light tank was "dangerously obsolete" for armor-versus-armor combat[3] and ill-suited for taking on any enemy tank, as it was so drastically outgunned. It required a "lucky" hit, at very close range, on the tracks or optics in order to disable a German tank. That task was comparable to stalking a bear in the woods armed only with a butter knife. One military historian and former World War II infantry company commander went so far as to opine that the 37-mm main gun in the Stuart tank was of "no value" except in support of defensive operations.[4] However, the Stuart "still had its uses" as it was needed for reconnaissance missions, so it was pressed into service despite its many deficiencies.[5]

In accordance with then-current U.S. cavalry doctrine, reconnaissance squadrons with their M5A1 light tank companies were instructed to "engage in combat **only** to the extent necessary to accomplish the assigned

---

[1] Andy Rooney, *My War* (Holbrook, MA: Adams Media, 1995), 253-254. By December 1944, the Sherman tank was considered by some in the know to be "almost obsolescent." MacDonald, *A Time for Trumpets*, 82.
[2] Reynolds, *Men of Steel*, 23.
[3] Rottman, *World War II US Cavalry Groups: European Theater*, 15.
[4] MacDonald, *A Time for Trumpets*, 82.
[5] Rottman, *World War II US Cavalry Groups: European Theater*, 15. Early in the war, obsolescence was not confined to the U.S. Army, e.g., two-seat British *Swordfish* biplanes with bracing wires, struts, and spars, were also well beyond their prime; yet, in May 1941 several outdated *Swordfish* torpedo bombers torpedoed the German battleship *Bismarck*, wrecked her steering and made her an easy target for British warships. Ronald H. Spector, *At War at Sea: Sailors and Naval Combat in the Twentieth Century* (New York; Viking Penguin, 2001), 166-168; the biplanes not only caused the *Bismark's* sinking, but all attacking *Swordfish* returned safely. Burkard Freiherr von Mullenheim-Rechberg, *Battleship Bismarck* (Annapolis: Naval Institute Press, 1990), 208-209.

mission."[1] Suffice it to say, they were warned to make every effort to avoid enemy contact and detection while performing flank screening, reconnaissance, or security missions, and most importantly, to avoid decisive engagement with any German armor.

During World War II, the U.S. Army's mechanized cavalry was intended to extend the eyes, ears, and reach of the infantry commander on the battlefield. They were to shield the friendly force's presence and probe for information as to the enemy's strength and any obstacles that might hinder the maneuver of the friendly force. Intended to be the vanguard, they were tasked with the goal of shielding a much larger force.

One might construe the mechanized cavalry as the land equivalent of the navy's destroyers, acting as the outer protective edge of any formation (albeit eggshell thin), searching for traces of the enemy; their offensive capability was largely an afterthought, except in the defensive mode against enemy infantry, where their fire support came in handy. Yet, while the cavalry's firepower was significant, holding ground required large numbers of infantrymen, and that was a job for an infantry battalion's more numerous riflemen with their bandoleers of extra ammunition. The cavalry squadron's small arms, mostly M1 carbines, were basically too short-ranged and lacked the stopping power needed to be fully effective when facing strong enemy resistance.[2]

In fact, when main forces engaged the enemy, U.S. cavalry squadrons were most often withdrawn and tasked with reconnoitering missions to find favorable routes of advance to bypass or outflank the enemy. Cavalry squadrons were also used to quickly seize key terrain against light resistance and holding it until the arrival of friendly forces. Furthermore, using the tactic of reconnaissance-by-fire, they could challenge the enemy to counterattack, thereby discerning their power and strength.[3] On locating the enemy, the cavalry would use what arguably was its best weapon, the

---

[1] War Department Field Manual FM 2-20, *Cavalry Reconnaissance Squadron, Mechanized*, 24 February 1944, 2.; War Department Field Manual FM 100-5, *Field Service Regulations, Operations*, 15 June 1944, 9-10.

[2] The .30 caliber M1 carbine was a valuable upgrade in firepower to any GI with only a sidearm for defensive purposes. Patrick Feng, "The M1 Carbine," *On Point: Journal of Army History*, Army Historical Foundation. Vol. 22, no. 4 (Spring 2017), 14-17.

[3] Rottman, *World War II US Cavalry Groups: European Theater*, 17, and 21-22.

radio, to call higher headquarters and "set in motion events leading to the destruction of enemy forces they observed."[1]

Prior to the Second World War the Chief of Army Ground Forces, Lt. Gen. Lesley J. McNair, redesigned the U.S. infantry into a **triangular**, three-regiment division from the more unwieldy **square**, four-regiment version of the First World War era.[2] That restructuring eliminated the brigade as a level of command. Thus, each World War II U.S. infantry division became a force of around 15,000 troops in three infantry regiments, four artillery battalions, a combat engineer battalion, a medical battalion, a cavalry reconnaissance troop, a signal company, and various other service-support units.[3]

The U.S. infantry regiment in World War II contained three infantry battalions, as well as heavy weapons, headquarters, anti-tank, cannon, and service companies.[4] Each infantry battalion was made up of three rifle companies, and each rifle company had three rifle platoons and a weapons platoon. The smallest tactical unit was the twelve-member squad, including three 4-man fire teams. Those three rifle squads plus a small headquarters element made up an infantry rifle platoon of around forty men.

---

[1] Yeide, *Steeds of Steel*, 41.

[2] The U.S. infantry division during World War I consisted of two regiments (hence the term "square" division); it also included an artillery brigade and a battalion of engineers. John S.D. Eisenhower with Joanne T. Eisenhower, *Yanks: The Epic Story of the American Army in World War I* (New York: Free Press, 2001), 62; while that organization of four infantry regiments in two brigades was justified for trench warfare, it was later considered cumbersome, thus the new three-regiment infantry division was created. Dupuy, et al., *Hitler's Last Gamble: The Battle of the Bulge*, 386.

[3] In 1944, a major general commanded a U.S. infantry division and a brigadier general commanded the division artillery, having three 12-tube 105-mm light artillery battalions and one 12-tube 155-mm howitzer medium battalion. Ibid.

[4] The triangular organization allowed for deployment of a division with three regiments on line, or two forward in line and one in reserve. Similar deployment was possible at each subordinate echelon (battalion, company & platoon), and each regiment had a headquarters and headquarters company, including an intelligence and reconnaissance (I&R) platoon. Ibid., 388.

General McNair's organizational overhaul was intended to prepare the U.S. Army for modern warfare, to "expand an out-of-date force of a quarter-million men into an efficient modern army of almost eight million soldiers." His aim, according to one military scholar, was to make the U.S. infantry division leaner and more mobile in order to achieve the military principle of economy of force.[1] In the words of another, the "greatest strength of the U.S. Army in World War II was its unprecedented and unrivaled development of combined arms," incorporating infantry, armor, artillery, as well as naval forces, when needed, "into well-coordinated thrusts that multiplied the strength of each element, raising the intensity of combat to new heights."[2]

Concerning the U.S. Armored Force, throughout the Second World War the army had only two "heavy" armored divisions: the 2nd "Hell on Wheels" and the 3rd "Spearhead."[3] At the core of those heavies were two armored regiments, each of which included four medium tank battalions and two light tank battalions, containing three companies each. In support, they had three field artillery battalions, one armored infantry regiment, a signal company, an armored engineer battalion, and an armored reconnaissance battalion. With various other attached units, both heavy armored divisions entered battle numbering around sixteen thousand men.

Beginning in September 1943, the fourteen other U.S. armored divisions were realigned and became smaller.[4] Armored regiments were discarded and the infantry, tank, and artillery components of the new "light" armored divisions were equalized at three tank battalions each. Separate medium and light tank battalions were abolished, as each tank battalion consisted of three companies of medium tanks and one light tank company. Each tank company totaled seventeen tanks: five in each of three

---

[1] Russell F. Weigley, *Eisenhower's Lieutenants: The Campaign of France and Germany 1944-1945* (Bloomington: Indiana University Press, 1981), 22-25; Alwyn Featherston, *Saving the Breakout: The 30th Division's Heroic Stand at Mortain, August 7-12, 1944* (Novato, CA: Presidio Press, 1993), 8.
[2] Perret, *Old Soldiers Never Die*, 389.
[3] Dupuy, et al., *Hitler's Last Gamble*, 380.
[4] The ratio of tank to infantry battalions in the two heavy armored divisions was two to one, but in the U.S. Army's new light armored divisions, that ratio became one to one. Balkoski, *From Brittany to the Reich*, 203.

platoons and two at the company HQ. With the addition of headquarters and reconnaissance tanks, light armored divisions contained 186 M4 Sherman medium tanks and 77 M5 Stuart light tanks, totaling 263 tanks, compared with 390 in the two heavy armored divisions. The new-equalized tank, infantry, and artillery battalions in the light armored division were self-contained administratively. Thus, each battalion "could be assigned with complete flexibility to either of the division's two principal combat commands" (designated CCA or CCB) or to a newly created, reserve combat command (CCR).[1]

Early on, General McNair's forward vision led to the formation of the independent tank battalion, identical to a divisional tank battalion, containing three medium tank companies, one light tank company, a service company, and HQ company. Thus, it could be attached to any division, providing "greater flexibility and adaptability" to changing circumstances on the battlefield. Basically, the separate tank battalions were assigned to armies and attached to infantry divisions. Their mission was to operate, within range of supporting artillery fire, but fight the enemy at the pace of the infantry riflemen.[2] By late 1944, sixty-five separate, independent tank battalions slightly exceeded the fifty-four tank battalions in the other sixteen U.S. armored divisions.[3]

After World War I, American tank design lagged behind other nations due to the decision that U.S. tanks should not fight other tanks. Instead, it was decided they should be used to attack more vulnerable targets, particularly infantry. The American high command convinced itself that defense against enemy tanks "should be left to the anti-tank weapons of the infantry and artillery and to tank destroyers."[4] That concept was reinforced by early German success in North Africa. There, the enemy's numerous 88-mm *Fliegerabwehrkanone,* or "Flak" guns, were effective in the anti-tank

---

[1] Weigley, *Eisenhower's Lieutenants*, 18.
[2] Those who served in them called separate tank battalions, rotated from corps to corps and division to division, as "bastard" battalions. Ibid., 81.
[3] Yeide, *The Infantry's Armor*, 3-7. One separate tank battalion, the 761st Tank Battalion, manned by black personnel, saw its first action in November 1944 with the Third Army, and later fought in the Battle of the Bulge. Ibid., 324.
[4] Weigley, *Eisenhower's Lieutenants*, 20-21.

role against British armor, and the Germans saved their panzers for offensive use. Thus, the need for an American tank destroyer came about due to the vast numbers of German armored vehicles fielded during World War II, and because U.S. Sherman tanks were dependent on sheer numbers to defeat the thick frontal armor of the German Mark V Panther in combat. In that regard, Sherman tank crews quickly learned that to be most effective they had to swarm *en masse* and surround an enemy Panther in order to fire a lethal shot at its thinner flank or rear armor.[1]

Since U.S. doctrine designated tanks for use primarily as infantry support, the tank destroyer (or TD) was used to counter enemy armor. The sole mission for TD units was to destroy hostile tanks, and TD battalions operated as mobile reserves.[2] The TD's speed allowed for elusiveness, as it could shoot at enemy armor and scoot, rather than fight in stand-your-ground situations.[3] Regarding the "trinity" of armament, mobility, and protection, the latter (armor protection) was eschewed in the TD to allow for a larger main gun without limiting speed and mobility.[4]

Initially in Europe, the M10 TD (the "Wolverine") was armed with a 3-inch (76.2-mm) main gun, mounted on a M4 Sherman tank chassis.[5] Its open-roof reduced its weight and provided excellent battlefield vision, but made the five-man crew vulnerable to enemy fragmentation grenades, small arms fire and showers of sharp shrapnel from enemy artillery. Additional drawbacks of the M10 TD were its thin armor, the absence of coaxial and hull-mounted machine guns, and a lack of a power turret traverse, a major flaw in combat "as it took nearly eighty seconds to [manually] traverse the turret 180 degrees."[6] Due to those failings and the fact that the M10's main

---

[1] Ibid.

[2] War Department Field Manual FM 18-5, Tank Destroyer Field Manual: Organization and Tactics of Tank Destroyer Units, 16 June 1942, 7.

[3] The U.S. Army tactic for individual TD use was to fire several rounds at the enemy's flanks if possible, followed by rapid movement to an alternate position before firing again. Yeide, *The Tank Killers* (Havertown, PA: Casemate, 2004), 8-9.

[4] David Higgins, *The Roer River Battles: Germany's Stand at the Westwall* (Havertown, PA: Casemate, 2010), 123-124.

[5] See generally, Yeide, *The Tank Killers*, 124.

[6] Steven J. Zaloga, M10 and M36 Tank Destroyers 1942-53 (Oxford, UK: Osprey, 2002, 23; the 3-inch M10 GMC was powered by a Ford 8-cylinder

110

gun could not penetrate the frontal armor of the German Panther, the up gunned M36 TD (the "Jackson") with a 90-mm cannon was deployed to France in September 1944.[1] It proved to be a vast improvement over the M10 Wolverine, but similar weaknesses, including open-topped turrets and no hull-mounted or coaxial machine guns for suppressive fire made close encounters with enemy infantry a hazardous proposition. Yet, a self-propelled TD was easily recognizable on the battlefield, and their mere presence gave nearby U.S. infantrymen "a tremendous shot of courage."[2]

Regarding the German army, each of their infantry divisions began the Second World War with three infantry regiments, comprising three infantry battalions, an artillery regiment of three light field and one medium artillery battalion.

As the war progressed, the organization of the German infantry division underwent two major changes. Beginning in 1943, the infantry battalions within a regiment were reduced from three to two, due to the heavy casualties Germany incurred while fighting the Soviets on the Eastern Front. By mid-summer 1944, the enemy formed Volksgrenadier divisions to offset increased manpower losses, and those new formations included only six infantry battalions (instead of nine as earlier in the war).[3] That new class of German division was named "das Volk" essentially to appeal to the national, military pride of the German people.[4]

Due to a lack of available manpower late in the war, the Volksgrenadier division was less formidable, as it included hospital returnees and previously exempt industrial workers, and minimal time was available to train them and the remnants of the Luftwaffe (the German air force) and former

---

gasoline engine and had a maximum road speed of 30 miles per hour and a cross-country speed of 20 miles per hour. Patrick Feng, "M10 Tank Destroyer" On Point: Journal of Army History, Army Historical Foundation. Vol. 23, no. 4 (Spring 2018), 15 and 16.

[1] Higgins, *The Roer River Battles*, 124; Yeide, *The Tank Killers*, 175.

[2] Zaloga, *M10 and M36 Tank Destroyers 1942-53*, 23-24, 33.

[3] The Volksgrenadier division included around 10,000 men, instead of the 12,350 in a standard 1944 German infantry division. Balksoski, *From Brittany to the Reich*, 84.

[4] Charles B. MacDonald, *The Siegfried Line: U.S. Army in World War II: ETO*, (Washington, DC: Office of the Chief of Military History, 1963), 15.

sailors from the defunct Kriegsmarine (the German navy).[1] To compensate for the depleted artillery supply, Volksgrenadier divisions were furnished a higher allotment of anti-tank and assault guns, as rapid-fire weapons replaced standard bolt-action rifles to counter the lack of manpower due to attrition.[2]

During December 1944 German Bulge counteroffensive, the Volksgrenadier infantry company was found to have a massive firepower advantage, despite being roughly half the size of a U.S. Army rifle company. Of the 119 enemy soldiers in a German company, seventy-three were armed with automatic weapons, compared to only nine Browning Automatic Rifles (BARs) available in a 200-man U.S. rifle company. Moreover, the German assault rifle was eight pounds lighter than the BAR, and its thirty-round magazine contained ten more bullets than a BAR and twenty-two rounds more than the M1 rifle.[3] In addition, Germany's superb machine gun (the *Maschinengeweher* 42) fired 1,200 rounds per minute, providing a far superior volume of suppressive fire over anything available to the Allied armies.[4]

As to German armored formations in Normandy in June 1944, the panzer regiments of the Field Army and *Waffen-SS* were similar in composition[5] with the panzer regiment being the heart of the panzer division. The panzer regiment had two tank battalions: the 1st battalion comprised four companies, each with a top strength of seventeen Mark V Panther medium tanks. Counting the eight Panthers in each battalion HQ Staff Company (*Stabskompanie*), the theoretical total was 76 Panthers; and the 2nd battalion also had four companies with 22 Mark IV tanks each for a

---

[1] John McManus, *Alamo in the Ardennes: The Untold Story of the American Soldiers Who Made the Defense of Bastogne Possible* (Hoboken, NJ: John Wiley, 2007), 30.
[2] Except where noted otherwise, the prior two paragraphs draw on Forty, *German Infantryman at War*, 11-14; *Weigley, Eisenhower's Lieutenants*, 30.
[3] Balkoski, *From Brittany to the Reich*, 84-85.
[4] Beevor, *D-Day: The Battle for Normandy*, 254.
[5] *Waffen-SS* panzer divisions were larger, including more than 17,000 men, whereas a regular army panzer division's strength was nearly 14,000 personnel. As Hitler's favorites, the SS divisions usually had a higher allotment of motor vehicles and weapons, as well as a "first crack at new recruits." Dupuy et al., *Hitler's Last Gamble*, 411.

top strength of 96 Mark IVs, counting the eight tanks in their Stabskompanie.

German panzer divisions also had two panzergrenadier regiments (one motorized and one armored), a motorized artillery regiment, an assault gun (*Sturmgeschutz*) battalion and/or tank killer (*Jagdpanzer*) battalion, an armored reconnaissance battalion, a pioneer battalion (engineers) and other support units.

Mark VI Tiger tank battalions were not integral to the panzer division, but were allotted to army groups and sub-allotted to armies, corps and divisions, according to need. German panzergrenadier divisions had no tank regiment, but instead had a panzer battalion that was normally equipped with assault guns or Jagdpanzers, in lieu of tanks.[1]

---

[1] The prior three paragraphs draw from Lefevre, *Panzers in Normandy*, 6, 9-13.

9. ON THE CONTINENT AT LAST

On June 28, 1944, Dad wrote in his diary that the 15th Cavalry Group Headquarters and Headquarters Troop and the 15th Cavalry Recce Squadron, departed Trowbridge for the coast of England.[1] He indicated they left "in a big hurry, on short notice," and a little later he wrote concisely, "They go over before us."

The 15th Cavalry Group headquarters and Maj. Robert W. Fuller's entire 15th Cavalry Squadron sailed from Portland Harbor (Weymouth) on the fourth of July 1944. Shortly thereafter, they steamed across the English Channel to France and landed at Utah Beach on the following day.[2]

During the first week of July, Dad described the weather in Britain as cool and somewhat cloudy, and reported that he and his fellow crewmen were continuing the task of cleaning their tanks and making them ready for shipment across the Channel. Later, he mentioned that the drivers had moved their tanks down to the docks, and they all returned to the bivouac area and "started sweating", as they focused on the momentous task that awaited them.

The map on the next page depicts the separate routes and embarkation points used by the U.S. 15th and 17th Cavalry Reconnaissance Squadrons, as they were shipped to France in July 1944.

---

[1] The English Channel suffered its worst storm in forty years from June 19-21, 1944; it destroyed many of the prefabricated, artificial harbors that were erected following the initial Normandy landings, and brought all beach landings to a halt, causing the shipment of critical supplies, reinforcements, and equipment to fall way behind. Randolph Bradham, *"To the Last Man": The Battle for Normandy's Cotentin Peninsula and Brittany* (Westport, CT: Praeger Security International, 2008), 41

[2] TLR, 5.

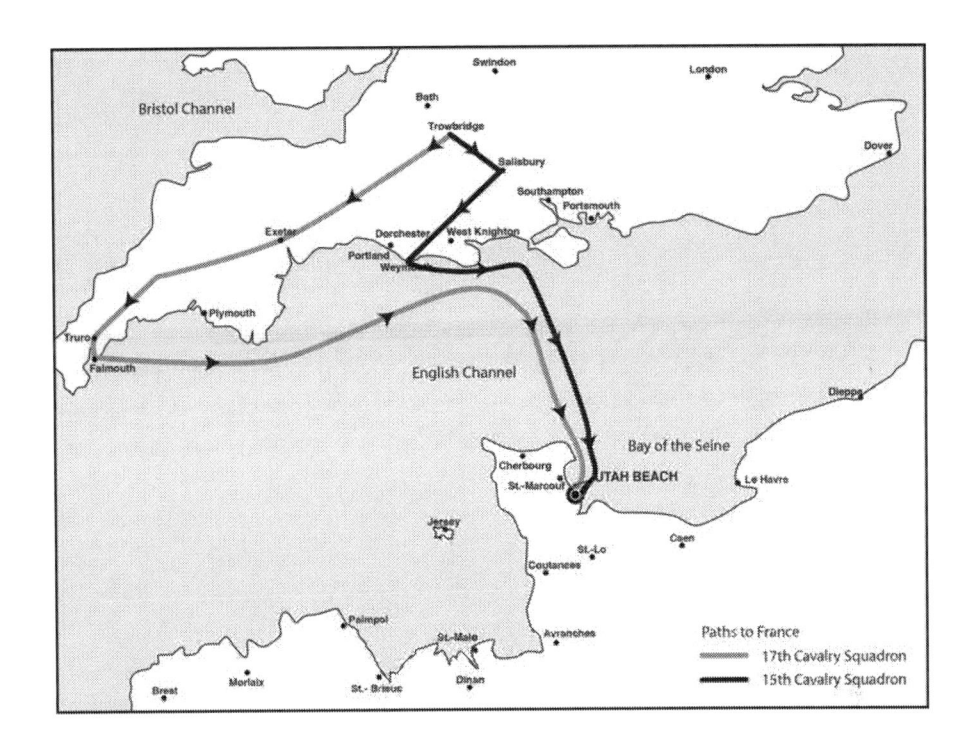

By July 9, 1944, the 17th Cavalry Squadron under the command of Lt. Col. Kenneth K. Lindquist had completed a 195-mile journey, winding their way southwest through the English countryside to their designated marshaling area near the city of Truro in Cornwall. On July 11, they traveled the last fifteen miles to the port of embarkation, Falmouth Harbor.[1] Not until the next day, did Dad document the fact that he joined a mass of olive-clad soldiers crowding together to board the Liberty ship[2] Stanton H. King. As the troops settled into their new surroundings, the ship slipped its moorings and moved slowly out into deeper water where she lay at anchor for the evening. Early the next morning, she weighed anchor and got underway, following the English shoreline to their naval

---

[1] "History of the 17th Cavalry Reconnaissance Squadron for Year 1944," Memorandum to The Adjutant General, Washington, D.C., 1 March 1945, 2; CAVS17,
Record Group 407, entry 427, National Archives II, College Park, MD.
[2] Shipbuilder Henry J. Kaiser produced these vessels during World War II, completing one every forty-two days on average. James D. Hornfischer, *The Last Stand of the Tin Can Sailors* (New York: Bantam Books, 2004), 68.

assembly point off the port of Southampton. There she joined a multi-ship convoy bound for the coast of France. Luckily, their passage was unopposed by the enemy as they crossed the windswept waters of the English Channel, and maneuvered into the Bay of the Seine, opposite the eastern shoreline of the French Cotentin Peninsula.

According to Dad's notes, their ship arrived off Utah Beach at 0945 on the morning of July 15, 1944 (D+39, thirty-nine days after the initial Normandy landings). After dropping anchor, the onerous task of unloading that vessel began promptly, but as the Liberty ship's large holds were packed tightly with cargo and heavy equipment, the task of offloading the tanks and vehicles was not completed until the following day. The ship's two large boom cranes were used to ease their equipment onto a flat-bottomed landing barge, which ferried them safely ashore when the tide was right. Nonetheless, Dad mentioned in his diary that he took off his GI-issue footwear and celebrated his arrival off the coast of France by washing his feet in the Bay of the Seine.

Although he and the other members of the 15th Cavalry Group had spent many months training hard in preparation for war, from that point on they began to realize the necessity of remaining constantly alert. Having only a general idea of what might befall them on the battlefield, they knew instinctively that they had to focus and use every shred of their military training to keep each other alive and in one piece. Beyond that, all was in the hands of God or fate.

Of great significance was the fact that by early July 1944, the millionth man of the Allied ground force had stepped ashore in Normandy.[1] By mid-July 1944, when my father and his squadron came ashore on the European continent, America had been at war for only around two and a half years. By comparison, the Chinese had been fighting Japan since 1937, and the United Kingdom had been at war with Nazi Germany for nearly five full years. Fortunately, great strides had been made toward victory, but it was only too clear to the Allies that much toil and bloody effort would have to be expended to make matters dramatically better.

Following Hitler's ill-advised invasion of the Soviet Union in 1941, the German Sixth Army was destroyed at Stalingrad, and only two years later

---

[1] Prados, *Normandy Crucible*, 2.

the Wehrmacht was in full retreat on the Eastern Front after their defeat by the Soviets at Kursk. U.S. forces on the South Pacific island of Guadalcanal had also achieved victory in early 1943, and the advance up the Solomon Island chain was about to commence. In addition, Allied forces had liberated the Mediterranean island of Sicily and the Germans had withdrawn across the Strait of Messina. Accordingly, Lt. Gen. Mark Clark's Fifth Army continued to pursue the enemy with amphibious landings at Salerno and Anzio, and together with the British Eighth Army, the Allies advanced toward Rome along the Apennine Mountains, bisecting the Italian Peninsula.

On the afternoon of July 16, 1944, (some forty days after the initial D-Day landings), the 17th Cavalry Recce Squadron finished the process of unloading and finally disembarked onto the soil of France at Utah Beach. After doing so, they mounted their mechanized steeds and moved off the sandy beach near the village of St.-Germain-de-Varreville. Then, they hurriedly drove their jeeps, armored vehicles and light tanks inland into the rubble-strewn French countryside.

By early morning of the following day, they bivouacked in a grassy field for a few hours of needed rest and sleep. On awakening, Pop wrote that they continued their advance through three "major towns": St.-Mère-Église, Montebourg and Valognes on the Merderet River. He described each town they passed through as wrecked, revealing block after block of charred rubble. He expressed amazement that he "couldn't even see one complete house" left standing. As a newcomer to battle, he was awed by the sight of shattered trees demolished by high-explosive artillery fire, and was sobered by the fact that there was "nothing [left] but [isolated, free-standing] walls." Thus, he began to learn firsthand the terrible aftermath of combat.

By the next morning, Dad's cavalry unit was on the move again, this time in a northerly direction toward the port city of Cherbourg. Pop noted it was not tank-friendly country, as they had their first encounter with Norman hedgerows: centuries-old earthen and stone embankments, topped by trees, and filled with thick vegetation. The French farmers in the bocage[1] of Normandy used hedgerows to separate their small fields and to

---

[1] The bocage country of France amounted to all of the Cotentin Peninsula and much of eastern Brittany. The hedgerows in Normandy made ideal

corral their livestock in lieu of fences. It was not at all surprising that the German defenders used them to great advantage as defensive strong points and when setting up ambuscades. Tanks were particularly vulnerable to short-range, anti-tank weapons in such country, yet their use was required by the infantry, as a call for artillery fire support was too dangerous when the enemy was a mere one to two hundred yards away.[1] Pop described those barriers as about four to five feet high, two to three feet thick, "made of rocks, roots and earth" and "strong as cement." He said they gave them a lot of trouble, because their tanks were totally incapable of climbing over or pushing through them.

To the rescue of all U.S. tankers in Normandy came homegrown American ingenuity at its finest in the genius of Sgt. Curtis G. Culin, Jr., of the 102nd Cavalry Recce Squadron, 102nd Cavalry Group, who designed a hedgerow-cutting device made from German scrap iron, salvaged from beach obstacles and welded to the front of a tank. When so equipped, a tank or TD could be driven into a hedgerow, where the steel tusk-like prongs pinned the tank to the obstacle, preventing it from "bellying up" and presenting an easy target to the enemy. That allowed the armored vehicle to plow through the hedgerow without exposing its thin belly armor. Because the tanks were thought to resemble a rhinoceros with Sergeant Culin's invention attached to the nose, they came to be known as a "Rhinos". General Bradley was so impressed with the Culin "hedge cutter" that he ordered them mass-produced throughout his command. By the beginning of Operation Cobra (the Normandy breakout), they were installed on "three out of five First Army tanks."[2] That large iron-toothed device was called a "tank spade" by General Patton, who thought them magnificent because they cut through hedgerows "like a spoon through warm butter."[3]

German infantry delaying positions. George S. Patton, Jr., *War as I Knew It* (New York: Houghton Mifflin, 1947), 96.
[1] Close, *Tank Commander*, 108.
[2] Weigley, *Eisenhower's Lieutenants*, 149; Stephen E. Ambrose, *Citizen Soldiers: The U.S. Army from the Normandy Beaches to the Bulge to the Surrender of Germany, June 7, 1944-May 7, 1845* (New York: Simon & Schuster, 1997), 67; Stephen E. Ambrose, *The Victors: Eisenhower and His Boys: The Men of World War II* (New York: Simon & Schuster, 1998), 217.
[3] Rooney, *War as I Knew It*, 96.

Prior to the Culin device's existence, Sherman bulldozer tanks and high explosives were used to penetrate the hedgerows. Those techniques however were fraught with danger, as the Germans quite naturally figured it out "and quickly aimed AT [anti-tank] weapons at any gap that suddenly appeared in the far hedgerow."[1]

Another ingenious U.S. Army field modification was the vertical L-shaped stanchion made from scrap angle iron welded to the front bumper of most American jeeps in the ETO. That metal, wire-breaker was intended to catch and sever any downed telephone, power line or intentionally rigged piano wire strung at neck level across a road by retreating German soldiers. It likely prevented the decapitation of many an unwary U.S. Army jeep occupant in Normandy.[2]

From July 18-20, 1944, Dad reported that his unit had moved to the western, Atlantic side of the Cotentin Peninsula. There they were assigned "mop-up" and security missions in the vicinity of the small French village of Les Pieux, guarding installations within the Com-Z and the area up and down the west coast of the peninsula "from Cherbourg to Lessay" against enemy landings by sea or airborne attack. As an additional assignment after landing on the European continent, the men of the 15th Cavalry Group provided active, continuous protection of the lines of communication for U.S. forces in Normandy, north of the line from Carteret to Valognes. On Friday, July 21st, the 15th Cavalry Group headquarters moved from La Glacerie, south of Cherbourg, to Chateau Sotteville, near Les Pieux.[3]

By way of historical reference, all organized German armed resistance at Fortress Cherbourg, and the city itself, ended on June 27, 1944. That feat was accomplished by 4th Cavalry Squadron troopers and soldiers from the 4th, 79th ("Cross of Lorraine"), and 9th ("Old Reliable") Infantry Divisions of the U.S. VII Corps, commanded by Maj. Gen. J. Lawton ("Lightning Joe") Collins, a veteran of the Guadalcanal campaign. Capture of the deep-port city of Cherbourg signaled accomplishment of the main objective of the cross-Channel phase of Operation Overlord; however, by the time of their surrender, the Germans had managed to wreck the port, "leaving it a

---

[1] Yeide, *The Tank Killers*, 128.
[2] Beevor, *D-Day: The Battle for Normandy*, 255; Caddick-Adams, *Snow & Steel*, 435.
[3] TLR, 5, 19.

tangled mess that took several months to become functional again."[1] Nevertheless, a month of hard fighting remained, as by July 1, 1944, the Normandy lodgment was no more than five to six miles deep. Also, in no place was it more than 25 miles in depth and the cities of Caen and St.-Lo were still under German military control.[2] However, by mid-July, American forces succeeded in capturing St.-Lo.

During the month of July 1944, the 17th Cavalry Squadron continued its traditional cavalry mission of rear area security, and was assigned a secondary role as a mobile fighting reserve for Gen. Omar Bradley's First Army.

The arrival of Friday, July 14, 1944, however, turned out to be a very memorable occasion in Cherbourg, as some fortunate personnel in the 15th Cavalry Group were picked to join the patriotic townspeople as they celebrated the first post-liberation Bastille Day with a parade. On that day a large crowd of locals were understandably emotional to see their tricolored flags waving again in the breeze. They were also thrilled at the opportunity to sing the French national anthem, La Marseillaise, as the Germans had banned it during the previous four years.

Yet, all was not joyous for everyone in Cherbourg that day, as French Resistance members took out their pent-up fury on females, who were accused of adultery for consorting with German occupiers. While the rowdy crowds cheered, they were shepherded into public areas and their hair was shorn to the scalp. Then, *les femmes tondues* ("the sheared women") were publicly humiliated by being "paraded through the streets in the bed of a truck beneath a sign" that read "The Collaborator's Wagon."[3] Similar embarrassment was afforded French women in Paris during 1944, for their alleged misbehavior with occupying German soldiers. Journalist Andy Rooney observed the anger of the crowd and hoped "they got the right women because there was no such judicial nicety as a presumption of

---

[1] After the deep-water port of Cherbourg was repaired, it "was barely able to supply 50 percent of the tonnage [of supplies] required by First Army and Patton's Third Army." D'Este, *Eisenhower: A Soldier's Life*, 545.
[2] Patrick Delaforce, *Smashing the Atlantic Wall* (London: Cassell, 2001), 64; Atkinson, *The Guns at Last Light*, 123.
[3] William I. Hitchcock, *The Bitter Road to Freedom: A New History of the Liberation of Europe* (New York: Free Press, 2008), 35, 47-49.

innocence."[1] Other potential victims undoubtedly had the good sense to flee with their lovers to Germany, knowing that certain individuals among the French public would seek revenge for their *collaboration horizontale*.[2]

Also noteworthy for the officers and men of the 15th Cavalry Group was July 20, 1944, since on that date they provided escort for Great Britain's Prime Minister Winston Churchill, as he toured Fort du Roule, the docks and arsenal, and the former V-1, flying buzz bomb launch sites in Cherbourg.[3] Those well-camouflaged launch sites had narrow ramps roughly 180 feet long, and they were very nearly impossible to observe from the air.[4]

In the sixth volume of his Second World War memoir, Churchill described his July 20 cross-Channel visit, flying "direct in an American Army Dakota [the British designation for the C-47 troop transport]" to a landing on the Cherbourg Peninsula. He described seeing "for the first time a flying bomb launching point" and mentioned his shock at the damage done by the Germans to the town of Cherbourg and its harbor. Noting that the harbor basins "were thickly sown with contact mines," he realized the inevitable delay in getting the port open. Nevertheless, he paused to admire the divers who were working "day and night disconnecting [naval mines] at their mortal peril."[5]

According to Dad's diary entry for July 25, the war was at last brought home to him in violent fashion when an enemy "booby trap" exploded, killing two staff officers from the 17th Cavalry Squadron's headquarters, Maj. Charles J. Donohoe and First Lt. Harold W. Linesay. Sadly, Dad mentioned that the former officer had been promoted to the rank of major that very day. From that unpleasant instance, he and his squadron mates

---

[1] Rooney, *My War*, 207.
[2] Such women were considered guilty of having slept with the enemy and became scapegoats for entire communities in Western Europe. In France, some 20,000 women suffered such degradation in front of large crowds from their local population. Ian Kershaw, *To Hell and Back: Europe, 1914-1949*, 474.
[3] TLR, 5-6.
[4] Geoffrey Perret, *Winged Victory* (NY: Random House, 1993), 300, 308.
[5] Churchill, *Triumph and Tragedy*, 25.

came to a more certain understanding that from that moment on they were playing for keeps.

Concerning the danger of enemy booby traps, the army listed certain booby-trapped items for the soldiers' safety, e.g., "fence posts, teacups, doorbells, light switches, window curtains, inkwells." In addition, American GIs were told that German bodies were often booby trapped with grenades to maim or kill GI souvenir hunters. They were duly "warned that bodies being picked up on the battlefield should be jerked by a rope at least 200 feet long."[1]

Around the time the 17th Cavalry Squadron sustained its first wartime fatality important events were taking place elsewhere in France. While traveling by staff car to his headquarters at Chateau de La Roche-Guyon, Germany's Field Marshal Erwin Rommel, commander of Hitler's Atlantic Wall defense of northern France, was gravely wounded by strafing Royal Air Force "Spitfire" aircraft.[2]

Even better from the Allies standpoint, on July 20, 1944, certain disillusioned members of the German military, led by Col. Claus von Stauffenburg, had attempted an assassination of Hitler by exploding a bomb at his field headquarters, the "Wolf's Lair" (or *Wolfsschanze*) in East Prussian near Rastenburg, Poland. That event planted "poisonous mistrust" in the German officer corps between the fanatical loyalists and those in the Wehrmacht, who by then despaired of victory.[3]

From July 24-27, 1944, General Bradley's First Army engaged in a four-corps (fifteen-division) assault to break out of the Normandy lodgment. That plan (Operation Cobra) was designed to end the relative stalemate in Normandy. Bradley's intention was to blow a gaping hole in the German lines to allow a rapid penetration "along a stretch of road west of the Vire River and St.-Lo."[4] It was preceded by two days of carpet-bombing by the U.S. Army Air Forces (USAAF) in a concentrated area along the road

---

[1] Atkinson, *The Guns at Last Light*, 129.
[2] David Fraser, *Knight's Cross: A Life of Field Marshal Erwin Rommel* (New York: HarperCollins, 1993), 513.
[3] Hastings, *Overlord*, 279.
[4] Stephen R. Taaffe, *Marshall and His Generals: U.S. Army Commanders in World War II* (Lawrence: University Press of Kansas, 2011), 189-190.

connecting Periers with St.-Lo. On July 25, 1944, more than two thousand USAAF four-engine heavy bombers (B-17 "Flying Fortresses" and B-24 "Liberators") and twin-engine medium bombers dropped over four thousand tons of high explosive and fragmentation bombs in the Cobra area. The Earth literally shook, as it was "the largest single bombardment of the war until Hiroshima."[1]

Unfortunately, on both days the pre-assault bombardment was bollixed, as "dumb" gravity bombs of that era were dropped short of their planned target area due to human error. As a result, more than 600 hundred American GIs were killed or wounded.[2] Among those killed by that errant bombing was Lt. Gen. Lesley J. McNair, commander of U.S. Army Ground Forces, the highest-ranking general officer in the U.S. Army to be killed in action in Europe during World War II. "Only McNair's shoulder patch and stars betrayed any hint of what had once been a lieutenant general."[3] Despite that fratricidal disaster, the St.-Lo breakout was otherwise a huge success for U.S. ground forces, as German defensive units in the area of that tactical bombing attack suffered a crippling blow.[4]

---

[1] Blumenson, *Breakout and Pursuit*, 234; Cooper, *Death Traps*, 54.
[2] For those who have never worn the uniform, the situation described above makes clear that precision in military matters is not always achieved. During World War II, soldiers had acronyms for all sorts of events. **SNAFU**, was the most common, indicating an ordinary military screw up: a Situation Normal, All Fouled Up. A superlative was coined around the time of the Battle of the Bulge for a situation **worse** than SNAFU, it was **TARFU**: Things Are Really Fouled Up. The short-bombing fiasco, described above, was an appalling disaster, requiring escalation to an even stronger superlative, SNAFU on steroids, or **FUBAR**: Fouled Up Beyond All Recognition. Davidson, *Cut Off*, 30. (Note, however, the author has modified the acronyms above intentionally, as military language is quite coarse; not surprisingly, however, these phrases continue to have currency within modern military vernacular.)
[3] John C. McManus, *The Americans at Normandy: The Summer of 1944–The American War from the Normandy Beaches to Falaise* (NY: Forge, 2004), 295.
[4] The German Panzer Lehr Division was annihilated by the air bombardment at the St.-Lo-Periers line. Hastings, *Overlord*, 256; Williamson Murray and Allan R. Millett, *A War to be Won: Fighting the Second World War* (Cambridge, MA: Belknap Press of Harvard University Press, 2000), 429.

Regarding that tragic "short-bombing" episode, a high-ranking officer in the 30th ("Old Hickory") Infantry Division said sarcastically, "As a fiasco, this operation was a brilliant achievement." As historian Rick Atkinson put it, the men raged against the "American Luftwaffe" as the 30th Old Hickory Division sustained more casualties on July 25 than on any other day from enemy fire.[1] Some U.S. soldiers were so angered that they actually "opened fire on their own aircraft, a not uncommon practice among all the armies in Normandy when suffering at the hands of their own pilots."[2]

By July 29, the French town of Coutances fell as both Collins's VII Corps and Middleton's VIII Corps advanced steadily down the Cotentin coast. That signaled the collapse of German positions in western Normandy, as they were forced away from the coast and "their left flank hung in the air."[3]

The official U.S. Army Signal Corps/National Archives photograph below shows several U.S. Army vehicles advancing into Coutances, some 18 miles west of St.-Lo.

[1] Ibid., 143.
[2] Hastings, *Overlord*, 253.
[3] Murray and Millet, *A War to Be Won*, 429.

By late July 1944, the 4th Armored Division, commanded by Maj. Gen. John S. Wood, had captured Avranches, and by noon on August 1, 1944 (D+56), the Third Army first became operational under the command of Lt. Gen. George S. Patton, Jr.[1] On that day, the 15th Cavalry Group was assigned to the Third Army at Avranches to be its "eyes and ears." Gen. Omar Bradley became commander of the newly activated 12th Army Group and Lt. Gen. Courtney Hodges succeeded him as commander of the First Army.[2] Around that time, Bradley informally loaned the VIII Corps to Patton's Third Army for its planned advance into Brittney; nevertheless, it remained technically under the command of General Hodges.[3]

---

[1] Based on his performance in North Africa and Sicily, the Germans were convinced that Patton was a most capable battlefield commander. In early 1944, his mythical First Army Group (FUSAG) in southeast England used a fictitious troop concentration, rubber replica tanks and false wireless messages to help carry out a subterfuge that convinced Hitler and his commanders that the landings in Normandy were a feint, and that the real invasion would take place at the most logical place, the Pas-de-Calais region. Carlo D'Este, *Patton: A Genius for War* (NY: HarperCollins, 1995), 593, 626.
[2] D'Este, *Eisenhower: A Soldier's Life*, 562; Charles M. Province, *Patton's Third Army* (New York: Hippocrene Books, 1992), 17.
[3] Bradham, *"To the Last Man"*, 94.

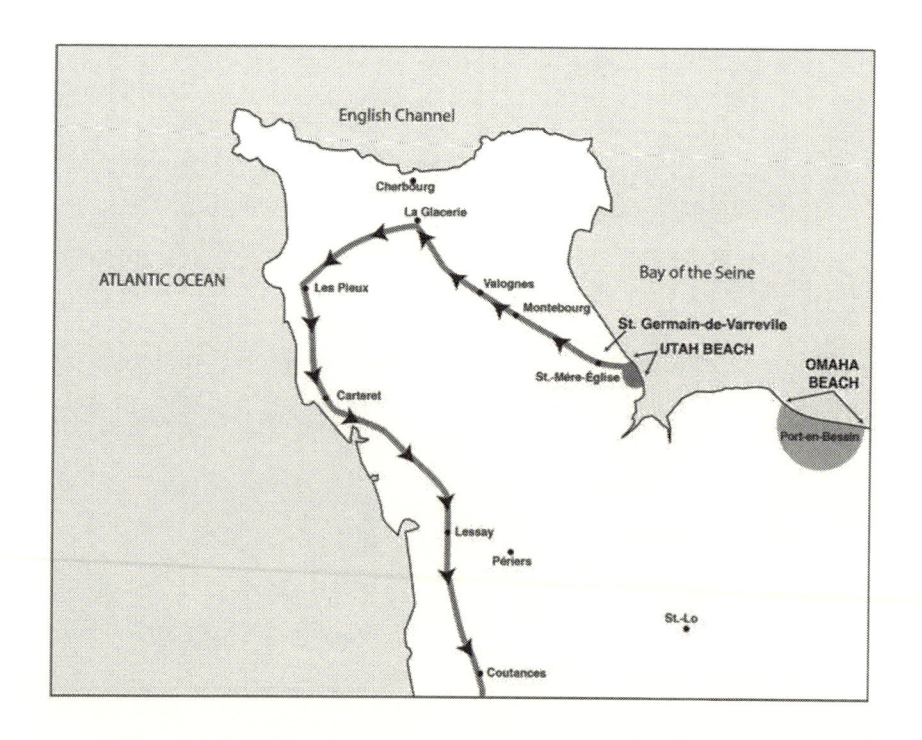

The map above reveals the path of the 15th Cavalry Group (Mechanized), as it advanced northwest across the coast of the French Cotentin Peninsula and then turned south down the Cherbourg Peninsula toward Avranches.

By early August, it became apparent that the First Army had defeated German defenses along the Periers–St.-Lo Line, as armored and motorized infantry units advanced rapidly south along the west coast of France, past the towns of Gavray and Avranches. At that point, "the entire western portion of the German line had collapsed, leaving only scattered remnants to keep up the contest." Clearly, the Normandy Campaign had entered "a new phase."[1]

The mission of Patton's Third Army, initially with only Middleton's VIII Corps, was to pass through the corridor of Avranches-Pontaubault, make a sharp right turn and proceed westward to clear the Brittany Peninsula of enemy forces and ultimately seize the port cities of St.-Malo,

---

[1] Taaffe, *Marshall and His Generals*, 190.

Brest, Lorient, and St.-Nazaire.[1] That strategy seemed important because without those ports and harbor facilities, supply to the Allied armies in France would be hampered greatly. As a well-executed success, Operation Cobra swung the door wide open for the U.S. mechanized cavalry and armored force to begin the great race south at a "gallop."[2]

By early August 1944, the time was considered ripe for a swift exploitation of the Cobra breakout through enemy lines. Thus, a three-pronged mechanized force, trailed by infantrymen, surged into Brittany. General Wood's 4th Armored Division led the advance by cutting south toward Rennes and beyond, while Maj. Gen. Robert Grow's 6th ("Super Sixth") Armored Division attacked to the west along the central plateau of the peninsula toward the naval port of Brest, some two hundred miles away near the tip of the Brittany Peninsula. Such "sweeping [mechanized maneuvers] were vintage Patton, fostered in the [pre-war] Louisiana and Texas maneuvers, which taught him to think in terms of swift drives over long distances."[3]

On August 2, 1944, a brigade-size, highly mobile mechanized force, Task Force A, (TFA) was assembled at La Repas, a few miles north of Avranches, and it became the third prong of the attack to Brest along the all-important rail line that ran along the north coast of Brittany.[4]

Brig. Gen. Herbert L. Earnest assumed command of TFA, the principal components of which were the 15th Cavalry Group (with its two squadrons) and the 6th Tank Destroyer Group. In addition, they had an assortment of supporting troops attached, including the 705th Tank Destroyer Battalion, combat engineers from the 159th Engineer Battalion,

---

[1] It was to St.-Nazaire that the German battleship *Bismarck* was heading after it had been badly damaged by British air and naval forces in late May 1941. That French port was valuable as it had a large dry dock and it was a good point of departure for operations against enemy commerce in the Atlantic. Mullenheim-Rechberg, *Battleship Bismarck*, 156; Misch, *Hitler's Last Witness*, 83. Denial of German submarine access to the Atlantic Ocean from Brittany bases was an important goal for the Western Allies following the successful Normandy landings. Spector, *At War at Sea*, 226-227.
[2] Delaforce, *Smashing the Atlantic Wall*, 80-81. Yeide, *Steeds of Steel*, 170.
[3] Alan Axelrod, *Patton: A Biography*, (NY: Palgrave Macmillan, 2006), 136-137.
[4] Yeide, *Steeds of Steel*, 170; Patton, *War as I Knew It*, 98.

and a Bailey bridge company (the 509th Engineer Light Pontoon Company), all operating under the control of headquarters of the 1st Tank Destroyer Brigade.[1] Depending on the mission assigned significant augmentation was provided by the attachment of a tank destroyer battalion and engineer support to assist with bridging tasks was not at all that uncommon.[2]

For the 15th Cavalry Group, their role was designed to be a classic "whip-and-spur" cavalry mission, using speed and maneuverability to dash forward, reconnoiter and protect the flanks of TFA. Their orders were to proceed as rapidly as possible across the northernmost route of Brittany, probing for the enemy in the vicinity of Brest and through the intervening towns of Avranches, Pontorson, Dol-de-Bretagne (hereinafter referred to as "Dol"), Dinan, St.-Brieuc, Guingamp, and Morlaix.

General Earnest's TFA was directed to "drop off small guard detachments" at each town until they were relieved by elements of the 83rd ("Thunderbolt") Infantry Division. At the same time, General Grow's Super Sixth Armored Division advanced along the same route as far as Dinan, but they were ordered to turn south at that point. TFA's mission was to clear the route to Dinan and establish an assembly area midway between Dol and Dinan for use by the Super Sixth on August 2-3. Then, TFA was to make full use of the assembly area on the night of August 3-4, 1944.

---

[1] Blumenson, *Breakout and Pursuit,* 349; Yeide, *The Tank Killers,* 141.
[2] Rottman, *World War II US Cavalry Groups: European Theater,* 29.

10. COMBAT ON THE BRITTANY PENINSULA

On August 1, 1944, Dad wrote in his diary that the officers in his outfit[1] were called to a meeting at squadron headquarters, and when they returned, the entire camp was "abuzz with excitement." At that squadron officers' briefing, the 15th Cavalry Group commander, Col. John B. Reybold,[2] had described their mission with TFA: to secure the estuary bridges along a double-track railroad from Rennes to Brest. Reybold explained: "It's all about the supply line, Boys. Brest does us no good without it. We've been told to button up these routes tout [de] suite."[3] Sometime thereafter he wrapped up his briefing by announcing that, since the task force came under General Patton's Third Army command, "Every man—to a one—will wear their neck-down." That meant the curious notion of going into combat wearing a necktie.

No one complained about the mission, but the absurdity of wearing neckties in combat apparently caused much agitation among the men.[4] In a recent book about the life of a former enlisted member[5] of Troop B, 17th Cavalry Squadron during World War II, the author wrote: "Before Eyeball could hear the complaints, he had Sgt. Cottone dismiss the troops."[6]

Dad scribbled a hasty note that evening that his company had been assembled and informed of the mission: "This is it, the Big Show—we're in

---

[1] To be clear, Dad always used the term "outfit" when discussing the U.S. 17th Cavalry Recce Squadron.
[2] Men in the U.S. 15th Cavalry Group, apparently nicknamed their West Point-educated commander "Eyeball" because "every time he'd go over a hill, he'd puff his eye up, shouting 'Faster! Faster!'" It was disclosed that "one fellow did an excellent impression of the man. 'I want no weaklings in combat,' he'd say." Meyers, *Teacher of the Year*, 198-199.
[3] Ibid., 200-201.
[4] GIs refer to "petty, meaningless tyranny by self-important officers" as "chicken shit." Bill Davidson, *Cut Off*, (New York: Stein and Day, 1972), 115.
[5] Pvt. Edwin D. Barlow was wounded in action in September 1944 during the Battle of Crozon, France, and was awarded the Purple Heart Medal. TLR, 29; History of the 17th Cavalry Reconnaissance Squadron for Year 1944, 6.
[6] Meyers, *Teacher of the Year*, 201.

it!" His excitement was undeniable, and the adrenaline rush was clearly evident. Such youthful pre-battle cockiness was not at all uncommon early in the war, as they all looked forward to testing their mettle against that of their opponents; in most cases, however, the bravado abated when the men of the 15th Cavalry Group had their first encounter with the enemy and "saw the elephant", the beast in all its fury.[1] That hard lesson provided much-needed battle experience, which undoubtedly contributed toward their chances at future survival in battle.

General Earnest's TFA, as part of Patton's Third Army, was initially ordered to clear the route to Dinan and establish an assembly area midway between Dol and Dinan. They were to advance to the fortified town of St.-Malo, and bypass it, in order to meet up with General Grow's Super Sixth Armored Division. Then TFA was to continue on and render any necessary assistance in the envelopment of the fortified seaport of Brest.[2]

By August 1, the 4th Armored Division had reached Rennes[3], and by that evening, the Super Sixth had taken Pontorson, south of the French landmark of Mont St.-Michel. Later, in describing that operation, General Patton strongly criticized the 6th Armored for having "lost a battery of self-propelled guns, due to stupidity." Specifically, he indicated that the "guns were too far to the front, too close together, and had no security detachment." He continued by mentioning that the officer responsible was killed in that action.[4]

On August 2, TFA took on seven days of K rations, gasoline for 250 operational miles, a combat load of ammunition, and other essential equipment preparatory to embarking on their assigned mission. Allied air identification panels were determined necessary and their prominent display was required for all units as a safeguard to prevent Allied fighter-bombers from shooting at them accidently.[5]

---

[1] "Seeing the elephant" is a metaphor dating back to at least the American Civil War and refers to the psychological and physical passage through a first battle encounter with the enemy that a green soldier must endure before becoming a combat veteran.
[2] Yeide, *The Tank Killers*, 142.
[3] Ibid., 143.
[4] Patton, *War as I Knew It*, 98-99.
[5] TLR, 6.

Concurrent with that activity, my father diarized that the upcoming mission of TFA was to proceed through Avranches and close with the enemy in order to "take and secure Brest." That entry makes the point that their squadron scuttlebutt (the rumor mill) was working quite well on that occasion.

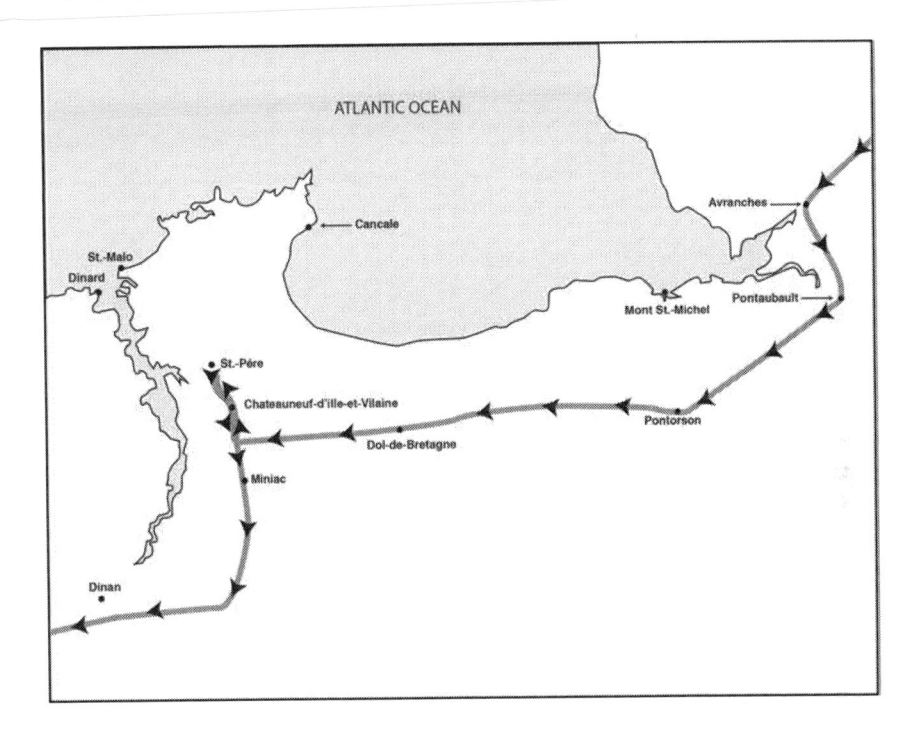

[Map showing the Atlantic Ocean with locations: Avranches, Pontaubault, Mont St.-Michel, Cancale, St.-Malo, Dinard, St.-Père, Chateauneuf-d'Ille-et-Vilaine, Dol-de-Bretagne, Pontorson, Miniac, and Dinan, with arrows tracing a route from Avranches south through Pontaubault, west through Pontorson, Dol-de-Bretagne, and toward Dinan.]

Shortly thereafter, the order was given to "Mount Up", and during the early morning hours of August 3, 1944, the fully mechanized 17th Cavalry Squadron began to crank its engines; then, with great enthusiasm, they took the point and led the advance of TFA out of the bivouac area.

The map above traces Dad's diary account, as they headed south from Coutances through Avranches, and then turned west into Brittany. With Troop C in the lead, the order of march for the troop was as follows: 3rd Platoon, 1st Platoon, troop headquarters, 2nd Platoon, and the remainder of the squadron, including Fox Company (Dad's light tank company), Troop E (the assault gun troop), and squadron headquarters. Their reconnaissance mission was to determine the strength of the enemy near the port of St.-Malo, by driving in its advance elements. (Those eager newcomers from America were soon to lock horns with an experienced

131

enemy. The lesson they learned would prove to be unpleasant, but highly instructive.)

They traveled a dangerous stretch of road in one column through Pontorson on their way toward Dol. At all times during that advance, the 15th Cavalry Group commander, Colonel Reybold, rode up front with the lead platoon of Troop C, near the head of the column, "as if leading a horse cavalry charge", noted one author.[1]

The column made first contact with the enemy shortly after 0600, when the advance guard experienced sniper fire and the lead platoon was ambushed at a wooded bend in the road, roughly two and one-half miles east of Dol. The trap consisted of a heavily defended roadblock, covered by German mortars, anti-tank and machine-gun fire with dismounted enemy flankers on each side of the road for several hundred yards. It was set by the enemy exactly at the point of maximum exposure for the lead element of the column.

According to the 17th Cavalry Squadron's official history, the lead platoon leader, 2nd Lt. Harold S. Garrison, and seven enlisted troopers from the squadron were killed in action (KIA).[2] Several other troops were later reported missing in action (MIA), including the overzealous 15th Cavalry Group commander, Col. John B. Reybold, whose jeep was hit immediately and burst into flames. Those not killed in the initial burst of enemy fire were described as having had to jump from their vehicles into ditches on each side of the road.

To extricate the men not killed in the opening gunfire and recover the dead and wounded,[3] assault guns of Troop E near the rear of the column moved to a nearby hill crest and returned gunfire at the suspected enemy

---

[1] Morton, *Men on Iron Ponies*, 153.
[2] Memorandum to The Adjutant General, Washington, D.C., 1 March 1945; CAVS-17-0.1, Record Group 407, entry 427, National Archives and Records Administration II, College Park, MD; History of the 17th Cavalry Reconnaissance Squadron for Year 1944, 4, 5; those men killed on that occasion were: "Tec 5 Manuel Gonzalez, Tec 5 Henry C. Haynes, Pvt. Robert B. Rands, Sgt Omar F. Hawes; PFC Ferd A. Dunn, PFC Walter J. Gutkowski, and Pvt. Libero M. Rogo." As Colonel Reybold was presumed killed in action, the battle report listed 9 KIAs.
[3] Eight enlisted troopers were reported wounded in action (WIA) and ten more were described as MIA after that ambush and firefight. Ibid., 4.

positions, using mainly smoke and high-explosive rounds. Troop A, the second troop in the column, covered the beleaguered Troop C with fire as the squadron gradually pulled back and reorganized. As further progress was not possible down that road, the entire column then went off road, bypassing to the south, and proceeded by an alternate route to their assigned assembly area near Lenhellin, eight miles south of Châteauneuf d'Ille-et-Vilaine (hereinafter referred to as "Châteauneuf.")

After contact with the enemy was broken, Colonel Reybold was reported "missing, presumed dead" and the executive officer, Lt. Col. Robert J. Quinn, Jr., assumed command of the 15th Cavalry Group. Upon their arrival at the assembly area, Col. Logan C. Berry took over command of the 15th Cavalry Group and ordered both squadrons to reconnoiter northward at once in the direction of St.-Malo. The 15th and 17th Cavalry Squadrons then moved out shortly after 1800 hours to locate and determine the enemy's strength, but they soon met heavy enemy artillery, mortar, and small arms fire, which together with the loss of daylight caused "considerable trouble." Radio communications also reportedly failed, making it difficult for commanders to coordinate their units as evening darkness approached; further action was called off at 2100, and the two squadrons reorganized "generally along an East-West line running through Miniac."[1]

The botched episode described above emphasized the strong vulnerability of a road bound, mechanized column. It removed any doubt as to the need and importance of maintaining a tactical march formation when conducting a movement to contact, even when the advance route was presumed clear.

After the war, a U.S. Cavalry Journal article noted: "Had Troop C been preceding the main body by a half a mile in the approved formation for an advance guard" there would have been adequate warning time to allow the commander "to dispose" his squadron effectively, "and for the group commander to employ" his reserve forces. That tragic ambush also emphasized the fact that the proper place for a cavalry group commander was "not up [front] with the point corporal."[2]

---

[1] The prior four paragraphs draw on: TLR, 7 and "An Ambush in Brittany," *Cavalry Journal*. Vol. 54, no. 5 (September-October 1945), 3.
[2] Ibid.

Pop's diary describes that first actual combat encounter with the enemy as a chaotic scene. After realizing that his baptism of fire was behind him he wrote, "What a mess . . . We [lost] our heads . . . Just like a bunch of rookies."

Notwithstanding his frustration concerning the initial panic, their action the following day at the village of Pianfour was described favorably in another postwar Cavalry Journal article, written by two actual participants. They mentioned that, with Troop A in the lead, the 17th Cavalry Squadron proceeded south of its bivouac below Miniac, followed by Fox Company, Troop E, and Squadron Headquarters. Then the column swung to the northeast and moved into the village of Pianfour, where the men of Troop A immediately encountered around fifty German soldiers "dug in at a crossroad and prepared to hold their position." Troop A quickly dismounted their vehicles, and supporting light tanks from Fox Company maneuvered its 1st Platoon to their right and overran the enemy positions. Troop A followed closely behind, cleaning out enemy emplacements, while the indirect fire of Troop E's assault guns shelled the rear of the town, "cutting off the enemy's line of retreat." That engagement was reported to be fast and furious: "over in about 20 minutes", producing 38 enemy killed and 3 captured compared to the "loss of one [GI] killed and none wounded."[1]

Dad described the captured enemy soldiers as "just kids," appearing to be no more than sixteen years of age. Kids or not, he did not consider them innocent adolescents, as they wore the enemy's uniform, were highly indoctrinated, and appeared very fit. He reconciled his actions and felt little remorse, as in virtually every instance the young combatants were heavily armed and fought with great determination. Even so, he wrote: "It was very difficult, their bodies were still warm," and it seemed to him very strange and awkward, looking at human remains, as if they were dead animals.

As one American cultural and literary historian observed, "War must rely on the young, for only they have the two things fighting requires: physical stamina and innocence about their own mortality." By late 1944, German manpower losses on two different war fronts had created such

---

[1] Lt. Col. G. J. Dobbins and Capt. Thomas Fiori, "Cavalry and Infantry at St. Malo," *Cavalry Journal* Vol. 54, no. 6 (November-December 1945), 15-16.

desperate need that, "boys of the Hitler Jugend, [Hitler Youth] aged sixteen and seventeen, and a few as young as fourteen or even twelve, were being thrown into the German line."[1]

Before offensive action toward St.-Malo got underway, the 17th Cavalry Squadron found it necessary to advance through the neighboring village of Châteauneuf. Prior to that attack, General Earnest visited the Troop B assembly area. He, of course, felt the loneliness of independent command, but was not one to abandon common sense. He was described as "a fine old general who strode confidently among the troops," but it appeared as though he was intent on some kind of inspection. After passing several troopers, he came to an abrupt stop and said, "Get those damn things off," referring to the neckties. Then, he turned and strode away.[2] The uniform neckties were duly stripped off by everyone, and thus ended the legacy and necktie mandate of Col. J.B. Reybold.

Thereafter, Fox Company took the lead, and their reconnaissance mission continued, as they fanned out right and left on roads leading to Châteauneuf.[3] In his diary Pop mentioned "a change in orders" required them to road march north in support of infantry from the 83rd Thunderbolt Division, attempting to take St.-Malo. On moving to Châteauneuf, he mentioned being "greeted by a bunch of 88's" and coastal artillery fire coming from the direction of St.-Malo.

Consequently, they withdrew to a wooded area and called in friendly artillery fire. While the enemy gunfire continued, Pop described the roar of outbound[4] American 105-mm rounds as "sweet music" to his ears. That supporting gunfire came directly from the Thunderbolt Division's field artillery, which along with the rest of the 83rd Infantry Division had moved from Dol into TFA's zone. Later, Dad mentioned he was "tired and dirty," but there would be no rest for the weary, as they dug their positions during the night, some one thousand yards south of Châteauneuf.

---

[1] Fussell, *Wartime*, 52, 53.
[2] Meyers, *Teacher of the Year*, 205.
[3] TLR, 7.
[4] Among the skills vital to a GI's survival in combat was the ability to distinguish the shell-sound of friendly, outgoing gunfire from hostile, incoming enemy artillery and automatic weapons fire.

Dad's photograph below reveals one of the Wehrmacht's most feared direct-fire weapons of World War II, the 88-mm dual-purpose (anti-tank/anti-aircraft) gun that "greeted" them in early August 1944, while they made their advance to Châteauneuf.

The firepower of the German Flak guns, turned tank killers, was tremendous: an armor-piercing round making a direct hit on the frontal armor of an Allied tank did not bounce off, but rather sliced clear through the interior compartment and continued out the back of the vehicle. Rarely did any tank crewman survive the incoming hit itself, as the ricochet of metal fragments inside the tank ("spalling") led to an inevitable concussion and residual internal bleeding.[1] According to a former lieutenant from the 103rd ("Cactus") Infantry Division, except for the atomic bomb, the German 88-mm gun was the most frightening single weapon of World War II.[2]

(Most of the photographs that appear in the following pages were taken with a 35-mm single lens reflex "Exakta" camera, which my father liberated

---

[1] McManus, *The Americans at Normandy*, 321.
[2] Fussell, *Wartime*, 268; in a ground role, the German 88 gun was "terrifying and accurate, even from a mile away."
Beevor, *D-Day: The Battle for Normandy*, 256.

from the enemy somewhere in France. He was allowed to keep the camera as his company commander declared it in writing a trophy of war under pertinent U.S. Army authority.[1])

By early the next morning, my father mentioned that they were up and off, "a little wiser, and [years] older too." He noted that their next move was to force their way into Châteauneuf, but the men of Troop A's 1st Platoon were met with heavy artillery fire and a strong roadblock. That brought the tank destroyers of TFA into action. They maneuvered into position, and with only a few rounds of direct fire, knocked out the enemy 88-mm, anti-tank gun that was guarding the roadblock: a massive barrier made of concrete, thick iron rails, and bridge girders. After the engineers' attempts to destroy it with demolitions were unsuccessful, General Earnest called up a single M10 Wolverine TD to fire point-blank at the obstacle and blow it to smithereens; however, that effort was to no avail. Finally, an army "tank retriever"[2] came forward and successfully removed the weakened obstacle from the roadway, allowing the reconnaissance platoon to push through the break and continue their support of advancing infantry.[3]

The photograph of an M10 Wolverine TD in action in France is shown on the next page in an official U.S. Army Signal Corps/National Archives photograph. It clearly illustrates the awesome firepower of the 76-mm rifled cannon.

---

[1] Section III, Circular 353, War Department, August 1944.
[2] The U.S. tank recovery vehicle in 1944 was an old, obsolescent M3 Lee/Grant tank converted for tank recovery work with a power crane, boom and winch. Max Hastings, *Victory in Europe* (NY: Little, Brown, 1985), 34.
[3] Dobbins and Fiori, "Cavalry and Infantry at St. Malo," 16.

Throughout the day of August 5, 1944, dismounted infantry and light tanks of the 17th Cavalry Squadron forced their way through Châteauneuf. Dad indicated that they buttoned up their tank and moved cautiously into town with friendly infantry in support on both flanks.[1] While they were intent on flushing the enemy out of that French village, indirect mortar fire or assault gun artillery was considered too indiscriminate and dangerous to the safety of friendly forces. Thus, the decision was made to bring up the direct fire support of tanks with the flat-flight trajectory of their cannons.

While advancing, Pop's adrenaline surged to such an extent that he had to suppress the urge to shoot anything that moved. In short order, however, as the infantry searched from house-to-house, a radio call came over the net reporting an enemy machine gun was firing down the street from a second-story window in the next block.[2]

---

[1] Troops were often unsettled about having tanks around them in World War II. They disliked being too near a tank because it always drew enemy fire. On the other hand, when the battlefield became "hot" they would "pray for a tank to come up and start blasting with its guns." Pyle, *Brave Men*, 442.

[2] Tanks are most vulnerable to attack from above when maneuvering through narrow urban streets. Something as primitive as an ignited rag

On hearing that message, their driver picked up the pace, and Dad later wrote, "We cut to the other side of the street." By that maneuver to the opposite side of the street, they obtained a tactical advantage, providing the infantry a clear field of cover fire. With their hatches buttoned up, Pop's vision from the gunner's seat was limited, but he could see well enough through his periscope, as they closed on the building; looking through his optical gun sight, he fired a burst of coaxial machine-gun fire when the cross hairs settled on the target. By observing the strike of the red tracer rounds[1], he locked on to the second-floor window as they crept closer. Finally, on hearing the cannon's breechblock slam shut, he fired the first of three rounds at the target.

Later, he mentioned in his diary with great satisfaction that they had knocked out a chunk of the wall of that masonry building and showered the street below with rubble and dust. Then he reported, the infantrymen rushed in and took control of the building. As they reached the second floor, he described seeing the GIs kick six German helmets out of the window, which by then was nothing but a large gaping hole.

From his written portrayal of urban combat at Châteauneuf, it is clear that Pop took great pride in having mastered the tank warfare skills needed to defeat the enemy. His training kicked in, and by working with the rest of the crew, their chances of surviving the war improved. Crowded street fighting was a "slow, tedious business" and teamwork between the tankers and GIs on the ground was vitally important. As one military historian noted, "Too many soldiers took delight in destruction to write off that phenomenon as an aberration."[2]

Subsequently, Fox Company was detached from 17th Cavalry Squadron control and sent forward with a battalion of infantry from the 83rd

---

attached to an empty wine bottle filled with gasoline, a "Molotov cocktail," thrown on the top of a tank could quickly cause a lethal inferno. Infantry support in urban settings is important since tanks are normally buttoned up and move slowly due to reduced vision. Cooper, *Death Traps*, 39, 236.
[1] Every fifth bullet in the machine gun belt was a red incendiary round, allowing the gunner to adjust his aim on the target while conserving main gun ammunition. (The Germans were known to use green tracer rounds.)
[2] Peter S. Kindsvatter, *American Soldiers: Ground Combat in the World Wars, Korea, and Vietnam* (Lawrence: University Press of Kansas, 2003), 184.

Thunderbolt Division, commanded by Maj. Gen. Robert C. Macon.[1] Advance elements of Dad's squadron then pushed into St.-Père, maintaining the movement north toward St.-Malo. Both the previously cited 1945 Cavalry Journal article and his diary indicate that tanks in his outfit had "shot up" some German soldiers found riding in a captured American jeep, a few of whom were identified as Waffen-SS.[2] Later he wrote, without any sign of remorse that "all three died [the] next day."

With infantry on their flanks skirmishing with small enemy detachments, the Stuart tanks of the 15th and 17th Cavalry Squadrons maintained the momentum of advance and provided sufficient fire support to capture several prisoners and accounted for many German dead and wounded before moving to the assembly area around Lenhellin.[3] Then, in order to maintain continued pressure on the enemy, the 17th Cavalry Squadron leapfrogged forward into the lead and fanned out to find good fire-supporting positions. Constant radio communication during that operation and teamwork between the infantry and cavalry allowed immediate tank fire support when needed.[4]

Immediately following that action at Châteauneuf, Capt. W. S. Parker (the 15th Cavalry Group's German-speaking dental surgeon) conducted an interrogation of several German prisoners of war (POWs), which revealed some very interesting intelligence.[5] They stated they were so short of officers that a first lieutenant was in command of their battalion, the "II Parachute Machine Gun Battalion, 3rd Parachute Division." Dr. Parker recorded in his August 1944 POW report that "very often" the prisoners

---

[1] TLR, 7; Weigley, *Eisenhower's Lieutenants*, 128; General Macon was a 1912 graduate of Virginia Polytechnic Institute (precursor to what is now popularly known as Virginia Tech) and its highly esteemed corps of cadets.
[2] The *Schutzstaffel* (*SS*) were Hitler's ceremonial/security bodyguard before the war; later, they became the *Waffen-SS*, consisting of many divisions by war's end, though they remained less than 10 percent of the *Wehrmacht*. George H. Stein, *The Waffen SS: Hitler's Elite Guard at War, 1939-1945* (Ithaca: Cornell University Press, 1966), xxx-xxxi, 17, 60.
[3] TLR, 7.
[4] Dobbins and Fiori, "Cavalry and Infantry at St. Malo," 16.
[5] The best time to gather useful information from German POWs was "as soon after their seizure as possible, when fear loosened their tongue." Balkoski, *From Brittney to the Reich*, 82.

mentioned their fear and awe of American artillery.[1] That useful information made it clear that the enemy had developed a distinct dislike for "Time-on-Target" coordinated-artillery fire concentrations[2] and airbursts caused by the new proximity fuzes on U.S. high-explosive artillery shells.[3]

As a consequence of the fighting in early August 1944, it became apparent that capture and destruction of enemy defenses around St.-Malo would require a lengthy siege operation. Thus, the VIII Corps commander, Gen. Troy Middleton, decided to use his infantry to lay siege to the town, and he released TFA during the night of August 5th, ordering General Earnest "to continue the mission of sweeping Brittany's north shore."[4]

With the addition of the 3rd Battalion of the 330th Infantry Regiment and Battery C of the 323rd Field Artillery Battalion (each from the 83rd Thunderbolt Division), the TFA with both the 15th and 17th Cavalry Squadrons broke contact with the enemy and detached from Macon's 83rd Thunderbolt Division.

At dawn on August 6, 1944, they set out to secure three railway bridges in the vicinity of St.-Brieuc, some thirty miles west of Dinan. With the 15th

---

[1] August 4, 1944 POW Report, CAVG-15-0, entry 427, Record Group 407, National Archives II.

[2] A time-on-target or (TOT) artillery barrage happens when a U.S. fire direction center coordinates the massing of artillery gunfire from separate artillery batteries onto a designated an enemy target so that the shells from each battery arrive at the target simultaneously. The effect of such a bombardment was devastating, "making the U.S. artillery the best in the world in World War II." Dupuy et al., *Hitler's Last Gamble*, 392-393.

[3] The proximity or variable time (VT) fuze was a huge improvement over the traditional time-fire fuze; it contained a small radar system that became armed when the projectile was fired from the gun tube. As it neared its target, the radar signal caused the artillery shell to detonate at the desired height, spilling a cone of hot steel fragments on the enemy below. Those VT fuzes were extraordinarily lethal since they did not require actual observation and could be fired at targets beyond a ridgeline and deep into the enemy's rear area. Cooper, *Death Traps*, 206-207.

[4] Blumenson, *Breakout and Pursuit*, 391; as it turned out, St.-Malo fell to Macon's 83rd Thunderbolt Division on August 8, but the Citadel held out until August 21, 1944. Patton, *War as I Knew It*, 102; Province, *Patton's Third Army*, 21-22.

Cavalry Squadron in the lead, they bypassed Dinan to the south, as it was still strongly held by the enemy, and by early evening, they reported having reached the outskirts of St.-Brieuc. Dad noted in his diary that it had been a "dry, hot and dusty" day, and he mentioned that little was happening, "but by civilian reports, we are [only] hours behind the [retreating] Boche."[1]

On reaching the periphery of St.-Brieuc, lead elements of TFA discovered that the Germans had fled hastily without blowing three small railroad bridges; by that afternoon, contact was made with a local group of irregular French Resistance fighters under "Colonel Eon, who was already in possession of St.-Brieuc." Then having determined that the three bridges near town were intact, TFA secured and placed them under guard.[2] Thereafter, the Free French partisans reported "a hostile force of some 1,000 Germans and Russians were in an area about five miles west of town." They indicated also that the enemy "might be ready to surrender to the Americans, if properly approached."[3]

Relying on that intelligence, both squadrons went into bivouac and the 15th Cavalry Squadron's commander, Lt. Col. Robert W. Fuller III, along with a French officer rode out in a jeep to contact the Germans,[4] while waving a white flag. On finding the enemy, Colonel Fuller and his French military companion dismounted, but at that moment an aircraft appeared overhead. Apparently startled by the unexpected, the enemy opened fire, wounding both men, and they were evacuated that night for medical treatment. Thereafter, command of the 15th Cavalry Squadron was turned over to Maj. Albert W. McGrath.[5]

By the next day, TFA got back on track with their mission, which required a sweep of the north shore area of the Brittany Peninsula to clear enemy resistance along the route from St.-Brieuc to Guingamp. On learning that the enemy was in close proximity (near Châtelaudren), the

---

[1] German soldiers were sometimes referred to as "Boche" by the Allies.
[2] Blumenson, Breakout and Pursuit, 391.
[3] TLR, 8.
[4] Those hostile troops were likely elements of an enemy force that had previously occupied Morlaix (the German 266th Division); on August 8, they departed to seek refuge in Brest. Blumenson, *Breakout and Pursuit*, 392.
[5] TLR, 8.

15th Cavalry Squadron advanced west along their route, applying continuous pressure, while the 17th Cavalry Squadron circled around to the south. Prior to that encirclement, air identification panels were deployed, as friendly air support was called in, and the area was strafed "with good results." Some enemy soldiers made their escape to the north toward Paimpol and the coast, but many of the hostile force were either killed or captured. Similar tactics were used that day as TFA continued its advance toward Guingamp.

The methods employed and described above were typical of those used by TFA as it continued its sweep through the Brittany countryside. Troopers of the 15th Cavalry Group reconnoitered along their axis of advance to find the enemy; after fixing them in place, they withdrew slightly, allowing friendly air support to "soften up" the German positions. Then, after "a short preparation" of artillery fire, the cavalry and infantry advanced to capture and/or destroy the enemy force.[1]

Thereafter, the night of August 7 was reportedly spent in restful bivouac west of Guingamp. By the following morning, it was decided that the 17th Cavalry Squadron would spearhead the TFA column west toward Morlaix. Since enemy resistance had been scattered and disorganized, the squadron commander decided to attach himself to Troop A of the lead the squadron. The order of march was: a reconnaissance platoon, a light tank platoon from Fox Company, the troop command section, an assault gun platoon from Troop E, one platoon of men in half-tracks detached from Troop C, and Troop A's two remaining reconnaissance platoons.[2]

On the morning of August 8, my father indicated they left the assembly area at the break of day "took off west on [National Route] N12" advancing toward the town of Morlaix. He wrote that they knew they were "getting closer" to the enemy, as the road was littered with abandoned vehicles, guns, and other military equipment.

By around 0900, east of Plouigneau, he mentioned that two enemy 40-mm anti-tank guns, situated under a railroad trestle, had opened up on them

---

[1] Ibid.
[2] Anonymous, "Seizing Strategic Installations," *Cavalry Journal,* Vol. LIV, no. 5 (September-October 1945), 7.

with steady gunfire. Then, he wrote, "The point [of the column] immediately pulled into hull defilade[1] and returned fire."

The lead tank platoon leader came forward and "sized up the situation with the reconnaissance platoon leader." As no anti-tank weapon larger than 40-mm was seen, he quickly decided to attack the anti-tank guns by running two tanks abreast down the road, assigning each an enemy gun to take out. With dismounted infantry in support, success was achieved in knocking out both 40-mm guns and their advance continued. More enemy personnel were spotted on the other side of the rail trestle, so the tanks advanced, firing steadily as they went. Within minutes, more than seventy German troops were taken prisoner.[2]

The map on the next page reveals a broad overview of Task Force A's overall progress under the command of General Earnest from the beaches of Normandy through the Brittany Peninsula to Brest, and on to the north shore of the River Loire.

---

[1] Tanks do their most deadly work when firing from "hull down" positions, where the mass of the armored vehicle is concealed from the enemy and the tank commander observes from the turret and assists the gunner adjust fire. War Department Armored Force Field Manual, FM 17-12, *Tank Gunnery*, 32.

[2] Anonymous, "Seizing Strategic Installations," 7.

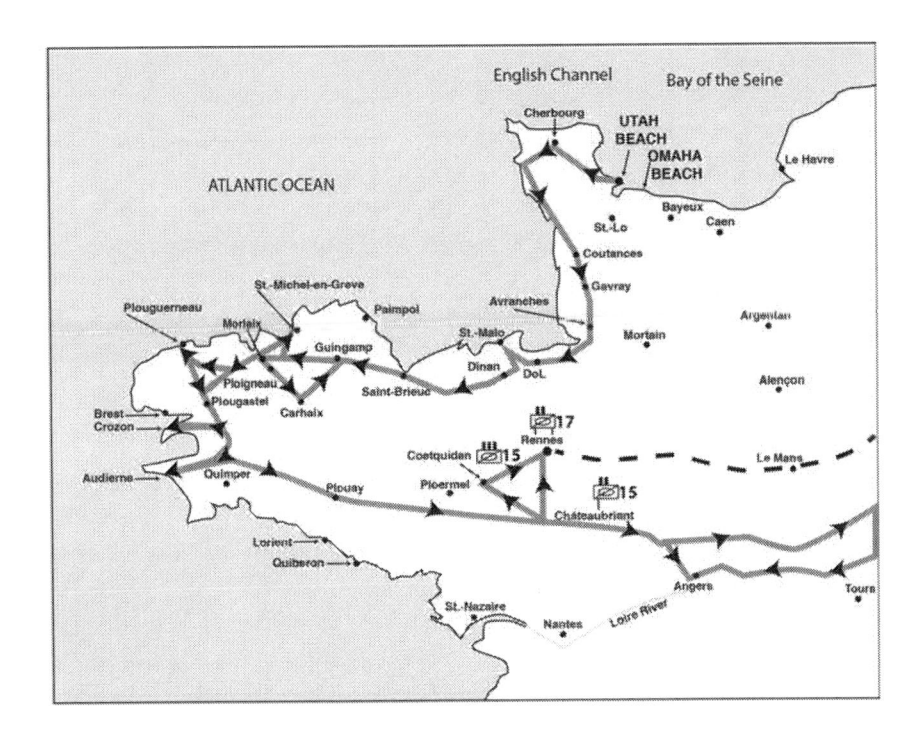

After passing through Plouigneau, Troop A sent a platoon to Morlaix via a parallel road "south of Highway 12." At the same time, Troop B, minus one of its reconnaissance platoons, got orders "to move by secondary roads and enter Morlaix from the north." However, due to several minefields and numerous, large anti-tank obstacles, neither Troop A nor Troop B was able enter the town.[1]

By noon, as the lead jeep came within sight of Morlaix, an unmanned, 20-mm enemy light Flak gun was detected straight ahead, again under a railway trestle. Before the Germans could fully man that gun, however, it was knocked out and set on fire. Immediately afterward, troopers in the two lead scout jeeps dismounted and advanced alongside an M8 armored car. They soon spotted another German light Flak gun positioned under a second railroad trestle some 200 yards away. As the enemy began to load that weapon, the armored car opened fire and knocked it out, but subsequent machine gun and small arms fire pinned down the dismounted GIs.

---

[1] Ibid.

Consequently, the Troop A commander came forward to reconnoiter and decided to dismount a portion of his 3rd platoon and troop headquarters. Positioning those GIs behind hedgerows about 200 yards on either side of the column, he called forward a tank platoon and some men from the attached platoon of Troop C. With the benefit of supporting small arms fire, the platoon of five tanks then advanced rapidly down the road with dismounted troopers from Troop C. They promptly massed their fire at the enemy in and near a chateau on the right and along the railroad embankment.

Realizing that the Germans were on high alert and fearing the worst, the squadron commander ordered forward an attached infantry company to follow the railway embankment into Morlaix in order to capture the big bridge and hold it "at all costs." Within ten minutes, the infantry company was reported to have captured their objective intact and Troop A took "over 270 enemy [prisoners] in and around the chateau".

After reorganizing, the squadron began their move into Morlaix, but on encountering sniper fire, tanks were called forward to suppress the enemy's fire, raining down on them from several buildings. By the time that was accomplished, the enemy surrendered "so quickly and in such numbers" that Troop A had all it could handle.[1]

Several hours after that hot pursuit, Dad remarked in his diary that they had "captured numerous German soldiers and 7 officers." Later, he wrote it was "unknown how many [we] killed?"

With the assistance of bands of Breton Maquisards,[2] General Earnest reported on August 9, that his task force had completed its mission to liberate the city and capture the large railroad bridge south of Morlaix. The total number of German soldiers captured by TFA was 1,200, and

---

[1] Ibid., 7-8.
[2] Gen. Charles de Gaulle created the *Forces Françaises de l'Interior* (the FFI) in early 1944; they were French guerillas most often referred to as the *Maquis* or Free French Resistance. Lt. Col. Will Irwin (USA-Ret.), *The Jedburghs* (New York: Public Affairs, 2005), 86. The FFI in Brittany numbered around 20,000 armed fighters under the command Col. Alfred M. Eon. Blumenson, *Breakout and Pursuit*, 354; they cut telephone lines, blew up bridges, mined roads, derailed trains and captured some 10,000 German prisoners. Waller, *Wild Bill Donovan*, 237.

American and FFI losses were described as "very small."[1] Afterward, troopers from the 17th Cavalry Squadron mounted guard details and forward observation posts throughout the surrounding area to protect "the long and vulnerable railroad bridge" at that location, while the remainder of TFA assembled in bivouac several miles west of Morlaix.[2]

The photograph below is one Dad took of the Morlaix railroad station, shortly after its capture, revealing quite a traffic jam of U.S. trucks and M8 armored cars. Fortunately, the Allies had established air supremacy; otherwise, the Germans would have had a field day, reducing most of those vehicles to smoldering rubble. Of special interest is the proud display by the local citizens of the French Tricolour, the vertically striped blue, white, and red national flags, hanging from the upper window of the station. It showed how pleased the French citizens were to have been liberated after four long years of German occupation.

With respect to the bridges on the French double-track railway that required seizure by American forces in early August 1944, the most valuable one was at Morlaix: "an arched stone structure some thousand feet in

---

[1] Blumenson, *Breakout and Pursuit*, 392.
[2] TLR, 8.

147

length and two hundred feet in height." It was the largest railroad viaduct in France, spanning a defile that was 250 feet deep and 200 yards wide.[1]

Due to the U.S. lack of appropriate heavy construction equipment, destruction of that bridge by the Germans would have been disastrous and would have paralyzed "the Brest-Rennes railroad line indefinitely." Without that rail line, the capture of the port of Brest would have served no useful purpose.

Throughout the effort to seize those important railroad bridges, there was basically a total lack of information concerning the opposing enemy, which made planning and coordination of attack nearly impossible. The enemy was also without adequate communication and it was evidently quite disorganized; they knew as little about the attacking American force as the Americans knew about them. That confusion made it highly advisable for the lead troop of the 17th Cavalry Squadron to attack rapidly as a small task force and knock out the enemy before they got organized. The lesson learned that day was: while in pursuit of scattered enemy resistance, at a time when neither side knows the status or whereabouts of the other, the head of the column should be "loaded with a hard wallop, in order to overwhelm the enemy before he can organize any resistance."[2] That experience proved so satisfactory that it was made standard operating procedure for the remainder of Brittany Peninsula operation.

My father mentioned in his diary that he and his squadron mates had bivouacked on the train station platform that night. Ever observant, he also commented, "Morlaix has an awful lot of beautiful women."

By August 8, 1944, a portion of the town of St.-Malo was under the firm control of General Macon's 83rd Thunderbolt Division. However, by the time the entire port surrendered in mid-August, it was so badly damaged by the Germans that it was inoperable and essentially useless. That's when General Patton ordered Middleton to use the three divisions of his VIII Corps to advance rapidly to secure the port of Brest, as a priority mission over the capture of Lorient.[3]

---

[1] Blumenson, *Breakout and Pursuit*, 392.
[2] The previous two paragraphs draw on the *Cavalry Journal* essay: Anonymous, "Seizing Strategic Installations," 7-8.
[3] Delaforce, *Smashing the Atlantic Wall*, 79-92; Blumenson, *Patton*, 230.

Several days earlier, during the evening of August 2, Bradley realized he would not need to use Patton's entire Third Army to seize the seaport of Brest, as events had outrun his original attack plan. Thus, Patton's VIII Corps under Middleton was left to clear out the Brittany Peninsula, while the XV Corps under Haislip[1] and Walker's XX Corps were launched in the opposite direction, due east into the heart of France.[2]

On August 9, General Earnest endeavored to make contact with Grow's Super Sixth Armored Division, but to no avail. He radioed: "Where is Six Armored Division's right flank?"[3] As Middleton's response was vague out of necessity, reconnaissance was initiated by the 15th Cavalry Group to locate them in order to gain their support. Previously, Grow's men had taken the middle, more direct route through the Brittany Peninsula to Brest, thereby reaching the outskirts of Brest by the evening of August 6. However, they "lacked the strength alone to storm the place, and by the time reinforcements arrived" the enemy had dug in and prepared for the siege.[4] When contact was finally established with elements of the Super Sixth by late afternoon, "liaison parties" were sent out to coordinate 15th Cavalry Group activities. Meanwhile, TFA assembled in bivouac near Ploudaniel, north of Landernau.[5]

In the interim, Adolf Hitler exacted appalling revenge on certain high-ranking German Army officers based on their alleged complicity in the July 20 bomb plot to assassinate him at his headquarters in East Prussia. The plotters were convicted in a show trial, and hung from ceiling meat hooks with nooses of wire wrapped around their necks. To make matters more horrifying, the execution was filmed with the specific purpose of creating

---

[1] Wade Hampton Haislip was a West Point-educated Virginian and World War I combat veteran. He was also one of General Eisenhower's oldest friends; yet, as Haislip's background was infantry, Patton playfully noted: he's "been sitting around the War Department in swivel chairs so long, he's muscle-bound in the ass." Featherston, *Saving the Breakout*, 157.
[2] McManus, *The Americans at Normandy*, 344.
[3] Blumenson, *Breakout and Pursuit*, 392.
[4] Taaffe, *Marshall and His Generals*, 192-193.
[5] TLR, 9.

shock and fear in the German population.[1] The death toll ultimately numbered around two hundred individuals, but according to one historian: "it was Hitler's last triumph."[2]

On another matter, when TFA first got underway in early August 1944, it was decided that the old adage regarding strength in numbers applied. Thus, unit supply trains were combined to afford them better protection from enemy air and ground attack. That requirement resulted from the fact that a combat element was not regularly attached to the train convoy; they had to furnish their own protection. Thus, care was taken to distribute the more heavily armed vehicles at intervals along the column, placing a sufficient number with antiaircraft weapons in the lead and tail vehicles. Those vehicles were mainly half-tracks, two light tanks from each squadron's maintenance section, and three armored cars, mounting .50 caliber machine guns. At that time, very few of their supply trucks were equipped with ring mounts.[3]

On August 9, 1944, Dad recorded in his diary that at 1000 in the morning, Fox Company was alerted to provide assistance to the 15th Cavalry Group's supply column, which had become detached due to heavy fog from the rest of the TFA supply train.[4] They were bivouacked some eight miles east of Morlaix, near Plouigneau, and had come under enemy attack earlier at around 0700 hours. Their first instinct was to make a run for it, but soon they learned a German force of some two hundred enemy soldiers had surrounded them with light horse-drawn, 20- and 40-mm anti-tank weapons. As the supply-train support vehicles possessed inadequate,

---

[1] Field Marshal Erwin von Witzleben was one of those hung in August 1944, as he had been selected by the July 20 conspirators to command the German Army after Hitler's overthrow. Kershaw, *Hitler: 1936-45: Nemesis*, 692.
[2] Kershaw, *Hitler: 1936-45: Nemesis*, 693.
[3] Capt. Clark R. Larson and Capt. Frank C. Horton, "Trains Have to Fight Too," *Cavalry Journal*, Vol. 54, no. 5 (September-October 1945), 5-6.
[4] An army's supply train should not be confused with a railway operation. Rather, it is the service and supply element of a military force, consisting mostly of truck convoys, furnishing essential items, including food, ammunition, and fuel in the field. While advancing in combat, they became increasingly vulnerable to enemy attack.

organic firepower, they were forced to set up a defensive firing line around their area, "covered wagon style."[1]

Capt. Herman M. Marlow, commander of the 17th Cavalry Squadron's Headquarters Troop, was reported to have dashed forward in an armored car to the outskirts of Morlaix where he successfully made contact with members of a tank platoon from Fox Company. Thereafter, "a hot fight ensued" and the enemy was repulsed by a "fire brigade" tank platoon led by Lt. John O. Conway of the 17th Cavalry Squadron, which "attacked full speed up the road, firing as it came."[2] Ultimately, the additional firepower of those light tanks allowed the detached 15th Cavalry Group supply convoy to break contact and move out of the area in order to rejoin the rest of Task Force A's trains, which were situated on the outskirts of Morlaix.[3]

Sadly, one of Pop's closest brother-in-arms (Pvt. William J. Scott) was killed in action during the course of that operation.[4] In his diary, he mentioned that when he heard the news it shocked him to the core. He apparently took it pretty hard, as he and "Scotty" (as he called him) had trained for several months together in the California desert during 1943; once again, he was reminded of the dangers inherent in his work as tank crewmen. After mourning Scotty's death for some time, he thought back to the vow he made to his bride: to return in one piece; thus, he resolved to continue to stay alert, but to keep his head down and do nothing too daring or stupid, or both.

For his actions during the "Battle of 'Plouigniau'" (actually Plouigneau), Private Scott was awarded the Bronze Star Medal (posthumously).[5] Today, his grave and those of several other 17th Cavalry Squadron troopers[6] are

---

[1] Larson and Horton, "Trains Have to Fight Too," *Cavalry Journal*, 6.
[2] TLR, 9.
[3] Larson and Horton, "Trains Have to Fight Too," *Cavalry Journal*, 6.
[4] History of the 17th Cavalry Reconnaissance Squadron for Year 1944, 5, 7.
[5] Ibid.; TLR 24 and 28.
[6] The other 17th Cavalry troopers buried at the Brittany American Cemetery are: Tec 5 Henry V. Haynes, Sgt. Omar F. Hawes, 2nd Lt. Harold S. Garrison, Tec 5 Donald F. Fulton, Cpl. Clarence C. Braziel, Pvt. William Barna, Pvt. John J. Amrick, Jr., PFC Ferd A. Dunn, Pvt. Liberio M. Rogo, PFC Walter J. Gutkowski, SSgt. Charles L. Trimble, 2nd Lt. Russell J. MacDonald, PFC John T. Sutter, Cpl. George M. Romaniello, PFC Delbert D. Kindle, PFC Norman P. Gillings, and Tec 5 Cosmo P. Coccitti.

located at the Brittany American Cemetery and Memorial near St.-James, France. Currently, they are maintained with great care under the supervision of the American Battle Monuments Commission.

By early August 1944, Hitler made a disastrous situation far worse by personally concocting his own battle plan to defeat the Cobra breakout of U.S. forces from Normandy. Designated Operation Luttich, the commanders of the four remaining German panzer divisions in Normandy (the 1st SS-Leibstandarte Adolf Hitler, 2nd SS-Das Reich, 2nd Panzer and 116th Windhund), and the 17th SS-Panzergrenadier Division were directed to counterattack against the American spearhead and thrust west to the Atlantic coast at Avranches.[1] Hitler's intention was to isolate Patton's Third Army, which was slicing south into France and west into the Brittany Peninsula. German Field Marshal Günther von Kluge mentioned in his diary: "The attack represents the decisive attempt to reverse the situation in Normandy. If it succeeds, the enemy who has advanced into Brittany will be cut off."[2] Nonetheless, that scheme was doomed from the start, as it failed to consider the fact that German troops would be operating in the open without air support or an inadequate anti-aircraft defense. Such incompetent planning by Hitler inured to the benefit of the Allies, as his underestimation of Allied air strength set in motion a terribly lethal reception for his divisions.

Forewarned of German intentions through decryption of intercepted Ultra[3] messages, the 30th Old Hickory Division of "Lightning Joe" Collins's VII Corps was rapidly positioned in the vicinity of the French town of Mortain. There, the seasoned Old Hickory Division "earned fresh laurels mounting a desperate defense", as they took on the full brunt of the German attack.[4]

---

[1] McManus, *The Americans at Normandy*, 367-369.
[2] Hargreaves, *The Germans in Normandy*, 176.
[3] "Ultra" was the code name for the super-secret intelligence gleaned from successful deciphering of the German Enigma machine. Eisenhower, *Eisenhower: At War, 1943-1945*, 166-167.
[4] Barr, *Eisenhower's Armies: The American-British Alliance during World War II*, 392; General Bradley ultimately provided the 30th Division with additional divisions from Patton's Third Army and two more from the First Army as reinforcements. Stephen E. Ambrose, *The Supreme Commander: The War*

Predictably, that German offensive was repulsed in a hard-fought battle, aided by tactical air support in the form of Allied fighter-bombers: U.S. P-47 Thunderbolts[1] and RAF rocket-firing Hawker Typhoons. The latter were described as the "real tank busters" at Mortain, firing 20-mm cannon and rockets, as "a single rocket hit was usually enough" to destroy the best-armored German tank.[2]

Out of the Allied envelopment, a total rout ensued as remnants of the Fifth Panzer Army, the German Seventh Army and Panzer Group Eberbach, scrambled to the east to escape the Falaise pocket: the deadly kill sack formed following the German defeat at Mortain. Yet, the situation grew worse as Allied forces gradually surrounded the wrecked German divisions retreating to the area between the French towns of Falaise in the north and Argentan to the south. But as British, Canadian, and Polish forces in the north attempted to link up with the Americans in the south near Chambois to trap the enemy, a fifteen-mile wide escape route remained open to the east until August 19. Thus, small, isolated groups of Germans continued to escape across the Dives River until August 21, when the pocket became airtight.[3] It became known as the "Corridor of Death" as Germans by the thousands died trying to escape.[4] That battle destroyed von Kluge, as he was relieved of command and ordered to report to a furious Führer. Knowing what awaited him, he swallowed a cyanide capsule and ended his life the next morning.[5]

Concerning the average German division that escaped the Falaise cauldron, no more than 300 men were left. As to the remnants of seven panzer divisions, which reassembled on the far bank of the River Seine, "their total strength after fleeing amounted to 1,300 men, 24 tanks, and 60

Years of General Dwight D. Eisenhower (Garden City, NY: Doubleday, 1970), 473.

[1] The P-47 amounted to flying artillery with its eight .50 caliber machine guns, making German reinforcement extremely tenuous. Rooney, *My War*, 165.
[2] Featherston, *Saving the Breakout*, 132-133.
[3] Blumenson, *Breakout and Pursuit*, 554.
[4] Prados, *Normandy Crucible*, 194-239.
[5] Weigley, *Eisenhower's Lieutenants*, 215; Murray & Millett, *A War to Be Won*, 433.

artillery pieces."[1] At the end of that battle, the Germans were said to have suffered a loss of some 50,000 men captured and 10,000 dead.[2] As a consequence, German Army Group B was totally ruined.[3]

Walking through the carnage a few days after the Allies succeeded in closing the gap south of Falaise, General Eisenhower was appalled at what he saw: scenes that could be described only by Dante. He wrote, "It was literally possible to walk for hundreds of yards at a time, stepping on nothing but dead and decaying flesh."[4]

By one estimate up to 40,000 troops escaped that Allied encirclement, but they were described as mostly noncombatants, including "a good many headquarters personnel around whom the Germans would reconstitute their units."[5] Yet, other historians believe around 50,000 Germans escaped the wreckage of the Falaise pocket, describing them as "the toughest soldiers in the German Army."[6] No matter how you slice it, the enemy was dealt a mauling of historic proportions near Falaise in August 1944.

On the heels of that defeat of the enemy, Patton's Third Army continued its plunge deeper into the French countryside, as Nancy, Rennes, and Nantes fell, the ports of Brittany were invested, and American spearhead units continued to close on Paris.[7]

While the major events described above were occurring a few hundred miles to their east, TFA was given the mission of protecting the north and northwest flank of Grow's Super Sixth Armored Division in Brittany. On the morning of August 10, 1944, the 15th Cavalry Squadron conducted a reconnaissance in force[8] and a hostile pocket was encountered in the afternoon near Plouguerneau, producing nearly two hundred POWs. On

---

[1] Esposito (ed.), *The West Point Atlas of American Wars, 1900-1953,* Vol. II, Map 55; Barr, *Eisenhower's Armies,* 395.
[2] Blumenson, *Breakout and Pursuit,* 557-558; McManus, *The Americans at Normandy,* 435, 437.
[3] Hastings, *Victory in Europe,* 51, 52.
[4] Eisenhower, *Crusade in Europe,* 279.
[5] Taaffe, *Marshall and His Generals,* 196.
[6] Murray and Millett, *A War to Be Won,* 432.
[7] Hargreaves, *The Germans in Normandy,* 185.
[8] A reconnaissance-in-force is far more aggressive than a basic cavalry reconnaissance mission. It's akin to stirring up a wasp nest to see if anyone is home. Rottman, *World War II US Cavalry Groups: European Theater,* 17.

returning to their assembly area near Lesneven, the squadron observed a flight of U.S. medium bombers, flying through "heavy flak" as they emptied their bomb loads on Brest.[1]

By early to mid-August 1944, the resupply situation became critical, as Patton's Third Army was outrunning its supply lines. Consequently, TFA was ordered by VIII Corps to secure a badly needed beachhead for Third Army use. A supply shortfall had developed because with each day's advance Patton's forces became farther removed from Third Army supply dumps. For example, before the port of Brest fell it was not uncommon for ammunition trucks to have to travel 500 miles round-trip to obtain certain kinds of artillery ammunition. Omaha Beach was the closest resupply site for 76-mm ammunition for TDs attached to TFA and up-gunned Sherman tanks in VIII Corps.[2]

As supply stocks dwindled, a special round-the-clock trucking service (called the "Red Ball Express") was established in Com-Z to speed delivery of military supplies, especially gasoline.[3] As an emergency expedient, it was crewed mainly by African American soldiers and was required to haul supplies on round trips from the Normandy beaches. Those Red Ball cargo trucks were described as "a band of stage-coaches making a run through Indian country." They reportedly kept their wheels moving, and tried hard not to get lost or killed.[4] That was at a time when most of the units of both U.S. armies in Northern Europe were on the move, and their daily gasoline consumption exceeded 800,000 gallons.[5] Patton's Third Army alone used more than 275,000 gallons of gas daily and received "on average only about 202,000 gallons a day" throughout the month of August.[6]

After a long road march without encountering any hostile force, Task Force A successfully secured a small beachhead near St.-Michel-en-Grève, providing Patton's forces a much-needed supply terminus, northeast of

---

[1] TLR, 9.
[2] Maj. Glenn E. Font, "Group Supply Problems," *Cavalry Journal,* Vol. LIV, no. 5 (September-October 1945), 5.
[3] Province, *Patton's Third Army,* 30.
[4] Blumenson, *Breakout and Pursuit,* 354.
[5] Ibid., 690-691.
[6] Taaffe, *Marshall and His Generals,* 237.

Morlaix. Thus, they satisfied a vital need, providing a supply point much closer to combat activity in northern Brittany.[1]

By the late afternoon of August 11, 1944, cargo ships had dropped anchor and began the task of offloading to landing craft the most urgently needed items: type K and "10-in-1" rations, ammunition, and gasoline.

To clarify, K rations were meant to be a single meal for individual GIs. Each cardboard K ration box was flammable and proved useful in warming the meal and brewing coffee; they came labeled specifically for breakfast, dinner, or supper, with breakfast being the "least evil"[2]; the latter consisted of a fruit bar, Nescafe, sugar, crackers, and a small can of ham and eggs. Dinner and supper amounted to a can of cheese or potted meat, crackers, and a bouillon cube, topped off by chocolate candy and sticks of chewing gum.[3]

The "slightly more appetizing" 10-in-1 rations were intended to feed ten men for one day or one man for ten days. They came in a large box, containing a variety of small canned items.[4] Type C rations amounted to canned food that was intended by the War Department to feed one soldier for one day. Also available were type D rations, which were hard chocolate candy bars intended for emergency purposes mostly.

Furthermore, it was not at all uncommon for GI rations to be "supplemented" by a stray French chicken and some eggs.[5] Also, American GIs were known to augment their K and C rations by pulling up raw vegetables (carrots, turnips, beets, and cabbage) from French gardens, and sampling apples and other fruit from orchards they came upon along the way.[6]

On August 12, Maj. Garrett J. Dobbins took command of the 15th Cavalry Squadron, and he wasted little time putting his squadron to work combing the area around the St.-Michel-en-Grève beachhead, finding it clean of any enemy force. Next, TFA moved through Morlaix on August

---

[1] TLR, 9.
[2] MacDonald, *Company Commander*, 29; Slaughter, *Omaha Beach and Beyond*, 68.
[3] Province, *Patton's Third Army*, 301.
[4] Ibid.
[5] Cooper, *Death Traps*, 63.
[6] Joseph H. Ewing, *29 Let's Go! A History of the 29th Infantry Division in World War II* (Washington, D.C.: Infantry Journal Press, 1948) 89-90.

13 and to the southeast to clear the triangle: Carhaix to Guingamp to Morlaix. In doing so, no enemy forces were detected and they encamped that night near Callac.

By August 15, General Earnest's TFA advanced to the northeast to reduce a hostile enemy position at Tréguier. Following a "stiff fight" around five hundred more POWs were removed from the battlefield. TFA then patrolled eastward on August 16, and after a struggle in which they employed all arms of the task force, the town of Lesardrieux was captured. A reconnaissance-in-force mission was also undertaken that day on the peninsula to the north of Lesardrieux, but no resistance was encountered, except at Île à Bois where another two hundred POWs were rounded up. On August 17, TFA secured the coastal town of Paimpol and the area to its north, culminating in the capture of around six hundred more POWs. That action successfully ended all major enemy resistance on the northern Brittany Peninsula between St.-Malo and Brest. Then, the 15th Cavalry Group, the largest single element of TFA, moved from near Lesardrieux on August 18, to the vicinity of Landerneau. On that occasion, the 15th Cavalry Squadron relieved Dad's outfit from its security mission around Morlaix and the beachhead of St.-Michel-en-Grève.

As TFA arrived at Pleuneventer, the 17th Cavalry Squadron was ordered to reconnoiter the southern flank of Middleton's VIII Corps, which had relieved the 6th Armored Division, and was making final preparations for an assault on Brest. The 17th Cavalry Squadron then advanced its security screen to the south as far as Châteaulin and Sizun.

On August 20, the 15th Cavalry Squadron pushed into the Daoulas Peninsula on a line running roughly north and south through Plougastel. There they encountered stiff resistance, and on August 21st, the 3rd Battalion, 330th Infantry Regiment of the 83rd Thunderbolt Division moved in abreast of the 15th Cavalry Squadron for support. Intelligence estimates reported a probable enemy strength of from three to five thousand troops.

By the evening of August 22, another task force (TFB) assumed command of the 3rd Battalion of the 330th Infantry, and the 50th Infantry Battalion of the super Sixth Armored Division became attached to TFA. At that time, the 15th Cavalry Squadron was given the mission of maintaining contact with the two infantry battalions until its redeployment

157

in a southerly direction to the Crozon Peninsula, the extreme northwestern corner of France.[1]

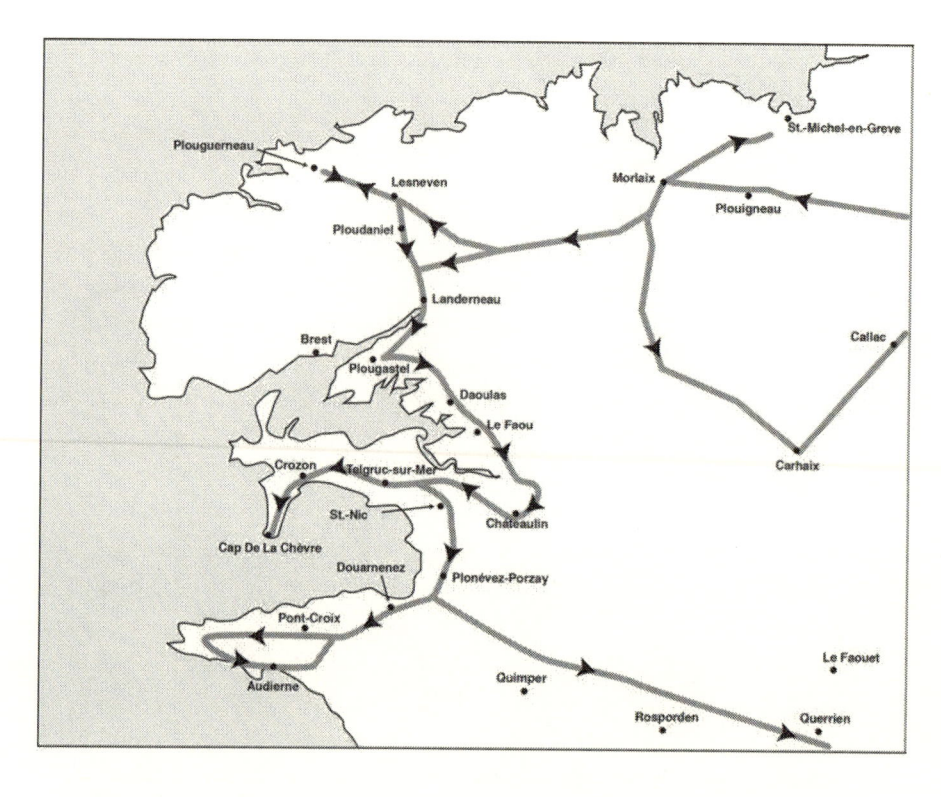

The map above reveals the path of the 15th Cavalry Group's operations while assigned to Task Force A during August 1944.

On August 23, Dad described his unit's movement through the town of Landerneau where he "never saw such narrow streets; [we] had hardly enough room to maneuver [our] tanks." His commentary made clear the agility of the Stuart tank: its smaller size relative to the Sherman allowed much greater maneuverability in tight urban areas. Given its lighter weight and agility, the Stuart tank could travel across muddy ground where a Sherman would bog down.

---

[1] The previous six paragraphs draw on TLR, 9-10.

158

11. FIGHTING ON THE CROZON PENINSULA

At that moment in the fighting, one might question the Allies decision to lay siege to a seaport at the western end of Brittany Peninsula. The answer requires an understanding that Brest had been an important port during the First World War for American forces arriving in Europe.[1] War Department planners were already familiar with Brest, and it had symbolic value to veterans of the Great War like Generals Marshall and Patton ("Old Blood and Guts"), as that was where they first set foot on French soil in 1917. More importantly, since the captured harbors of Cherbourg and St.-Malo had been so badly damaged prior to their capture, the Brest harbor took on increased importance to supply Allied troops on the continent with food, fuel, and ammunition; its large roadstead was fourteen miles long and four miles wide.[2]

The assault on Brest by the three subordinate infantry divisions (the 2nd, 8th, and 29th) of Middleton's VIII Corps began on August 25, 1944. The 29th Blue-Gray Division formed the right flank of the VIII Corps attack on the port city, as the 8th Pathfinder Division attacked from the north and the 2nd Indianhead[3] Division swung down from the east. The capture of Brest required hard fighting for almost a month and ultimately cost around ten thousand American casualties.[4]

On August 26, 1944, the U.S. Eighth Air Force launched an attack on Brest using over 170 B-17 heavy bombers. The RAF Bomber Command also joined in the attack, and the city fortress "was bombarded from the sea by large warships."[5]

---

[1] The port of Brest was considered ideal, as the Allies in World War I used it extensively; it was the largest landlocked port in Europe, serviced by an excellent French railway system. Bradham, *"To the Last Man"*, 135.

[2] Delaforce, *Smashing the Atlantic Wall*, 92.

[3] The U.S. 2nd Infantry Division is nicknamed "Indianhead" by virtue of the American Indian warrior depicted on its soldier's shoulder insignia.

[4] Ewing, *29 Let's Go!*, 123; Perret, *Winged Victory*, 315.

[5] Perret, *Winged Victory*, 315.

In a personal aside, my father recorded in his diary on August 26, that he had been promoted back to the enlisted rank of corporal. Of far greater importance to the war effort, the 17th Cavalry Squadron that day set out south on a reconnaissance mission to the Crozon Peninsula with an attached combat engineer platoon, a TD platoon and a field artillery battery from the 83rd Thunderbolt Division.

By August 28, they encountered a strong enemy force positioned along a line running generally through St.-Nic, Menez-Hom, and Brigneum. Army intelligence had indicated that a reinforced German battalion held that line.[1] Also, on that day the 15th Cavalry Squadron, minus Troop A (left at Daoulas Peninsula), moved to the northern flank of the Crozon Peninsula and took over the zone formerly occupied by Troop A of the 17th Cavalry Squadron.

Also, on August 28, the newly promoted Lt. Col. Garrett Dobbins was wounded and Lt. Col. Robert J. Quinn, Jr., assumed temporary command of the 15th Cavalry Squadron, and he continued in that capacity until September 12, when Colonel Dobbins recovered sufficiently to resume command.[2]

In a postwar *Cavalry Journal* article, it was noted that after nearly five hundred miles of motorized operations on the Brittany Peninsula during August 1944, the 15th Cavalry Group engaged the enemy mostly as dismounted infantry within a containing screen[3] from August 27 to September 15, 1944, on the Crozon Peninsula, south of Brest. The mounted phase of that operation ended quickly as the initial enemy defensive line was encountered on the first day, and the squadron vehicles were parked in defilade. Thereafter, the mission became a grimy assignment, filled with many unknowns, and it was accompanied by very little restful sleep. That dismounted mission resulted from the hilly terrain with ridges and deep narrow valleys intertwined by high-banked streams, making the use of mechanized vehicles of any type unsuitable. To assist the

---

[1] TLR, 10
[2] Ibid., 10, 11.
[3] This type of mission was "intended to counter enemy reconnaissance and warn friendly forces of their presence; the cavalry would repel or destroy enemy patrols, and warn of the enemy's main-force approach." Rottman, *World War II US Cavalry Groups: European Theater*, 18.

mission, mutually supporting strong points were established with unobstructed, interlocking fields of fire along the front to allow maximum use of each squadron's automatic weapons.

The deployment of both squadrons of the 15th Cavalry Group was necessary due to a shortage of U.S. infantrymen in Brittany. That arrangement was anything but the preferred use for cavalry since it did not have the equivalent capability of two battalions of infantry. Those dismounted cavalry squadrons lacked powerful automatic weapons (e.g., BARs) and they had only a few M1 Garand rifles on hand; their carbines and submachine guns were useful for close-in defensive work, but such short-ranged firepower made them far less desirable as primary combat weapons.

That blocking screen was established to prevent enemy infiltration, with the squadrons essentially on line: the 15th Cavalry Squadron covered the northern sector of the Crozon Peninsula, and the 17th Cavalry Squadron had responsibility for the southern flank. Each squadron deployed two reconnaissance troops forward with the third recce troop and their light tank company in squadron reserve. The assault guns of Troop E in each squadron were placed in battery to provide defensive, harassment and interdiction fire, as needed. Also, an attached field artillery battery augmented the fires of each squadron in direct support, while the 35th Engineer Battalion and M18 "Hellcats" of the 705th TD Battalion provided general support to the entire 15th Cavalry Group. The engineers were trained to fight as infantry when necessary, and the fact that TDs were attached indicated they expected heavy enemy resistance. To supplement their defensive positions, each troop conducted daily foot patrols to try and identify the location of enemy positions and search for signs of offensive intentions.

During that operation on the Crozon Peninsula, the Germans "showed little if any desire for offensive action." Yet, they defended stubbornly, bringing down heavy fire on all dismounted patrols, and flatly repulsed one attempted reconnaissance in force of their position by a combat group, consisting of Troop A of the 15th Cavalry Squadron, supported by tanks, assault guns, and M18 tank destroyers.[1]

In his diary, Corporal Gough wrote that it took them two days to take St.-Nic, and on September 1, he reported accompanying several other troopers on a dismounted reconnaissance mission. As noted previously, a typical cavalry mission involved movement and observation; Pop referred to it as a hasty, "sneak and peak." In any event, their job was to locate the enemy and report their position to headquarters; their instructions and prior training told them to avoid getting "bogged down" by fighting the enemy.[2] As they were required to travel by foot beyond their own lines through a contested "no-man's land," arm and hand signals were necessary, as noise discipline was important to assure their safe return.

During the course of their reconnoitering Dad wrote, "No sooner did we get outside St.-Nic, when we were fired on, and pinned down." He indicated they took cover until more help could be brought up, allowing them to break contact with the enemy and withdraw. During that firefight he also reported seeing a flock of chickens, and after opening up on them he and his pals enjoyed fresh chicken later for supper. (Of course, that would not be the last time my father and his mates took notice of the occasional "abandoned" European poultry to supplement their rations.) As a consequence, many fowl went missing in the ETO, and those that survived undoubtedly learned early to roost high in the trees or face dire consequences.

---

[1] The prior four paragraphs draw on: Maj. William R. Kraft, "Cavalry in Dismounted Action," *Cavalry Journal*, Vol. 54, no. 6 (November-December 1945), 10-12.
[2] Rottman, *World War II US Cavalry Groups: European Theater*, 24.

The photograph above shows my begrimed father, standing second from the right with a group of equally grubby buddies. They certainly appear to have been successful in their combat foraging mission. While the birds appear quite scrawny with their feathers freshly plucked, Pop and his mates were not at all disappointed. On the contrary, they appear quite happy and ready to finish the job by cooking them up for supper.

As Task Force A had been sent to the south of Brest, their mission was to push west up the Crozon Peninsula as far as possible until they met strong enemy resistance. Then they were to engage the enemy and prevent any of the nearly 40,000 entrenched German defenders in the Brest area from escaping by water south across the harbor, and by land eastward down the peninsula. The enemy's first line of defense on Crozon had collapsed by early September 1944, due to "the surrender of a considerable number of Russian labor battalions"[1] holding the northern flank of the promontory of Menez-Hom. Those troops were mostly Red Army POWs, captured by the Germans on the Eastern Front who had been persuaded to work on coastal defense projects as forced-labor conscripts with the *Organisation*

---

[1] Adam Tooze, *The Wages of Destruction* (NY: Viking Press, 2006), 519-521.

Todt,[1] in lieu of starving to death in German POW camps.[2] Some were later armed and press-ganged for garrison duty in Normandy or used as static defense forces (*Osttruppen* or Eastern troops in German) to free up regular German units for frontline mobile duty.[3]

As mentioned earlier, the enemy on the Crozon Peninsula held their defensive positions stubbornly with the assistance of intense automatic weapons, anti-tank, and 88-mm artillery fire. They showed little to no interest in offensive operations, but brought down heavy fire on all daily squadron patrol activity.[4]

On September 3, my father wrote that his tank platoon had advanced up a hill and through the town of Telgruc (now known as Telgruc-sur-Mer). As they waited west of town for further orders, his "complete unit" was bombed and strafed by U.S. P-51 Mustang fighter-bombers. He reported they immediately put their tanks in motion, fanned out madly, waved their bright air identification panels, and fired smoke grenades and flares, but still the friendly air attack continued. He mentioned bombs landed within "200 yards from my tank," and ".50 cal[iber] bullets [were] what I was worrying about."

After the first few bombs fell, Pop said, "We took off." They passed back through Telgruc, made it safely and watched the town burn "just 800

---

[1] Fritz Todt,'s construction firm for the German military relied entirely on POWs and millions of forced laborers. Speer, *Inside the Third Reich*, 193-195.
[2] More than 3,000,000 Soviet POWs died in the Second World War. The mortality rate for Soviet POWs in German hands exceeded fifty percent; as many British and Americans died in German POW camps during the war as died in Soviet POW camps in one day. Mazower, *Hitler's Empire*, 161-163. By contrast, only one in twenty-five American POWs died under Nazi captivity, while one in three died under Japanese incarceration. Iris Chang, *The Rape of Nanking* (New York: BasicBooks, 1997), 173.
[3] After the war, Stalin demanded repatriation of all Soviet soldiers who had been German POWs, deeming them traitors. On their return, many were promptly executed, while others faced "a slower death" in Soviet forced labor camps, known as the Gulag. Norman Davies, *No Simple Victory* (New York: Viking, 2007), 272, 328-334; Gilbert, *The Second World War*, 728. By December 1946, 1.5 million Red Army POWs were sent to the Gulag or to penal labor battalions in Siberia, where they faced near certain death. Antony Beevor, *The Fall of Berlin 1945* (New York: Viking, 2002), 423.
[4] Kraft, "Cavalry in Dismounted Action," 12.

yards away." However, Recce Troop A was not so lucky, as they lost several men and some jeeps. That "mix up" baffled him since the town had been "cleared of Huns since yesterday." He also mentioned with regret that many civilians were killed in Telgruc that day.

After they returned to the town three hours later, he described it as shattered with trees uprooted and buildings in broken ruins. He wrote: "Every house is damaged, and the streets are covered with debris and bodies. Some are still burning." The sight of that devastation, together with the stench of death from the many charred corpses and body parts strewn on the ground caused him understandable distress.

That complete foul-up was mentioned briefly in Part I of the history of the 15th Cavalry Group, *The Lion Rampant*, a pamphlet published on September 20, 1945. There, on page 11, it was reported that an Allied air strike was conducted on known enemy targets along the front, but after scoring several hits on a roadblock east of "Tel-ar-Groas" (presumably Telgruc) one plane in the flight had a "hung" bomb,[1] which dropped accidentally on the 17th Cavalry Squadron's command post on Hill 146. Seeing what they thought was a legitimate target, a subsequent flight of fighter-bombers dropped more bombs and strafed Recce Troop A. To make matters worse, a follow-on squadron of B-17s released their payloads on Telgruc, and more "friendly" aircraft bombed and strafed the town while ambulances and medical personnel attempted to tend to the wounded. Sadly, the number of casualties from that unfortunate episode of fratricide[2] totaled no fewer than thirty-three men, all of whom were from the 17th Cavalry Squadron. (No doubt that day's events qualified as an enormous FUBAR, but such was war and the men simply sucked it up and continued their mission.)

On September 4, 1944, Dad reported, "Our job today is to draw enemy fire." At that time, he observed that the Germans "must have poor gunners" as we gave them two hours to "zero in" and "they miss[ed] us by 50 feet." Afterward, he described withdrawing through Telgruc and going

---

[1] A hung bomb is one that after being toggled for jettison fails to fully disengage from an aircraft's bomb rack; it may dangle precariously or break loose and cause unintended, tragic consequences.
[2] Fratricide is the military term for the accidental killing of soldiers by their own side. Kindsvatter, *American Soldiers,* 61.

about three miles where again "we [drew] more 88 fire." He indicated things were getting too hot, so they decided to back up behind a cut in the road and wait it out. Then, he wrote anxiously, "Three shots cross[ed] my bow." As luck would have it, shortly after that they were recalled to their squadron area, and he wrote it had been "one rough day for our nerves."

By the following day, he wrote: "Again we go out," this time with the 3rd Platoon of Fox Company. "We sit and wait," but on three occasions that day the "88s chase us." By the end of that patrol, he described being "very jumpy . . . My hands are shaking, and I have a terrible time lighting a match."

On the next day, his crew remained on alert status only, thankful that they "did not have to go out that day." Later, he explained that they were used like sitting ducks: "We show ourselves to draw enemy fire, then our [howitzers] counter the enemy's artillery fire." His tank platoon had been used in a dangerous cat-and-mouse game with the enemy, acting much like catnip in order to lure German gunfire from hidden positions. It was a *ruse de guerre*, and if it proved successful, their artillery forward observers would call down counterbattery fire on the enemy's location.[1]

In essence, they were baited hooks intended to unmask the enemy's presence; on completion of that mission, they gladly pulled back into camouflaged positions. (Surely Pop did not volunteer for that hazardous decoy mission; rather, he and the rest of the tank crew were likely "volun-told" to do their duty, and they did it well. Like most other GIs in combat, however, he no doubt preferred the role of shooter to being a target.[2])

---

[1] A safer alternative to search out the presence of the enemy would have entailed simply shelling a suspected wooded area, but that would waste ammunition. In the American Civil War, the Confederate Army of Northern Virginia called that "feeling out fire." Douglas S. Freeman, *Lee's Lieutenants:* (vol. 2) *Cedar Mountain to Chancellorsville*, (New York: Charles Scribner's Sons, 1943), 606.

[2] Dad's experience as a "lure" was not all that uncommon. In the 12th "Hellcat" Armored Division, Stuart tanks were reportedly found to be "so useless that they were often employed as 'anti-tank gun bait' for the division's M4 Shermans." Seelinger, "The M24 Chaffee Light Tank," *On Point: Journal of Army History*, 16.

Dad next described his position on the Crozon Peninsula as directly across from Brest. He wrote anxiously, "We can see and hear the fighting going on over there."

On September 7, 1944, he mentioned they had heard news on the radio that "the only fighting in this section is in Brest." In apparent astonishment, he wrote, "I sure would like to know where all this 'big stuff' and small arms fire is coming from, keeping us on our toes?"

By September 11, Pop reported they were just outside Telgruc, awaiting the outcome of the combat to take Brest. He also mentioned being very happy that finally they were getting a new issue of clean GI clothing: shirts, trousers, socks, undershorts and undershirts.

He expressed the belief that they had been long overdue for that uniform reissue, as they had worn "the old grimy stuff" for more than a month, through long days of mud, sweat, and greasy toil. He also mentioned with relief that they had finally had the opportunity to take a long-overdue GI bath, which amounted to a quick clean-up for soldiers in the field using his steel helmet as a wash basin: first he rinsed, then a short lather-up session was followed by a final dousing with whatever water was left.

On completion of that delightful experience, he described the fact that they then enjoyed heaping their old soiled clothes onto the company burn pile.

The map on the next page reveals the movement of the 17th Cavalry Recce Squadron of the 15th Cavalry Group, as they fought and struggled along to destroy what remained of the enemy's force through the Crozon and Douarnenez Peninsulas of western France during September 1944.

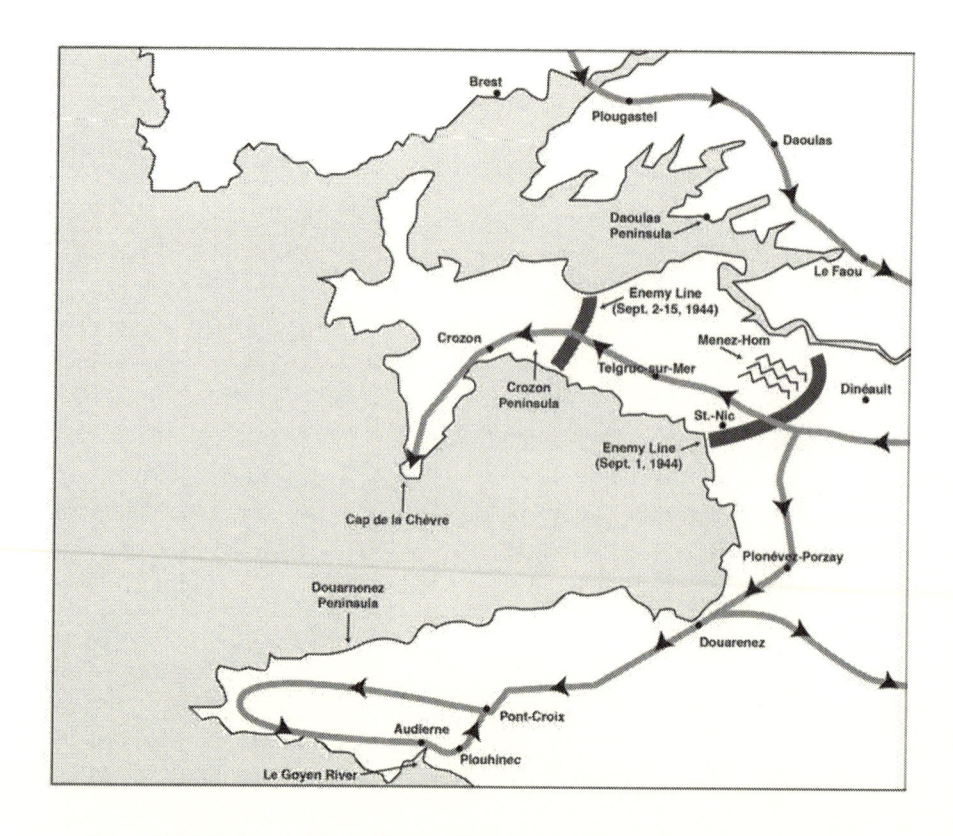

From September 4-15, 1944, the 15th and 17th Cavalry Reconnaissance Squadrons continued to push their daily patrols forward of their lines to maintain contact with the enemy and further develop the hostile Main Line of Resistance (MLR). Finally, in the early hours of September 15, Maj. Gen. Donald Stroh's 8th Pathfinder Division relieved the 15th Cavalry Group in place. On the following day, the 8th Pathfinder infantrymen passed through their lines and attacked the enemy MLR. After initial gains were made and while the infantry was proceeding against their secondary objectives, "the 15th Cavalry Group moved in between Combat Team 28 on the north and Combat Team 121 on the south", thereby facilitating the efforts of both combat teams to maintain contact with each other. [1]

By September 18, Dad recorded in his diary that they had pushed into the town of Crozon and continued in a southerly direction, gathering up enemy forces as they went along. He said it was "tough going, as the Huns

---

[1] TLR, 11.

had their backs to the sea" and they fought hard. He reported they were fighting dismounted and were receiving heavy small-arms fire from dug-in positions around Dolmen. Then, "the artillery behind us cut loose on the town" and "blew it to Hell." He also indicated that P-51 Mustang fighters had bombed and strafed the town for about a half hour. He described the battle-ravaged town as "burning and smoking" while they entered, but the enemy had retreated to strong, cement pillboxes, which required point-blank, tank fire to finish them off. By the end of that fierce fight, around 1800 hours, the men of Troop A of the 17th Cavalry Squadron had captured several hundred POWs, including the commander of the German 343rd Infantry Division, Gen. Erwin Rauch, and his entire staff.[1]

The cost in casualties to the 17th Cavalry Squadron's battlefield success on the Crozon Peninsula, including the fight at Cap de la Chèvre, amounted to forty-five troopers: ten of whom were killed in action[2] and the remaining thirty-five men were treated for a variety of wounds. (Specially mentioned on September 19, 1944, was the heroic action of Tec 5 Vernon C. Wheeler of the 17th Cavalry Squadron's medical detachment, who earned the Silver Star Medal near Cap de la Chèvre.)

The attack on Brest, the main seaport of Brittany, was a hard-fought battle. It proved as intense as the taking of Cherbourg, but it finally fell in mid-September 1944 when German Gen. Hermann B. Ramcke, a devoted Nazi[3] and hero of the 1941 Battle for Crete, surrendered his forces to the U.S. VIII Corps commander, General Middleton. That surrender came despite Ramcke's promise to the Führer that his force would defend the city "to the last man." When Brest finally fell, it was clear that it had been an

---

[1] Ibid., 11-12.
[2] The 17th Cavalry Squadron troops killed on the Crozon Peninsula were: 2nd Lt. Harold T. McKenna, Tec 5 Robert D. DeLorenzo, Tec 5 Bruce C. Byrd, Tec 5 Donald F. Fulton, Tec 5 Cecil E. Fry; Cpl. Clarence C. Braziel; Cpl. Harvey M. Menden; Cpl. Fred P. Gildner, PFC John C. McMonagle, and Pvt. Harold E. Billings. History of the 17th Cavalry Reconnaissance Squadron for Year 1944, 6.
[3] Blumenson, *Breakout and Pursuit,* 387; General Ramcke was also famous for having commanded the German 1st Parachute Division in its defense of Monte Cassino in Italy. Ewing, *29 Let's Go!,* 121.

"even tougher nut to crack than Cherbourg,"[1] as the elite German 2nd Parachute Division constituted the core of the defense of Brest.

Thereafter, the usual German port destruction had to be cleared, as the enemy had methodically destroyed the city by fire and explosives. By the time the harbor was made safe for operations, the war had moved well to the east, leaving Brest far behind, obviating any possible contribution to future Allied logistic needs.[2] That fact alone explains why the Allies were no longer in any hurry to attack the port cities of Lorient and St.-Nazaire. Thus, they left those German "static"[3] defensive forces, surrounded and guarded by American infantry and thousands of French Resistance fighters (the FFI) until the finally capitulation at war's end.[4]

By that point in the war, "a great crescent" extended across the map of France from Brittany in the west to nearly Belgium in the east. It was packed with more than two million Allied soldiers and some 400,000 vehicles. By that point in the war the Allies had a two-to-one personnel advantage over Germans in Western Europe, and a twenty-to-one edge in tanks. General Bradley's 12th Army Group contained twenty-one divisions and British Field Marshal Bernard L. "Monty" Montgomery's 21st Army Group had another fifteen divisions that had just overrun the German V-1 flying bomb launch forces. The last "buzz bomb," fired from France by the Germans occurred on September 1, 1944. By then the rout was so ignominious that those German troops in Western Europe, who wanted out of the war and were unable to find white flags, "surrendered by waving chickens."[5]

By September 11, 1944, the Allies had succeeded in reaching a point which pre–D-Day planners had expected it would take them 330 days to achieve (i.e., May 2, 1945). They were ahead of schedule by more than 200 days, but the most encouraging surprise was the fact that total Allied casualties (killed, wounded, missing, and POWs) since the Normandy

---

[1] D'Este, Eisenhower, 563.
[2] Ibid., 564-565.
[3] Static units in the German Army were not first-line troops; they fought from fixed positions and were mostly partially disabled soldiers and foreign "mercenaries" from Eastern Europe. Ambrose, *D-Day, June 6, 1944*, 157.
[4] Weigley, Eisenhower's Lieutenants, 185, 285.
[5] Atkinson, *The Guns at Last Light*, 219-220.

landings were much "lighter than expected," a total of over 224,500, only slightly more than 10 percent of the total force committed. However, by then the Germans had lost around 300,000 men, "while another 200,000 were penned [up] in various redoubts."[1]

On September 15, an important event occurred when Patton's Third Army linked up with the 6th Army Group of Lt. Gen. Jacob Devers as it drove north, following their landing on the French Riviera in August 1944. Only then was a junction made of the Operation Dragoon[2] forces and General Eisenhower's overall command, which had advanced from Normandy since the Cobra breakout in mid-July 1944. At last, the Allies in Western Europe were united in a "broad front", from north to south: Monty's 21st Army Group, Bradley's 12th Army Group, and Devers's 6th Army Group, making preparations to continue their drive to the German frontier.[3]

Also on September 15, 1944, a relevant article appeared in the daily newspaper of the U.S. Armed Forces, in which war correspondent G. K. Hodenfield wrote: "the German Army was racing across France in headlong retreat to the Fatherland," while the U.S. cavalry reconnaissance force was "nipping at their Nazi heels like a terrier pup chasing a tramp down the alley." It was reported also that, since the U.S. Army had gone into action on the Cotentin Peninsula in July, "they've been doing a lot of chasing," especially following the breakthrough near St.-Lo. The article went on to point out that, while the American troopers were in France and Belgium, they "got a lot of help from civilians, who gave them the latest information and often accompanied them in their search for the enemy." That newspaper article also noted that the cavalry's mission was to maintain contact with the German armed forces "to keep pressing against the enemy."[4]

---

[1] MacDonald, *The Siegfried Line: U.S. Army in World War II: ETO*, 4, 5.
[2] Operation Dragoon (the Allied invasion of southern France) culminated in the capture of the large, relatively undamaged French port facilities of Marseilles and Toulon. Murray and Millett, *A War to be Won*, 433.
[3] Weigley, *Eisenhower's Lieutenants*, 355, 356.
[4] *Stars and Stripes*, Vol. 1, no. 54, Tuesday, September 15, 1944, 2.

On September 21, TFA was officially dissolved and on the following day, Col. Logan C. Berry turned over command of the 15th Cavalry Group to Lt. Col Robert J. Quinn, Jr.

After being placed under the command Maj. Gen. Harry J. Malony of the 94th "Pilgrim" Infantry Division at Châteaubriant, the 15th Cavalry Group was assigned a priority mission to a mop up a pocket of 300 or more German soldiers near Audierne on the Douarnenez Peninsula. Thereafter, Troop C of the 15th Cavalry Squadron moved south to Plouhinec to block the enemy from escaping to the southeast, while the remainder of the 15th Cavalry Group and its attached TDs advanced southward from the Crozon Peninsula to Plonevez-Porzay.

Early on September 22, the 15th Cavalry Squadron and its attachments advanced in a single column toward Pont-Croix. Troops A and B with assault guns and TDs took the lead, followed by tanks and engineers in reserve. Group Headquarters and the 17th Cavalry Squadron brought up the rear. The column then divided into two formations on reaching Pont-Croix in order to envelop the enemy in a pincer movement. At that point, the 17th Cavalry Squadron continued west to the end of the Douarnenez Peninsula and turned south, making a wide sweeping reconnaissance toward the remote western fringe of Audierne. There it remained in reserve to provide fire support to its sister squadron.

Advancing from the north, Troop A drew first contact with the enemy when it was fired on near the outskirts of Audierne. That caused the men of Troop A to back off slightly, and they established an observation post in a nearby church steeple to call in and adjust the fire of its 75-mm assault guns. At the same time, Troop B made its advance into town and learned from friendly French citizens the approximate location of the German's positions. Troop B continued to advance under sniper fire and successfully cleaned out an enemy strong point, consisting of numerous emplaced machine guns. Troop C then moved west across the Le Goyen River and completed the envelopment from three sides. After the enemy surrendered, the processing of some 315 enemy POWs commenced, but that task soon became harried as the French citizenry demonstrated a strong hostile attitude toward the Germans.[1]

Shortly afterward, elements of the 15th Cavalry Group mounted a security patrol along the Loire River, the southern flank of Bradley's 12th Army Group, from Nantes in the to the Yanne River in the vicinity of Auxerre.[2] That mission was intended to seal off hostile incursions and conceal from the enemy the location and intentions of the friendly force. Its basic function was to be in a position to warn higher command of the imminent presence of any enemy force.[3]

After their arrival at Châteaubriant, some thirty miles or more south of Rennes, the headquarters of both the 15th Cavalry Group and the 15th Cavalry Squadron moved to Vendome, and Troop A road marched as far as Gien. By the evening of September 24-25, their screening mission ended.

On returning to Châteaubriant, the 15th Cavalry Group expected to relieve the 83rd Thunderbolt Division, only to learn that that division had already pulled out. Instead, the 15th Cavalry Squadron attached their tanks and assault guns to General Malony's 94th Pilgrim Division to provide some armor in reserve and to ensure that the enemy stayed put and remained out of the war while confined within the seaports of Lorient and St.-Nazaire.[4] As the Allies surrounded both harbors, the German submarine pens lost all value as dry dock and replenishment centers. The enemy could no longer resupply them; thus, it was decided that the best course of action was to leave them to wither on the vine, thereby avoiding further bloodshed. Consequently, those surrounded seaports became "self-supporting" POW camps.[5]

By December 10, 1944, the 15th Cavalry Group's strength was further reduced as the 15th Cavalry Squadron's Troop C was attached to the 66th "Black Panther" Infantry Division, which had previously relieved the 83rd

---

[1] The prior three paragraphs draw on: Lt. Col. Garret J. Dobbins, "Mopping Up an Enemy Pocket," *Cavalry Journal*, Vol. 54, no. 6 (Nov.-Dec. 1945), 17.

[2] TLR, 14.

[3] Rottman, *World War II US Cavalry Groups, European Theater*, 18.

[4] TLR, 14.

[5] Samuel W. Mitcham, Jr., *Retreat to the Reich: The German Defeat in France, 1944* (Mechanicsburg, PA: Stackpole, 2000), 212.

Thunderbolt Division.[1] In less than a month, the guard mission conducted by the 15th Cavalry Group (minus the detached 17th Cavalry Squadron) came to an end on January 2, 1945, as they became Mobile Reserve for the Atlantic Coastal Sector of the Ninth Army, at Coëtquidan.[2] In February 1945, the 115th Cavalry Group relieved the 15th Cavalry "demi-Group" of its duties in the Atlantic Coastal Sector.[3] It then reported to the XVI Corps, commanded by Maj. Gen. John B. Anderson, at his headquarters in Sittard, Holland.[4]

---

[1] The Germans surrendered the seaport of Lorient on May 10, 1945, and St. Nazaire surrendered the following day. Bradham, *"To the Last Man"*, 5.
[2] TLR, 14.
[3] The 115th Cavalry Group was originally a horse-mechanized Wyoming National Guard unit; it became fully mechanized and arrived in France in January 1945. Rottman, *World War II US Cavalry Groups, European Theater*, 41.
[4] TLR, 14.

12. DEFENSIVE SCREENING IN HOLLAND

Effective September 22, 1944, Dad along with the rest of the 17th Cavalry Squadron were detached from the 15th Cavalry Group, and assigned to the Ninth Army, which had just become operational at Rennes on September 5, 1944, and consisted of the 2nd Indianhead and the 8th Pathfinders of Middleton's VIII Corps. Their primary mission at that time was to guard the headquarters of Lt. Gen. William H. Simpson,[1] as the Ninth Army began its movement from Rennes, France, to Maastricht, Holland.[2]

By September 26, the VIII Corps headquarters and its two divisions began to move surreptitiously by railway to the Ardennes-Eifel area, and by October 1, the Ninth Army entered the line of battle.[3] Thereafter, the 17th Cavalry Squadron continued to perform its "palace guard" protection mission, screening and guarding Simpson's Ninth Army forward command headquarters throughout the month of October 1944.[4]

The photograph on the next page shows Pop perched atop his Stuart light tank (nicknamed "Werewolf") with the crew and a few other soldiers from Fox Company, 17th Cavalry Squadron. The painted Werewolf[5] face is barely visible on the left side of the hull.

---

[1] Gen. William Hood Simpson was the son of a Confederate veteran, who served in the American Civil War as a Tennessee cavalryman under the overall command of Gen. John Bell Hood, CSA. Higgins, *The Roer River Battles,* 140.

[2] TLR, 14; the area around Maastricht was known by American GIs as the "Dutch Panhandle." MacDonald, *The Siegfried Line,* 29.

[3] Weigley, *Eisenhower's Lieutenants,* 284, 355, 356.

[4] TLR, 14.

[5] Surely, my father was unaware that Hitler's field headquarters in Ukraine on the Eastern Front was codenamed "*Wehrwolf*". Lloyd Clark, *The Battle of the Tanks* (New York; Atlantic Monthly Press, 2011), 146. He was also clueless as to Hitler's "*Werewolf*" movement to recruit fanatics of the Hitler Youth generation for continuing resistance behind Allied lines. Evans, *The Third Reich at War,* 404, 738.

The practice of picking nicknames and hand painting "artwork" on Army vehicles was apparently quite common in the ETO. Even Lt. Col. Creighton Abrams (a future commander of U.S. forces in Vietnam and army chief of staff), who led the 4th Armored Division's relief column into Bastogne had a nickname for his tank: "Thunderbolt." Painted on the hull of his Sherman was a large white thunderhead cloud, pierced with three

176

lightning bolts. He and his crew went through several tanks during the war, winding up with "Thunderbolt VII" at wars' end.[1] Like Abrams, Dad finished the war in another tank, an M24 Chaffee, labeled "Werewolf II".

According to war journalist Ernie Pyle, names were painted on practically anything that moved during World War II: airplanes, tanks, jeeps, motorcycles, and even field artillery pieces. He described seeing girls' names and "trick names such as 'Sad Sack' [and] 'Hitler's Menace.'"[2]

While my father and his unit were fighting their way through Brittany, Patton's Third Army advanced east and liberated the French cities of Orleans and Chartres by mid-August 1944. On August 19, 1944, elements of Maj. Gen. Ira Wyche's 79th Cross of Lorraine Division of Haislip's XV Corps had crossed the River Seine northwest of Paris. At the time, Eisenhower's original desire was to bypass Paris and avoid the burden of feeding its large population. He knew it was a "strategic sideshow" and a logistical nightmare, but being aware of its obvious symbolic importance,[3] he eventually ordered its occupation to assist an uprising of local French Resistance fighters; consequently, Allied forces entered the city on August 25[4], as General Barton's 4th Ivy Division crossed over and secured the east side of the Seine.

As an aside, once the French capital was liberated, Ernest Hemingway set up what he called an "Advance Command Post" in the Hotel Ritz in Paris.[5] There, he aided soldiers of his self-proclaimed favorite regiment (the 22nd Infantry) liberate the Ritz wine cellar. Earlier, that hard-drinking writer declared the "Ivy League" his favorite division in the entire Army.[6] While accompanying the 4th Ivy Division on assignment for Collier's magazine, Hemingway met a staff sergeant whose duties with the Ivy Division entailed interrogating captured German POWs. (After the war, that soldier, J.D. Salinger, went on to author his own famous novel, The Catcher in the Rye.)[7]

---

[1] Sorley, *Thunderbolt*, 52-53.
[2] Pyle, *Brave Men*, 379.
[3] Terry Mort, *Hemingway at War* (New York, Pegasus Books, 2016), 49.
[4] Yeide, *The Tank Killers*, 157.
[5] Whiting, *Papa Goes to War*, 97; Mort, *Hemingway at War*, 207.
[6] Ibid., 152, 171.
[7] Ibid., 97; see also Caddick-Adams, *Snow and Steel*, 173.

As mentioned earlier, casualties among German forces in Western Europe after D-Day exceeded 300,000 with more than half of them were POWs. Among the casualties was Field Marshal Rommel, whose death occurred in mid-October 1944, by which time he had been implicated in the July 20 plot to assassinate Adolf Hitler. Ultimately, Rommel was "allowed" to commit suicide by cyanide capsule to protect his family from repercussions and to maximize Nazi propaganda interests through the pageantry of a state-sponsored funeral.[1] Disingenuously, his death was officially explained to the German public as resulting from the wounds he received earlier in France.

On October 2, 1944, Dad noted that they had obtained and fitted steel tracks on their tanks, which allowed better cross-country traction and footing in slippery mud and snowy conditions. They were an off-road improvement over the rubber block tracks they used throughout the summer months; that equipment adjustment demonstrated solid preparation for combat in the icy, rainy winter weather of Northern Europe. At about the same time, other personnel in the 17th Cavalry Squadron installed tire chains on their M8 armored cars to alleviate the effects of the slippery mud. Also, that day, Dad was pleased to note that Lt. John Conway of Fox Company would soon take over as the 17th Cavalry Squadron's new executive officer.

Pop next diarized that they broke bivouac on October 7, and left for the Rennes railway station where they loaded their tanks and equipment onto French flatbed railroad cars. Then they found their "quarters" for the train ride across France to Holland aboard old boxcars, which dated from the First World War. Those railroad cars were stenciled on the outside in French "40 hommes- 8 chevaux" and were referred to as "40 and 8s" by the Americans because they were designed to carry 40 soldiers or 8 horses.[2] They had to move with their equipment, and by that point in the war, flatbed railway cars were the preferred method of transporting tanks over long distances. It was much quicker to travel by train than to road march

---

[1] Atkinson, *The Guns at Last Light*, 171-178, 181; Fraser, *Knight's Cross*, 550-552.
[2] Alex Kershaw, *The Longest Winter* (Cambridge, MA: Da Capo Press, 2004), 146.

178

their vehicles, and it obviously saved a significant amount of tank track wear and tear.

Pictured below are several soldiers in Dad's outfit preparing for their eastbound rail trip from France through Belgium to Holland in a rickety World War I French "40 and 8" boxcar.

On the reverse side of the photograph, Pop identified the men, from left to right on the bottom row, as "Bernard, 'Penny' Penniplede, and Schmidt," and those standing were "Lyons, Kinder, Garvin, and Ramirez." (Some time later, he wrote on the back of that photo that S/Sgt. Miguel C. Ramirez had been shot and "killed [in action] in Holland outside a barn.")

After they climbed aboard those malodorous railcars, Dad and many other troops were immediately taken aback by their cramped and grimy condition. He commented sarcastically, "This train has all the comforts of home: one door, four walls, no toilets, no nothing." Then he described how one could maneuver to answer the call of nature. (His elaborate description has been omitted intentionally to spare the reader the graphic details, except for his observation that one must "watch out for the flying hot ashes.")

While on the train, Dad expressed displeasure with the lurching motion of their railway conveyance. However, he apparently settled down shortly thereafter upon seeing convoys of badly burned and wrecked enemy vehicles in the fields as the train traveled along. He mentioned that it had become mountainous before they entered Belgium by late afternoon of October 10, 1944, and he described the countryside as showing less damage than France. He indicated further that the weather was "wet with lots of fog." Apparently, there were many people standing along the side of the railroad track, and he described them as "happy to greet us." But later, he became concerned when he counted four long hospital trains heading in the opposite direction. He reported next passing through the city of Liège, and by midday on October 12, they arrived in Holland, "just 20 kilometers from the fighting."

Pop later mentioned on October 13 that he had spent the early morning hours on guard duty and saw the sky to the east all lit up by artillery fire in the approximate direction of Germany. On October 14, 1944, he noted it was his third year anniversary in the army.

At some distance from Pop's location near the Holland-Belgium border, General Eisenhower, had good reason to celebrate as he observed his own birth anniversary, his fifty-fourth on October 14, which also marked his third consecutive birthday overseas. On the following day, Eisenhower traveled with Bradley by automobile to First Army headquarters in Verviers, Belgium. There he and Bradley met with Generals Hodges, Patton, and Simpson, the First, Third, and Ninth Army commanders of the 12th Army Group, respectively. Also joining that august assemblage was King George VI of Great Britain, who by coincidence was making his own royal tour of the European front at that time.[1]

On Sunday, October 15, Dad noted that it had rained all day while he had been on detail guarding Gen. George Marshall's train at the railway station in Maastricht, Holland. Confirmation of that brief brush with a major figure in American history comes from Second World War military historian Forrest C. Pogue. In his multi-volume biography of Marshall, Dr.

---

[1] Atkinson, *The Guns at Last Night*, 306.

180

Pogue noted that President Roosevelt's top military advisor[1] had spent the night of October 10 at Simpson's Ninth Army headquarters in Arlon, Belgium. On October 11, Marshall's inspection included visits with Generals Middleton (VIII Corps), Gerow (V Corps), and Collins (VII Corps); later that day, he traveled to the vicinity of Aachen, "his first visit to German soil since 1919." On October 12, Marshall visited the commanders of the XIX Corps, the 2nd Hell on Wheels Armored Division and the 30th Old Hickory and 29th Blue-Gray Infantry Divisions. Shortly thereafter, Marshall moved on to XIX Corps headquarters at Maastricht and flew to Versailles that afternoon to spend the next day at General Eisenhower's headquarters.[2]

By October 16, Dad described the weather as terrible, and mentioned that he had caught a bad cold. He wrote, "Almost froze last night, while on guard [duty] at the station. All I had was one blanket." On the following day, he complained about the harsh weather: "It rained all night", and he described the area as unusually cold and wet.[3] Yet, little did he know that his lifestyle was about to undergo improvement, as around noon on October 17, he moved from their field bivouac area to the "Hotel Vancken" in the town of Valkenburg, Holland. At that time, he noted that his squadron was positioned "just outside of Maastricht", only a few miles northwest of the city of Aachen, Germany's westernmost city.

When he awoke the next day, Pop exclaimed, "Had a hard time sleeping last night," as he was so unaccustomed to a mattress and "soft bed." He stated further, "Now I can see how the Air Corps enjoys Florida." (That comment was likely a playful jab at his brothers, who were serving in the

---

[1] General Marshall, a 1901 graduate of Virginia Military Institute (VMI), was then the U.S. Army chief of staff. "In the 1900 season, his tackling on the football team helped VMI tie the University of Virginia, and he starred in the annual Thanksgiving Day game against VMI's chief rival, Virginia Polytechnic Institute." Pogue, *George C. Marshall: Education of a General*, 55.
[2] Forrest C. Pogue, *George C. Marshall: Organizer of Victory* (New York: Viking Press, 1973), 476-477.
[3] The fall and winter of 1944 in Europe produced weather of near record severity. Rainfall was far above average, and snow and freezing temperatures came early and lasted for long periods. MacDonald, *The Siegfried Line Campaign*, 35.

USAAF. He was apparently convinced that their army "air corps" service was light duty, compared to what he was experiencing.)

By October 20, he still couldn't believe his good fortune, "This life of a G.I. in a hotel is OK with me; could do it for the duration." That day he reported going on patrol and manning an outpost with Fox Company's 3rd Platoon, near "a beer-garden—run by two girls." Naturally, he mentioned that when off duty he and several others frequented that establishment, as it was warm inside, and they could get out of the weather, have a beer, write letters, and listen to a jukebox. He also noted cheerfully that they ate evening meals in the dining room "using silver ware and china." He said the girls were "only too glad to cook for us, and let us eat there since we bring our own food [army field rations] and they [dine] with us." On that occasion, my father and his mates seemed highly satisfied with themselves for having negotiated a win-win scenario, as they were able to enjoy some home-cooking indoors in civilized fashion, while sharing GI rations with their civilian hosts.

As the war progressed, it became clear that few soldiers in World War II failed to trade their cans of cold army rations for civilian food, when opportunity presented itself. Apropos of that phenomenon, one enlightened observer wrote, "It's funny to watch a civilian, sick of his potato soup, brown bread and red wine, wolf down one of those horrible K rations as eagerly as the soldier tears into the soup and bread and wine."[1]

Dad next mentioned that he had manned picket duty on October 21, and reported that, in the afternoon, they went back over to Belgium, where Fox Company had prepared two other defensive outposts. He said, "The fighting is tough and close." By the next day, he noted that their platoon was on a two-day outpost rotation. He also described performing maintenance on his tank for most of the day and fixing a flat tire on a scout jeep they had used.

Several days later, Pop visited a hospital full of "casualties from Aachen, both GIs and German civilians, mostly little kids." He described the children's wounds as an awful sight, and mentioned seeing numerous instances in which legs and arms [were] missing. Sadly, he expressed the belief that those hideous wounds resulted from senseless cruelty on the part

---

[1] Bill Mauldin, *Up Front,* (New York: W.W. Norton, 1995), 173.

of the Nazis since they won't let the civilians escape to a safe place, but keep them in town, where we end up shelling them by mistake.

Later, quite out of the blue, my father mentioned in his diary that his entire company had undergone "short-arm" and dental inspections. Most importantly, at the conclusion of those examinations, he proudly asserted, "I'm OK."

At around the same time, an American lieutenant described a salacious, but amusing episode he experienced in his 3rd Spearhead Armored Division maintenance unit, while advancing through Belgium. Traveling from town to town by convoy, he said many civilians, including young women, wandered into the streets as they passed by, giving out flowers and cognac to the troops in exchange for cigarettes and candy. On one occasion, however, his column came to a halt and he made good use of it by taking a catnap in his jeep. A short time later, he awoke and noticed his driver and the driver of the truck to his rear were missing. He then got out of the jeep to stretch his legs and search for their whereabouts. As he walked to the rear, he began to hear muffled "shuffling" noises coming from the steel deck of the truck bed "mixed with amorous moans." On reaching the back of the truck, he noticed the tailgate was up and the canvas curtains were closed. After announcing his presence, the commotion ceased and out came his missing driver with a "sheepish look on his face," followed by a number of other GIs and a young Belgian female, "straightening out her skirt and blouse, [and] grinning from ear to ear." When she got down from the truck, he noted that her shoulder bag was filled with cigarettes and chocolate candy bars. Then, while strolling away, she turned and announced, "*Vive l'Amèrique!*"[1]

While on this subject, it's worth noting that, by mid-October 1944, the rate of venereal disease (chiefly syphilis and gonorrhea) among soldiers in Europe had doubled. As one British historian noted, venereal disease was "the most serious affliction among troops in the [ETO] . . . and its prevalence[2] caused all military staffs to stress hygiene and to monitor

---

[1] Cooper, *Death Traps,* 116-117.
[2] By June 1945, about half a million American GIs in the ETO had some form of VD. Hitchcock, *The Bitter Road to Freedom,* 94.

prostitution."[1] Thus, Eisenhower placed all brothels and similar establishments off-limits to the troops. Moreover, "mandatory 'short-arm' inspections by medical 'pecker checkers' increased sharply."[2]

For those unfamiliar with the military's time-honored "short-arm" inspection, it is a mandatory, periodic medical check of a soldier's genital area to detect the presence of venereal disease[3]; it stands in stark contrast to a rifle inspection, which of course is a "long-arm" inspection.

Initially, the short-arm inspection for males begins with soldiers forming a line and dropping their pants so that a medical officer or enlisted medic may visually examine the pertinent area for evidence of redness, swelling, ulcer, or telltale "runny nose," which may indicate of the presence of a sexually transmitted disease.[4] Following the examination, the soldier is dismissed, but if positive clinical findings are evident, a referral for appropriate medical attention is mandatory.

During World War II, "soldiers excused from duty while being treated for syphilis or gonorrhea were said to be 'whores de combat,' and the Good Conduct ribbon became known as the 'No-Clap Medal.'"[5] (Solely for the sake of accuracy, I am compelled to report that my father's DD-214 (Enlisted Record and Report of Separation and Honorable Discharge) specifies that he was the recipient of the U.S. Army's Good Conduct Medal "with Clasp".)

Later, on October 26, Dad recorded in his diary that he had retrieved various objects from a souvenir pile, including a German steel helmet and bayonet, and several other war artifacts for shipment home to his father. Apparently, that was not an unusual practice in the ETO, as individual soldiers wanted to impress their family and friends back home. Such behavior showed their "desire for recognition on the home front."[6] Yet, as

---

[1] Davies, *No Simple Victory*, 260.
[2] Atkinson, *The Guns at Last Light*, 401.
[3] Neill, *Infantry Soldier*, 6; for additional details about the short arm examination, as practiced in the 26th ("Yankee") Infantry Division, see Robert Kotlowitz, *Before Their Time* (New York: Alfred A. Knopf, 1997), 87-90.
[4] *Current Medical Diagnosis & Treatment*, (NY: McGraw-Hill, 2012), 1258, 1412.
[5] Atkinson, *The Guns at Last Light*, 401.
[6] Kindsvatter, *American Soldiers*, 266.

far as I know, he never helped himself to anything other than a little wine, confiscated along the way, an assortment of discarded war paraphernalia and, of course, the occasional free-range chicken.

The same cannot be said for others, as historian Rick Atkinson observed in volume III of his superb work, The Liberation Trilogy. There he explained that the battlefields in Europe had become "a world to be looted", and the phenomenon became much worse as Allied forces crossed into Germany in 1945. A soldier in the 29th Blue-Gray Division reported, "We're advancing as fast as the looting will permit." Some plunderers were referred to as the "Lootwaffe", and a soldier in the 45th ("Thunderbird") Infantry Division facetiously described the typical infantry squad of twelve men as "two shooting and ten looting."[1]

During the Rhineland campaign, a soldier in the 116th Infantry Regiment of the 29th Blue-Gray Division noted, "Our own rear echelon medical personnel sometimes robbed wounded soldiers blind." He described once watching "a ghoulish soldier bayonet-chop a dead man's finger to get his wedding band."[2]

Students of military history know only too well that deplorable activity such as looting was nothing unique to the Second World War.

During the American Civil War, the citizens of Fredericksburg, Virginia, learned of such behavior when Union soldiers pillaged their city in 1862; likewise, Pennsylvania farmers became acquainted with such conduct when Confederate soldiers ransacked their homes in 1863. Foraging for food and provender is one thing, but the malicious destruction of private property which occurred in Fredericksburg, and the willful larceny in Pennsylvania, prior to and during the Gettysburg battle, are quite another.[3]

As regrettable as the looting by American GIs was in the final year of World War II, the great majority of those cases were limited to little more than petty theft and the occasional "liberation" of alcoholic beverages and food items for personal consumption. Yet, in some cases U.S. soldiers did misbehave, and they were brought up on charges and punished

---

[1] Atkinson, *The Guns at Last Light*, 544-545.
[2] Slaughter, *Omaha Beach and Beyond*, 170.
[3] George C. Rable, *Fredericksburg, Fredericksburg* (Chapel Hill: University of North Carolina Press, 2002), 271; see also Harry W. Pfanz, *Gettysburg: The Second Day* (Chapel Hill: University of North Carolina Press, 1987), 11.

appropriately. In other instances where robbery, murder or brutality occurred, the accused were given the opportunity to defend themselves, and if tried and convicted by courts-martial, they were sent to the stockade.[1]

Contrast that with the barbarity of the Nazis during their reign of terror where highly organized, state-sponsored genocide of millions of Jews, political prisoners and others occurred. In addition to murdering many thousands in irrational and sadistic medical experiments, they enriched themselves through systematic theft of thousands of paintings from European galleries that fell under their control. Also, innumerable valuable artworks were stolen from private collections during the 1930s and '40s.[2]

Recently, it was noted that, "Hitler and the Nazis pulled off the 'greatest theft in history,' seizing and transporting more than five million cultural objects to the Third Reich."[3] Proof of their untiring looting comes from the plundering by Nazi *Reichsleiter* Rosenberg's task force, which stole "ownerless cultural property" and priceless art objects throughout Europe.[4] Not to be outdone by the larcenous Nazis, when the "Monuments Men"[5] got to Berlin after the war ended they found that our Soviet Allies had helped themselves, deeming it appropriate and equivalent to "war reparations."[6]

Based on my study of the subject and my father's commentary, the typical American soldier in World War II was content to perform his duty and do whatever it took to get home from war in one piece. Unlike the Nazis, American soldiers were actively discouraged from engaging in

---

[1] Hitchcock, *The Bitter Road to Freedom*, 51.
[2] Many packing crates containing art looted by the Germans were found after the war in a salt mine in the Austrian mountains at Alt Aussee, southeast of Salzburg. David Stafford, *Endgame, 1945* (NY: Little, Brown, 2007), 334-338.
[3] The *Einsutzstab Reichsleiter* stole the famous Vermeer painting *Astronomer* for Hermann Goering's personal collection "right off the wall of Edouard de Rothschild's sitting room." Robert M. Edsel with Bret Witter, *The Monuments Men* (New York: Center Street, 2009), 247.
[4] Artwork was declared "ownerless" after the rightful owners were ejected from their homes and sent to death camps in Eastern Europe. Ibid., 218.
[5] That group of American and British soldiers recovered thousands of art masterpieces stolen by the Nazis. Edsel et al., *The Monuments Men,* xiv, 405.
[6] *Wall Street Journal*, Wednesday, January 29, 2014, D5.

mayhem and cold-blooded murder, and were under strict orders to refrain from wanton destruction and thievery. Also, peer pressure played a major role in deterring bad behavior among the young GIs, as the official policy at the highest level, and at every step along the chain of command, made it perfectly clear that malicious cruelty was totally unacceptable. Keeping soldiers in line required commissioned and noncommissioned officers alike to set an example and regularly interact with the lower ranks to ensure proper discipline. Of course, our GIs were not choirboys and always models of decorum,[1] but compared to what we know about the deliberate, methodical plundering of the Nazi regime, it is hard to imagine the contrast being more striking or absolute.[2]

Returning to Dad's wartime odyssey, the activity described in his diary makes it clear that in the last week of October 1944, he and his comrades had gotten into a pretty steady routine, and daily life had become quite tolerable. During that brief "rest-and-refit" phase, they had re-equipped and savored the rare opportunity to recover while off duty. Yet, as most good things in life and wartime are apt to come to an end, their short respite from the reality of war ended rather abruptly.

Beginning on October 31, 1944, Dad's beer-garden, jukebox days came to a sudden halt when the 17th Cavalry Squadron (less Troop A), was assigned to Maj. Gen. Raymond McLain's XIX Corps for combat operations.[3] By November 1, the entire unit was bounced unceremoniously from the hotel where they had resided since mid-October, and they were

---

[1] During the winter of 1944-45, General Eisenhower became so disgusted with reports that certain American GIs had raped local women while liberating Europe that at one point he thought the only solution was to line up the perpetrators and shoot them. Mark Perry, *Partners in Command* (NY: Penguin, 2007), 409; Evan Thomas, *Ike's Bluff* (NY: Little, Brown, 2012), 6.

[2] For GIs in Europe during World War II, predations like plundering or pillaging private property for pecuniary gain were prohibited under the Articles of War, as the Uniform Code of Military Justice (UCMJ) did not become effective until 1951.

[3] On October 18, 1944, General Bradley relieved the prior commander of XIX Corps (Gen. Charles "Cowboy Pete" Corlett) and replaced him with General McLain. MacDonald, *The Siegfried Line Campaign*, 319-320.

posted to dug-in, defensive positions within sight of the enemy near Sittard-Born, Holland.

According to the brief unit history, the 17th Cavalry Squadron moved to the north and was positioned on the left flank of Simpson's Ninth Army, which General Bradley had deployed between the British 21st Army Group to the north and Hodges's First Army to the south. There they were told to hold "a line of some 3,000 yards in length until the 17th of November."[1] Their mission at that time was to maintain contact between widespread friendly divisions and to be alert for enemy infiltration of the lines.

By November 2, the 17th Cavalry Squadron was officially attached to the 113th Cavalry Group (Mechanized) as its mobile reserve, becoming the reinforcement element on the picket line.[2] Later that month, Pop described being on guard duty at a forward observation post within sight of the enemy, a mere "500 yards of open ground" in the distance. He reported "hip-high grass" and two canals separating them from the German lines. While there, dismounted foot patrols were used to probe the enemy's lines and test the German defenses.

Dad reported spending most of his nights either on guard duty or manning the radio, and mentioned that changing the outpost guard was a dangerous job, done only after sunset, as the enemy had them under close observation.[3] He wrote that it had "rained for the last three days," making life miserable for everyone around him. On November 7, he mentioned that two German soldiers had "deserted their army and crawled over to us" during the cold and rainy "pitch black night" to surrender. He described them as dressed in only their summer uniforms without any hats or topcoats.

By Wednesday, November 8, 1944, he indicated they had heard the returns from the U.S. presidential election; Pop mentioned that he was pleased with the result: "Roosevelt won again." Along with him, most of

---

[1] TLR, 15.
[2] Rottman, *World War II US Cavalry Groups: European Theater*, 47.
[3] The most terrifying frontline chore for a soldier was manning an outpost beyond friendly lines in no-man's land. That job required one to watch, listen, and report back to higher command all that was observed. Such duty was a leap of faith, as a man's entire survival depended on the hope that the enemy would never attack in strength. McManus, *Alamo in the Ardennes*, 17.

his cavalry mates were happy about that news, as they could barely envision a world without FDR at the helm of national affairs. Nevertheless, while he had been re-elected for an unprecedented fourth term, many members of the media worried that he would not survive a full term of office due to his obvious poor health.[1]

On November 11, 1944, the twenty-sixth anniversary of Armistice Day (also known as Veterans Day), Dad found himself on frontline guard duty near Born, Holland. At the end of that day, he wrote sorrowfully in his diary, "two of our men got it today." He specified that PFC Norman P. Gillings was killed, but Sgt. Lincoln E. Babcock was "still alive and in the hospital." Both were described as victims of "a tree burst" from enemy mortar fire.

Writing further, Pop mentioned that their main threat was incoming German mortar fire, which occurred every morning at dawn and in the evening at dusk. In that respect, the enemy was particular cunning in choosing those as the times most propitious to shell American troops. They obviously surmised that dusk and dawn were the occasions when they could best catch GIs out in the open, attending to their personal needs and gathering in groups at the chow line.

To be clear, indirect mortar fire is extremely accurate and lethal in the hands of an experienced crew; mortars are favored weapons of infantrymen because they are relatively easy to transport and maintain, and they are much easier to resupply with ammunition than artillery.[2] As noted by one military historian, mortar fragments were very life-threatening as they "caused some 70 percent of the battle casualties among four U.S. Infantry divisions" during the Normandy campaign.[3]

On November 12, Dad mentioned that the prior evening was quite eventful, as the squadron had finally gotten some needed infantry support. He wrote: "The infantry came in and took their positions between [the

---

[1] Regrettably, that prognostication concerning his health was spot on, as FDR was suffering from several life-threatening diseases, including congestive heart disease and severe hypertension. Steven Lomazow, M.D., and Eric Fettmann, *FDR's Deadly Secret* (New York: Public Affairs, 2009), 147.
[2] Kindsvatter, *American Soldiers*, 83.
[3] Atkinson, *The Guns at Last Light*, 112.

spread of] our tanks. His gratitude was clear: "Geez, it sure feel[s] great to have them here with us . . . but it sure was hell, sweating it out up here by ourselves." He mentioned, "two more [Fox Company men] got hurt" that day: Staff Sgt. Miguel C. Ramirez was killed[1] and Sgt. Henry O. Olson was "hit in the leg by shrapnel."

By morning of November 14, Dad mentioned that Troops B and C of the 17th Cavalry Squadron along with some infantry had been sent out on a dismounted reconnaissance mission the previous night. He said they returned with useful information regarding the enemy's activities.

One day later, Pop breathed in the chilly air and mentioned with delight that his unit was in the process of being relieved by a group of British troops, the "Irish Guards." He noted they came in and took over on the line around 0930 hours. Yet, contrary to any spirit of hands-across-the-sea, but true to his ancient Hibernian ancestry, he wrote disdainfully: "Most of them [appear to be] Limeys."[2]

He next reported traveling all day in a road march on November 16, in very frigid weather, and he mentioned that his feet and hands had been cold "as never before". Prior to bivouacking for the night near the small Dutch town of Epen, the squadron was put on notice that they were then assigned to the XIX Corps mobile reserve.

Within only a very short time thereafter, he described hearing "an awful weird noise in the sky": a vibrating rumble that prompted his first glimpse of what he learned later was a German V-1 flying bomb. Around two hours later, he heard the pulsating sound of another one flying overhead, but as he watched, it went "hay-wire," made "a half twist" in flight and plunged to the ground, exploding about 1,800 yards to their front.

The strange objects Pop mentioned on that occasion were early forerunners of modern-day cruise missiles; they were Hitler's V-1 buzz

---

[1] Both PFC Norman P. Gillings and S/Sgt. Miguel C. Ramirez, were killed in the vicinity of Born, Holland, while the 17th Cavalry Squadron was holding defensive positions near the border with Germany. TLR, 28; March 1, 1945 memorandum to The Adjutant General, entitled: "History of the 17th Cavalry Reconnaissance Squadron for Year 1944," 6.

[2] Pop's derogatory term for Englishmen likely came from the Royal Navy's early practice of adding citrus juice to a sailor's daily rum ration to prevent Vitamin C deficiency (scurvy) on long sea voyages. See http://en.wikipedia.org/wiki/Limey.

bombs, which the British referred to as "doodlebugs" due to the noise they made traveling overhead. They were pilotless aircraft, measuring twenty-five feet in length with a seventeen and a half-foot wingspan. Crude pulsejet engines powered them to a maximum velocity of 350 miles per hour with a range of around one hundred miles. Each was packed with nearly a ton of high explosive that detonated on impact with the ground. They were cheap to build and easy to launch, but were vulnerable to Allied fighter aircraft and antiaircraft artillery gunfire. It was calculated that only about 80 percent of the V-1s landed within a target circle eight miles in diameter. A small propeller in the missile's nose was set to rotate a certain number of times with each revolution representing a fraction of the distance from the launch site to the target. When the correct number of revolutions was reached a signal cut the engine and the flying bomb "dropped like a stone."[1] (See graphic illustration below.)

---

[1] Marshall De Bruhl, *Firestorm: Allied Airpower and the Destruction of Dresden* (New York: Random House, 2006), 109 and 110.

13. THE SIEGFRIED LINE & ROER PLAIN

Preceded by an artillery barrage and the most massive supporting air bombardment yet seen in Northwestern Europe (roughly 2,400 U.S. Eighth Air Force and Royal Air Force heavy bombers with some 200 medium bomber and fighter sorties), the Ninth Army's XIX Corps and XIII Corps launched an attack north of Aachen, Germany, and the First Army's V and VII Corps widened the advance south of that city on November 16, 1944. Against stubborn enemy resistance, that air-land attack, code-named Operation Queen, successfully penetrated a portion of Adolf Hitler's vaunted *Westwall* defenses.[1]

One day later, the headline story in *Stars and Stripes*, the daily newspaper of the U.S. Armed Forces, reported that Simpson's Ninth Army, "last heard of at Brest, materialized out of the Dutch bogs last night and smashed across the German border." It was described as the "Mystery" Force, the "will-o'-the-wisp" Ninth Army, by combat journalists, as its location had been "kept under wraps" for security reasons. That article also noted that the Germans were taken totally by surprise by the Ninth Army's "sudden attack, which was launched 800 miles from its last appearance" months earlier on the Brittany Peninsula.[2]

By then, Simpson's Ninth Army, along with Hodges's First Army, Patton's Third Army, and Alexander Patch's Seventh Army[3] were reportedly in the process of pounding most of Germany simultaneously from Holland to the Swiss border. War correspondents reported that the Ninth Army had attacked on a narrow, seven-mile front "north of the First Army's sector above Aachen," and by nightfall had taken the villages of Immendorf, Floverich, Euchen, and Bettendorf, just inside the German border. The Ninth Army's success in deceiving German intelligence as to their whereabouts was described as the product of a classic screening

---

[1] MacDonald, *The Siegfried Line Campaign*, 412.
[2] *Stars and Stripes*, Vol. 1, no. 117, Friday, November 17, 1944, 1.
[3] General Patch's Seventh Army had landed on the French Mediterranean coast between Nice and Marseille in mid-August 1944 to support the Allied forces in Normandy; facing minimal enemy resistance, they quickly moved north to join Lt. Gen. Jacob L. Devers' Sixth Army Group. Waller, *Wild Bill Donovan*, 264.

mission by vast numbers of American forces. That deception was made clear by reported German broadcasts, which placed the Ninth Army far to the south of France, between either the First and Third Armies or the Third and Seventh Armies, many miles away from their actual location west of Aachen.[1]

On the extreme right of the photograph my father stands with a wry smile on his face and his arms folded. On the rear of the photo he identified his squadron mates (standing, from left to right, on Dad's left): Hakim and Johnson, and (kneeling, left to right) Stalzer, Rosenberger and Morrical. The soldier in the front row on the left (Len Stalzer) appears to be making an effort to proudly display his M3 "grease" gun[2], while the soldier on the right (Harold Morrical) seems more matter of fact about the M1 carbine, cradled between his arms.

---

[1] *Stars and Stripes*, Vol. 1, no. 117, Friday, November 17, 1944, 4.
[2] That .45-caliber submachine gun was called a grease gun because it was thought to resemble a mechanic's lubricating device.

193

A fair portion of the successful Allied security and screening effort may be attributed to Dad's 17th Cavalry Squadron, which along with many other U.S. soldiers entered the defensive line in early November 1944. They maintained observation and listening posts on the ground across from the enemy in order to disguise the strength and disposition of the American force. They also performed stealthy reconnaissance on foot to detect the location and intentions of the German forces opposing them. Due to the efforts of countless stalwart soldiers in the icy, sleet-filled November weather, another step toward final victory over the enemy was assured. Yet, as the Allies would soon learn, the Germans had also been busy planning a surprise of their own, and they were preparing to implement it as weather conditions in Northern Europe worsened.

The photograph on the prior page was taken by my father in an urban setting showing several buildings, including a bell tower or church steeple, and a mangled, perforated roof near Aachen, Germany. It reveals the type of collateral damage caused by American and German artillery duels and Allied bombers during the war.

Amazingly, the church spire in the background of the photo appears to be wholly intact. That seems strange, since Allied forces expended tremendous effort during the war to knock them out early since the enemy was known to install observers and snipers high in church steeples, together with spotters, to observe and adjust the range and accuracy of their gunfire. According to one author, many European church belfries fell victim to such "prophylactic reconnaissance by fire" on the theory that squandering ammunition was better than risking men's lives in a surprise attack from above.[1]

Dad took the photograph on the next page in November 1944. It shows a member of the 17th Cavalry Squadron's Fox Company examining the remains of a disabled German self-propelled assault gun, a *Sturmgeschutz* III (or StuG III). The distinctive rounded *Saukopf* ("pig's head" in German) gun mantlet on which the soldier was seated identifies it as a vehicle manufactured after the spring of 1944.[2] Earlier versions of the 22-ton StuG III were instead fitted with a bolted V-shaped gun mantlet. Their low silhouette (about seven feet high) allowed for easy concealment behind vegetation. That turret-less vehicle was most effective in a hull-down defensive position where it would stand fast and provide close fire support for infantry. It could also defeat armor at close or medium ranges and became a "real fireman" for the Germans when used as a tank killer in the final years of the war.[3]

The main gun of the StuG III could depress and elevate, but its main disadvantage was the lack of a maneuverable turret. Note the dangerous,

---

[1] Zaloga, *Sherman Medium Tank, 1942-1945*, 13.
[2] Niall Barr & Russell Hart, *Panzer* (Osceola, WI: MBI Publishing, 1999), 165.
[3] The Germans built over 9,000 StuG IIIs during the course of the war. Mike Dario, *Panzerjäger in Action* (Warren, MI: Squadron/Signal, 1973), 33, 35.

angled superstructure that contrasted greatly with the smoother, sloping front of the Jagdpanzer V. Also, quite apparent in the photo is an awesome muzzle brake at the end of the 75-mm cannon; its function was to reduce obfuscation of the target and lessen the cannon's recoil by redirecting propellant gases to the side of the muzzle. That reduced gun recoil was important for the crewmen seated within the restricted confines of that vehicle; it also allowed for maintenance of line of sight with the target, which was a huge bonus for the German gunner.

On November 21, 1944, the 17th Cavalry Squadron moved to the "Jülich-Düren" sector of Germany, and from there they held a line on the southern, right flank of the Ninth Army for the 30th Old Hickory Division under General Hobbs; later in the year, they performed the same vital duty for Maj. Gen. Charles Gerhardt's 29th Blue-Gray Division.[1]

Dad diarized on November 21, that they had moved out from their reserve position near Epen, Holland, and traveled well to the east. He said they "crossed the border" into Germany and passed some "smashed and

---

[1] TLR, 15.

burned out pillboxes" on the Siegfried Line. He mentioned it as an awful sight, as the first town they entered "was cut to ribbons" and in ruins with destroyed vehicles, smoldering buildings, and dead enemy soldiers scattered on the ground. He also noted some bloated horse carcasses were still in their harness traces, and the stench of rotting flesh was overpowering. He said that the place remained "under enemy artillery fire" for some while, and he surmised that the Germans had evidently put up a hard fight, from house to house. He was clearly awed by the devastation that he saw among the scorched gray stone buildings, writing sadly, "It reminded me of France."

Construction of Germany's *Westwall* (also known as the Siegfried Line) began several years before the war's onset. Its construction amounted to a Herculean effort by the Nazis; it was a long band of about three thousand steel reinforced-concrete pillboxes and bunkers that were mutually supporting and emplaced in depth. The Germans made good use of natural terrain conditions, situating the fortifications on the forward slopes facing west and recessed them into the sides of hills to better camouflage them.

In addition, minefields and concrete anti-tank obstacles (called "Dragon's Teeth" by the Allies) were combined with those formidable fortifications. But "the biggest problem facing the defenders of the West Wall was a shortage of troops to man it."[1] By late 1944, Hitler thought that his line of defense works was impervious, a trump card if you will, but their neglect in 1940 led to much deterioration, and the Germans had to work "furiously to put together a scratch force of 135,000 men to partially rebuild and man the line as the Allies approached."[2]

---

[1] Robin Neillands, *The Battle for the Rhine* (NY: Overlook Press, 2005), 175.
[2] Yeide, *The Infantry's Armor*, 190.

Pop's photograph above shows the remains of a steel-reinforced concrete fortification that the 17th Cavalry Squadron encountered while advancing through the Siegfried Line. Those mammoth pillboxes, placed several hundred yards behind the anti-tank obstacles, had concrete walls and steel-beamed roofs that were three to eight feet thick and generally twenty to thirty feet wide, forty to fifty feet deep, and twenty to twenty-five feet high with half the structure being below ground level. Each pillbox had several rooms and living quarters for its troops, but only a few had escape hatches. While their fields of fire were limited to an arc of some fifty degrees, they all had the advantage of interlocking fields of fire from nearby supporting pillboxes.[1]

A variety of tactics were used during the war to destroy those pillboxes, however Allied tank crews soon discovered that their main guns were ineffective in knocking out most of them, head on. Only self-propelled artillery, "Long Toms", firing 155-mm shells were able to penetrate the hardened concrete, "but tank destroyers firing armor-piercing rounds at the embrasures caused casualties from concussion."[2]

---

[1] MacDonald, *The Siegfried Line Campaign*, 34-35; Harry Yeide, *The Longest Battle* (St. Paul, MN: Zenith Press, 2005), 26.
[2] Beevor, *Ardennes 1944*, 28.

Consequently, tanks were limited to firing high-explosive rounds at the embrasures of the pillboxes to keep the enemy defenders' heads down while brave GIs attacked on foot. An equally effective technique used to convince the enemy to surrender was to drop a fragmentation or white phosphorus hand grenade down the ventilation shaft, and if that proved unsuccessful, tank dozers were called in to block the airshaft with soil and assorted rubble.[1]

The photograph below reveals multiple rows of Germany's infamous concrete, anti-tank obstacles (known as *panzersperren* in German) that lined much of Germany's western boundary. That *Westwall* network ran for about 400 miles, starting north of Aachen on the border with Holland and continuing along the Belgian, Luxembourg, and Franco-German frontier, coming to an end in the south at the Swiss border.

---

[1] Yeide, *The Infantry's Armor*, 191; Beevor, *Ardennes 1944*, 29.

The intent of the builders of the Siegfried Line was not to construct a line of self-contained fortresses (like the French Maginot Line), but rather to create a concrete and steel barrier to buy time and delay an invader until German mobile reserves could assemble, counterattack and eliminate any penetrations.[1] Where there were natural obstacles, such as lakes, rivers, or dense forests, they were incorporated into the defense system as passive protection from Allied tanks. Elsewhere, rows of anti-tank Dragon's Teeth (each "tooth" a pyramidal-shaped, concrete obstacle) were set in rows of four or five, rising gradually from three feet in height in the first row to over five feet in the last row. They were intended to stop tanks by forcing them to "belly up", exposing their thin armored underside to easy destruction by German anti-tank weaponry.

As noted earlier, the West Wall (as it was known by the Allies) turned out to be much less than an impregnable barrier for the Third Reich, since it was basically a hollow shell due to a lack of continuous maintenance following the German Blitzkrieg into France and the Low Countries.[2]

According to one author in particular, it was described as something of a Potemkin village by 1944, as its formidability was based on "an old, unearned reputation."[3] That was due to the fact that its usefulness was heavily damaged years earlier when Hitler ordered its weapons removed and installed in the so-called Atlantic Wall (*Festung Europa*) shore defenses prior to the D-Day landings.[4]

The next map discloses the convoluted path of the 15th Cavalry Group as it traveled into Germany in late November 1944, then returned to the "Dutch Panhandle" of Holland during the Nazi Bulge counteroffensive and attempted breakout, prior to a final advance and ultimate crossing of the Rhine River in 1945. It also reveals the approximate location of the German defensive barrier, the Siegfried Line or West Wall, as it related to their area of operation.

---

[1] The problem was that "in early fall of 1944 no strong [German] reserves existed." MacDonald, *The Siegfried Line Campaign*, 31.
[2] Weigley, *Eisenhower's Lieutenants*, 299-300.
[3] MacDonald, *The Siegfried Line Campaign*, 31 and 34.
[4] Caddick-Adams, *Snow & Steel*, 22.

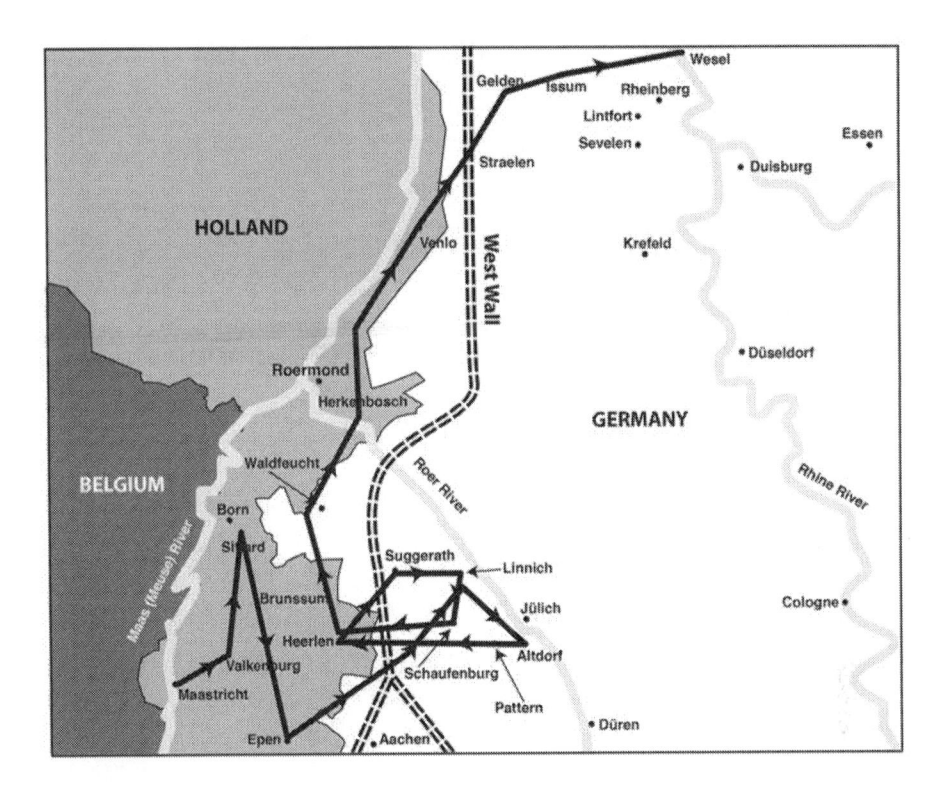

From November 21-23, 1944, Dad's unit followed on the heels of the advance of the 30th Old Hickory Division, and they occupied various German villages, as the enemy vacated them. General Gerhardt of the other division in the XIX Corps "believed the November mud made a battleground whose trials the infantry might surmount, but in which tanks would surely founder." As a consequence, the 29th Blue-Gray Division attack made "little use of tanks."[1]

On November 22, Dad mentioned that Recce Troops A, B, and C of the 17th Cavalry Squadron went ahead, while his light tank company remained behind in reserve, ready to deliver supporting fire. That arrangement most probably resulted from the damp weather conditions and the nature of the terrain of the Roer Plain.[2] It was interlaced with small

---

[1] Weigley, *Eisenhower's Lieutenants*, 426.
[2] Earlier in September 1944, excessive autumnal rainfall had washed out and turned secondary roads into gluey, "muddy quagmires" turning streams in the area between the Wurm and Roer Rivers into significant barriers to

canals, numerous anti-tank mines, and sticky, glutinous winter mud, which greatly impaired tank movement. Clearly the rationale expressed above by General Gerhardt occurred simultaneously in General Hobbs's mind, persuading him to follow suit with the advance of his Old Hickory Division.

In any event, on November 22 he wrote that they searched and gained control of a German village from which the surviving residents had apparently decamped. He mentioned that they found a few civilians living in a church basement, and they were subsequently placed under guard. In addition, he casually observed that there were a "few chickens running around." He indicated further that they subsequently killed about forty birds on that occasion, and everyone in the troop had chicken for dinner. (That chicken dinner was undoubtedly hailed as a vast improvement over their regular pre-packaged K rations.)

In a similar vein, it was far from rare for GIs on guard duty during World War II to "accidently" shoot wandering animals, especially at night, thinking they might be under attack by the enemy. Land mines sown by the Germans also killed their share of stray cattle, sheep, deer and hogs in the ETO. When that occurred, fresh beef, mutton, pork or venison became available to supplement ordinary rations.

While traveling in Normandy in 1944, a famous Pulitzer Prize-winning journalist noticed another source of supplemental protein available to both American and German soldiers. He described the European countryside as "a land of rabbits" that roamed throughout fields and farmyards.[1] Needless to say, any rabbits found wandering about the battlefield became fair game and a welcome addition to a hungry GI's supper.

The photograph below provides even clearer evidence of that culinary phenomenon in practice, as Dad and a coterie of sidekicks from his company appear to be eagerly preparing fresh meat to include in their meal. There is little doubt that such a treat went a long way toward improving their morale while they were on campaign in the field. (My father appears

---

vehicular traffic. That precipitation "morphed into a continual freezing rain, with only the briefest breaks in the weather" during October 1944. Higgins, *The Roer River Battles,* 64.
[1] Pyle, *Brave Men,* 412.

to be one of the individuals in the background carving away with his left leg propped on a log for leverage and fully intent on alleviating his appetite.)

For Thanksgiving Day 1944, General Eisenhower issued an order that every GI under his command was to be furnished a full turkey dinner for the holiday.[1] When the day arrived on November 23rd, Dad described having a special supper with four of his mates[2] in a soggy cellar of a heavily damaged German house. He said they rummaged around for a while until they found an old wooden table, a dark blue tablecloth, as well as a few dishes and eating utensils. With the use of a tank battery, he mentioned they were able to rig up some lighting. After a brief scavenging effort, they apparently found a few "luxury items" (red cherries, pears, and a quart of German whiskey), and they ate their turkey and celebrated the holiday about as well as could be expected under the circumstances. He said it proved to be an unforgettable picture, inscribed in his memory, and it was

---

[1] Beevor, *Ardennes* 1944, 78.
[2] In his diary, Dad identified his Thanksgiving 1944 dinner companions as "Red" Williams, Roy Miller, Eddie Bernard and "Penny" Penniplede.

especially momentous, as they were all very thankful to be "alive and in one piece".

Pop later mentioned in his diary that it had been raining steadily for nearly a week. Thus, finding nightly shelter in various damp cellars of demolished German houses was imperative while advancing across the Roer Plain. He described enduring three successive days of bitter cold, biting wind, and pouring rain on November 26th, and as a result, he announced they were "wet, cold, muddy and miserable."[1] However, on November 27 and 28, he was delighted to report that the weather had cleared and the sun shined down brightly and warmed them up.

Adding to their comfort, those improved weather conditions paid immediate dividends, as American tactical airpower in the form of several P-51 Mustang fighters suddenly appeared overhead. He described them roaring in at treetop level and making what looked like observation turns, as they peeled away, one by one. Within minutes, however, they returned and pounced on their prey, strafing the enemy beyond their positions with .50-caliber machine gun fire. He and his mates were thrilled by that show of friendly force. They were likewise ecstatic that the weather had finally cooperated to make their life a little better. With the prospect of more sunny days ahead, they knew the enemy would soon have additional worry concerning "death from the sky."

By November 29, my father noted that the fields they passed were heavily "pockmarked by mortar, artillery and bomb craters." He wrote that many of the houses and farm structures had collapsed and were "all knocked to hell" and in total ruins.

Dad also mentioned the grotesque sight of enemy torsos displaying *rigor mortis* and putrid animal carcasses, lying in the fields, their legs pointing straight into the air.[2] Not surprisingly, he described the smell of death and

---

[1] The fall and winter of 1944 produced "weather of near record severity." Rainfall was "far above average, and snow and freezing temperatures were to come early and stay for long periods." MacDonald, *The Siegfried Line Campaign*, 35. By then, Dad's battle dress tanker uniform included olive drab wool-lined, bib-front over trousers and a front zippered, wool-lined jacket. Rottman, *World War II US Cavalry Groups: European Theater*, 59.

[2] The bellies of those animal carcasses became swollen with gas trapped inside, causing them to roll onto their backs; they were found in shocking death poses with four feet pointing up to the sky. Rooney, *My War*, 160.

decay as extremely unpleasant. The corpses were rotting, and he said the smell became thick and hung heavy in the air. Apparently, the sight of dead cattle was not uncommon during World War II when modern, highly mobile armies fought over large areas of agricultural land. Many innocent animals were killed, mainly due to the concussion from exploding artillery rounds.[1]

He also wrote on November 29th that he had seen two knocked out German "Tiger Royal" tanks (known also as King Tigers) in a field "just 200 yards" from Pattern, Germany. He reported that one of them had sustained two 76-mm holes, but was "still in good running condition." The other was described as "burned up inside" and contained five dead German crewmen.

He next reported that the scene "sure looks awful, but it is war after all." Evidently, the horror of burned and blackened German corpses, an abundance of voracious flies and hungry maggots, as well as the powerful stench of death from decomposition did little to deter Pop and his fellow crewmen from a quick examination of those crippled prizes. Apparently, the opportunity to closely inspect two heavily armored enemy vehicles proved simply irresistible.

---

[1] Even during cold winter weather, the frozen animal corpses bloated up and were found smelling "fearsomely" lying on their backs with all four hooves "extended stiffly in the air." Davidson, *Cut Off,* 25-26.

It is likely that spalling killed the dead crewmen inside the German armored tracked vehicle, numbered "121", in the photograph above. That occurs when an AP round penetrates the outside armor protection and breaks off steel fragments and splinters that ricochet around the inside of the tank, showering the interior space to lethal effect.[1]

Despite Pop's belief that the vehicles were King Tigers, the above photograph, as well those on subsequent pages are inconclusive, since 70-ton German Mark VII King Tiger tanks were a very rare sight on the battlefield during World War II. Moreover, armored vehicle 121 does not appear to possess the rounded nose and sleek lines of a King Tiger's Porsche-designed turret.[2] And since that was the first mention in his diary of such a monster, it is safe to say that he had never actually seen a King Tiger prior by late 1944; thus, his apparent error is certainly understandable.

One troublesome aspect regarding the photographs is the extensive vegetation that hung along the front of vehicle 121's hull, masking its sharp lines. That fact seemingly prevents a valid determination as to whether 121 actually had a turret. An important fact that we know for certain is that all

---

[1] Green & Green, *Panther,* 136.
[2] Barr and Hart, *Panzer,* 137, 141.

"tanks" have rotating gun turrets; that, of course, makes them more combat effective and costly to build.

Another matter of concern is the apparent lack of a nearly hemispherical gun shield on the front of vehicle 121.[1] Instead, it appears that hidden under that vegetative camouflage was a thickened cast armored *Geschuetznische* (gun recess) bolted to the front glacis plate, a characteristic of the *Jagdpanther V*.[2] Therefore, given the apparent absence of a hemispherical gun shield, I believe that vehicle 121 was either a Jagdpanther V or a Mark VI Tiger tank. However, the latter choice is conditioned upon the indiscernible presence of a standard Henschel production-revolving turret.

Finally, what I find most telling is the fact that long after Dad had the photographs developed, he scribbled on the back of each photo, identifying both vehicles as German "self-propelled 88s." By then, he had apparently revised his analysis and knew they were not Tigers. As to the enemy vehicle with the deceased crew still aboard, he wrote, "Boy do they stink."

---

[1] The Mark V Panther had a distinct, nearly hemispherical gun shield that covered most of the width of the turret front. Green & Green, *Panther*, 147.
[2] Barr and Hart, *Panzer*, 260, 264.

The photograph above appears to have been taken sometime later that day from a slightly different angle than the first. It includes two American GIs standing in the foreground, which adds perspective and clearly reveals vehicle 121's low profile, a hallmark of the German Jagdpanther V.

Solely for the purpose of information, the numeral "121" proximate to the AP kill shot of that tracked vehicle identified it as belonging to the commander of the second platoon of the first company of a German armored battalion. Also, of note in the two prior photographs are vertical metal panels (called *schürzen*) that were attached to the side of the tank to protect the tracks, suspension, and the flat sides of the hull chassis, providing protection from incoming anti-tank rounds. When newly installed, those metal side skirts were effective, but they tended to break off during movement through dense woods, thick underbrush, especially while fighting in the hedgerows of Northern France.[1]

The photograph below reveals two side-by-side penetration holes in the left flank of the armored hull of another disabled enemy vehicle in the foreground. In the background is enemy vehicle "121". In contrast to the prior photographs, it is quite clear that the near vehicle was turret-less. Instead, it had a fixed armored casemate, providing a larger fighting compartment for its five-man crew. That fixed casemate confirms that it was none other than the deadly efficient Jagdpanther V, the enemy's formidable tank killer, which first "rolled off the factory floor in January 1944."[2]

---

[1] Hastings, *Overlord,* 112.
[2] Green & Green, *Panther*, 263.

Since both of the German tracked vehicles in the photograph above were protected by thick sloping frontal armor, the flank kill shots in this instance were in complete accord with the preferred technique for most U.S. tanks in World War II, as they were encouraged to strike the enemy's more thinly armored flanks by shooting them in the tracks, the side of the hull, or in the rear of the enemy vehicle whenever possible.

In viewing the prior three photographs, it is important to note that German tank killers were very vulnerable on the battlefield due to their slow rate of fire and lack of all-around fighting capability. Yet, they mounted the deadly 88-mm anti-tank gun, but the crews suffered from limited vision due to the absence of adequate viewing ports on the front and sides of their vehicle. While buttoned up, they were virtually blind, and had to rely on the roof-mounted commander's scissor-type telescope, and the driver's periscope and gunner's periscope gun sight.[1]

That 51-ton Jagdpanther V was built on a Mark V Panther tank chassis, having 80 mm thick frontal armor, overlapping, interleaved road wheels,

---

[1] Ibid., 263-266.

and rugged torsion bar suspension, making it one of the most effective tank killers of World War II. However, the Germans were estimated to have produced only 413 Jagdpanthers during the war before their factories "were overrun by the Allies in April and May 1945."[1]

Moreover, despite its fierce appearance, the Jagdpanther V was far from indestructible. Because it had no turret, its fixed armored casement greatly limited the main gun's traverse to a maximum of 15 degrees to each side. Also, its main gun tube "could be elevated and depressed only 12 degrees and 9 degrees, respectively."[2] Thus, to fire a round at a target to either the right or left, beyond its maximum traverse, the vehicle's entire chassis had to be put in motion and pivoted sideways. The delay inherent in such a maneuver made it very vulnerable to Allied tanks, which were far more numerous,[3] maneuverable, and had 360-degree power-traversing turrets. With the faster turret traverse, an American tank gunner had the ability to fire well-aimed shots much quicker than the enemy. Also, American tankers could fire on the move, which the Germans rarely attempted, because to do so with any accuracy required a gyrostabilizer.[4]

Considering all of the above, my conclusion is that the same Allied armored vehicle caused the lethal penetration holes in both German vehicles shown in Dad's photographs, as they appear to have been fired basically from the same quadrant. Also, my guess is that German vehicle 121 was the first battle casualty in this case.

With that threat removed and out of action, the two side kill shots on the Jagdpanther V in the foreground appear to have been fired in quick succession. The Allied tank gunner would have activated the turret's traversing mechanism, acquired the target through the gun scope and commenced firing. It is most likely that a U.S. M10 Wolverine, M18 Hellcat TD, a British Firefly or a long-barreled, second-generation M4A3 Sherman tank accomplished that task. Each of the aforementioned boasted a 76-mm main gun barrel of greater length than the original M4 Sherman, bringing with it increased muzzle velocity and much greater killing power.

---

[1] Ibid., 264.
[2] Ibid., 269, 270.
[3] The U.S. manufactured almost 50,000 M4 *Sherman* tanks during World War II. Marks, "The M4 Sherman Medium Tank," 14.
[4] Green & Green, *Panther*, 233.

(As one former U.S. Army Ordnance officer explained, the larger the caliber of the main gun, the longer the barrel had to be to give the propellant time to expand against the projectile, producing a higher muzzle velocity.[1])

The U.S. Army Signal Corps/National Archives photograph below shows an M18 Hellcat TD in April 1945, preparing to fire its 76-mm main gun. With that longer barrel, modifications to the M4 chassis were required, including installation of a muzzle brake to reduce the cannon's recoil, and a distinctive rear turret counterweight to add support for the heavy gun barrel and provide stability and balance.

It is important to note that the only American weapons capable of consistently knocking out a German Tiger tank were the 90-mm cannon, mounted in the M26 Pershing heavy tank, and the M36 Jackson TD.[2] Yet,

---

[1] Cooper, *Death Traps,* 230, 232.
[2] MacDonald, *A Time for Trumpets,* 82-83; the M36 tank destroyer was named after Gen. Thomas J. "Stonewall" Jackson, C.S.A.; it was essentially an M10 redesigned to accommodate a 90-mm cannon. Weigley, *Eisenhower's Lieutenants,* 10; much like the German 88-mm gun, the 90-mm gun mounted in the M36 TD was converted from an antiaircraft gun.
Yeide, *The Infantry's Armor,* 231.

Tigers were anything but indestructible, as they were prone to mechanical breakdown and known for their clumsy maneuverability. Also, they entered battle with a further serious handicap: a slow manual turret traverse. Moreover, their twelve-cylinder, gasoline powered Maybach engines guzzled fuel, getting less than a half-mile per gallon and most roads were ill suited for those behemoths, especially in the Belgian Ardennes where finding a suitable bridge to handle a Tiger tank was a major challenge. They were models of German over-engineering, made with no fewer than 26,000 separate parts, causing many to spend half their time in workshops or under local repair due to the ordinary wear and tear of field service.[1] With the benefit of hindsight, it is clear that their technological sophistication was essentially a luxury, as they were irrelevant in the face of superior numbers of Allied armor. U.S. official postwar estimates revealed that only about 250 Tiger tanks took part in the Battle of the Bulge; the rest were Panzer IVs[2] and Panthers.

While German Tiger tanks were "extraordinarily rare" on World War battlefields[3], "many Allied action reports remark that any tank encountered was a King Tiger."[4] Also, military historian Dr. Caddick-Adam concluded that the similar sloping front shared by the Mark VI Tiger and Mark V Panther might explain the problem of their frequent misidentification on the battlefield.[5]

In the early morning hours of November 22, 1944, German forces ejected the advance of the 29th Blue-Gray and 30th Old Hickory Divisions from the villages of Bourheim and Lohn, several miles northeast of Aachen, Germany. Both divisions of McLain's XIX Corps spent the remainder of that day attempting to regain lost ground and resume the advance, but to no avail. They were then so close that the enemy had a distinct advantage: they

---

[1] Neillands, *The Battle for the Rhine*, 273; an example of the over-engineering by German designers: it took around 300,000 man-hours to manufacture a Tiger tank, compared to some 55,000 for a German Panther and 48,000 for an American Sherman tank. Caddick-Adams, *Snow & Steel*, 65.
[2] The Panzer Mark IV comprised roughly half of the German tank strength in the Ardennes. Dupuy, et al., *Hitler's Last Gamble*, 413.
[3] Balkoski, *From Brittany to the Reich*, 169.
[4] Neillands, *The Battle for the Rhine*, 273-274.
[5] Caddick-Adams, *Snow & Steel*, 485.

could bring down "smothering" artillery barrages onto the Americans from the relative safety of the east bank of the Roer River.[1]

Later in November, the XIX Corps chose to advance in a more cautious fashion against the enhanced enemy resistance, alternating days of attack with days of consolidation. That was necessary because to their south Collins's VII Corps and Gerow's V Corps of the First Army were still heavily engaged in savage fighting in the *Hürtgenwald* (the infamous Hürtgen Forest), east of Aachen. Thus, Simpson's Ninth Army advanced slowly and carefully over the last few miles to the river. The Old Hickory Division eventually reached the Roer by capturing the tiny German town of Altdorf during the evening of November 27-28, 1944, and "then gradually closed up to the [Roer] river along its whole front."[2] While the Ninth Army's progress was slow, by the end of November they had successfully closed in on the Roer River.[3]

Daylight dawned bright and clear on Friday, December 1, 1944, according to my father's diary. On that morning, he saw in the sky several U.S. P-51 Mustangs, their shiny wings flashing in the early morning sun. The next thing he knew, they circled their position, rolled in overhead and gave "the Huns the business." He reported later that his cavalry squadron had been "constantly under artillery fire, both day and night." But "so far [we've been] lucky" as the incoming rounds "have not hit very close." In addition, he mentioned his first actual sighting of the German *Luftwaffe* in flight that day, in the form of six German Messerschmitt (Me-109) fighters, flying low in two flights of three planes each. Two enemy planes were reportedly knocked down by anti-aircraft fire, and he speculated: "They could have been on recon [as] they had no bombs and did no strafing." He also mentioned the regular receipt of "incoming mail" (enemy artillery fire) every night and described a regular nuisance, "bed check Charley," a German plane that paid them a nightly "social call", flying over their lines late in the evening near midnight.

On the following day, December 2nd, Pop chronicled an episode in which a German plane "caught us [walking] on a straight open road" in

---

[1] Weigley, *Eisenhower's Lieutenants*, 429.
[2] Ibid.
[3] Taaffe, *Marshall and His Generals*, 250.

broad daylight; after dropping a load of bombs, it came around, leveled off at low altitude, and strafed the entire length of the highway. At that moment, my father, together with Sgt. Glenn "Gimp" Overlander and T/Sgt. Leonard Stalzer, realized the mistake they made by failing to "hug" the tree line during daylight. Consequently, they had to seek cover by belly flopping into a nearby roadside ditch. Shortly after diving into a gully, a quick personal inventory revealed that no one was injured, so out of the mud and slime they came, soaked to the skin and covered in all manner of foul-smelling detritus. While their pride was damaged, they shared a good laugh and by the end of that day my father observed the obvious: "One doesn't look for a dry spot when being shot at."

His subsequent diary entries over the next several days centered on nothing more than complaints about the cloudy wet weather that continued unabated. He went on to mention that it was causing them unceasing maintenance problems with the ankle-deep mud and slush.

By Sunday afternoon, on December 10, Dad wrote that he, Bill Welsh, Joe Miller, and Lowen Rosenberger were ordered to advance their tank two miles forward to "Charley" Troop (Troop C) to establish a frontline command post and communications relay. Before setting out, they attached steel grousers to their tracks for better traction, knowing full well that they would be traveling across a stretch of muddy and icy terrain. Since the Germans were positioned on the commanding "high ground" east of the Roer River, they had superior observation and could easily hammer them with their artillery during daylight hours. Thus, they waited until dark to get under way. He described that trip as an "awful slow" event, crawling along, skidding and sliding in the heavy winter mud like an elephant on ice skates. He also mentioned being aware of enemy mortar and artillery fire raining down all around them, but he noted later that the Germans could only hear our engine noise and the squeak and clatter of our tracks. Fortunately, the darkness of night conspired against the Germans, as "they could not see us thank God."

Within several hours, they had made it to the tiny town of Altdorf, just a few miles south of Jülich, Germany, very near the Roer. On their arrival, Pop mentioned that the place was "a wreck." Shortly thereafter, he and the crew were able to grab some much-needed rest in the cellar of a bombed-out dwelling. Within minutes, after collapsing with fatigue, they settled into their musty resting place and sleep came easily, as a steady chorus of heavy snoring no doubt ensued. For several days afterward, he mentioned they endured more German artillery fire and repeated strafing attacks from low-flying enemy planes.

By December 15, 1944, they finished their mission in Altdorf, and returned to the command post in Pattern. They spent the rest of the day cleaning, refueling, and rearming their tank. Later, they were fortunate enough to find some space to stretch out for the evening, and they hunkered down and were soon dead asleep. Again, no doubt, more snoring likely erupted in another dank, dark European cellar.

The photograph below of a burnt shell of a building reveals the type of abandoned shelter available to Dad and his squadron mates, as they advanced into Germany during the winter of 1945. Artillery had shattered the roof and the walls and windows were heavily pockmarked with gaping holes. Nothing remained but a shell of a building with piles of broken glass and crumbled bricks. The cellar was their only refuge for a good night's rest, providing a much-needed sanctuary from the rain and a place to dry off and stretch out.

Pop identified the gutted building above as a former German café that had been converted to a command post near Pattern, Germany.

215

By December 9, 1944, Simpson's Ninth Army had full control of the west bank of the Roer River throughout its entire sector. It had taken twenty-three days to cover the twelve miles from the start line of the advance to the Roer, despite the fact that the Rhine, Germany's "sacred river", located farther to the east was the actual, initial objective of their advance, not the Roer.[1]

Although that advance had brought the Allied forces closer to the Rhine, it had not lived up to General Bradley's expectations, because the patchwork assortment of German divisions had held and inflicted more than 10,000 battle casualties on the Ninth Army. Yet, German losses included more than 8,000 POWs captured and approximately 6,000 killed. In any event, the battle of the Roer was over.[2]

As Ike pointed out to his subordinate, General Bradley, the campaign was not simply about taking ground it had become attritional. Since the German losses were far greater than those suffered by his troops, Ike considered it a success.[3]

---

[1] Neillands, *The Battle for the Rhine*, 237.
[2] Weigley, *Eisenhower's Lieutenants*, 430-431; MacDonald, *The Siegfried Line Campaign*, 577-578.
[3] Lloyd Clark, *Crossing the Rhine* (New York: Atlantic Monthly, 2008), 246.

14. TROUBLE IN THE ARDENNES

On completion of their advance to the west bank of the Roer, General Bradley directed the First Army to seize a series of dams on the upper Roer near Schmidt, Germany, prior to crossing the river and proceeding to the Rhine. That strategy was intended to prevent the intentional flooding of the Roer Plain by the Germans. At that time, Simpson's Ninth Army was positioned north of the First Army, awaiting improvement in the weather and their anticipated attachment to the British 21st Army Group, prior to resuming the offensive.[1]

Nevertheless, the effort to save the dams from destruction broke down before it ever began due to the mid-December 1944 German counteroffensive: Adolf Hitler's ill-advised *Wacht am Rhein*, "Watch on the Rhine", later renamed *Herbstnebel*, meaning "Autumn Mist." The enemy intended that counterattack to deliver a massive blow to the Allies by repeating the May 1940 German victory achieved through the rugged Ardennes region. It was a huge gamble by Hitler intended to drive a wedge deep enough in the Allied camp to thwart their insistence on unconditional surrender terms.[2] In every way possible, the German troops in the field faced long odds in their effort to reverse the Allied juggernaut in Western Europe.

That German counteroffensive (the Battle of the Bulge, as we know it) amounted to a last-gasp commitment of the bulk of Germany's final reserves in men and materiel. Hitler himself predicted that its outcome would mean "life or death for the German nation."[3] It began as a three-pronged strike into Belgium and Luxembourg along a 75-mile front bounded by the German cities of Monschau in the north and Echternach in the south.

SS Gen. Josef Dietrich's Sixth Panzer Army was the *Schwerpunkt*, the center of gravity of the offensive. The Fifth Panzer Army was ordered to protect its flank in the initial assault while the Seventh Army opposite Luxembourg guarded against counterattack. In a secondary role, the

---

[1] Morton, *Men on Iron Ponies*, 172.
[2] Yeide, *The Infantry's Armor*, 212.
[3] Reynolds, *Men of Steel*, 41.

Fifteenth Army was poised to the north to cover the right flank and engage U.S. forces near Aachen.

That German operation consisted of thirty divisions, around 250,000 troops with some 1,500 tanks and assault guns, and 2,600 artillery pieces. The objective was to smash the U.S. First Army in the southern Ardennes, then. proceed rapidly to the River Meuse and capture the Belgian port of Antwerp. Hitler's goal was to split the British 21st Army Group away from the rest of the American combat forces to the south.[1]

At that point, Allied manpower on the continent was enormous, totaling nearly three million men.[2] Yet, directly in the path of that surprise German offensive were only around 83,000 American troops.[3] As the Ardennes region was considered to be a quiet sector, only a smattering of inexperienced and exhausted troops were there to defend it. Nevertheless, in the early morning hours of December 16, 1944, the Germans opened a surprise attack which benefited from a heavy fog, which descended over the snowy Ardennes and denied the Allies their usual tactical air cover.

The overstretched VIII Corps of the First Army took the brunt of the initial German attack. Its front covered an area much larger than the recommended coverage for a corps, and they had to defend in place without immediate reserves. Overextended as they were, Gen. Middleton had deployed all three of his infantry divisions to the front: the 106th ("Golden Lions") in the north; the 28th ("Keystone") in the center; and to the south in Luxembourg, the battle-weary 4th Ivy men and a brigade-size, combat command of the 9th Armored Division.

To patrol and screen the vulnerable five-mile avenue of approach into the area that was the Losheim Gap, Middleton inserted Col. Mark Devine's 14th Cavalry Group. There, Colonel Devine positioned his 18th Cavalry Squadron with the 99th ("Checkerboard") Division, across the corps boundary north of the Losheim Gap.[4] In addition to the cavalry troopers, a small group of some twenty soldiers of Lt. Lyle J. Bouck's Intelligence and

---

[1] Atkinson, *The Guns at Last Light*, 393-396; Blair, *Ridgway's Paratroopers*, 357.
[2] Caddick-Adams, *Snow & Steel*, 82.
[3] Perry, *Partners in Command*, 340.
[4] Caddick-Adams, *Snow & Steel*, 169-172; Morton, *Men on Iron Ponies*, 172-173.

Reconnaissance (I&R) Platoon of the 394th Infantry Regiment, 99th Division, were deployed at a key road junction near Lanzerath, Belgium.[1]

At the outset, Dietrich's Sixth Panzer Army was located directly across from the inexperienced 99th Checkerboard Division of V Corps. To the south of the Losheim Gap were the equally overstretched lines of the 106th Golden Lions of VIII Corps, who were even newer to combat than the 99th Checkerboarders.[2] As one author noted, in addition to being new to battle, the men of the Golden Lions Division were "under armed, under led, and entirely unprepared psychologically for what was to face them in a sector of the battlefield where they were expected to receive a gentle introduction to war."[3]

The fact that such a small force was assigned to defend that vast area demonstrated complacency on the part of the American high command. They had deceived themselves into believing that a German attack in the Ardennes was only a remote possibility.[4] Nonetheless, the American cavalrymen and Lieutenant Bouck's platoon manned their forward outposts in muddy foxholes while covering that potential enemy avenue of approach. Undoubtedly, they were aware of their role as a thin human tripwire.

Near daybreak, the many divisions of Dietrich's Sixth Panzer Army crashed westward with tsunami-like power and swept over that small American screening force.[5] But the Germans soon lost their traction as

---

[1] Each echelon of all U.S Army maneuver units, from regiment to corps, had a dedicated reconnaissance unit: infantry regiments had a 25-man, jeep-mounted I&R platoon, infantry divisions had a 143-man mechanized cavalry troop, and each armored division had a mechanized cavalry reconnaissance squadron. Rottman, *World War II, US Cavalry Groups: European Theater*, 7.

[2] Maj. Gen. Alan Jones's 106th Infantry Division had been in the line of battle for only five days. Taaffe, *Marshall and His Generals*, 262-263.

[3] Hastings, *Victory in Europe*, 108. Among the soldiers in the 423rd Infantry Regiment of the 106th Infantry Division was PFC Kurt Vonnegut, who became a POW during the Battle of the Bulge. He witnessed the Allied bombing of Dresden and used that experience to write his 1969 novel, *Slaughterhouse-Five*. Caddick-Adams, *Snow & Steel*, 179, 662.

[4] MacDonald, *A Time for Trumpets*, 83.

[5] At the Battle of the Bulge, the 14th Cavalry Group "suffered horrendous casualties, losing 20 percent of its officers and 33 percent of its enlisted men." Morton, *Men on Iron Ponies*, 175.

they became entangled with Gerow's V Corps defensive positions. There, the remnants of the shattered 99th Checkerboard Division, reinforced by men of other battle-hardened units held fast to the northern shoulder of the battlefield on the Elsenborn Ridge, while Simpson's Ninth Army counterattacked to the south and seized control of the First Army's VII Corps' defensive frontage.[1]

By then, Manteuffel's Fifth Panzer Army had smashed the inexperienced 106th Golden Lions and the battered 28th Keystone Division to the south, forcing its way through the Losheim Gap that split the seam between Gerow's V Corps and Middleton's VIII Corps. Striking that vulnerable seam was important to the enemy because at that location command responsibility was less settled and supporting U.S. firepower was less able to concentrate its firepower. Suddenly, little resistance appeared in the way of a rapid German push into Belgium to the Meuse River, but success relied on their gaining access to Allied fuel and supply dumps.[2]

Meanwhile, as GIs ran out of ammunition and were forced from their defensive positions, the order came down to destroy their equipment and save as many men as possible. Since they could not burn the bulk of their equipment without giving away their positions to the enemy, some GIs solved the problem by putting sugar in the gas tanks of their vehicles, wrecking their radios, and placing thermite grenades in the barrels of artillery pieces. Others disabled firing pins and buried the breechblocks of their heavy weapons in the snow, while machine guns were dismantled and their parts scattered in the fields and woods of the Ardennes.[3]

As to the matter of the Wehrmacht's transportation in the Ardennes, they were greatly hindered by the fact that, for every tank deployed in the offensive, they relied on up to forty horses to pull their supply and ammunition wagons. Ironically, while they captured many American vehicles at first, fueled up and ready to go, the Germans were unable to

---

[1] Ibid., 176.
[2] Weigley, *Eisenhower's Lieutenants*, 445-449, 475; Atkinson, *The Guns at Last Light*, 425, 433; Neillands, *The Battle for the Rhine*, 273.
[3] Cooper, *Death Traps*, 178.

continue their advance because so few of them knew how to operate a motor vehicle.[1]

At that stage of the war, Dad's unit was situated roughly one hundred miles north of the Belgian Ardennes with Simpson's Ninth Army, just inside the German border. On December 16, he wrote they had observed a lot of bombing and low-level strafing over their sector by German Me-109 fighter aircraft on both days. He mentioned that those aerial attacks seemed highly unusual. (Also, on a personal note, he was reminded that his bride Christine would celebrate her birthday on the following day.)

On that particular Sunday, December 17, 1944, the 30th Old Hickory Division, positioned on the 29th Blue-Gray Division's right flank, withdrew from the line and redeployed south to the area of the German breakthrough. Responsibility for that 3,000-yard void in the front was initially assumed by the 17th Cavalry Recce Squadron, which had recently been attached to the Blue-and-Gray. The scuttlebutt circulating throughout his unit on the following day was that the First Army was "getting pushed back by the Nazis," Dad observed. He also noted a report that Nazi paratroopers had landed behind their lines. Later that day, he wrote that he "saw a 'Charley jeep' [a jeep bearing Troop C markings] with two enemy captured, one dead and one wounded, both very young."

By December 20, the 1st Battalion of the Blue-Gray's 116th Infantry Regiment, took responsibility for the left portion of the 17th Cavalry Squadron's sector; it was relieved on the following night, by the Blue-Gray's 1st Battalion, 175th Infantry Regiment, at which point, the 17th Cavalry Squadron reverted to regimental reserve. Further juggling of Blue-and-Gray infantry battalions and companies followed, but it was not until December 24, before the 17th Cavalry Squadron was detached from the 29th Division.[2]

Unbeknownst to my father and his colleagues, horrific war crimes occurred on December 17, as SS panzer troops ran amok in the Belgian countryside some fifty miles to the southwest of their position. The most infamous incident was the massacre, which occurred three miles south of

---

[1] Caddick-Adams, *Snow & Steel,* 221-222, 267; Morton, *Men on Iron Ponies,* 185.
[2] Ewing, *29 Let's Go,* 200-201.

the town of Malmedy. At that location, around 150 lightly armed American soldiers from Battery B of the 285th Field Artillery Battalion were captured and executed summarily by machine-gun fire. Only a few GIs survived by feigning death, as German soldiers walked among them administering the *coup de grâce* by pistol. That disgraceful deed was committed by troops from the 1st *SS* Panzer Division, led by Lt. Col. Joachim Peiper.[1] For his role in the murder of the American soldiers at Malmedy, Peiper was later convicted of war crimes by an American military court and condemned to death.[2]

On the evening of December 18, 1944, General Bradley ordered the Saar Offensive, occurring farther to the south of France, suspended. By the next day, Eisenhower ordered Bradley to redirect Patton's Third Army north, directly into the left flank of the German Seventh Army.[3] Devers's 6th Army Group would then fill much of the Third Army's sector. Patton was so pleased with that decision that he pointed to the maps and boasted: "Brad, the Kraut's stuck his head in a meat grinder . . . this time I've got hold of the handle," while turning his fist in a grinding motion.[4]

In keeping with the old adage that fortune favors the bold, by December 22, Old Blood and Guts turned his force ninety degrees to the north and launched a three-division attack to rescue the outmanned American forces in the path of the German blitz.[5] At that time, Dietrich's Sixth Panzer Army was stuck on the Elsenborn Ridge in the north, and the U.S. 4th and 28th Infantry and 10th Armored Divisions stopped the enemy's advance near Echternach, Luxembourg, on the southern shoulder of the Bulge.[6]

Earlier on December 20, Eisenhower divided the Bulge by transferring all American forces north of the map line from Givet to Houffalize, Belgium, to Prüm, Germany, to the 21st Army Group. Thus, Hodges's

---

[1] Stein, *The Waffen SS*, 278; Weigley, *Eisenhower's Lieutenants*, 475-477; Atkinson, *The Guns at Last Light*, 423, 424.
[2] Stein, *The Waffen SS*, 280; Reynolds, *Men of Steel*, 290, 291; Beevor, *Ardennes 1944*, 363-364.
[3] Neillands, *The Battle for the Rhine*, 285.
[4] Caddick-Adams, *Snow & Steel*, 412-414; Axelrod, *Patton*, 149.
[5] Patton's III Corps, commanded by Maj. Gen. John Millikin, made that attack with the 4th Armored Division, the 26th ("Yankee") and 80th ("Blue Ridge") Infantry Divisions. Axelrod, *Patton*, 146-148.
[6] Caddick-Adams, *Snow & Steel*, 508-509; Blair, *Ridgway's Paratroopers*, 360.

First Army and Simpson's Ninth Army were brought under the temporary command of British Field Marshal Montgomery, while the forces located below that map line, including Patton's Third Army, remained under Bradley's command.[1]

Before long it became clear to Eisenhower that the German counteroffensive had created an opportunity for the Allied forces. As the battlefield widened and the bulge grew in size, the flanks of the enemy became vulnerable to counterattack. In discussing the situation with one of his aides, Ike remarked: "It is easier and less costly to kill Germans when they are attacking than when they are holed up in concrete fortifications in the Siegfried Line."[2]

On December 19, 1944, Dad witnessed his first aerial dog fight. He noted observing four planes "go down in flames," but as they were "high and far away," he could not tell if they were "theirs or ours." By December 20, he mentioned that his unit had heard a report that Nazi troops "were behind our lines dress[ed] as G.I.'s." As a result, they increased the watch and posted three men to guard each of their forward listening posts, but he wrote later, "Nothing happened all night."

Pop's concern about Nazi soldiers in their midst was caused by SS Lt. Col. Otto Skorzeny's men, who engaged in behind-the-lines sabotage to assist Dietrich's Sixth Panzer Army. Using bogus identification documents and GI uniforms garnered from American POWs, those English-speaking German troops began to instill chaos with some forty captured American jeeps, trucks, and tanks, each disguised with the U.S. white star design painted on their sides and turrets. Their mission was to advance sixty miles west to seize three bridge crossings over the Meuse River, but no German forces made it that far, in part due to a lack of fuel. In the end, those German saboteurs caused little tactical advantage, as they created only localized confusion by switching a number of directional road signs,

---

[1] Vincent J. Esposito (ed.), *The West Point Atlas of American Wars*, Vol. II (New York: Praeger, 1967), Map 61.
[2] Harry C. Butcher, *My Three Years with Eisenhower, 1942 to 1945* (New York: Simon & Schuster, 1946), 730.

sending false messages, cutting telephone lines, and misdirecting a small amount of American military traffic.[1]

Nevertheless, a major outcome of the frenzy sown by Skorzeny's malefactors was increased scrutiny by American military police and suspicious GI sentries. Consequently, soldiers appearing at roadblocks were interrogated for the identity of the "Windy City," or asked questions like: "Who is Mickey Mouse's girlfriend?" One widely reported incident involved the movie actor David Niven, a British officer in Montgomery's 21st Army Group. When stopped at a checkpoint by suspicious GIs, he was asked, "Who won the World Series in 1940?" He replied he had no idea: 'But I do know that I made a picture with Ginger Rogers in 1938.'"[2]

On December 21, 1944, Dad described the prior night as bitterly cold and dark, but quiet. He wrote, "The Huns are still pushing on the 1st Army front and [the] latest report [was] they started pushing north." He noted that all the civilians were gone from their area, but ten of them had been present earlier and enemy artillery fire had killed one female civilian and wounded two others. Therefore, he indicated they had chased the remainder of the civilians away for their own safety. Dad then observed that he and several other soldiers had become "farmers" by corralling a few horses, cows, and pigs into a field and feeding them some hay. He also reported eight chickens running loose, and they, of course, were captured and consumed that evening. He likewise was very pleased with himself, as he mentioned milking his first cow. Later, Dad wrote that he received a package from "Chris," on December 22, "the 4th so far—all for Xmas" and wrote tenderly, "Gee, I love that woman."

Around noon on December 22nd, some fifty miles to the southwest of the 17th Cavalry Squadron's position, German troops encircled American forces at the important crossroads town of Bastogne. Except for stragglers staggering to the rear in shock, every available American soldier at Bastogne (including cooks, bakers, and clerks) had to find a weapon and hold the line.

---

[1] Atkinson, *The Guns at Last Light*, 443; Weintraub, *11 Days in December* (New York: Free Press, 2006), 58.
[2] Atkinson, *The Guns at Last Light*, 444,445; Beevor, *Ardennes 1944*, 176; Weintraub, *11 Days in December*, 59.

Though heavily outmanned by the enemy, they were full of fight following reinforcement by parachute infantrymen from the 101st Screaming Eagles.

Savage fighting ensued for many days, but as the defenders were surrounded, they had one natural advantage: interior lines. By establishing an emergency group of responders from various units, called "Team SNAFU", they were able to concentrate their limited forces and deploy them swiftly to repulse attempted German incursions around the perimeter. Having taken up an all-around defense, that concept of interior lines[1] multiplied the effect of their short-handed force and helped to lessen the dire situation of the defenders at Bastogne. With that, the attitude of the defending American GIs became: "They've got us surrounded—the poor bastards!"[2]

Later, when German General von Lüttwitz demanded the surrender of Bastogne, the acting commander of the 101st Airborne Division, General McAuliffe responded, "Nuts."[3] Responding their bewilderment, the enemy was notified that the reply meant, "Go to Hell," in plain English.[4] Not surprisingly, that infuriated the Germans, and they continued to apply pressure all around the length of the perimeter.[5] However, shortly afterward, the sky cleared enough so that the hard-pressed troops could be resupplied with ammunition and rations[6] by air. By that time, the

---

[1] The defensive concept of "interior lines" is important because "the party occupying the interior lines or center of a circle" has the advantage "against the adversary who operates around the circumference, or on the exterior lines." That principle of war is based on the fact that a straight line is always shorter than a line that curves, i.e., the chord of a circle is shorter than its arc. When an armed force is surrounded, reinforcements may be rushed to a point of enemy attack more quickly by use of shorter, interior lines. Gary W. Gallagher ed., *Fighting for the Confederacy* (Chapel Hill, University of North Carolina Press, 1989), 219.
[2] Caddick-Adams, *Snow & Steel*, 490-494; Beevor, *Ardennes 1944*, 231.
[3] "Nuts" was slang meaning "the hell with you." Rooney, *My War*, 234.
[4] Weigley, *Eisenhower's Lieutenants*, 517, 518.
[5] Blair, *Ridgway's Paratroopers*, 383.
[6] While airdropped ammunition was a priority, the Belgians shared what little food they had with the American troops. Rations were supplemented with beef, venison, and rabbits that ran into trip-wired mines. Beevor, *Ardennes 1944*, 263-264.

uncertainty of battle was downgraded "two full degrees" from FUBAR through TARFU, all the way "to ordinary SNAFU."[1]

On Saturday, December 23, 1944, dawn broke cold and bright for Dad and his crewmates; on that cloudless day, he wrote that they had gotten the word that "we move tomorrow." Gathering up his personal gear, he joined them to make sure their tank was battle ready: using a bore brush, they scrubbed the main gun tube, and cleaned their mud-caked tracks, machine guns and side arms. They also loaded additional ammunition in the turret, filled up with fuel, and stashed a few extra ration boxes on the back deck of the tank. Despite the immediate nature of those preparations for combat, he mentioned the hope that their next move would be "back—not forward."

On December 24, he pondered his first wedding anniversary and remembered fondly one year earlier, hoping "my darling is having a better time than I [am]." That day, his unit left Pattern, Germany, in the morning, and began a road march west, back toward Maastricht, Holland. With some relief, he wrote, "Our destination is Heerlen, Holland," where they moved into a building at a colliery. On arrival, they dismounted and pulled maintenance on their tanks that afternoon. He also mentioned his great fortune to have received some hot chow and needed rest that evening.

On Christmas morning Pop described attending Catholic Mass in a large church in Heerlen, and he observed, "It was beautiful and well decorated." Later that day, he wrote that he obtained some "Christmas cheer—two shots of White Horse Scotch" from Captain Fiori and Lieutenant Conway. That episode could be construed as improper enlisted/officer fraternization, but given the circumstances, the display of seasonal spirit and concern was understandable. To Dad, the morale value of that kind act was incalculable[2].

Prize–winning World War II cartoonist Bill Mauldin observed correctly that the U.S. Army was a "citizen army" during World War II. He also noted that the army had historically maintained certain customs to prevent

---

[1] Davidson, *Cut Off*, 137.
[2] Military leaders learn early that to maintain the morale and fighting spirit of their men, they must walk among them, show them they care for their welfare, and share in their hardships and danger.

undue fraternization between officers and enlisted members on the theory that familiarity bred contempt; however, "most combat outfits scrap tradition, as they scrap many others things, when they go into battle." That's because the officer who was dependent on the men under his command "not only for his success, but for his very life" was not likely to allow them to be distressed unnecessarily, if he had good sense.[1] Thus, it is clear that the generosity bestowed on Dad by his company officers that Christmas morning in 1944 was well received, despite the potential for danger in an active combat setting.

As it so happened, Generals Patton and Bradley also attended church services that Christmas season at a cold and crowded Episcopal Church in Luxembourg City. Despite the fact that it was one of the holiest nights for all Christians, the ever-pugnacious Patton left the church service, glanced at the sky above, and was heard to mutter: "Noel, Noel, what a night to give the Nazis hell."[2]

Actually, by December 24, 1944, the German counteroffensive had reached its "high-water mark," and the enemy would not advance farther west than the east bank of the Meuse River at Dinant. Their concern at that point was the "stout U.S. resistance and a chronic lack of fuel."[3] Yet, the brilliant, blue skies provided great flying weather for Allied fighter-bombers to strafe the attacking German forces.

On December 26, Lt. Col. Abrams led the 4th Armored Division's 37th Tank Battalion, as they battered their way north into Bastogne.[4] Losses were heavy on both sides, and the fighting continued through January 4, but by the 7th of January, it became clear that the contest was over, as the Germans were in full retreat to the east.[5] By January 25, 1945, the Allies had pushed the enemy back to their original starting point and had "all but crippled the Wehrmacht."[6] After more than a month of furious fighting, it

---

[1] Mauldin, *Up Front,* 184-186.
[2] Atkinson, *The Guns at Last Light,* 465, 466.
[3] Neillands, *The Battle of the Rhine,* 295-298.
[4] Atkinson, *The Guns at Last Light,* 467.
[5] Neillands, *The Battle for the Rhine,* 299, 300; Esposito (ed.), *The West Point Atlas of American Wars,* Vol. II, Map 62.
[6] "Ardennes-Alsace Campaign," *On Point, Journal of Army History,* Vol.

became the largest engagement in American military history. Ultimately, no fewer than twenty-nine American divisions were involved in the Battle of the Bulge, "nearly half of all the divisions the army deployed against the Germans in the entire war."[1]

Among the 600,000 American GIs involved in the Ardennes fighting, the toll in casualties from the beginning on December 16, through to the elimination of the Bulge in late January 1945, was roughly 81,000 men. The number of German casualties is unknown, but the estimates run from about 82,000 (the lowest German guess) to at least 100,000 men killed, wounded, and captured. Both sides lost heavily in weapons and equipment, but that battle had thoroughly exhausted Germany's last reserves of manpower.[2]

As an example of how bad it was for the *Wehrmacht* by that time, German industry produced fewer than 25,000 tanks by the end of 1944, only a handful of which were Tiger tanks. On the other hand, the British made slightly more tanks than the Germans, but the Americans manufactured a staggering number: more than 88,000, most of which were Sherman medium tanks.[3] Clearly, the simplicity of design and greater mass-production capability of American industry was a big advantage.

---

19 no. 3 (Winter 2014), 4.
[1] Taaffe, *Marshall and His Generals*, 274.
[2] Weigley, *Eisenhower's Lieutenants*, 574; Atkinson, *The Guns at Last Light,* 489; MacDonald, *A Time for Trumpets*, 618; Reynolds, *Men of Steel,* 41.
[3] Ambrose, *Citizen Soldiers,* 64.

15. INTO THE RHINELAND

On December 27, 1944, the 17th Cavalry Squadron was positioned squarely on the left flank of Simpson's Ninth Army, which was headquartered at Suggerath, Germany, and later at Linnich. After holding the Roer River line on the northern flank for some time, Dad's squadron enjoyed a short rest before returning to its screening position on the Ninth Army's left flank.[1] To their immediate north was Montgomery's 21st Army Group, containing the British Second and the Canadian First Armies.

The eventual outcome of the battle in the Ardennes had become clear by the first week of 1945, and the Allied forces renewed their focus on the battle for the interior of Germany.[2] By that point, Eisenhower had at his disposal seventy-one divisions and he anticipated an increase to a total of eighty-five divisions by the spring of 1945; it consisted of sixty-one American, sixteen British and eight French divisions. Ike's plan was to use them in three phases: to destroy the remaining German forces west of the Rhine and close up to the river along its entire length; seize bridgeheads across the Rhine, from Emmerich and Wesel in the north to Mainz and Karlsruhe in the south; and advance from the lower Rhine into northern Germany and from the Mainz-Karlsruhe area to Frankfurt and Kassel.[3]

The German Third Reich, by contrast, was rapidly approaching its nadir. Matters were in total free fall thanks to Hitler's misguided Ardennes counteroffensive. The troops he squandered in the Battle of the Bulge were the best Germany had available, and they were irreplaceable. Among those not living in total fantasy by that point was Albert Speer, Hitler's armaments minister, who knew that Germany had shot its bolt, and concluded sadly: "The failure of the Ardennes offensive meant that the war was over."[4]

---

[1] TLR, 15.
[2] Edward G. Miller, *A Dark and Bloody Ground* (College Station: Texas A&M University Press, 1995), 190.
[3] H. Paul Jeffers, *Taking Command* (New York: NAL Caliber, 2009), 177.
[4] Speer, *Inside the Third Reich*, 420.

For the remainder of December 1944, Pop reported his unit performed duty at a routine pace: resting in place, cleaning weapons and equipment, restocking ammunition racks, going on and off alert status and manning defensive security positions at forward observation outposts. While manning those posts at night, checking for the presence of enemy activity, he described the weather as "cold, clear and frosty."

On the night of December 29, he wrote that his tank was set up in position to guard and monitor a crossroads, but during that evening a friendly café owner (a Dutchman presumably) came across the street and offered some "hot coffee and a couple of shots of gin." Of course, he gladly accepted the gesture, as the refreshment apparently "helped" him withstand the cold. Later, he commented in his diary that the night was full of dark shadows and sometimes it seemed that "houses move and fences [took] forms." (My guess is there may have been a nexus between the gin consumption and my father's observation of house motion and sinister fence forms.)

By the morning of December 30, he and his cohorts were still on guard duty, but by noon, they were relieved by Charley Troop. Then they moved to the vicinity of the squadron command post near the small village of Schaufenburg, Germany, where they got a full nights-rest on New Year's Eve 1944.

By the first of January 1945, Dad diarized his wish that the New Year would bring an end to war, so he and his squadron mates could return to their families. He also mentioned that among the mail he received that day were five letters and two Christmas cards from his "sweet wife, Chris."[1]

Two days later, Pop noted with delight that he was ordered to report to "Easy Troop" for a few days so that he would get hands-on training with respect to a brand-new American tank. On that occasion, he was referring to the new M24 light tank, which mounted a sleek new turret with electric-power traverse, and more importantly, the 75-mm main cannon that had been standard on the M4 Sherman all along.

On January 3, he was temporarily assigned to "Sgt. Gordon Zumbach's tank" and given the "dope" on the new tank's telescopic gun sight. After a

---

[1] There can be no question as to the most anticipated event of any day for a GI far from home during World War II: mail call. The company clerk would come around and deliver each piece of mail to its recipient.

short familiarization with the main gun, they reportedly received a fire order. Pop wrote that Sergeant Zumbach "worked the sight, and I loaded." First, they fired two rounds, and then they fired "Full Battery, six guns, twelve rounds. The next order was three rounds, each gun, rapid fire." Although he had heard that the 75-mm cannon had been somewhat ineffective in the Sherman tank, he nevertheless thought it a huge improvement over the puny, 37-mm armament mounted on their Stuart tanks. Obviously, he was happy to get acquainted with a gun that would do some damage to the enemy.

That new, 19-ton M24 light tank was nicknamed the "Chaffee" in honor of Maj. Gen. Adna R. Chaffee, Jr., the father of the U.S. Armored Force prior to World War II.[1] It had a lower silhouette and was technically state of the art when it entered European service in the winter of 1944-45. It was faster and better armed than its predecessor, the Stuart, but not so much as to tempt its crew to routinely take on the enemy in a tank-on-tank slugfest, most especially if it involved a deadly Mark V Panther or Mark VI Tiger tank. Nonetheless, such a situation would not be as hopeless as before in a Stuart tank.

The Chaffee's frontal armor was no thicker than its replacement (a mere 25 millimeters thick), but it had the advantage of being more sloped, and its slightly wider steel tracks and torsion bar suspension made it a more stable gun platform.[2]

According to data assembled by the 12th Army Group staff, the M24 Chaffee proved to be the "premier reconnaissance tank in all armies" in the ETO.[3] Similar to the M5 Stuart, the M24 Chaffee was intended for mainly light tank missions, such as mechanized infantry support, scouting, flank security and protective screening. Quantity over quality and size was the Army's doctrine at the time: faster and lighter tanks should exploit breakthroughs, not fight other tanks.[4] In addition to the 75-mm cannon, the new M24 mounted two internal .30-caliber machine guns, and a more

---

[1] Ibid., 25; Morton, *Men on Iron Ponies*, 81.
[2] Rottman, *World War II US Cavalry Groups: European Theater*, 33.
[3] Morton, *Men on Iron Ponies*, 166.
[4] Ambrose, *Citizen Soldiers*, 63.

potent .50-caliber machine gun on the outside of the turret for air defense.[1] (As to the .50-caliber M2 machine gun, known to most GIs as "Ma Deuce," Dad once explained to me his affinity for it in terse fashion: "It made a lot of noise and scared the hell out the Germans.") Along that same line, a former World War II Ordnance officer observed that the enemy was terrified of the M2 machine gun because of its massive .50 caliber "slug." He explained that once the .50-caliber round penetrated a person's torso, "the hydraulic shock would generate a virtual explosion inside the body."[2]

See Dad's photo below of the M24 Chaffee tank. Note the white identification star painted on the front hull, which served as a perfect aiming point for German gunners.[3])

---

[1] One .30-caliber machine gun was mounted alongside the main gun in the turret and the other .30-caliber machine gun was mounted in the front hull. Matthew J. Seelinger, "The M24 Chaffee Light Tank," *On Point: Journal of Army History*, Army Historical Foundation. Vol. 22, no. 3 (Winter 2017), 16.
[2] Cooper, *Death Traps*, 62.
[3] Patrick Feng, "8th Tank Battalion" *On Point: Journal of Army History*, Army Historical Foundation Vol. 25, no. 1 (Summer 2019), 26.

Naturally, when the M24 Chaffee was first introduced to the troops in Europe, it had to be driven around to various American units to acquaint the troops with the new light tank design. The rationale for this on-site introduction, of course, was to prevent any mistaken identity situations, and thereby reduce the risk of accidental, friendly fire incidents.[1]

The first M24 Chaffee tanks arrived at forward army depots in Europe in December 1944; however, deliveries in quantity during the following year provided most U.S. cavalry squadrons with full allotments by February 1945.[2]

During the first frigid days of 1945, the 17th Cavalry Squadron continued the task of maintaining security and screening outposts to the north on the Ninth Army's left flank, along the Roer River line. When not on duty, the squadron alternated in and out of short rest, resupply and refit status in preparation for their next mission.

By January 5, Dad wrote that he and his company were glad to be back under the cover of a roof at the colliery in Heerlen, Holland, as it had snowed about three inches the night before and turned much colder. That day he mentioned they "didn't do much . . . just cleaned our small arms." He mentioned that it continued to snow on January 6, "getting deeper and colder," so he and his crewmates became involved in friendly snowball fights. He indicated he spent all morning "pegging snowballs." That afternoon, he said he went into Heerlen on a 24-hour pass and saw *Sergeant York*, a movie about an American soldier from Tennessee, who earned the Medal of Honor for bravery during World War I.[3]

Later, on January 9, he commented, "this country [Holland] goes in for snow balls in a big way; everyone throws snow, young and old. It's their national sport." He also described getting pelted playfully by some Dutch

---

[1] Zaloga, *Stuart U.S. Light Tanks in Action*, 40, 43; due to its similarity to the German Mark V Panther tank, the M24 was nicknamed the "Panther Pup." Seelinger, "The M24 Chaffee Light Tank" *On Point: Journal of Army History*, 16.
[2] Yeide, *Steeds of Steel*, 253. The M24 Chaffee began production in the spring of 1944.
[3] In October 1918, York (a former conscientious objector in the 82nd Division) captured a large number of German soldiers in the Argonne. Kyle and Doyle, *American Gun*, 143-147; Eisenhower, *Yanks*, 237-239.

youngsters, who were standing alongside the road when they drove by in a jeep.

As the old saying goes, matters then went from the sublime to the ridiculous. Pop reported on January 10, 1945, that the weather was so bright and clear that he and a few of his sidekicks decided to go hunting and shot four quail in an open field behind the colliery. He noted there were plenty of birds in the field, so he and "all the guys are out hunting." Rather casually he observed that, for effectiveness, the carbine[1] was the best weapon to use while hunting, as the M1 Garand rifle bullet "cuts [the birds] in half."

Fortunately for all concerned, no one got hurt in the cross fire and those gallant "hunters" eschewed the use of an automatic weapon like the M3 grease gun during that quail shoot. It is also quite fortunate that, to my knowledge, there were no casualties reported among the citizenry of Heerlen on that occasion. (Only the fact that Pop wrote in his diary that he gave away the four dead quail "to a [hungry] Dutchman", makes this curious episode worthy of any mention at all.)

According to a postwar *Cavalry Journal* article, the 17th Cavalry Squadron was assigned a mission on January 12, 1945, to establish and man 24-hour-a-day observation posts to pinpoint enemy positions across from them on the Roer River line at Linnich, Germany.[2]

Initially, foot patrolling was limited because the enemy was thought to be well entrenched and had heavily mined the opposite riverbank. However, patrolling had been conducted to the north and northeast of Linnich, where the enemy still held ground on the west bank of the Roer. Entrenchments were seen, but no enemy movement was observed. Although the ground was snow covered, neither paths nor enemy footprints were seen in the snow near the trench line, but noises at night

---

[1] As the M1 carbine weighed only five pounds, it was more popular than the larger, 10-pound Garand rifle in cavalry squadrons. However, given its short range, the carbine was at a disadvantage during dismounted combat. Yet, with its 15-round magazine, tank crews favored the M1 carbine since it provided more firepower and range than a pistol. Rottman, *World War II US Cavalry Groups: European Theater*, 13.

[2] Capt. James M. McGuire, "Reconnoitering an Enemy Position," *Cavalry Journal*, Vol. 54, no. 6 (November-December 1945), 13.

made them very suspicious. Later, a series of foot patrols through the area confirmed the fact that the enemy occupied the entrenchments, but only during certain hours of the day. Because it was considered advantageous to seize the unoccupied entrenchments, a plan was devised to reconnoiter the positions to determine the most opportune time to attack.

In the early afternoon of January 14, a six-man night patrol was selected and taken to an observation post nearest the objective. Remaining there for several hours, they studied the terrain and picked their route of advance. Later, they were furnished mission-specific gear, snow-camouflage capes and two-way radios. Before departing, all potentially noisy equipment was discarded and telephone wire was laid to connect the squadron command post with the outpost; the sound-powered telephones between the outpost and the S-2 (the squadron intelligence officer) provided direct communication with the patrol at all times.

After darkness, the men moved to the jump-off point and began their advance across the snowy terrain. Prior to departure, supporting artillery laid harassing fire on the objectives; that gunfire was lifted and placed on other known enemy positions as they advanced. On reaching the entrenchments, they found them unoccupied, and that was reported back to the S-2 at the command post.[1]

As the patrol withdrew, activity at a nearby bridge drew their attention, and using hand and arm signals, they moved to within one hundred yards of the bridge. There they remained for about thirty minutes, attempting to observe the enemy, but heavy fog hampered their view; from the noise however, they concluded that the enemy was working to repair the bridge. Accordingly, they backed off a short distance and called in an artillery concentration on the bridge location to scatter the enemy. After the troopers returned from their recon mission, forward elements of the 17th Cavalry Squadron moved in and occupied the enemy entrenchments without any loss of life.[2]

More than likely Pop played no role in the night patrol described, as his diary is silent about it. That makes complete sense as a dismounted reconnaissance mission was more normally assigned to men in Troop A, B

---

[1] The previous three paragraphs also draw on: McGuire, "Reconnoitering an Enemy Position."
[2] Ibid., 14.

or C. Because Dad was a tank crewman, he would not have been a likely candidate for that mission, even though on occasion tank crewmen were required to dismount and take turn on patrol or outpost duty. Nevertheless, this episode illustrates the communication and planning required for a successful nighttime foot patrol, prior to any pursuit/mop-up mission involving a cavalry squadron.

On February 4, 1945, he reported that the weather was almost spring like: a "bright day and the sun and air force [were] out." By the next day, he noted it was "still like spring [as] all the snow is gone." He reported being on outpost duty on February 6, and that it had been rainy and windy that night. He also reported that, for the past three days the Ninth Army had been advancing, "night and day it keeps rolling forward." He guessed the unit's days at that position were numbered, surmising, "We'll be moving any day now."

Three days later, he mentioned that the 11th Cavalry Group[1] had relieved them, and the 15th Cavalry Group was ordered to travel north with the British under Montgomery's command. Later that day, they arrived at Waldfeucht, Germany, and he described the place as in dreadful ruins with "lots of English and German tanks, all over the place—[all] knocked out."

For the next four days, Pop described the condition of the roads as exceedingly muddy; yet, he thought all they needed was "a good frost" to allow the roads to hold their tanks. Over the next several days it rained and they continued to wait for more optimum conditions, but he noted that the mud was well over his ankles, and the roads were "terrible."

During the period from February 11-12, 1945, they stayed busy washing mud from their tank tracks and cleaning their equipment and weapons; he described watching some British engineers, who were fixing the roads ahead with "bricks and stones." Pop also wrote: "They come along and tell the Huns [they have] 20 minutes to clear out." Once the German civilians were evicted from their homes, the engineers "slap T.N.T. around the houses and BANG [more road] Road Material!"

---

[1] The 11th Cavalry Group arrived in France in November 1944, entered Holland in February 1945, and advanced into Germany with the XIII Corps. Rottman, *World War II US Cavalry Groups: European Theater*, 36.

Allied bombers brought in the New Year by continuing their unrelenting strategic bombing campaign against German factories and cities. By February 1945, most of the cities and industrial centers in Germany were described as resembling Stone Age ruins. For example, the massive Krupp Steel complex in Essen, Germany, was pounded to such an extent that it was reported "incapable of producing a hairpin." But even Lt. Gen. Carl Spaatz, commander of the U.S. Strategic Air Forces in Europe, had his doubts about "'the chimera of bringing Germany to her knees from twenty thousand feet."[1] Only continued ground assault, conquest, and occupation would bring an end to the German Third Reich. Thus, Dad's unpleasant European "adventure" continued.

Yet life soon improved for my father when he, T/Sgt. Stalzer and several other troopers in his unit were granted a 72-hour pass to Paris. Beginning on February 14, with Captain McGuire in charge, they began a long ride in the back of an army truck, traveling all the first day and half the next. (Pop was lucky enough to grab a seat near the tailgate where the air was fresh, and escape was possible in case of an emergency.) By the time they reached their destination in the afternoon of February 15, 1945, their joints were surely stiff and their bottoms sore from the hard-wooden benches and the constant jolting of their truck ride to Paris.[2]

He noted in his diary that they spent several nights at the Hotel Modern in Paris, and he characterized his visit to the City of Light as "very exciting, tiresome and educational." Yet, he also mentioned that "most of the time we were out of it." (The contradiction here seems obvious to me, as Pop used his time wisely, "drinking in" the high culture and sophistication of Paris. In theory, I suppose he may have seen some of the sights of the city, but for my money, the evidence is persuasive: following their arrival in Paris, he and his pals soon became pie-eyed GIs out on a well-earned bender.)

Dad's stroke of good luck in acquiring that three-day pass to Paris came about because the Germans had flooded the Roer Plain by opening the floodgates and wrecking discharge valves on many of the Roer River dams

---

[1] Atkinson, *The Guns at Last Light,* 534, 536.
[2] His mode of transport on that occasion was likely an army deuce-and-a-half, the standard 2.5-ton, canvas-covered army truck with wooden benches running the length of both sides of the cargo bed.

south of Düren. That upriver destruction and swift downstream flooding caused an indefinite delay[1] in Simpson's plan to advance his Ninth Army over the Roer, and ultimately across the Roer Valley to the Rhine. Such action by the retreating Germans put a vast portion of the west bank of the Rhine "ahead of the American forces under three feet of water."[2] According to one historian, not only was the Roer a raging torrent (estimated at about ten miles per hour), but also above the town of Linnich, it stretched a thousand yards across, instead of the usual one hundred feet from bank to bank.[3]

Returning from Paris on February 19, Pop observed that his company was still bivouacked in the vicinity of Waldfeucht. On the following day, he reported on his visit to Paris to Captain Fiori. Not surprisingly, the other "guys in the company" also had many questions for him, which he answered to the best of his ability. He wrote: "They mentioned I look[ed] weak and tired. Are they kidding?"

Later, on February 20, he noted in his diary that "T/4 [Claude E.] Scramlin," had returned to their outfit from the hospital. By way of explanation, he wrote that his fellow crewman and friend had been wounded previously in Pattern, Germany.

On the next day, he described an inadvertent tragedy, which struck his squadron earlier that day: a "Baker trooper" (a member of Troop B) was killed in a booby trap explosion. Also, that day he learned that the 17th Cavalry Squadron would rejoin its parent organization, the U.S. 15th Cavalry Group, including the 15th Cavalry Squadron and Group Headquarters, which was then completing its move into Holland. He explained, "We left them in France, last summer, when we left Brest."

In the early afternoon on February 22, Dad mentioned witnessing a particular shocking sight when a truck loaded with six combat engineers, their equipment, and an unnamed second lieutenant passed by their

---

[1] It took two weeks before the Roer River waters became stabile enough to allow Simpson's Ninth Army to risk a crossing. Taaffe, *Marshall and His Generals*, 282.
[2] Barry Turner, *Countdown to Victory: The Final European Campaigns of World War II*, (NY: William Morrow, 2004), 189; the dam destruction by the Germans on February 9, held up the Ninth Army's attack for another two weeks. "Battle of Germany," *Army Talks*, Vol. IV, No.2 (May 22, 1945), 8.
[3] Atkinson, *The Guns at Last Light,* 537.

position and triggered an enemy mine in the road. He wrote, "It blew every one of them to nothing." He described it as a particularly awful experience that "turned a lot of stomachs", as they were unable to find even "one [whole] body [among all] the mess." That night he mentioned that elements of the 8th ("Thundering Herd") Armored Division were "coming in" to relieve his outfit so they could leave their positions on line and return to Holland to rejoin the 15th Cavalry Group.

By the middle of February 1945, the 115th Cavalry Group[1] relieved the 15th Cavalry Group (minus the detached 17th Cavalry Squadron) of its security mission in the Atlantic Coastal Sector (the Brittany Peninsula and its environs). The 15th Cavalry Group then reported to the XVI Corps, at Sittard, Holland. By February 17, the 15th Cavalry Group completed its rail and motor march across France into Belgium. At last, it reassembled as a complete unit near the small Dutch town of Brunssum, south of Sittard, after it regained administrative control over the previously detached 17th Cavalry Squadron.

On February 18, the entire 15th Cavalry Group was attached to Maj. Gen. Paul Baade's 35th ("Santa Fe") Infantry Division, and assumed responsibility for the sector of the Roer River front that had formerly been held by the 17th Cavalry Squadron alone. By February 27, the 15th Cavalry Group returned to XVI Corps control and began the mission of relieving the 8th Thundering Herd Armored Division along the front facing Roermond, Holland.

On the following night, the 15th Cavalry Squadron advanced into the town of Roermond. At the same time, the 17th Cavalry Squadron sent patrols across the Roer and reported "no enemy contact." Then, the 35th Santa Fe Division pushed across the river, and its lead elements became situated north of Herkenbosch, Holland.[2]

General Eisenhower continued with his "broad-front" strategy, in which forces under Bradley and British Field Marshal Montgomery

---

[1] The 115th Cavalry Group (Mechanized) arrived in France in January 1945, and was attached to the VI Corps, seeing combat in France before entering Germany later in 1945. Rottman, *World War II US Cavalry Groups*, 41.

[2] The prior three paragraphs draw on material from TLR at 14 and 15.

advanced slowly and steadily to the east. Ike's idea was to push Monty's 21st Army Group, reinforced by the Ninth Army, across the Rhine into the north of Germany, while the First and Third Armies of Bradley's 12th Army Group crossed the Rhine south of the Ruhr Valley to link up with Monty's forces east of the Rhine. While this twin advance took place, Devers's 6th Army Group was tasked with shielding the right flank of the 12th Army Group.[1]

Finally, on February 23, 1945, the conditions were deemed suitable for General Simpson to launch Operation Grenade, the Ninth Army's crossing of the Roer, between Düren and Roermond, with ten divisions advancing east on a forty-mile front. Simpson's troops were positioned essentially abreast; from left to right, they were Anderson's XVI Corps, Gillem's XIII Corps, and McLain's XIX Corps, reinforced on the southern, right flank by Collins's VII Corps of Hodges's First Army.

That attack completely surprised the Germans, as the waters of the Roer were still some eighty yards wide with a current running at five to eight miles an hour. Out of all the divisions advancing across the Roer Plain, Macon's 83rd Thunderbolt Division was the first to reach Düsseldorf, and make the claim: "first to the Rhine."[2] By March 1, Simpson's Ninth Army reached the Rhine and men of McLain's XIX Corps nearly reached the bridge at Krefeld when the Germans blew it up in their faces. At that point, Anderson's XVI Corps was ordered to clean up the remaining pockets of enemy resistance in his sector west of the Rhine.[3] Later, they linked up with the Canadian First Army to their north before crossing the Rhine and continued their planned encirclement of the Ruhr region, Germany's industrial heartland.[4]

By the afternoon of February 27, Dad and his mates were told to straighten up their duffle bags and store them away. He then wrote,

---

[1] Derek S. Zumbro, *Battle for the Ruhr* (Lawrence: University Press of Kansas, 2006), 66; Atkinson, *The Guns at Last Light,* 406.
[2] Turner, *Countdown to Victory*, 189, 206.
[3] Taaffe, *Marshall and His Generals,* 282-283.
[4] John S. D. Eisenhower, *The Bitter Woods* (NY: G.P. Putnam, 1969), 438; Atkinson, *The Guns at Last Light,* 536; Weigley, *Eisenhower's Lieutenants,* 606.

somewhat ungrammatically, "This don't look good at all," indicating his belief they were moving out that evening.

On March 1, 1945, his diary indicated, "[We] started our push into Germany; crossed the Roer River." He described the weather as rainy, windy, and cold, making for poor visibility. They continued to on into the dark of night, but could not use their lights, as they were in enemy territory.

Their progress was reduced to a snail's pace as combat engineers had the very dangerous and time-consuming job of walking ahead of their vehicles to detect and remove mines. They had metal detectors to do the job, but often had to get down on their hands and knees to probe the ground with bayonets, feeling their way, yard by yard, to clear the road in "pitch blackness." Pop noted that some of the anti-tank mines were concealed in piles of cow dung along the roadway, while others were "doubled-decked"[1] (one stacked on top of another) and others were buried deep in the ground and had to be deactivated on the surface or blown in place.

As much as he admired the skill and courage of the demolition specialists, Dad resisted the urge to dismount his tank to get a better view of the demining process; rather, his diary makes plain that he and the rest of the crew remained right where they were, in their armored vehicles. Their discretion was likely a consequence of the many warnings they had received concerning various anti-personnel mines typically sown near those buried by the enemy on roads, including the S-Mine (the "Bouncing Betty") and the Schu mine. The former, when tripped, was extremely lethal as it bounced out of the ground waist high and sprayed jagged metal in all directions, out to a range of twenty-five to thirty yards. The German Schu mine or "toe popper," was made of wood to avoid detection and was designed to maim, not kill at least not immediately, as it would blow off a soldier's foot once the pressure pad was released.[2]

---

[1] When a tank detonates a mine, the explosion may break the track or tear off a bogey wheel. But when the Germans stacked mines, one on top of another, they were far more lethal, and that doubling up generated sufficient force to blow a hole through the thin armor on the belly of the tank and likely kill the entire crew. Cooper, *Death Traps*, 89.
[2] McManus, *The Dead and Those About to Die*, 144-145; Balkoski, *From Brittany to the Reich*, 281.

Dad also described an incident involving the 17th Cavalry Squadron's lead vehicle, which had stopped earlier that day to obtain information in "Rathenbock." In trying to catch up with the lead tank in the column, the jeep ran over a mine in the road, which blew the jeep (driven by one of his pals[1]) and a lieutenant, "clear off the road." He indicated that, "Gimp was OK, but frightened" while the lieutenant was in bad shape, suffering "chest injuries and three compound fractures of the leg." He noted the terrible irony of the situation: two entire recon troops, the medics, and seven tanks had rolled over the exact same spot where the "little jeep" was "blown to Hell."

From that episode, Pop relearned a disturbing fact: becoming a casualty can result from simply being in the wrong place at the wrong time. He saw again that there was randomness to death in combat and that fate clearly played a role. That was an especially troubling discovery because it meant that their experience, physical skills, weapons and tactical training, honed over time might ultimately be for naught.[2]

A short time later, Dad seemed fully recovered from the shock of that traumatic incident, as he wrote in his diary, "still in Holland" and he observed that the people ran out to greet them, "just like in France, without the wine and beautiful girls."

On the first day of March 1945 the 15th Cavalry Group along with an attached battery from the 691st Field Artillery Battalion and a company of engineers, crossed the Roer River at "Oersbeck." Their mission was to proceed north and reconnoiter a narrow zone through dense forest and the Siegfried Line toward Venlo, Holland, paying special attention to the Roermond–Venlo Road.

By late afternoon, the 15th Cavalry Group, with the 17th Cavalry Recce Squadron in the lead, reached Herkenbosch. However, as the roads were heavily mined, the situation demanded they come to a complete halt while the attached engineers worked in darkness again to carefully clear the minefields.[3]

---

[1] Sgt. Glenn E. Overlander, a soldier in the 17th Cavalry Squadron, received the Bronze Star Medal (Meritorious) and Purple Heart Medal based on his service in World War II. TLR, 28-29.
[2] Kindsvatter, *American Soldiers,* 59-60.
[3] TLR, 15.

In the morning hours of March 2, the 17th Cavalry Squadron found an out-of-the-way route north to Venlo through some forest firebreaks, arriving there around dusk, following a brief skirmish with some German soldiers in the woods. In the meantime, Troop B pushed north toward Straelen, Germany.

On the night of March 2nd, the mission of the 15th Cavalry Group was changed to provide protection to the left flank of Task Force "Byrnes" (the 35th Santa Fe Division) as it turned from Straelen and proceeded to the Rhine. The entire group was then given the task to maintain contact with the British Second Army, which was advancing from the north.[1]

Pop diarized that most of the day they traveled in the woods toward Venlo, "cross country style," and for mile after mile they saw nothing but spruce and pine trees. He reported that their advance went through what looked like a German training area. He described seeing tank traps and gun emplacements, and he described entrenchments that ran for "miles and miles." He remarked that they ran their vehicles in all directions, careening around in "zig-zag" style through the area, until they came to the main road leading to Venlo. That helter-skelter technique sounds somewhat reckless, considering the many casualties they had sustained earlier from German mines, but time then was of the essence, as they were in hot pursuit, racing against the clock to encircle and capture a retreating enemy before they could get to the river and demolish the bridges across the Rhine.

In the villages they passed, Dad noted seeing only a few civilians, "mostly old people and little kids." Yet, he observed that practically all those still residing in the area had hung white bedding material outside their windows to indicate their non-hostile intentions.

On entering Venlo, Holland, he observed happy civilians scrambling out of their homes in order to stand along the streets and wave welcome. He noted that they crowded around and greatly slowed their progress. He also made a curious observation, "everybody in the city wore Orange." (He apparently had no clue that Orange is the color of the Dutch Royal family.)

In the next photo, the animated crowd of townsfolk lining the street appear pleased to welcome the American 17th Cavalry Squadron as they entered their village.

---

[1] Ibid.

On the back of the photograph, Pop wrote that the men of the liberated town wanted to shake their hands, and the women wanted to give them hugs and kisses. He identified "Mike, my driver," on the left and Captain Fiori (their company commander, or "CO" for short) in the sunglasses, who was struggling to exercise his command authority; he was likely telling them to put away their chocolate candy bars and cigarettes in order to avoid unauthorized fraternization with those friendly Dutch females.

Troop B of the 17th Cavalry Squadron pushed on through roadblocks and light opposition beyond Straelen on the morning of March 3, and advanced close to Geldern, Germany. By that afternoon, the squadron made contact with British forces at Geldern and Walbeck.

Next, the 15th Cavalry Group obtained an additional mission to seize the town of Issum to cut off the German force on the Geldern–Issum Road that was delaying the British advance. The 15th Cavalry Squadron then proceeded via Sevelen toward Issum, Germany, while the 17th Cavalry Squadron pushed in from the west. As Troop A of the 17th Squadron approached Sevelen, a German delaying force opened fire on them, while attempting to escape to the north. Sixty German POWs were reported captured, while Troop A sustained only slight casualties in that skirmish.

By the morning of March 4, the 15th Cavalry Squadron reached Issum, exactly at the moment the enemy blew the bridge across a stream beyond the town. A mop-up operation in and around Issum was accomplished on the morning of March 5, and by the end of the day, the British were able to make their advance into town.[1]

---

[1] The previous three paragraphs draw on TLR, 15-16.

In a March 5, 1945 *Stars and Stripes* article, a war correspondent reported that the German bridgehead west of Wesel (northeast of Issum) had "shriveled into an escape gap only ten miles wide" as the Ninth Army had spread out along the banks of the Rhine across a thirty-mile front. It was reported that the only sizeable German concentration west of the Rhine in that area had been trapped along a bend in the river northwest of Duisberg, and the 2nd Hell on Wheels Armored Division had wiped it out. It was also reported that a small pocket of enemy resistance had been "nearly cleaned out" by the 35th Santa Fe Division in the Geldern area, and that the 15th Cavalry Group was continuing its drive to the northeast toward the Rhine.

By March 6, 1945, Krefeld and Homberg, Germany, were cleared of all enemy resistance and the Santa Fe Division had captured Rheinberg. Thus, the Ninth Army was on the Rhine on its whole front, except in the extreme north; the enemy had evacuated all supply and administrative units to the east side of the Rhine and the wounded were ferried across the river at Büderich.[1]

The British attacked astride the Issum–Wesel road on March 6, while the 15th Cavalry Group command post moved to Sevelen, Germany, and the 17th Cavalry Squadron went into reserve.[2] By March 7, General Hodges reported that Cologne had fallen. Not only that, but also the Hohenzollen Bridge, connecting the city to the east bank of the Rhine had been blown into the river.[3]

By then it was clear that the Allied push to the Rhine had been a resounding success. The Ninth Army had advanced more than fifty miles from the Roer River to the Rhine in less than two weeks. It had linked up with the Canadian First Army of Monty's 21st Army Group on March 3rd at Geldern, Germany, west of Duisburg. In doing so, the two forces together suffered "23,000 casualties while capturing 51,000 Germans and killing and wounding 38,000 more." However, in spite of their terrible

---

[1] "Battle of Germany," *Army Talks*, Vol. IV, No.2 (May 22, 1945), 8; Zumbro, *Battle for the Ruhr*, 124.
[2] TLR, 16.
[3] Atkinson, *The Guns at Last Light*, 546.

losses, the surviving enemy had made their escape across the Rhine River after destroying the final six bridges between Duisburg and Wesel.[1]

Their next mission for the Allied forces was to capture an existing bridge or two. Absent that, the alternative would require a full-fledged amphibious assault across the Rhine.

The photograph above shows Dad and members of the headquarters section of Fox Company, 17th Cavalry Squadron, catching a breather somewhere in the European countryside. From left to right, he identified Rosenberger, himself, John Hakim, Captain Fiori and Lieutenant Bomba.

As they continued their advance, Dad described seeing "lots of dead Huns and smashed bazookas" all along the road on March 5. The enemy "bazooka" he referred to was the cheap, but powerful *panzerfaust*, a light man-portable, hand-held anti-tank weapon, roughly the equivalent of a U.S. bazooka. The major difference between the two was that the *panzerfaust* (meaning "tank fist" in German) could pierce up to 200 millimeters of American armor, while a U.S. crew-served, 2.36-inch bazooka could not

---

[1] Ibid., 541.

penetrate the frontal armor of any German tank.[1] It was a highly effective one-shot, disposable weapon. A single German soldier could fire that recoilless device with a minimum of training. From the crook off his arm, he would trigger a toggle switch atop the metal tube launcher to fire a devastating shaped-charge warhead, capable of knocking out virtually any Allied armored vehicle.[2]

During early March 1945, the 15th Cavalry Group continued its mission of maintaining contact between the right flank of the First Canadian Army and the left flank of Simpson's Ninth Army. By March 12, Pop diarized the good news that their unit was finally getting their hands on the new light tank (the M24 Chaffee), which mounted the more potent 75-mm cannon.

Their Stuart tanks were replaced on a one-for-one basis, whereupon he wrote enthusiastically, "We can shoot now." As indicated by his remark, acquisition of that 75-mm main gun did much for the American cavalryman's confidence; finally, they could take on enemy armor on a more equal footing, so long as they got close enough to shoot at a German panzer's thinner flank or rear armor.

Dad's diary entry actually mentioned the "T26," which eventually became the M26 Pershing tank, named after First World War Gen. John J. Pershing. That tank evolved from the M4 Sherman and was equipped with a 90-mm main gun, but it was totally unsuited for cavalry reconnaissance missions. Thus, it is clear that he meant to reference prototype "T24", which became the M24 Chaffee that ultimately replaced his obsolescent Stuart. Moreover, the M24 was the tank to which he had been introduced, and in which he received training back in January 1945. The clincher is that only a small number of M26 Pershing tanks ever made it to Europe during World War II, and the 3rd Spearhead and 9th ("Phantom") Armored Divisions of the First Army were the tankers who put them to use in February 1945.[3]

Pictured below is my father leaning proudly on his new Chaffee tank, which came equipped with the same power plant as the Stuart tank: twin

---

[1] Reynolds, *Men of Steel*, 23.
[2] MacDonald, *The Siegfried Line Campaign*, 25.
[3] Steven J. Zaloga, *M26/M46 Pershing Tank: 1943-1953*. (Botley, UK: Osprey Publishing, 2002), 18, 19.

220-horsepower Cadillac 8-cylinder liquid-cooled engines with two Hydramatic drive transmissions. (Note the steel tracks and leather muzzle cover on the end of the main gun to keep dirt, dust, moist weather, and other obstructions out of the gun barrel.)

The M24 Chaffee's gear changes were controlled by engine load and the tank's transfer unit mechanically selected speed ranges (two forward and one in reverse); also, its turret compartment was much larger, measuring about 60 inches in diameter, compared to less than four feet of turret diameter in the Stuart. That increased roominess allowed for a crew of four or five men. If a fifth man was available, his duty was to serve in the turret as cannoneer/loader in combat.

One of Dad's crewmates, Tec/4 Claude Scramlin, is shown above peering out of the driver's hatch. His was a very demanding job since the M24, like the Stuart, had no steering wheel. Instead there were two steering brake levers, right and left, which when in the forward position allowed the driver to advance the tank with the use of the accelerator foot pedal. To turn the tank, the driver pulled the lever toward the direction desired. To turn the tank to the right, he pulled back on the right-hand lever; to make a left turn he pulled back on the left-hand lever. Pulling on both steering

249

levers allowed the driver to slow down or stop, depending on the effort applied.[1]

The glacis plate of the M24's welded front steel hull had a thickness of no more than an inch, but it was sloped sixty degrees from the vertical, and from the bottom it sloped upward forty-five degrees, forming a "V". Also, the sides of the hull sloped inward seventy-eight degrees at the bottom.[2] Those hull sloping improvements made the Chaffee much less vulnerable than its predecessor. The Stuart, by contrast, possessed unbelievably dangerous vertical side armor, without any slope whatsoever. Only the addition of stacks of sandbags to the sides of those antiquated vehicles provided any level of protection from German anti-tank fire.

By Monday, March 12, 1945, the 15th Cavalry Group had moved to Lintfort, Germany, west of Sevelen and Geldern, and passed to the control of Maj. Gen. Ray Porter's 75th Infantry Division of Anderson's XVI Corps, Ninth Army. Their mission was to provide security by patrolling along the Orsay–Büderich road to the east, while Allied planning and preparations were being made for the Rhine River crossing.[3]

---

[1] *Driving Instructions: Light Tank, M5, M5A1, Motor Carriage, M8*, 5, 12 and 13; *Department* of the Army Technical Manual, TM 9-729, *Light Tank M24*
[2] U.S. Army Technical Manual, TM 9-729, *Light Tank M2*, (Washington, D.C.: U.S. Government Printing Office), published from 1944-1951, 5.
[3] TLR, 16.

16. ACROSS THE RHINE & INTO GERMANY'S RUHR VALLEY

As the Allies encountered German conscripts on the battlefield, aged between sixteen and sixty, it became clear to them that the war's end was fast approaching. Those individuals lacked proper training and they were not made of the same material as the heel clicking, goose-stepping troops of the early 1940s. Instead, they were the last-ditch levy, the Volkssturm (the "People's Storm") that had been gathered up to save what remained of Hitler's Thousand-Year Third Reich.

Intended to replace the massive losses of manpower incurred during 1944, the Volkssturm were the bottom of the manpower barrel. They were all that was left of the soldier material then available to throw at the advancing Allies in a rapidly shrinking Germany. They constituted a sad group of aging men, young boys, and convalescing, disabled veterans, deemed still able to use a weapon. Most of them wore civilian clothing, as they had been given very little in the way of uniforms.[1] In general, they lacked the usual steel helmets; instead, they wore a motley assortment of civilian caps, and armbands emblazoned with the words: "*Deutsche Wehrmacht.*"[2] Recruited in desperation as replacements, they were a mob of untrained civilians having little combat value; their officers referred to them as "casserole" since they were a mixture of old meat and green vegetables.[3]

In many cases, those last-ditch replacements were armed with foreign and outdated weapons, and only a few received more than perfunctory training of between ten to fourteen days.[4] Nonetheless, when members of the *Volkssturm* were encountered by American GIs, they had to be on their

---

[1] To avoid being shot as irregulars, members of the *Volkssturm* were outfitted in a variety of uniforms from the stocks of the police, railways, border guards, postal service, National Socialist truck drivers, the Reich Labour Service, the Hitler Youth and the German Labour Front. Stargardt, *The German War*, 458.
[2] Zumbro, *Battle for the Ruhr*, 60-70; Clark, *Crossing the Rhine*, 278.
[3] Beevor, *The Fall of Berlin 1945*, 316.
[4] Stargardt, *The German War*, 457. As unimpressive as they were, no fewer than 175,000 *Volkssturm* were killed fighting the professional military forces of Russia and the Western Allies. Evans, *The Third Reich at War*, 676.

toes. Although most of those ill-trained militiamen were inept in terms of military effectiveness, there remained a few who were dangerous and still fanatically loyal to Hitler after years of heavy indoctrination.

By the end of February and into early March 1945, Eisenhower commanded a vast military force numbering some four million men, including Monty's 21st Army Group in the north, Bradley's 12th Army Group immediately below and Devers's 6th Army Group next even farther to the south. All together this force included twenty-one army corps and seventy-three fully mechanized divisions.[1]

The Germans, on the other hand, were having extreme difficulty countering the rapid advance and mobility of the Allied forces, consolidating along the west bank of the Rhine. The bulk of the enemy army in Western Europe had been pushed east across the Rhine River, but rear-guard forces remaining on the west bank faced capture or destruction, as they continued to be compressed into an ever-tightening pocket near the town of Wesel.[2]

Planning for the Rhine crossing had begun well before the Allies landed in Normandy, and bridging equipment and assault boats had been assembled for that purpose. However, a fortuitous event occurred for the Americans on March 7, 1945 when the Ludendorff Railway Bridge was captured intact, but somewhat damaged, at Remagen. Although German engineers had wired the bridge for destruction, the main charge failed to detonate properly and the explosion was insufficient to drop it into the river. When the charge was triggered, the bridge still stood after the black smoke cleared.[3] Dismantling the explosive charge as they advanced, forces from the 9th Phantom Armored Division of Hodges's First Army charged across to the east side of the Rhine. By the evening of March 8, eight thousand GIs occupied a bridgehead two miles wide and a mile deep.[4] At last, Allied forces in the west had made their way to the east bank of the Rhine. According to one British military historian, it was the first time an

---

[1] Charles B. MacDonald, *The Mighty Endeavor* (New York: Oxford University Press, 1969), 406; Zumbro, *Battle for the Ruhr*, 85.
[2] Ibid., 124.
[3] Charles B. MacDonald, *The Last Offensive: U.S. Army in World War II, ETO* (Washington, DC: Office of the Chief of Military History, 1973), 217.
[4] Atkinson, The Guns at Last Light, 547-552.

"enemy or invader had crossed the Rhine into Germany since Napoleon had done so in 1805."[1]

The fast flowing Rhine was as much a psychological barrier as it was a physical barrier, and once the Americans and British crossed it, German morale plummeted and Hitler was forced to rely on his ever-decreasing band of zealots for survival.[2] By that point, there was no doubt as to the outcome of the war.[3]

General Eisenhower was delighted to hear the news by telephone of the capture of the Ludendorff Bridge. Bradley asked if pushing his entire force over the river (more than four divisions) would interfere with his plans. Ike responded, "Go ahead and shove over at least five divisions instantly, and anything else that is necessary to make certain of our hold."[4] Consequently, Eisenhower altered his original plan for the First Army to drive south and link up with Patton's Third Army near Koblenz. With the capture of the last intact bridge across the Rhine at Remagen, all available U.S. forces were pushed rapidly toward and across that bridge.[5]

By March 9, 1945, the First Army had enlarged the Remagen bridgehead to a depth of more than three miles. Immediate German efforts to destroy the Ludendorff Bridge by air and artillery were unsuccessful. At the same time that troops were pouring across that bridge, American engineers were installing floating treadway bridges. When the Ludendorff Railroad Bridge finally collapsed on March 17, three pontoon bridges had been completed and were in full use by American forces.[6]

On March 21, three corps from Patton's Third Army had reached the Rhine.[7] Two days later, the 5th ("Red Diamond") Infantry Division of Manton Eddy's XII Corps had crossed the Rhine "with hardly a casualty." Patton telephoned Bradley, "tell the world we're across. I want the world to know the Third Army made it before Monty starts across!"[8]

---

[1] Gilbert, *The Second World War: A Complete History*, 648.
[2] Turner, *Countdown to Victory*, 319.
[3] Rooney, *My War*, 255.
[4] Eisenhower, *Crusade in Europe*, 380.
[5] Zumbro, *Battle for the Ruhr*, 97, 98.
[6] Ibid., 100.
[7] Atkinson, *The Guns at Last Light*, 557.
[8] Eisenhower, *The Bitter Woods*, 440.

Within a day, the Red Diamond Division had established a bridgehead on the far side of the Rhine that was five miles deep. Within days, Patton celebrated his transit over the Rhine by riding halfway across a pontoon bridge at Oppenheim and exiting his vehicle, he undid his fly and urinated in the river.[1] According to one historian, the general's efforts produced "a long, high, steady stream."[2] It was another of his theatrical wartime exhibitions, as Old Blood and Guts announced with glee, "I have been looking forward to this for a long time."[3]

Although Patton was often profane and less than politically correct (to borrow a current phrase), FDR was quite enamored of the old cavalryman, whom he considered "a carry-over" into modern times of old-fashioned spirit and dash. In fact, much earlier in the war he said of Patton: "He is our greatest fighting general, and sheer joy."[4]

Among U.S. Army generals in World War II, Patton may be considered second only to the greatest American military thespian: the vainglorious Douglas MacArthur. Both had massive egos and made full use of a variety of props during the war. Patton wore a lacquered, highly polished helmet with bright shiny stars, as well as jodhpurs, cavalry boots and a brace of holstered, ivory-handled revolvers. MacArthur, on the other hand, had his trademark corncob pipe, aviator sunglasses, and an old, crumpled uniform cap, adorned with a mass of spaghetti-like gold braid. Both were incredible self-promoters, but in Dad's mind, the imperious MacArthur took the prize for pomposity when he waded ashore at Leyte in the Philippines and

---

[1] On March 25, 1945, Churchill also showed his contempt for Hitler and the Nazi regime by relieving himself in the Rhine after crossing in a landing craft with British Field Marshal Montgomery. Caddick-Adams, *Snow & Steel*, 669.

[2] Stephen E. Ambrose, *The Victors* (New York: Simon & Schuster, 1998), 329.

[3] Blumenson, *Patton*, 257; Atkinson, *The Guns at Last Light*, 558.

[4] D'Este, *Patton: A Genius for War*, 755; Larrabee, *Commander in Chief*, 486. FDR believed MacArthur was a threat to democracy and the most dangerous person in America. Brands, *Traitor to His Class*, 261; Truman referred to MacArthur as "God's right-hand man" and ultimately fired him for insubordination during the Korean conflict. H.W. Brands, *The General vs. the President* (New York, Doubleday, 2016), 176, 398.

grabbed the headlines by announcing, "I have returned!"[1] (Despite his everlasting distaste for the late General, I realize that MacArthur was not then, nor is he now, without a large cadre of strong admirers; yet, I tend to agree with Dad's evaluation.)

The operational plan for the invasion of Germany, developed long before D-Day, called for the main effort across the Rhine to be made in the north. As Monty's 21st Army Group had remained on the left of the line throughout the campaign, his forces were charged with making the main assault, but since he had only fifteen divisions in the 21st Army Group, he requested the attachment of Simpson's Ninth Army for the crossing, together with two airborne divisions, bringing his strength to over twenty-nine divisions.[2]

On the night of March 23-24, 1945, the crossing of the Rhine in the north took place at Wesel during Operation Plunder; by the morning of March 24, "thirteen U.S. infantry battalions held the east bank on an eight-mile front." The two assault units in Anderson's XVI Corps, the 30th Old Hickory and 79th Cross of Lorraine Divisions, also participated in that "Plunder" assault upstream from Wesel near Rheinberg, suffering only minimal casualties in that operation.[3] After Montgomery's forces got across the Rhine, the 21st Army Group, north of the Ruhr drove to the east and northeastward from Wesel, and Simpson's Ninth Army, spearheaded by Anderson's XVI Corps established bridgeheads north of Duisberg. By March 25, all organized enemy resistance west of the Rhine was finished.[4]

On March 28, Ike informed Montgomery that Simpson's Ninth Army would revert to Bradley's 12th Army Group command "once he linked up with Bradley in the Kassel-Paderborn area." Not surprisingly, that order was not well received by the British Field Marshal; to him, it was perceived

---

[1] Unger and Hirshson, *George Marshal: A Biography,* 345. Nonetheless, one distinguished military historian argues that the photograph of MacArthur with "his face inscribed with a stern 'sense of destiny'" while coming ashore at Leyte was not a staged theatrical performance. See Richard B. Frank, *MacArthur* (New York: Palgrave Macmillan, 2007), 105-106.
[2] Eisenhower, *The Bitter Woods,* 441.
[3] Atkinson, *The Guns at Last Light,* 441, 561; Taaffe, *Marshall and His Generals.* 291.
[4] "Battle of Germany," *Army Talks,* Vol. IV, No.2 (May 22, 1945), 9.

255

as "a last indignity."¹ Without Simpson's Ninth Army, Monty had inadequate strength to advance to Berlin. Eisenhower was not of a mind to sustain the significant American casualties that such an endeavor would entail; he and General Marshall knew that those forces would most likely be needed later against the Japanese in the Pacific. As an aside, many other American commanders in Europe were pleased with that result, as it showed Monty, the Hero of El Alamein, that Ike was in charge and was "his own ground commander."²

South of the Ruhr region, Hodges's First Army left the bridgehead at Remagen and linked up with Patton's Third Army, coming up from the south. Then, on April 1, 1945, Easter Sunday, the First Army turned north and raced to complete its junction with the Ninth Army in the vicinity of Lippstadt, east of Paderborn.³ That link up occurred when the 3rd Spearhead Armored Division of Collins's VII Corps made contact with the 2nd Hell on Wheels Armored Division of the Ninth Army's XIX Corps.⁴ The convergence of those two divisions "snapped shut" the American pincers. It completed a full encirclement of the Ruhr, trapped Germany's Army Group B in a massive cordon, measuring some seventy-five miles wide by fifty miles deep. In his excitement, Ike called it the largest double envelopment in military history.⁵

Included in the Ruhr Pocket were the German Fifteenth Army, the Fifth Panzer Army, two corps of the German First Parachute Army and elements of many other enemy forces, totaling more than 300,000 enemy troops, who fought on until the middle of April. Among that group were

---

[1] The friction and distrust between Montgomery and the American high command dated from 1943 during the Allied campaign in Sicily, when many U.S. officers thought that Monty was trying to grab all the glory for the British forces and relegate the Americans to nothing more than a supporting role. Yeide, *The Longest Battle*, 21.
[2] Atkinson, *The Guns at Last Light*, 577-578; Mark Perry, *Partners in Command* (New York: Penguin Press, 2007), 354-355.
[3] John P. Irwin, *Another River, Another Town* (NY: Random House, 2002), 28; "Battle of Germany," *Army Talks*, Vol. IV, No.2 (May 22, 1945), 10.
[4] Eisenhower, *The Bitter Woods*, 451.
[5] Atkinson, *The Guns at Last Light*, 583-584; MacDonald, *The Last Offensive*, 362.

twenty-six generals and an admiral of the defunct *Kriegsmarine*.[1] That gathering of German POWs amounted to the largest number taken during the entire war, including those captured at Stalingrad or at Tunis in North Africa.[2] Later that month, German Field Marshal Walter Model ordered Army Group B disbanded. On April 21, the day after Adolf Hitler's fifty-sixth birthday, Model walked into the woods near Düsseldorf and "blew his brains out" with his service pistol.[3] He had declared earlier in the war that honor required a German field marshal to never surrender and become a prisoner of war.[4]

The loss of the industrial cities of the Ruhr was Germany's death knell. That region extended east from the Rhine about sixty miles and it included the cities of Duisberg, Essen, and Dortmund. Bordered on the north by the Lippe River, it was critically important to Nazi survival, as it constituted the heart of Germany's chemical and munitions industries, and was their primary source of steel production and coal.[5]

As part of the Allied strategy to encircle the Ruhr, the 15th Cavalry Recce Squadron was the first element of the 15th Cavalry Group to cross the Rhine. Its mission was to relieve a battalion of the 30th Old Hickory Division facing Lippendorf on the "Rhine Island" between the Lippe River and the Lippe Canal.

On March 26, the remainder of the 15th Cavalry Group followed, including the 17th Cavalry Recce Squadron, and by March 27, the entire 15th Cavalry Group became Anderson's XVI Corps mobile reserve. Two days later, the 15th Cavalry Group passed to the control of McLain's XIX Corps, and by the following day, it had advanced to a crossing of the Lippe River at Dorsten, Germany.[6]

In his diary, Pop wrote that he crossed the Rhine on the afternoon of March 26. On seeing the river for the first time, he observed that it was not

---

[1] Zumbro, *Battle for the Ruhr*, 260; Taaffe, *Marshall land His Generals*, 292.
[2] Atkinson, *The Guns at Last Light*, 585; Perry, *Partners in Command*, 356; MacDonald, *Company Commander*, 188.
[3] Atkinson, *The Guns at Last Light*, 584; Evans, *The Third Reich at War*, 730.
[4] Model had been highly critical of German Field Marshal Friedrich Paulus for surrendering to the Russians at Stalingrad in 1943; Model announced, "Such a thing is just not possible." Blair, *Ridgway's Paratroopers*, 485.
[5] Zumbro, *Battle for the Ruhr*, 38; Atkinson, *The Guns at Last Light*, 223.
[6] TLR, 16.

as large as he had expected, but he did think it comparable to the Schuylkill River in Pennsylvania. His guess was accurate as to the width of the Rhine, but what he didn't understand was that the Rhine "formed an extraordinary moat against invasion from the west." While it may not have impressed him as being that large, what he did not understand was the Rhine River's steep banks and strong currents, "fast enough that engineers compared any crossing to 'a short sea voyage.'" It was not fordable anywhere, "even at low water," as winter flooding had whipped up the currents in some stretches to almost eleven miles per hour.[1]

According to his diary entries for March 27-31, 1945, he noted: "These last five days, were tough ones." Pushing forward and advancing from early morning to late at night, sometimes we don't hit the bivouac area until around midnight." He mentioned sleeping in his cold and cramped tank turret when he wasn't sleeping on the ground.[2] He wrote that they could not make use of the damaged German structures for shelter, as the buildings couldn't be trusted due to the potential hazard of booby traps while advancing into Germany's interior.

Pop commented nervously that they had bypassed "many Huns which means we are right in the middle of them, and they are all around us." All along the road, he described seeing a "steady stream of civilians coming toward us." He said they had been informed that those poor souls, fleeing to the rear were mostly displaced persons (DPs), who had been liberated from German work camps.[3] He described seeing very hungry people the day before, "cutting meat from a dead horse" lying along the roadside. He expressed sadness for that throng of tired and worn-out men and women, shuffling along the road with nothing but despair on their faces. Observing them carefully, he remarked they "look undernourished and awfully tired"

---

[1] Atkinson, *The Guns at Last Light*, 546-547.
[2] Due to limited space, sleeping in a tank was anything but comfortable. The crew slept in their clothes with blankets spread around the interior. No one got to stretch out, but the "worst spot" was the gunner's seat (Dad's position) where a man had to sleep "half sitting up." Pyle, *Brave Men*, 268.
[3] The Nazis incarcerated foreign workers (male and female) and forced them to work as slaves in German factories, mines, and farms. Hundreds of Polish soldiers had their POW status stripped away and were assigned to German farms to bring in the harvest. Mazower, *Hitler's Empire: How the Nazis Ruled Europe*, 295-297.

in their ragged, threadbare clothing. At the time, he also observed with suspicion some of those he saw along the way, who looked well fed and of military age, and he wondered if any were enemy soldiers who perhaps had recently changed into "civvies." Without having the chance to check them, they continued on their way, churning the dust while advancing deeper into Germany. He wrote, "All we do is keep our eyes open and guns handy."

As the American forces pushed their way through the Ruhr Valley, they encountered ever-increasing numbers of freed forced laborers, "primarily from Russia, Poland and Serbia." Many of them had been coerced to work in the heavy industrial plants of the Ruhr, while others toiled on neighboring farms. After their liberation, hordes of uncontrolled individuals exacted revenge on their former Nazi masters, plundering "every corner of every building in search of valuables, while others simply sought food."[1] They wandered the German countryside carrying deadly contagious diseases, such as tuberculosis, diphtheria, chronic dysentery, and lice-borne typhus.[2] Each had likely contracted a life-threatening disease in the work camps under Nazi brutality, as they were denied medical care and a proper diet.

---

[1] Zumbro, Battle for the Ruhr, 329.
[2] Atkinson, *The Guns at Last Light*, 329.

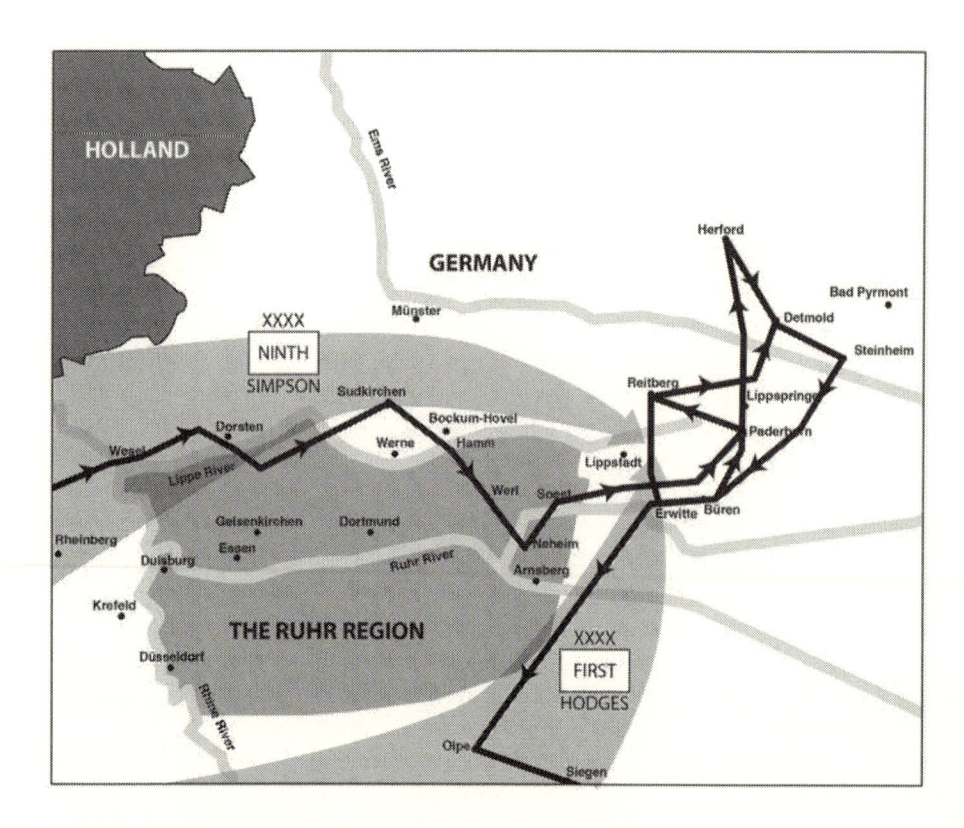

The map above traces the convoluted, twisting path of the 15th Cavalry Group during 1945 while they were assigned to Simpson's Ninth Army.

By late March 1945, McLain's XIX Corps had advanced from the Rhine eastward to the Elbe River with such speed that its penetration into enemy territory left "numerous organized enemy forces on both flanks" capable of attacking across the Lippe River to relieve pressure from the Ninth and Third Armies. Several units of the German 116th Panzer Division were scattered in the area south of the Lippe, and they launched coordinated tank and infantry attacks on two occasions against the 83rd Thunderbolt Division's bridgehead at Hamm, but U.S. artillery barrages drove them back.[1]

---

[1] Maj. Morton McD. Jones, "Seizing and Holding a River Line," *Cavalry Journal,* Vol. LIV, no. 6 (November-December 1945), 14.

On March 31, the 17th Cavalry Recce Squadron received orders to tighten the noose around the encircled enemy forces in the Ruhr Pocket by pushing rapidly across the Lippe Canal with a combat team from the 83rd Thunderbolt Division. Their mission was to seize and hold all bridge crossings over the Lippe in its assigned zone near Hamm, but if the crossings were found to be safe and intact, they were to reconnoiter south of the Lippe River and the nearby Lippe Canal. A secondary mission was to establish a counter-reconnaissance screen along the north riverbank, preventing infiltration by either enemy forces or civilians. That evening, the 17th Cavalry Squadron moved from their assembly area in Sudkirchen. In the approach march, they advanced east to the assigned zone, and turned south toward the Lippe River. Then they divided their zone into two sectors: Troop C on the right and Troop A on the left. Each recon troop was assigned a light tank platoon from Company F and forward artillery observers (FOs) from Troop E. Troop B, minus two sections plus an attached light tank platoon from Company F, became the 17th Squadron's mobile reserve. (Pop was apparently with the mobile reserve, since his diary entries for that period relate only to a discourse concerning the composition and health of the POWS they had gathered up.) Troop E (the squadron's self-propelled howitzer troop) went into battery near the squadron command post, and began plotting defensive fire concentrations while they still had some daylight left.[1]

Troop A made contact with some civilians, who reported an estimated battalion of enemy infantry was known to be in the tiny village of Bockum. Five additional POWs were captured by Troop A, and many German soldiers and a tank were reported lurking in the adjacent small village of Hovel. Due to the darkness of night and the heavy roadblocks encountered, Troop A formed a protective screen on the northern outskirts and planned to reconnoiter Bockum-Hovel (as that municipality is known today) at daybreak. Based on Troop C's scouting effort, it was determined that the center span of the bridge at the nearby town of Werne had been destroyed. Thus, Troop C established a screen along the Lippe River and its entire front, ultimately establishing contact with the 15th Squadron. During that evening the east boundary of the 17th Squadron was extended to include the area north of Hamm.

---

[1] Ibid., 14-15.

Several hours before sunrise, Troop B relieved Troop A and then moved to expand the new 17th Cavalry Squadron boundary screen to the east. At daylight on, April 1, 1945, Troop B with its tank platoon reconnoitered toward Bockum from the west; at the same time, Troop A sent one of its platoons along with a tank platoon into Hovel from the east. When Troops A and B linked up in Bockum-Hovel later that day, they reported capturing around 465 POWs, four 88-mm guns, and two 20-mm anti-aircraft guns.

Also, on April 1, Troop E moved its battery position to the vicinity of Horst to obtain greater range on targets south of the Lippe River. The FOs for the assault guns of Troop E established forward outposts in Stockum, Bockum-Hovel, and Werne, and they unleashed fire on mortar positions and other dug-in enemy targets south of the Lippe. By moving their FOs closer to the Lippe River to better vantage points, Troop E achieved excellent results adjusting the fire of their howitzer assault guns on the enemy.[1]

Writing months later in a postwar *Cavalry Journal* article, a lesson learned from the aforementioned operation was that the new M24 Chaffee light tank, with its 75-mm main gun, had all the direct, suppressive fire support needed to assist reconnaissance troops perform their job. As a result, the M8 (HMC) self-propelled howitzers could be used in battery for indirect fire to support the entire squadron front. Also, it was concluded that reconnaissance of enemy territory at night by mechanized cavalry was impractical in extreme darkness because enemy elements could be bypassed, causing "a false sense of security" for those friendly units being screened.[2]

By April 3, the 15th Cavalry Group had moved to Herbern, Germany. On the following day, they were detached from McLain's XIX Corps and attached to Maj. Gen. Harry Twaddle's 95th (Victory) Infantry Division of Anderson's XVI Corps. From April 4-12, 1945, the 15th Cavalry Group screened the Lippe River line to the north, while the 75th and 95th Infantry Divisions attacked across its front on the south bank.[3]

---

[1] The prior four paragraphs draw on the article by Maj. Morton McD. Jones, "Seizing and Holding a River Line," 14-15.
[2] Ibid., 15.
[3] TLR, 16, 17.

On the morning of April 3, Dad mentioned that he had had a hard night as he "drank too much cognac and wine." He described, "running into a warehouse full of liquor, all French stuff" in one of the towns they had searched for snipers. He reported rescuing a few cases and splitting it up so all the troops got some, "even enough for the 15th Squadron." He also mentioned that it tasted like "paint remover." Yet, he said it was good enough, so they drank it anyway.[1] More to the point, he noted that he was situated that day in reserve with Recon Troop A, but that the 1st Platoon of Fox Company was "still out" on a reconnaissance mission with Troop B, and the 2nd Platoon was with Troop C, near Hamm.

On April 4, he wrote, "Last night one of the 1st Platoon tanks, got hit" by German 88-mm gunfire. He described it as "Penny's Tank," (referring to his friend, Al Penniplede), and reported matter-of-factly that it was the third or fourth tank that "they were knocked from under."

During the period from April 6-7, Pop reported that while Fox Company was in reserve status, they were called on to provide "some indirect firing" on German-held positions at a crossroads in the distance. Their apparent intent was to discourage further German tenancy in that vicinity. Of course, forward observers directed their fire, and again he wrote, "Anything that moves gets hit."

While tanks normally engage the enemy with direct, flat-trajectory gunfire. Indirect tank fire is another possible method, where the tank's cannon is used as artillery, firing high angle HE shells at distant or out-of-sight targets. To perform that function, the tank was normally driven up the side of a hill or earthen embankment to angle the tank chassis upward. In that position, maximum elevation of the tank's main gun mimics the army's artillery arm by firing a projectile on a parabolic path down on top of the enemy.

By April 10, 1945, the remaining security zone was determined to be small enough to allow the 15th Cavalry Squadron to take over. The 17th

---

[1] On that occasion, Pop likely encountered a brand of French firewater, known by GIs in Europe as *eau de vie*. It was thought to be a "savage liquid made by boiling barbed wire, soapsuds, watch springs, and old tent pegs together." Some drank it and afterward tears ran down their cheeks, caused by "violent efforts to avoid clutching their throats and crying out in anguish." Pyle, *Brave Men*, 378.

Cavalry Recce Squadron was then attached to Task Force Faith (the 95th Victory Division) to assist in making contact with the First Army on the Mohne River, between Frienehol and Neheim, south of Hamm. On April 11, the 15th Cavalry Recce Squadron was released from their security positions along the Lippe River and they subsequently relieved the 88th Reconnaissance Battalion along the Mohne River, between Neheim and Dellwig. At that point, the 15th Cavalry Group had responsibility for the entire security zone, while the Victory Division "attacked across the front to the south of the river."[1]

On April 11, 1945, Dad reported leaving Horst very early in the morning with the knowledge that they were to advance "by way of Hamm" toward Werl and Soest. He described the conditions on that occasion as being "very dark, but surprisingly warm." When dawn broke, he observed that he was barely able to make out the shapes of objects, as a dense fog shrouded the fields and forest, as they advanced along "a ribbon like road." As the fog lifted, he described seeing scattered debris and two huge, knocked-out German 155-mm field guns, as well as the artillery tractor that pulled them out into the field.

By 0655 that morning, he reported entering Hamm, by "a round-about way." Apparently, they traveled through two bomb-damaged buildings, over a "filled-in bomb crater" into a railroad yard, and then they followed the rail line into the heart of the city. "Boy, this is one city that is really wrecked," he wrote in amazement, and the "street cars still stand in the middle of town, as if waiting for passengers." However, as they approached, he saw the windows were smashed and many holes "polka dot" the charred vehicles, which attested to the intense street fighting prior to that town's "liberation." In addition, he observed that nearly every house had white bed sheets and pillowcases flapping from the windows as makeshift surrender flags. Most if not all of the larger buildings were also flying what seemed to be a sea of white cloth; he mentioned that it was almost humorous, since it looked as if the townsfolk had just hung out their wash to dry. To his eye, it was apparent that the German civilian population had had enough, so they continued their advance through the broken brickwork of Hamm, and were soon on their way to Werl and Soest.

---

[1] TLR, 17.

As they proceeded south through the countryside, he also mentioned that the road was littered with shards of glass, rubble and all sorts of discarded German war equipment, including both large and small arms. He described the German people standing along the road, staring blankly and appearing like "statues, with hate glaring from their eyes." He wrote, "We just go by and shower them with dust from our fast-moving tanks and vehicles."

As the 17th Cavalry Squadron rumbled along providing left flank security for the advance of Simpson's Ninth Army in the Ruhr Region, they encountered many scenes of wreckage and destruction. Thus, as was his wont, Pop dismounted his tank and took the photograph below showing remnants of a demolished airplane, the victim of German antiaircraft gunfire or a successful Luftwaffe fighter attack. The roundel marking on its fuselage clearly identifies it as a British aircraft, and since human remains were not evident, he reasoned that the "flyboys" had safely bailed out prior to ground impact.

At this point in the narrative, the reader might share my curiosity about what Dad and his cohorts experienced while bouncing along in their claustrophobic tanks, advancing rapidly across Northern Europe in pursuit of the enemy. Their mission was a grueling one, and speed was of critical importance. Yet, long hours passed for the crewmen without personal relief, as they had been ordered to stop only to engage the enemy or to refuel from supply trucks that accompanied the formation when necessary. Those tank crews were scared no doubt as they continued their journey, but consider the adjustments they had to make to answer the call of nature, as so-called "pit stops" were absolutely forbidden.

The solution comes from a former tanker in the 3rd Spearhead Division who wrote: "Whatever spectators there might have been were treated to the ridiculous spectacle of men urinating from their tanks or 'dumping' into their steel helmets and tossing it away as they traveled, rarely without unwelcome consequences."[1] To be sure, Pop and his mates did what they had to do since "desperation is the mother of heroic expedience."[2]

During April 1945, Pop continued to remark in his diary about the sad state of the slave laborers he observed walking along the roadways and heading to the rear. Passing them on the roadside, he wrote, "There must be millions of them." He reported counting more than three thousand during one, thirty-minute period, describing their faces as drawn, blank, and expressionless. He continued his chronicle of those sad individuals, as their silent staring eyes denoted people who were in complete and utter despair.

By April 12, he was positioned at an outpost south of Neheim, on the side of a mountain looking directly down on the small village of Arnsberg, some eight hundred to a thousand yards away. Through his telescopic gunsight he could see many enemy troops milling around, but very few civilians. He wrote, "Unless they are asking for it, we don't fire on them." His entire tank company was apparently on a security mission and they set up a significant distance from the enemy on favorable terrain to observe, provide early warning, and buy reaction time in the event the enemy attempted an attack.[3]

During the next day, Friday the 13th, 1945, nothing unlucky happened while moving through Arnsberg toward their squadron assembly area. The weather was again thick with a misty fog, and for miles along the winding

---

[1] Irwin, *Another River, Another Town*, 41.
[2] Ibid., 58.
[3] Rottman, *World War II US Cavalry Groups: European Theater*, 18.

road they encountered smashed and smoldering German motor convoys (mostly armored hulks, knocked-out trucks, disabled guns, and burned-out personnel carriers), stark testimony to the violence of past battles. In overly cynical fashion, Dad mentioned seeing bits and pieces of enemy equipment, shredded body parts, and field-gray German uniforms adorning the branches of nearby trees. That harsh reminder of the deadly work of Allied artillery fire prompted him to write: "They look like ornaments hanging from a Xmas tree." His observation made clear that his attitude toward the enemy had undergone a process of dehumanization as the war neared its end. Like many other GIs, he felt nothing but intense dislike for the enemy. Surely, the memory of wounded and deceased friends with whom he had served played a large role in his antipathy toward German soldiers.

By early April 1945, farther to the east, General Bradley's 12th Army Group had begun to converge on the Elbe River. U.S. armored units were continuing to advance rapidly along a wide ribbon of concrete, the central *autobahn*[1] of Germany, while massive refugee columns "numbering in the thousands" headed toward safety in the west. Periodically, U.S. cavalry troops were called on to clear refugees and DPs from the roadway to keep the main roads open so essential military traffic and supplies could move toward the front. The sight of that endless column of long-suffering people greatly disgusted my father. Yet, reality required them to end the inhumanity by continuing to chase down and destroy every vestige of Hitler's Third Reich.[2]

In the late afternoon of April 11, elements of the 2nd Hell on Wheels Armored Division first reached the Elbe. On the next day, Ike informed Patton of his decision to stop at the Elbe River and leave the capture of Berlin to the Soviets. Thereafter, "Eisenhower repeatedly checked the great joy-ride of Patton's Third Army" to make certain his forces at the end "maintained a more or less straight frontage" relative to the enemy and the advancing Soviet forces.[3] To Ike, it was more important strategically to

---

[1] That dual motorway was begun in Germany in 1933, and it became "the most durable of the propaganda exercises mounted by the Third Reich." Evans, *The Third Reich in Power* (New York: Penguin Press, 2005), 323.
[2] Perry, *Partners in Command*, 356.
[3] Hastings, *Armageddon*, 426.

capture the Ruhr industrial region and the Saar basin of Germany, rather than the heavily devastated capital city of Berlin.[1]

Eisenhower's decision to avoid Anglo-American involvement in the Battle for Berlin was absolutely correct. No amount of death and suffering by Allied soldiers would have altered the decisions made previously at the Tehran and Yalta Conferences, guaranteeing each of the Allies a postwar occupation zone in Berlin. In the words of Second World War historian Max Hastings: "What would Eisenhower have said to the mother or husband of an American or British soldier killed in a battle for Hitler's capital, which at best would have yielded only a symbolic triumph for the Western Allies? . . . Wherein lay the purpose of losing American and British lives to gain territory destined to become the responsibility of the Red Army?" The wisdom of that decision was magnified by the fact that more than 350,000 Russians became casualties in Berlin, including around 78,000 deaths. Given the butcher's bill up to that point in the war, it was considered too high a price to pay.[2]

The large number of Russian casualties in the operation to capture Berlin was due in no small measure to Stalin's low regard for the lives of his soldiers. Those losses were needlessly high "due to the race to get to Berlin before the Western Allies and partly to packing so many armies into the assault" to such an extent that they bombarded each other.[3]

---

[1] Caddick-Adams, *Snow & Steel*, 82.
[2] Hastings, *Armageddon,* 422-424, 475; Unger et al., *George Marshal,* 337.
[3] Beevor, *The Fall of Berlin 1945*, 424.

17. THE WAR ENDS IN EUROPE

On the 14th of April 1945, Pop announced in his diary that by 1220 in the afternoon, the 17th Cavalry Recce Squadron had gotten underway and first entered the German autobahn, "a four-lane job," at Milestone 340. By 1435 hours, however, they had discontinued their travel on that high-speed highway at Milestone 251.5, heading in the direction of Paderborn. While barreling down that road, he observed no civilian motor traffic due to the lack of fuel supplies in Germany by that point in the war. The few German civilians he saw along the roadside were riding bicycles or pulling handcarts filled with all their worldly possessions. Some were walking barefoot, and he described the procession of shattered humanity as virtually unending.

Subsequently, he reported they lost some time in their road march when Charley Troop (Troop C) took a wrong turn that cost them almost forty-five minutes getting turned around and back on course. To recover for lost time, he said they went "as fast as our tracks will fly" and did well until they got to the middle of the town of Höxter. There, he noted the third tank in the 1st Platoon (the number 3 tank in the column) skidded on the street and "slid into some GIs, who were watching us fly by." As they were on an urgent mission, they stopped for only a minute, and he remarked rather callously, "only one guy got hurt" as the tank ran over his right leg and "must [have] broke it in 3 or 4 places." In his most empathetic fashion, he observed they were "lucky more than one wasn't hurt." Clearly, such unfortunate events were the unpredictable hazards and vagaries of war.

Upon arrival at their destination, Steinheim, at 1645 that afternoon the 17th Cavalry Squadron assumed a military governance mission for several days, as the country was in total breakdown. Chaos reigned, and there was no coherent government in most of what remained of Germany. As one might imagine, the duties they performed were mainly administrative, but they were also responsible for establishing control, maintaining the peace, and filling the power vacuum left by the retreating German authorities. In that capacity, the Allied military occupation forces did yeoman service, quelling minor disputes, imposing curfews, preventing acts of revenge, and restoring order under lawless conditions.

In his diary, Dad wrote that Captain Fiori began early in the morning of April 14 interviewing "all Germans between the ages of 16 to 75, and what a line of people are waiting to enter his office." At that point, he was likely trying to identify those residents who could help get the city back on its feet. He was also clearly intent on keeping the civilians on his side because he needed to ascertain whether there were any high-ranking Nazis in their midst, especially those of the *SS* persuasion.

Pop mentioned that Fox Company was located in the middle of Steinheim with one platoon manning an outpost and another on guard duty at the POW cage. He noted that those on outpost duty had been told to bring to the command post (the CP), anyone found walking along the road without a pass on their person. He also wrote that they were delighted to have welcomed three British troops and one Canadian soldier, former German POWs who had just "come in" to the CP to be repatriated back to their regular units.

Also, on the morning of April 14, Pop and his squadron mates were stunned and saddened to learn the news that President Franklin Roosevelt, had died two days earlier.[1] The official report indicated the cause of his death was a cerebral hemorrhage[2] that occurred at the Little White House, his cottage in Warm Springs, Georgia.

Dad greatly lamented the loss and wrote in his diary that the late president had been "like a father to us" over the years. He seemed uncertain about how the president's death would affect the war, but he thought perhaps the troops would fight harder to honor his memory. He also wondered who "the new guy" was, and pondered: "Where did he come

---

[1] While the president was relatively young in terms of age, his health had been in steep decline. Barr, *Eisenhower's Armies*, 453.

[2] FDR's death certificate lists cerebral hemorrhage as the primary cause of death, but an autopsy was never performed. A recent review of the medical evidence suggests that FDR developed malignant skin cancer, a deadly melanoma, over his left eyebrow in the late 1930s that later metastasized to his abdomen and brain, and was likely the underlying cause of his death. As the treating physicians had overlooked the lesion and its medical implications, Lomazow and Fettmann, *FDR's Deadly Secret*, 63-66, 91, 161-169; ironically, FDR had teased Churchill years earlier for wearing a homburg at the Casablanca Conference in January 1943. Churchill said he wore it to keep the sun out of his eyes and suggested FDR do the same. "I was born without a hat," FDR replied, and "I don't see any reason for wearing one now." Atkinson, *An Army at Dawn* (NY: Henry Holt, 2002), 292-293.

from?" He mentioned that they all hoped he would be "half as good" as FDR. That thought was surely prophetic, as just two weeks later President Harry Truman first learned of the super-secret Manhattan Project together with the fact that one atomic bomb could potentially destroy an entire city and most of its population.[1]

By the middle of April 1945, the 17th Cavalry Recce Squadron had been in almost continuous motion advancing through Germany for distances of from 50 to 150 miles per day. They had been tactically employed to thwart numerous pockets of resistance in the Ruhr Valley and had performed screening missions and rear-area security, when it was determined to be necessary. On April 15, following the elimination of the Ruhr Pocket, the entire 15th Cavalry Group essentially withdrew from all combat activity and resumed its work as a military government detachment, headquartered in the city of Bad Pyrmont, northeast of Steinheim, Germany.[2]

By April 16, Dad mentioned that they had been very busy that day, disarming German prisoners of their knives, swords and weapons of all kinds. By the following day, it had quieted down somewhat, and on the morning of April 18, it was officially reported that all organized German resistance had ceased in the Ruhr district.[3]

On the next day, his squadron was ordered to move out after morning chow for their new destination, the town of Herford, farther to the north and west of Bad Pyrmont. He described passing through country with "lots of pretty scenery," and noted that some farmers were out in their fields, "planting again." He took that as a good sign for all concerned.

Next, he reported arriving in Herford by mid-afternoon, and by April 20, he mentioned they had parked their tanks outside of town and were billeted in a large house, about four hundred yards from the German autobahn. As his company had been designated the squadron reserve, they shut down their engines, and spent the time either on guard duty or pulling routine maintenance on their vehicles. That short amount of down time

---

[1] David McCullough, *Truman* (New York: Simon & Schuster, 1992), 376-377.
[2] TLR, 17.
[3] Forrest C. Pogue, *The Supreme Command, U.S. Army in World War II, ETO* (Washington, D.C.: Office of the Chief of Military History, 1954), 440; Weigley, *Eisenhower's Lieutenants*, 680.

also allowed the tank crew the opportunity to walk around and shake out the cramps in their legs.

By April 25, 1945, Germany had been essentially cut in two as American troops in the First Army's 69th Infantry Division met their Soviet counterparts, troops of the 175th Rifle Regiment for a ceremonial handshake at Torgau, Germany, on the Mulde River, a tributary of the Elbe.[1] Only a few days later, Italian partisans captured Benito Mussolini (Hitler's fascist partner), executed him, and hung his body and that of his murdered mistress upside down in a square in Milan, to be vilified by an angry mob.[2] Whether Hitler knew of that event is unclear, but had he known of it, he undoubtedly repeated orders that his body and that of his bride be destroyed "so that nothing remains."[3]

Shortly after midnight, on Sunday, April 29, as Russian troops closed in on the Reich Chancellery in Berlin, a frail Adolf Hitler[4] married his longtime mistress, Eva Braun. By mid-afternoon on April 30, they ate lunch in the underground *Führerbunker*, and as Soviet forces came within a mile of the bunker, they retreated to the inner sanctum where they committed suicide together: he by pistol and she from cyanide poisoning.

Shortly after 3:30 p.m., the news spread throughout the bunker: "*Der Chef ist tot!*" (The chief is dead!) Their bodies were then wrapped in blankets, carried up to the Chancellery garden, doused in gasoline, and burned in the presence of several Nazi officials. Afterward, the charred remains were gathered and buried nearby.[5] Thus did Hitler's abhorrent twelve-year regime come to an abrupt end.

---

[1] Ian Kershaw, *The End* (New York: Penguin Press, 2011), 339; Atkinson, *The Guns at Last Night,* 607; Evans, *The Third Reich at War*, 682.
[2] Denis Mack Smith, *Mussolini* (New York: Alfred A. Knopf, 1982), 320.
[3] Hugh R. Trevor-Roper, *The Last Days of Hitler* (New York: Macmillan, 1947), 196; Kershaw, *Hitler 1936-45: Nemesis*, 826.
[4] At 56 years of age, Hitler was a physical wreck and looked very old; he was stooped and pallid in appearance. Misch, *Hitler's Last Witness*, 145, 147-148.
[5] Hitler's personal servants referred to him as *"der Chef."* Among those present at the funeral pyre were Martin Bormann, Hitler's private secretary and Josef Goebbels, the Third Reich's propaganda minister. Hugh R. Trevor-Roper, *The Last Days of Hitler*, 200-202; Evans, *The Third Reich at War,* 725-726.

Not until the evening of the first of May was Hitler's death announced to the German public. Only a few years earlier, a similar broadcast of his death would have shocked the nation.[1] But by spring of 1945, the majority of the surviving German population had endured enough death and destruction. Weary from all the sacrifices made over nearly six years, they understood the futility of any continuation of a war that was already lost. At last reality set in for the general population; they no longer had any illusions about their future.

With Hitler's death, Germany's collapse came with gravitational certainty: the jig was up, observed author Rick Atkinson. By May 2, 1945, the last Soviet shells fell on Berlin. By then, Simpson's Ninth Army held the American left wing fifty miles west of the Elbe, while tens of thousands of screaming Germans fled the pursuing Red Army.[2]

On the morning of May 2nd, the 17th Cavalry Squadron was assigned a security mission in a wooded area where they checked all civilians whom they encountered "from the [age of] 17 to 50 for passes." Dad observed that the leaves of the surrounding trees had begun to open and were finally greening up. He also noted that Fox Company was using their tanks to cover the main roads, while dismounted men from Troops A, B and C maneuvered through the woods, continuing a security mission until May 3rd, at which time they returned to Herford.

One day later, Dad reported that he and other members of his outfit were called out at midnight to provide the MPs some needed assistance at the POW cage. He mentioned an astonishing number of German soldiers were "giving themselves up" and crossing the American lines in droves. One correspondent referred to it as a "Niagara" of POWs that was nearly overwhelming for the Americans.[3]

Pop wrote: "The Russians have them on the run and they are afraid to give up to them, so they come to us." He described the situation as chaotic: "all day on May 4, two complete divisions gave themselves up, driving their own vehicles directly into the POW stockade in Herford."[4] According to

---

[1] Kershaw, *The End*, 348.
[2] Atkinson, *The Guns at Last Light*, 615.
[3] Blair, *Ridgway's Paratroopers*, 486.
[4] The approach of Soviet troops greatly motivated the Germans to surrender. Their preference for giving themselves up to Americans rather

his diary, the street leading into the POW cage was "double parked with German trucks and men piled all over them." Those German soldiers apparently knew that further sacrifice was useless.

By the next morning, Dad commented that the POW cage had been expanded by extending bands of barbed wire all around a large open field; it "covered two city blocks [and was] jammed full." When his platoon was relieved finally at 1300 hours by newly arrived MPs, he reported how "damn glad he was, as you don't know what a pain in the neck the POWs had been." As you can imagine, he was a very happy GI to have completed that temporary duty, herding a massive crowd of German prisoners shouting "Hitler *Kaput*!" He described them as a thoroughly beaten, but strangely arrogant lot.[1]

In April 1945 the U.S. First and Ninth Armies had captured around 325,000 German POWs by the time the the Ruhr Pocket was reduced. That amounted to "the largest single surrender by the *Wehrmacht* during the Second World War."[2]

By the beginning of May 1945, Supreme Headquarters, Allied Expeditionary Force, reported that they were holding more than 4.2 million German POWs. That total continued to climb to over 7.4 million enemy POWs by June 1945, at which time "there are more German prisoners than U.S. troops in the American zone."[3]

As an example of how chaotic the POW situation had become, one GI in the 78th ("Lightning") Infantry Division started out escorting 68 German POWs, heading for a compound in Wuppertal, Germany. On arrival at his destination, "the sixty-eight [prisoners had] grown to twelve hundred." Many had walked for miles in order to find an American soldier "who was not to occupied with other duties" to accept their surrender.[4]

---

than to the Soviets "resulted in the surrender of an entire German division to the 29th, the largest surrender to the Blue-Gray Division [of the Ninth Army] since the capitulation at Brest." Ewing, *29 Let's Go!*, 256.

[1] In my early teens, I recall Dad saying rather emphatically that the German POWs were "a pain in the rear." He described the Nazi officers as prima donnas and the enlisted soldiers were "dumb jerks."

[2] Hastings, *Victory in Europe*, 140.

[3] Zumbro, *The Battle for the Ruhr*, 391, 395.

[4] MacDonald, *The Last Offensive*, 486.

By war's end, the 15th Cavalry Group was credited with having captured a total of 6,874 enemy POWs, mostly captured in Brittany prior to their repositioning to Holland.[1]

Dad's photograph below reveals an enormous mass of enemy POWs, corralled in a field somewhere in Germany. That hastily built, open-air holding pen shows them being held temporarily, while surrounded by barbed wire to ensure proper control.

Those prisoners look somewhat relieved to be out of the war and under U.S. military jurisdiction, instead of the not-so-pleasant alternative of enduring Soviet "hospitality" in captivity. There appear to be several *Wehrmacht* officers in the foreground of the photograph, including several high-ranking German officers, identified by arrow markings. Another

---

[1] "History of the 15th Cavalry Group," 5, 8.

seems to be facing in their direction, but he is partially obscured from view by a fellow POW standing to his left in a long leather overcoat.

One British historian noted recently the relative absence of *Waffen-SS* POWs in those holding pens. He declared they "were conspicuous by their rarity," opining it was either it had to do with "their determination to go down fighting," or because their captors merely shot them on sight.[1]

On May 5, Pop diarized: "We got word we are moving out tomorrow—peace rumors are [all] over the place—Hope it's true— Something's in the air." By the next day, he described leaving Herford in the morning, and motor marching south through Detmold, Steinheim, and Paderborn into Büren. He noted that, after they got under way, a steady, hard rain began and the blowing wind helped it along; he described it as a cold rain and wrote, "It really gave our faces a going over."

By Tuesday, May 8, he chronicled what happened that day, writing excitedly: "Unofficially, the war is over." Little did he know that the unconditional surrender document had been signed in the early hours of May 7, in General Eisenhower's headquarters in Reims, France. Gen. Alfred Jodl signed on behalf of the Germans, while the American signatory was Ike's chief of staff, Lt. Gen. Walter Bedell Smith.[2] Gen. Ivan Susloparov signed the instrument of surrender for the Soviet Union. By that act of capitulation, all military operations ceased at midnight (Central European Time) on May 8. Hence, May 8, 1945 was officially V-E Day, "Victory in Europe Day."[3]

At Stalin's insistence, a lengthier version of the capitulation document was signed later on the outskirts of Berlin. That second signing at Soviet headquarters was not completed until May 9, but it was backdated to the prior day to conform to the terms of the original document signed in

---

[1] Beevor, *Ardennes 1944*, 343. *Waffen-SS* soldiers were easily identified by the tattoo of their blood type, as it was applied to the skin under their left arms.

[2] Eisenhower's disdain for the Nazis was so great that he declined to be present at the surrender ceremony and delegated the task of signing the surrender documents to General Smith. D'Este, *Eisenhower: A Soldier's Life*, 702-703.

[3] Stafford, *Endgame, 1945*, 362.

Reims. Signing the document for Germany was Field Marshal Wilhelm Keitel, *der Führer's* obsequious lackey.[1]

Also, on May 9, 1945, the Wehrmacht issued its final report stating, "From midnight the weapons are silent on all fronts." On command of Admiral Karl Dönitz, Hitler's designated successor, Germany's "struggle" was over. The relevant metric was more than forty million lives lost in Europe alone, greater than four times the number of dead from the First World War, the so-called War to End All Wars.[2]

Peace was finally at hand in Europe. Following notification from Eisenhower, Bradley telephoned the army commanders of his 12th Army Group: Hodges (First Army) in Weimar, Patton (Third Army) in Regensburg, Simpson (Ninth Army) in Braunschweig, and Gerow (Fifteenth Army) in Bonn, and ordered them to stop in place to avoid further casualties. To a staff officer, Bradley said, "Now our troubles really begin . . . everyone will want to start for home immediately." He next opened his map board, which displayed the locations of all forty-three American divisions under his command, arrayed across a front of more than 600 miles. Clutching a grease pencil, Bradley wrote his final entry on the map, D+335.[3] (That meant 335 days had passed since the Allies made their initial landings on D-Day.)

After V-E day, there remained three more months of exhausting and dangerous challenges for U.S. and Allied military forces in the Pacific. On the European continent, however, the major task of drawing down and redeploying GIs by the tens of thousands began.

On May 9, 1945, Dad wrote that his unit had moved out from Büren, through Paderborn, to the small town of "Reithburg" (actually Reitberg), where his company was in squadron reserve. He said, "War was officially over today," but he didn't "feel any different." He described Paderborn as one grimy, skeletonized city: "there isn't a complete building standing. This is the worst city yet, everything was shot to Hell—nothing was spared."[4]

---

[1] Kershaw, *The End*, 371-372.
[2] Ibid., 376-377.
[3] Atkinson, *The Guns at Last Light*, 626-627.
[4] The destruction in and around Paderborn had much to do with the fact that it had been the site of one of Nazi Germany's panzer training facilities.

By May 10 and 11, Pop mentioned they were bivouacked two miles outside of Reitberg. He described their morning routine as staying busy cleaning mud and grime from their tank tracks and equipment, and by afternoon they played ball or soccer. He said they were simply waiting to see what would happen next. On May 15 and 16, they moved into the countryside and spent two days screening a wooded mountain region on foot. He noted they found no military age men, but the woods contained "lots of deer." (He also happened to mention that he shot at two, but "missed.")

Not long afterward, Pop described an interesting occurrence that took place on May 18: Captain Fiori got a "phone call" from squadron headquarters, but when he picked up the receiver, he couldn't "place the voice [of the person] talking to him." It was none other than Col. J. B. Reybold, their cavalry group commander, who had insisted earlier that his men wear neckties in combat. Dad wrote, "Every one gave J. B. up for dead long ago."

Instead, the Germans had captured him at Dol, France, in early August of 1944; he became a POW and was held on the Channel Island of Jersey for the remainder of the war. Dad wrote, "I sure pity the men there [his fellow POWs] and the Huns, I bet they suffered."

Actually, Pop was onto something with that sentiment, as the June 15, 1945 issue of *Yank* magazine reported a certain high-ranking POW (Colonel Reybold) had "repeatedly made written demands upon their German captors, consistently quoting the Geneva Convention, and signing his letters 'Eisenhower's Representative on the Channel Islands.'" As a consequence, their conditions improved due to old "Eyeball's" constant harassment of the German authorities.[1]

On the afternoon of Saturday, May 19 Pop wrote, the Colonel showed back up at headquarters: "he came in and shook hands with everyone, still the same, only he'd lost a little weight, but everything else was Col. John B. Reybold."

It was the scene of fierce fighting between *SS* Brigade Westfalen and taskforces of the 3rd Spearhead Division in the last days of March 1945. Zumbro*he Battle for the Ruhr*, 210-237.

[1] Meyers, *Teacher of the Year,* Appendix A, 297.

Shortly following the VE day celebrations, Dad sent a special V-mail request to his bride, showing his mind had switched to far more ardent thoughts. What he requested on that occasion was a "pin-up" picture of her. As the photograph on the next page makes very clear, Mom was more than happy to accommodate him despite the objections of her prim and proper mother.

While she gladly complied with his request on that occasion, there is little to no doubt in my mind that she would have objected mightily to my sharing it within these pages, as she was far too modest to ever wear such a scandalous outfit in public. Nevertheless, I take full responsibility for my action here and gladly reveal for all to see her warm and happy spirit, as well as her great ardor and affection for him.

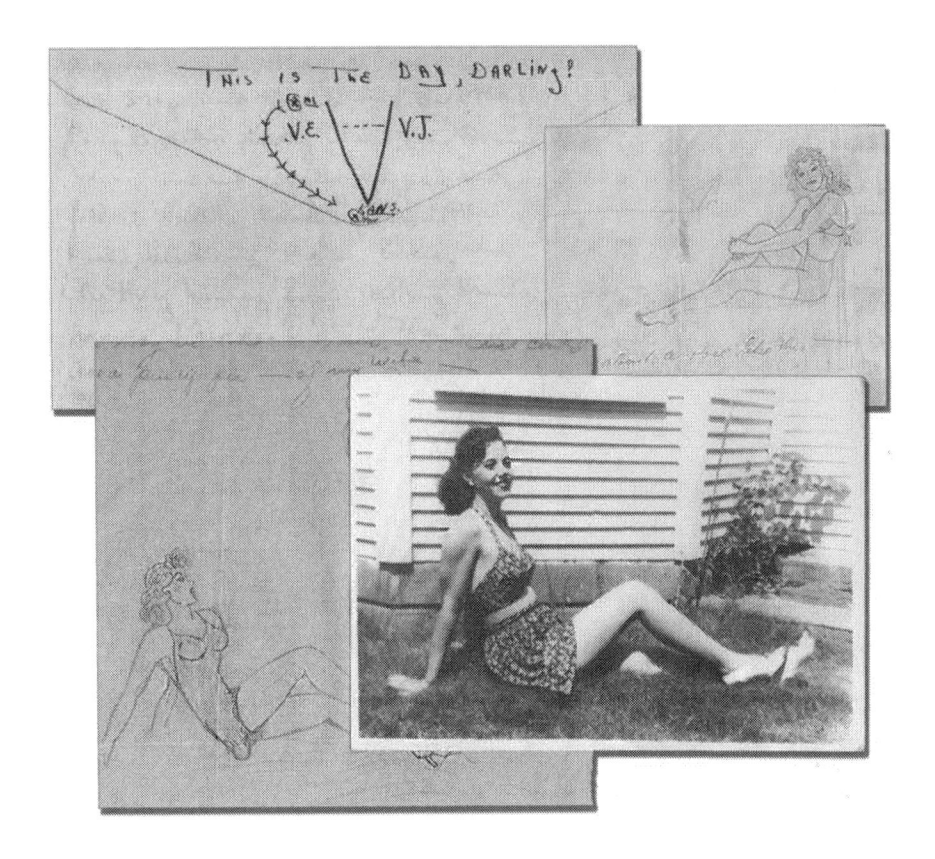

Later in May 1945, Pop decided to relieve the tedium by trying his hand at a little journalism. In the May 25, two-page mimeographed issue of *Cover the Front,* the 17th Cavalry Squadron's information bulletin, he wrote an article entitled, "Old 'Stud' Gone Away" that described the departure of their "Stud Duck," First Sgt.[1] William L. Thornton, from Quanah, Texas, who had accumulated "over 85 points"[2] and was about to depart for home in the first rotation. It noted that Sergeant Thornton had joined the outfit in 1943 at Camp Maxey, Texas, and that he was a great morale booster while imitating Fox Company's commanding officer during their pre-deployment Louisiana maneuvers.[3]

Dad wrote again in the May 26 edition of *Cover the Front*: "Every day this past week around Fox Company the boys have been doing a 'buzzin cousin'[4]—especially those with over 85 points." He also reported there were eleven new faces "around the campus" and he seriously questioned whether the "old army" men were essential any longer.[5]

In the May 29 edition of the squadron bulletin, a summary of the British Broadcasting Company included news that 750 American B-29 bombers had dropped tons of incendiary bombs on the Japanese port of Yokohama. Pop also reported on Fox Company's upcoming visit to the tank range near Bad Lippespringe. He mentioned that it was an old German *panzer* course, and that many relics would be available on the range to target. He also noted there would be an optimum time for the men, "particularly the new ones," to get in some much-needed gunnery practice.

---

[1] The backbone of an army company or troop is the first sergeant; he's the company's senior non-commissioned officer, the "Top Kick." Pyle, *Brave Men*, 73.

[2] To make demobilization fair, the rotation of soldiers back to the U.S. was done on a point system: 85 points or more allowed a first rotation home. The criteria were: one point for each month of service after a certain date; another point was added for each month of overseas service; and additional points were issued for certain combat awards and for having a dependent under age 18. Slaughter, *Omaha Beach and Beyond*, 188; Unger and Hirshson, *George Marshall*, 361.

[3] A BBC News summary in the May 25 issue of the squadron information bulletin reported SS-Reichsführer Heinrich Himmler died by suicide, and that a fierce battle was raging in Okinawa.

[4] "Doing a 'buzzin cousin'" was slang of the period for rumormongering.

[5] A BBC summary on May 26 in the bulletin included news that five hundred U.S. B-29 Superfortresses had dropped tons of incendiaries on Tokyo, Japan.

He concluded with the hope that no "Maggie's Drawers"[1] would be recorded while Fox Company was on the range.

On May 31, 1945, the 15th Cavalry Group was relieved from attachment to the XVI Corps, commanded by Maj. Gen. John B. Anderson. By then the group had suffered the loss of 82 men killed in action. As astonishing as it may seem, the fatalities sustained in the 15th and 17th Recce Cavalry Squadrons were equal: exactly 41 men killed in each.[2] As to the matter of military decorations, men of the 15th Cavalry Group had earned two Distinguished Service Crosses,[3] 31 Silver Star Medals, 66 Bronze Star Medals for valor, and 154 Purple Heart Medals. In addition, certain men in the group were awarded the following: one Legion of Merit, three Croix de Guerre (a French decoration for heroism), and four Soldier's Medals.[4]

In early June 1945, Company F of the 17th Cavalry Squadron conducted field-firing exercises at a gunnery range in the vicinity of Augustdorf, north of Bad Lippespringe. Dad reported that they took their tanks to the range and fired 75-mm rounds and small arms at an assortment of captured German tanks and armored vehicles.

The mostly idle M24 tank crews likely welcomed the break from dull monotony that gunnery practice provided them. Like Dad, most tank gunners enjoyed hearing the bark of their main guns. They also took great pride in the skill it took to operate their lethal equipment and they derived a significant sense of pride in their ability to deliver accurate gunfire down range

By the third of June, they had returned from the range, and only a few days later, Dad mentioned that they had left Reitberg in the morning and

---

[1] The phrase "Maggie's Drawers" is common U.S. military slang for a complete miss of the target on the target range.
[2] TLR, 23 and 24.
[3] The recipients of the Distinguished Service Cross, the second highest U.S. military award for extreme gallantry and risk of life, below only the Medal of Honor, were: Tec 5 Donald K. Davies and Pvt. William P. McPherson, both of whom were troopers in the 17th Cavalry Squadron. Ibid., 27.
[4] Ibid. 25-30.

drove all day, initially west and then southwest through a number of German towns, including Erwitte, Olpe, Siegen, Rennerod, Freilingen, arriving at their destination, Selters, that evening. He noted that they had to maneuver around a number of destroyed German vehicles and tanks during that dusty road march. The most heavily damaged town he saw on that trip was Siegen, which he described as "really a mess." He reported that the townspeople were beginning to clean away the rubble and dirt, but he "saw only a few houses that weren't completely ruined."

Around that time the 15th Cavalry Group became a military occupation force in the Paderborn area with headquarters at Bad Lippespringe, and on June 5, Col. David Wagstaff, Jr., assumed command. Shortly thereafter, the entire group traveled about 150 miles to the south to the Province of Hessen-Nassau, east of Koblenz, to occupy Landkreis Unterwesterwald, and later Landkreis Oberlahn.[1]

By then a curious phenomenon became evident in newly defeated Germany. For some reason, when dealing with the civilian populace, neither he nor any of his squadron mates could ever find anyone who would admit having ever been an admirer of Adolf Hitler or a member of the Nazi party. "Nicht Nazi! Nicht Nazi!" was the universal response. The reply was always that some other guy down the street was a Nazi, or a certain person in the neighborhood liked Hitler, but he or she had recently left town very hurriedly.[2] The process of dissociation from Nazism was obviously well under way, even at the grass roots level.[3] Needless to say, those less than forthright responses were met with GI skepticism and total disbelief.

In the spring of 1945, Martha Gellhorn, an American war correspondent and the estranged third wife of Ernest Hemingway, wrote a scathing article for *Collier's*, entitled "*Das Deutsches Volk.*" In that magazine report, she described the obvious dissembling and brazen amnesia on the part of the German population that she encountered in Germany's Ruhr Valley: "No one is a Nazi. No one ever was. There may have been some

---

[1] Ibid., 17.
[2] Slaughter, *Omaha Beach and Beyond*, 171.
[3] Kershaw, *The End*, 380.

Nazis in the next village." Not one person she interviewed admitted to knowing any Nazis, past or present.[1]

As to any mention of Jews, Ms. Gellhorn was deeply dismayed, as she heard the same lies over and over: "nearly everyone had a story about saving a Jewish neighbor or acquaintance" from the death camps.[2] They always replied: "Oh, the Jews? Well, there weren't really many Jews in this neighborhood . . . We have nothing against the Jews; we always got on well with them." She opined that the Germans could set their nonsensical refrain to music: "I hid a Jew for six weeks. I hid a Jew for eight weeks. All God's chillin hid Jews." Writing with bitter contempt, she commented that it wouldn't make their protests any more believable, but it would perhaps "sound better." In her outrage she reported, "To see a whole nation passing the buck is not an enlightening spectacle."[3]

Sometime later in June 1945, my father mentioned that Captain Fiori had been transferred to their sister squadron, the 15th Cavalry Squadron. He mentioned that he "hoped to get over there too" in short order. (His commentary reflected very clearly the confidence and respect he had for his prior CO, whose leadership had got him safely through the war.)

Pictured on the next page are three relaxed GIs who appear ready to accept a boat ride home and an honorable discharge. In military parlance, they appear to have "stacked arms." Pop stood on the left, with Al Garvin standing in the center and Al Penniplede on the right.

Clearly evident in the photo are their army-issue canvas "musette" bags, strapped to the outside of the turret of their tank. Each bag contained an individual crewman's personal items, which included a pair of clean dry socks, underclothing, a change of shirt or two, mess gear and other hygiene items, such as soap, toothpaste, toothbrush, a towel and a razor.

---

[1] Pringle, *The Master Plan*, 291-292.
[2] Ibid.
[3] Martha Gellhorn, *The Face of War* (New York: Atlantic Monthly Press, 1988), 162-163; Stafford, *Endgame, 1945*, 323; Hitchcock, *The Bitter Road to Freedom*, 181.

By the Fourth of July 1945, Dad wrote that his unit was situated in Selters, Germany. He mentioned being bored, with "nothing much to do, just play ball." On July 7, he noted that his company was moving out once again, yet he and several of his squadron mates had been awarded a short pass to a rest facility in Spa, the Belgian resort town that previously had been the Imperial German Army's headquarters on the Western Front during the World War I.[1]

On their arrival, they checked into a hotel and Pop once again observed that he had trouble sleeping on a soft bed between clean sheets. With some disappointment he wrote that he, "rolled all night."

On the following day, he and his pals walked around some and took a streetcar to Verveirs. On the following day, they went to the movies and a dance in Spa; he noted the Belgian band was very good and the girls were all "jitter bugs, but he was not." The next few days he wrote letters to his father and his bride, took a mineral bath, "loafed around," listened to some

---

[1] Generals Paul von Hindenburg and Eric Ludendorff directed the German armies more than twenty-five years earlier from their headquarters in Spa, Belgium. Caddick-Adams, *Snow & Steel*, 406.

music, and drank a little cognac. He wrote that he tried some Belgian beer, but described it as "too bitter" for his liking.

On the return trip from Spa on July 11, he reported passing "through the [the Ardennes] where the Germans made their counterattack last winter." He described seeing wrecked and burned-out equipment, both American and German, lying scattered in every direction. He mentioned passing through Aachen, Jülich, and Cologne, and he noted that all three cities had been absolutely devastated.

By the time of his return, he wrote that his "outfit" had relocated and he joined up with them after a nine-hour truck ride to the town of Weilmünster, east of Limburg, Germany.

In answer to a letter from Christine, my father's younger brother Bernard wrote in July 1945, beginning in his own affable fashion: "Howdy Doody to Youdy." In his letter, he mentioned that he hoped Francis would soon be "heading for home," indicating that their father would "feel a lot happier" to see him again since he had been gone for more than three years. He mused that after so much time it would be a great thing for all of them to finally "stand under one roof" again, as he hadn't seen his brother since 1941.

The photograph of Dad's brother Bernard on the next page fully captures his playful personality and *joie de vie*. He and my father were apparently very close while growing up.

"Bernie" (as he was known in the family) was an incredibly upbeat and cheerful person, who always seemed to have a twinkle of mischief and delight in his eye. During the war, he was more than pleased to have served his tour of duty while stationed at Hickam Field in Hawaii. Yet, from my standpoint, he appears in this photo to have just stepped off the set of *From Here to Eternity*, the movie based on a post-war novel by James Jones, which portrayed military life in Hawaii before the Japanese sneak attack on the U.S. fleet at Pearl Harbor.

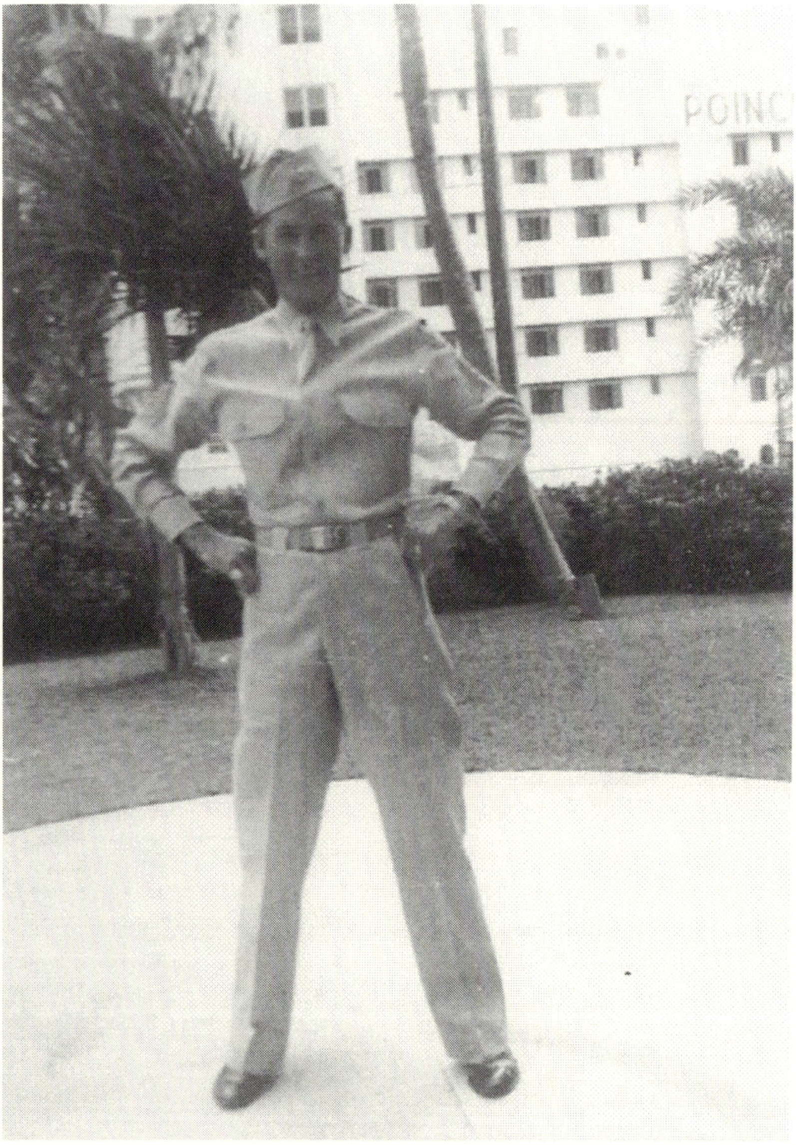
POINC

18. WORLD WAR II COMES TO AN END

Prior to the defeat of Japanese forces in the Pacific, the U.S. Navy spent much of 1943 recruiting, training, and rebuilding its fleet, aviation and land forces. Nine months passed before the Marine Corps stormed another Japanese-controlled island after Guadalcanal was secured in February 1943. That hiatus to rebuild the force was necessary, as the six-month campaign for Guadalcanal was "carried out on a shoestring." During that time, an Army task force retook the islands of Attu and Kiska in the Aleutians, and U.S. and Allied troops under MacArthur continued to wear down Japan's forces on New Guinea.[1]

After much discussion, it was decided that a series of amphibious landings across the Central Pacific was the best method to secure access to Japan's inner defensive perimeter. Thus, while Admiral Halsey's South Pacific force attacked Bougainville in the Solomon Islands in late 1943, Admiral Spruance's Fifth Fleet began its offensive by seizing the Tarawa Atoll. The march continued through the Marshall Islands and into the Marianas, as U.S. forces captured Saipan, Tinian, and Guam in the summer of 1944. Later, more bloody combat was necessary to capture Peleliu and the "island hopping" strategy continued into 1945 with the capture of Iwo Jima in March.

Beginning in April 1945, brutal fighting against Japanese forces continued on Okinawa, and not until mid-June 1945 was it finally secured. According to one authority, the number of Americans killed was around 12,500 with over 36,000 men wounded ashore and over 8,000 at sea."[2] Also, "a further 36,000 soldiers and Marines became non-battle casualties, many of them combat-fatigue cases."[3] Moreover, Admiral Spruance's fleet off Okinawa paid a heavy price in battle damage from Japanese kamikazes (suicide attack planes).

---

[1] James D. Hornfischer, *The Fleet at Flood Tide: America at Total War in the Pacific, 1944-1945* (New York: Bantam Books, 2016), 3.
[2] Hastings, *Retribution: The Battle for Japan, 1944- 45*, 386.
[3] Ibid., 402.

Returning to my father's narrative, by mid-July and into the month of August 1945, the 15th Cavalry Group Headquarters and the 15th Cavalry Squadron were categorized Class II, Strategic Reserve in the United States, while the 17th Cavalry Squadron prepared for deactivation. Later, they were re-categorized as Occupation Troops in the ETO.[1] With the war over in Europe, the Allies focused all their military resources toward ending the war with Imperial Japan.

On August 5, 1945, Dad wrote that his outfit was still posted in Weilmünster, Germany. He mentioned he kept himself busy working in the supply room, which he was soon destined to take over. His next diary entry, dated on August 8, noted that on returning to his room from CQ[2] the radio program was interrupted for a news flash: "Russia Declares War on Japan.'" He also mentioned having heard that the U.S. had developed a new weapon: the "Atom Bomb."

With the capture of Tinian in the summer of 1944, U.S. Navy Construction Battalions repaired and extended the Japanese runways for use by B-29 bombers. Ultimately, the 509th Composite Group, 20th Air Force deployed to the island of Tinian in July 1945 to perform their end-of-war mission.[3]

On August 6, 1945, Col. Paul Tibbets piloted a B-29 "Superfortress", the Enola Gay, which dropped the first atomic weapon ever used in war, code-named "Little Boy," on the Japanese city of Hiroshima. Tokyo had been eliminated as a target since it had been heavily damaged earlier by incendiary munitions and was considered "practically rubble" due to prior bomb strikes.[4] Instead, the city of Hiroshima was selected, as it was an intact target, which had been spared from previous attack; thus, the new bomb's effect would more likely register the desired psychological impression on Emperor Hirohito.

---

[1] TLR, 17.
[2] "CQ" is a military acronym for "Charge of Quarters" which amounts to assigned routine administrative duty for enlisted personnel around the company area, e.g., answering the telephone, signing people in and out, keeping order, etc.
[3] Richard B. Frank, *Downfall: The End of the Imperial Japanese Empire* (New York: Random House, 1999), 261.
[4] Ibid., 255, 264-265.

Only three days later, a second B-29 heavy bomber, named Bockscar, took off from Tinian to drop a larger, plutonium-implosion bomb, dubbed "Fat Man," on the Japanese city of Nagasaki. While the actual death toll from both bombs is unknown, the best estimate is between 100,000 and 200,000.[1]

As harsh as the fatality numbers were, it must be understood that in the summer of 1945 American planners believed an invasion of the Japan would produce a bloodbath, consuming some 100,000 American lives in the landing alone. Also, it was estimated that another million Americans would die to fully secure Japan's home islands, a sum far more than the combined casualties at Hiroshima and Nagasaki.

At the request of President Truman, General MacArthur, the Supreme Commander of the Southwest Pacific Area, studied the operation plan to invade the Japanese mainland and concluded that around a million U.S. troops would die in the invasions of Kyushu and Honshu alone.[2] Also, he estimated that the battle for Japan would rage on for another ten years "in the likely event that guerrilla forces retreated to the mountains." When considering prior predictions by MacArthur, it was known that his estimates of American casualties in prior battles in the Pacific during World War II had been uncannily accurate.[3]

On the other hand, the best estimates of probable total deaths in a mainland battle were about two million Japanese, and that number would grow much higher if civilian suicides and suicidal resistance caused hysteria, as was seen in the Guam and Okinawa campaigns.

Other U.S. estimates formulated during that summer of 1945 predicted that the "blood price" to defeat Imperial Japan by conquest would amount to five to ten million Japanese deaths, and the Americans would suffer between 1.7 and four million casualties, including 400,000 to 800,000 deaths.[4] As a consequence, U.S. war leaders deemed an invasion of the

---

[1] Frank, *Downfall*, 283-287.
[2] By memorandum to General Marshall from his deputy, Gen. Thomas T. Handy, it was estimated that avoiding a land invasion of Japan would save no less than 500,000 to 1,000,000 American lives.
McCullough, *Truman*, 400-401.
[3] George Feifer, *Tennozan* (New York: Ticknor & Fields, 1992), 572.
[4] Frank, *Downfall*, 340.

Japanese mainland absolutely unjustifiable. Admirals Nimitz and Halsey were of the opinion that the battle to reach Japanese soil would have been "apocalyptic" with American casualties approaching as many as one million men.[1]

Fortunately, on August 15, 1945, the Emperor's words were broadcast all over Japan declaring that Japan would accept capitulation. In his announcement, the Emperor made it clear "that the atomic bomb was the greatest reason for the surrender."[2] His close advisors thought that direct reference to the atomic bombs was indispensable and made surrender more palatable, as the Japanese people could save face by thinking they were defeated by science and not by a lack of spiritual power or through strategic errors.[3]

On August 29, Admiral Halsey's flagship, the USS Missouri, steamed into Tokyo Bay. By nightfall, nearly four hundred warships joined them and dropped anchor several miles out in the bay. Only a few days later, on September 2, 1945, MacArthur presided over the surrender of the Imperial Japanese on the deck of the Missouri, and the war with Japan came to an end.

Postwar revisionists and counterfactual historians have asserted that the war with Japan could have ended without our having to resort to atomic weaponry. However, it is undeniable that continued incendiary bombing by B-29 bombers for the remainder of 1945 would have vastly increased the death toll. Civilian casualties in the Japanese cities firebombed by early August 1945 had already far exceeded those at Hiroshima and Nagasaki combined. In addition, the U.S. strategic-bombing directive of August 11, if implemented, "would have caused far more loss of life by starvation than the atomic bombs exacted."[4]

Continuing with sound logic, historian Paul Kennedy wrote recently, "The only thing that seems certain is that the starving of the Japanese nation by submarine blockade or the blasting of the Japanese population by low-altitude bombing would have caused far greater loss of life than the

---

[1] John Wukovits, *Tin Can Titans* (Boston: Da Capo Press, 2017), 223, 225.
[2] Frank, *Downfall*, 320-321, 346.
[3] Ibid., 347.
[4] Feifer, *Tennozan*, 582.

atomic bombs that were dropped at Hiroshima and Nagasaki."[1] Also author Richard Frank put the matter in splendid perspective by noting, "Japan in 1945 was facing mass famine brought on by the destruction of her transportation system."[2] Starvation with the likelihood of accompanying fatal diseases would surely have caused a loss of life many times greater than that caused by "Little Boy" and "Fat Man." Without recourse to atomic weapons in 1945, Emperor Hirohito's surrender would have been delayed, and that postponement would have been far more costly in terms of American and Japanese lives.

Author James Hornfischer opined recently that Rich Frank's analysis in his book Downfall "stands like a tombstone over the tired argument that the bombs were a needless cruelty inflicted on an already-defeated country."[3] Besides, whether it was immoral for the U.S. to resort to atomic weapons to end the war, one former World War II combat infantry officer found it interesting that "the farther from the scene of horror, the easier the talk."[4]

From Dad's accounts, written while he was still exposed to orders for further combat in the Pacific Theater, it is beyond doubt that he was elated to learn that atomic bombs had finally put an end to the war. He and his companions had seen enough carnage and death, and they were completely incapable of summoning up moral outrage concerning the use of those weapons. They had seen the German soldiers surrender willingly with their own eyes and knew the Japanese were far more fanatical as a whole. Knowing full well that an invasion of Japan's home islands would increase the rate of fatalities exponentially, there was no enthusiasm for fighting further against people who were determined to expend their lives for their emperor, rather than surrender.[5]

---

[1] Kennedy, *Engineers of Victory*, 338.
[2] Frank, *Downfall*, 350.
[3] *Wall Street Journal*, Sunday, November 18-19, 2017, C18.
[4] Paul Fussell, *Thank God for the Atom Bomb and Other Essays* (New York: Summit Books, 1988), 19. Churchill was in complete agreement with Truman's decision to use atom bombs to end World War II. Manchester and Reid, *The Last Lion*, 947.
[5] Not one single Japanese military unit had surrendered during the entire war. McCullough, *Truman*, 438.

Reading Pop's diary so long after the fact, his relief on that occasion seems nearly palpable. Never had he or any of his fellow comrades imagined that the war would have end so rapidly.[1] It certainly made them grateful that their lives had been spared, and they came to the remarkable conclusion that they actually had a future ahead of them. Yet, with all their celebratory backslapping, they no doubt remembered with sadness the many others who had perished along the way.[2]

The mood of the average GI at that time cannot be described any better than by author Paul Fussell: "My division like most of the ones transferred from Europe, was to take part in the invasion of Honshu . . . I was a twenty-one-year-old second lieutenant of infantry . . . When the atom bombs were dropped and news began to circulate that . . . the invasion would not, after all, be necessary, . . . for all the practiced phlegm of our tough facades we broke down and cried with relief and joy. We were going to live. We were going to grow to adulthood after all."[3]

On August 15, 1945, Dad wrote, "Today is the big day," as the radio indicated to one and all: "The war is over." He was understandably very pleased, but he didn't feel any different, as he was still wearing an army uniform. Yet, demobilization was obviously underway as he reported with delight that they had turned in their tanks at the ordnance depot that morning. By then, however, he was surely irked, and the question that occurred to him was, "When will I be going home?"

By V-mail letter Dad wrote to his "Dearest Christine", venting his frustration concerning Victory Day. He was clearly in an awful mood, as he inquired whether "people back in the states" were enjoying their "wonderful day," while "people who really won this damn war, and who really suffered and felt its breath down their back and on their faces . . . were still sitting in some foreign land." He went on to wonder "if a guy

---

[1] By 1945, millions of men in no fewer than thirty U.S. divisions from the ETO were "on the way to the Pacific" for combat redeployment. Ibid.
[2] On the question of whether the U.S. owes Japan an apology in the context of that long and bloody war, Truman's authorization to use atomic bombs to end it was the "lesser of the evils available to him." Miscamble, *The Most Controversial Decision: Truman, the Atomic Bombs, and the Defeat of Japan*, 123.
[3] Fussell, *Thank God for the Atom Bomb and Other Essays*, 28; on this point, see McCullough, *Truman*, 455-456.

could only get drunk enough to forget all his miserable memories, on a day like this." He said that he was thankful to God to be alive and "said a few prayers" for his fallen buddies, "who weren't as lucky" as he had been. He also expressed relief at no longer having to "sweat out the [possibility of redeployment to the] Pacific or C.B.I. [the China-Burma-India Theater of Operations]," but registered his disdain for all the "'USO Commandos back in the States and the rear echelon" types, wondering whether they would be the first to be discharged from service.

The ire he expressed in that letter undoubtedly came from his belief that he and his cavalry mates were being forgotten on foreign soil, while those at home were "safe, comfortable and prosperous." To be still in uniform, while others were already celebrating, was galling to Pop. After getting it off his chest, he calmed down and told his "darling" that he very much looked forward to coming home, as "you know it will be for keeps."

Perhaps his rant from across the sea was understandable given the circumstances, but it gave his young wife much cause for concern. She promptly wrote her brothers-in-law, Joe Jr. and Bernard Gough, asking them for guidance. They both responded immediately by letter in September 1945. Taken together, their response was essentially identical: "stay positive, keep your chin up and everything would be fine once we get home and see each other once again."

Dad's next older brother Joe (photograph on the next page) wrote from McClellan Air Field in Sacramento, California. He explained that he "knew Francis better than the rest" of the family, and he thought that Dad would very likely be the same fellow as he was before, but he cautioned her to be patient, "as things over there might have changed him a little bit."

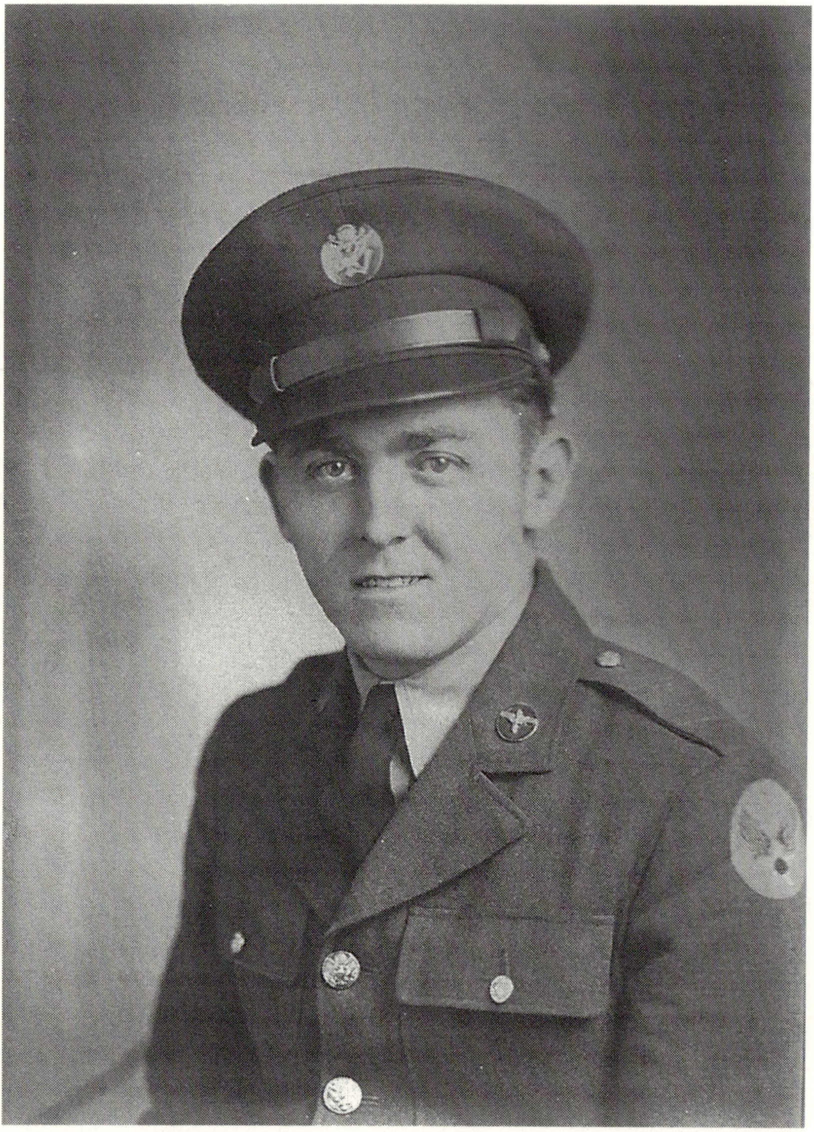

19. HOMEWARD BOUND

On September 2, 1945, Dad noted in his diary that he was one of only twelve men left in Company F of the 17th Cavalry Squadron; the rest, he indicated, had all been transferred over to the 113th Cavalry Squadron of the 113th Cavalry Group. He wrote, "I'm left in Weilminster, by myself, to check in [and account for] all the equipment and company property."

Above is an image of the shoulder patch of the "Red Horse" Cavalry, the 113th Cavalry Group (Mechanized), consisting of the 113th and 125th Cavalry Recce Squadrons.[1] They were a tough, battle-hardened cavalry group.[2] Although Pop was separated from military service wearing the red and yellow Red Horse Cavalry shoulder patch, he maintained primary

---

[1] Originally an Iowa National Guard unit, President Roosevelt called them into federal service in January 1941. Balkoski, *From Brittany to the Reich*, 121.
[2] The 113th Cavalry Group deployed to France in July 1944 and was attached to the XIX Corps, fighting at the Falaise Gap and in the Ardennes. Rottman, *World War II US Cavalry Groups*, 40.

allegiance and fidelity to the 17th Cavalry Recce Squadron of the 15th Cavalry Group.

By September 3, Dad reported he was finishing his duties in the supply room, noting that all books and "property turn-in slips" were cleared. By Wednesday, September 5, he wrote, "Today at 1300—[I] leave the 17th Cav —going to the 113th Cav — on my way home—Happy Days."

He noted on September 10, that he had left Germany "for good" early in the morning, heading for Camp Cleveland, France. They traveled by truck and spent the night in Metz. By the time he got to his destination early the next morning, he wrote, "The Red Cross girls had coffee and donuts waiting for us." He reported that they were in "Zone VI" and were sleeping in seven-man tents, and he described the days as warm, but the nights were "very cold." He later mentioned that they had been issued another blanket, but "Now we have three and it's still cold at night."

On October 2, 1945, he reported they were up early in the morning and left Camp Cleveland by truck for the railroad station. To his amazement, they were loaded onto passenger cars, six men to a compartment, with ten compartments per car. "What a [pleasant] surprise," he wrote, "We were lucky to have soft cushioned seats in the compartment", as he had expected to be assigned space on another awful 40 and 8 French boxcar, like the one in which he had traveled to Belgium in the fall of 1944. He mentioned the scuttlebutt that they were headed for a "cigarette camp"[1] and he hoped their stay there would be short and sweet. Naturally, the closer he got to home, the more he expressed his restlessness, indicating understandable impatience for the day he would finally get his "freedom [discharge] papers."

By the morning of October 3, Pop reported that they arrived at their destination by truck in the middle of a pine forest: Camp Twenty Grand.

---

[1] The hastily erected tent cities were situated in forests and fields near the French port city of Le Havre to process men redeploying to the U.S. in the spring of 1945. Each was named after a cigarette brand popular in the 1940s. "Camp Twenty Grand" was located in the vicinity of Henouville/Duclair, between Rouen and Le Havre. Nick McGrath, "Camp Lucky Strike France," *On Point: Journal of Army History,* Army Historical Foundation. Vol. 20, no. 3 (Winter 2015), 44-45.

There, they were assigned to large, twelve-man tents, and once they got their tents set up and cots made, he "hit the sack".

On the following morning, he described having slept "like a log", in spite of the cold weather. By the next day, he began his investigation of the vicinity and described it as "not so hot." He grumbled that the shower facility was about a half mile away and "the water was never warm."

While waiting their turn to board a ship back to the U.S., the soldiers were processed and afforded a physical examination, which of course included the inevitable short-arm inspection. Then, after slightly more than a week, Dad reported that he and his colleagues had received American currency in exchange for their French francs, and they left Camp Twenty Grand by truck on the evening of the eleventh of October.

He next described his arrival at the port of Le Havre, France, where he and his mates cheerfully clambered aboard a Liberty ship for the sea voyage home. Curiously, however, he failed to record the name of that vessel. Such oversight on his part makes very clear his wild excitement to be finally on the long-awaited trip home. Up until then, he had named every other vessel he boarded without fail, not to mention the countless towns and cities he passed through in Europe during the war.

By Friday, October 12, 1945, Dad noted that the sailors "dropped the gang plank" on the pier, cast off their mooring lines and two tugboats pushed them out of the harbor toward the blue waters of the English Channel. Within an hour or so of their embarkation, he described clearing the breakers and heading west across the Atlantic Ocean. After such a momentous day, he wrote sparingly: "Tonight we turn our watches back; food good, weather good."

On his second day at sea, he described how thrilled he was to have been served fresh milk and a cup of ice cream for dessert. He described it as the best refreshment he had tasted "since 1941 in PA." He also commented that all of the men he saw standing at the ship's rail were "looking forward, and to the left and right front—everyone had the same idea—no one cared where they had been, they were all looking to the open sea and America."

By Sunday, October 14, he mentioned having gone to Mass aboard ship that morning, and remembered it was his fourth anniversary as a soldier. Afterward, he described seeing a chart posted in the mess hall, which recorded their progress in crossing the ocean. He was pleased to learn that a member of the ship's crew updated it daily in red pencil. He again raved about the fresh milk and ice cream they received every day. Inevitably, their long days aboard ship grew monotonous; however, he specifically mentioned enjoying the movie *Johnny Angel*, which he viewed that evening along with many others topside near the ship's stern. He wrote thankfully that the movie was a great morale booster and gave him two hours of relief from what otherwise was a very tedious sea voyage.

On October 15, Pop wrote appreciatively, "The food seems to be getting better all the time." He noted there was nothing for him to do but go out on the crowded deck and walk around, shoot craps[1], or sleep. He commented that boredom set in, so he was doing lots of reading and sleeping, little or no gambling, and quite a bit of walking. He seemed to enjoy the fresh sea breezes, while looking out at the water, as the ship plowed its way through the endless waves.

By October 16, he wrote lyrically, "Still churning our way towards the U.S.A." That day, he described spending long hours staring at the endless, slate blue sea, and noted with interest that they passed another Liberty ship, headed in the opposite direction. Later that day while on guard duty, he described seeing the beautiful red glare of sunset. While viewing the horizon, he wrote that it reminded him of an old phrase: "Red sunset means sailor take warning."[2] Despite his confusion about that rhyme, his senses proved accurate because early the next day, bad weather became a reality, and they encountered whitecaps and rough, choppy seas that lasted all day. Pop diarized, "Some of the guys are getting sick, but I'm still OK." Since that Liberty ship was a much smaller and slower vessel than the ship he earlier cruised to Europe in, it is not surprising that some of his colleagues encountered nausea and seasickness on their journey home.[3]

By October 19, Dad observed that the sea had finally calmed and by keeping his eyes on the horizon he observed two whales, spouting in the

---

[1] "Craps" is an informal form of gambling in which money wagers are made against the outcome of the dice roll.
[2] I believe the actual weather-predicting rhyme goes something like this: Red sky at night, sailors' delight, red sky in morning, sailors take warning.
[3] Liberty ships were less than half the length of the RMS *Queen Mary* and their maximum speed was only 11 knots, propelled by one screw. By comparison, the *Queen Mary* cruised at 30 knots, propelled by four screws beneath the water. Nicholas A. Veronico, *Hidden Warships* (Minneapolis, MN: Zenith Press, 2015), 215.

distance. He mentioned astonishment at the size of those beasts, as they swam directly toward the ship, dove under the bow and soon reappeared far astern. Happily, the playfulness of those large creatures caused no structural harm to the ship.

Finally, that afternoon, after many long days looking out at the boundless ocean, they were told to assemble below to be briefed on the disembarkation procedure. He described great anticipation and the excitement he felt: "Tomorrow is the day we finally touch the soil we were away from so long and fought for."

Early on Saturday morning, October 20, 1945, Pop described his elation at seeing on the horizon, his first glimmer of America. To avoid the stale, fetid air below deck, he and his pals crowded the rail to enjoy the fresh smell of their native land, which lay beyond their view. He noted with excitement, that he "couldn't see the coast, but could see beacon lights off to our right." Then, as they arrived at the mouth of Boston Harbor, he was thrilled to see a "GI tugboat with a band onboard" there to greet them.

It was his first look at the Port of Boston, and he described the harbor as jam-packed with "Navy fighting ships." Very soon thereafter, a pilot launch came along side and several tugboats began to nudge the ship toward the dock. Their transport ship eventually made fast to the pier and they began unloading at exactly 0930 in the morning. In his diary, he recorded the total mileage of their sea cruise was 3,482 miles. "Gosh, but it was a funny feeling to come back," he wrote. His excitement rose to new heights as he described a tingling that ran down his spine. He thought to himself, "What a grand and wonderful sight, just to see the U.S.A. again."

Later around noon, my father and the rest of the troops disembarked from the ship and they boarded a train, only "25 yards from the gang plank." Yet, consistent with the army's usual practice ("hurry up and wait") they encountered delay and finally arrived at their destination: Camp Myles Standish, near Taunton, Massachusetts, where they found "nice soft beds" awaiting them in barracks. "For chow," he said simply, "we had steak." After that meal, he reported with enthusiasm that he topped off his evening with two glasses of "American beer!"

On awakening from a good night's sleep on October 21, Dad made special note of his first morning back in the U.S.A, "one year and eight months . . . God, it seemed like an awful long time." He was pleased that the familiar staccato notes of "reveille" had not awakened them that morning, and he mentioned great satisfaction of the taste of his first malted milk and sundae in over two years. Later that day, he enjoyed the thrill of being able to speak by telephone with his father, his eldest brother Bob and his sister Mary.

On the following morning, Pop boarded a train headed to Fort George G. Meade, an army post located half way between Washington, D.C., and Baltimore, Maryland. On his arrival at the demobilization center, he was welcomed, oriented and assigned to barracks. Later, he was allowed to travel to his father's home[1] in the District of Columbia, where he stayed up talking most of the night. It was a festive occasion, and he commented, "Geez, but Dad was glad to see me . . . but I was the happiest of them all."

Not surprisingly, the wheels of the military ground very slowly when it came time to demobilize so many personnel at war's end. The endless round of lectures, briefings, and inspections continued for most of the next day, but Dad was able to return to his father's home that evening. Later that evening, he attempted to place a telephone call to "Chris" back in Kansas, but he remarked: "no soap", after realizing that his request couldn't reach her. That upset him, as he had not heard her cheerful voice in nearly two years. However, his disappointment was assuaged somewhat later when Dad's Aunt Tess, Uncle "Scotty," and his first cousin Mary Ellen Scott, paid him a surprise visit. Before going to bed that evening, Dad observed that his father "looks the best of them all."

By the following day, his final physical evaluation[2] was complete, and he wrote, "Tomorrow we should be finished with Army life." Cheerfully that evening, he was finally successful in contacting Christine by telephone. Afterward, he wrote joyously, "Gosh, it was good to hear her voice—and she will come to D.C., soon."

---

[1] Sometime in the early 1940s, my Grand Pap moved to Washington, D.C., to begin employment working on the massive new headquarters for the U.S. War Department, the Pentagon. As a result, he eventually made a home on tree-lined Hobart Street in the Northwest Washington neighborhood of Mount Pleasant.

[2] On his separation physical examination, he was described as standing five feet and nine inches tall and weighing 152 pounds.

On October 25, 1945, he was mustered out of the military and returned to civilian status. He described it as his best day in over four years. Later that morning, he reported to the quartermaster shop, where he was issued a new cotton shirt and pair of trousers, and his "ETO" jacket that included a "ruptured duck" honorable discharge emblem sewed on. (Above is an image of that cloth emblem, which was sewn over the breast pocket of his uniform tunic.)

Of the many offices he visited that day, while out-processing from military service, the last and most important was the Finance station, where he gladly accepted his mustering-out pay in cash. Then, after receipt of his discharge papers, he caught the next bus bound for Washington, D.C., and returned to his prior, peaceful life. (Surely, no man received his honorable discharge papers from the army with greater pleasure than my father.)

By the morning of October 29, Christine's train squealed to a stop next to a platform at Washington's Union Station. Later, she wrote her mother about her arrival and said, "Fran[1] was there at the station, waiting to meet her." She noted, "He is fine, looks and acts like the same as ever . . . you wouldn't know that he had been through anything at all, but he doesn't want to talk about it." Continuing to soothe her mother's concerns she wrote, "It doesn't seem like we were separated for all those months; everything is just the same as it was 22 months ago." She also indicated rather hopefully that the nightmare he went through was now "set aside and

---

[1] Mom always called him Fran and his friends knew him as Frank.

forgotten." That was certainly the wish of all those worried wives and mothers who had waited so long to welcome home their returning loved ones from overseas.

By letter on Christmas Eve, Christine wrote her parents that they would celebrate their second wedding anniversary at a small family gathering, following their return from midnight Mass. She mentioned also that they were looking forward to finding an apartment of their own after the New Year. (At that time, the couple was sharing an apartment with Dad's youngest brother Adrian, who likewise had been separated recently from military service and lived on Park Road in Northwest Washington, D.C.) That living arrangement was necessary since housing was in short supply due to the droves of former servicemen returning to civilian life.

The photograph below is of a young Adrian Gough, a life-long bachelor and the most happy-go-lucky of all of Pop's siblings. During his USAAF service, he had trained to be a crewman on a twin-engine B-26 "Marauder" medium bomber during 1945. Fortunately, the war ended before he was assigned to flight duty overseas. Regrettably, however, his later years were encumbered by a self-inflicted disorder known by some as the "Irish flu", which ultimately led to his untimely demise due to chronic alcoholism.

20. THE POSTWAR YEARS

In early 1946, Christine Gough obtained employment with the U.S. Veterans Administration (the VA)[1]. Along with that clerical job in the VA's Central Office in Washington, D.C., came a salary of nearly $1,700 per annum. As Dad had also landed a position with the U.S. Government in Washington, they were at last beginning their married life together in reasonably good financial shape for those times.

After setting aside a decent sum of money, Dad made the decision to put his GI Bill educational benefits[2] to work by attending college. While studying for his degree, he minimized expenses by living at his maternal Uncle Frank McLaughlin's home on Chester Avenue in Philadelphia. To economize further, Christine returned to Kansas to await the birth of their first child at the home of her parents; my arrival[3] in late 1947 likely ended any chance for the quiet, peaceful postwar lifestyle they had longed for.

---

[1] By then, Gen. Omar Bradley as the new VA Administrator. In 1989, the VA transitioned from an independent agency to cabinet level status and is now known as the U.S. Department of Veterans Affairs.

[2] The original "GI Bill of Rights" arose out of the Servicemen's Readjustment Act of 1944 to provide VA educational benefits to millions of veterans who returned from World War II. Ferguson, *The Last Cavalryman*, 64.

[3] My birthplace, Caldwell, Kansas, in Sumner County is located about sixty miles south of Wichita. Nicknamed "The Border Queen", its southern town limits coincide with the Kansas-Oklahoma border. By the late 1800s, it was the terminus of the Chisholm Trail where trail drivers of Texas longhorn cattle proved fatal to "more law officers than any other Kansas community." Bill O'Neal, *Ghost Towns of the American West* (Lincolnwood, IL: Publications International, 1995), 32. By 1880, Caldwell became so infested by rowdy cowboys, prostitutes, whiskey peddlers, and livestock rustlers that its name became synonymous with violence. Robert R. Dykstra, *The Cattle Towns* (New York: Alfred A. Knopf, 1968), 114. The sight of a horse thief at the end of a rope under a cottonwood tree was not unusual and a marshal's term in office in Caldwell was about two weeks. Don Worcester, *The Chisholm Trail: High Road of the Cattle Kingdom* (New York: Indian Head Books, 1994), 130. In September 1893, Caldwell inhabitants witnessed the Cherokee Strip land rush as wagons and

After Dad's graduation from college in February 1948, he found a place for us to reside in the city of Washington, and Mom and I moved "back East" to be with him. By then, he had again garnered employment with the federal government in 1950. At that time, he commuted to work at the Pentagon and put in long hours that included duty on most weekends.[1]

By the early to mid-1950s, my siblings (Phil, Patti, and Jody, respectively) began to arrive in rapid fashion and became my lifelong companions. Shortly after my brother was born, Dad and Mom decided we had outgrown our one-bedroom apartment in the city. Hence, they packed up their worldly possessions and moved from the redbrick New Amsterdam building on 14th Street N.W. (near Meridian Hill Park), abandoning crowded city life for a new home in the bustling suburbs of Northern Virginia.[2]

While attending school in the years that followed, I recall having to fill out forms for school administrative purposes. As instructed by my father, I always reported that he was a U.S. Government employee. That was what he told me to do, and that was all I knew as a child. Only years later, after his retirement from the NSA,[3] did I come to understand the confidential nature of his work and grasp the importance of an event that occurred in

---

horseback riders stampeded early across the state line to stake land claims in Oklahoma. *Caldwell Messenger*, Wednesday, Sept. 8, 1993, 1.

[1] As a youngster, I remember the fun of streetcar and bus rides while accompanying my father to work on Saturdays; while he worked, I climbed on mail carts and rode them down sloped, polished corridors of the Pentagon. Of course, that was prohibited activity and I had been duly warned. Yet, as I couldn't resist, my fun came to an abrupt end when I crashed into a man wearing shiny stars on his shoulders; thereafter, I remained home with Mom on Saturdays.

[2] As a returning veteran with an honorable discharge, Dad was eligible for a VA home loan, requiring little or no down payment, making that new home purchase a reality.

[3] That ultra-secret agency of the U.S. Government is an outgrowth of the Second World War, known facetiously by some as "No Such Agency". Created in October 1952 by secret executive order signed by President Truman, the NSA engages in the global collection of signals intelligence and code-breaking activities that are absolutely essential for our nation's security. Michael V. Hayden, *Playing to the Edge* (NY: Penguin, 2016), 3, 31.

the early 1960s. Looking back with the clarity of hindsight, the pieces fell into place.

At some time during the fall of 1962, I overheard rumblings of a plan my parents concocted for Mom to take "the kids on an adventure to the country to see the fall colors". Being the eldest child, I was enlisted to assist her, but was told not to let on since it was intended to be a surprise for my siblings. Luckily, however, that trip never came to fruition.[1] I remember disappointment at the time, as I was unsuspecting of any connection with the ongoing missile crisis in Cuba. Indeed, it was fortunate for all of us that that dangerous situation came to a peaceful resolution.

Sometime earlier, Dad had undoubtedly discussed with our mother some emergency information, explaining his assembly area in the event of a national emergency. Yet families had to devise their own doomsday evacuations.[2] At that time his workplace was the U.S. Naval Security Station[3], located on an elevated tract of land on Nebraska Avenue in Washington, D.C., near American University. From his building it was reportedly possible to see the Pentagon in good weather, and that location provided a line-of-sight view of numerous foreign embassies.[4]

---

[1] The destination of that proposed outing was unclear, but looking back I realize that her maternal instincts for survival were working overtime. She enlisted my help to pack and load the family station wagon, and in return, she agreed to allow me to bring along our dog, "Socks". Unaware of the danger at hand, I recall thinking at the time that such an abrupt trip was unusual since my parents were total strangers to spontaneity.

[2] Dobbs, *One Minute to Midnight*, 311.

[3] As a youngster, my annual birthday treat was a trip to old Griffith Stadium to watch the opening day baseball game of the Washington Senators. Dad left me in the car in a barbed wire enclosed parking lot until noon, as there I caught up on my homework. The marine guards allowed me to pass into the lot with him, but I was barred from exiting the vehicle for any reason. In hindsight, the basis for that curious requirement makes sense to me now.

[4] That location was formerly the campus of a private women's college, Mount Vernon Seminary; within weeks after the Japanese attack on Pearl Harbor, the U.S. Navy commandeered the school while the students were home on Christmas break. Up went a chain-link fence guarded by U.S. Marines, and it became an intelligence station designed to monitor radio

At that time, NSA employees at Fort Meade, Maryland, were ordered to make their way north to a prepared facility in Pennsylvania in the event of an emergency. Dad's orders, on the other hand, were to proceed south to a specified location in rural Virginia. That place was Vint Hill Farms Station in the Blue Ridge Mountain foothills of Fauquier County, Virginia, where on occasion he took my brother and me fishing on weekends as youngsters. Little did we know then, as we fished a little and horsed around a lot, that beyond the woods was a top-secret cryptographic signals-intercept and electronic warfare site.[1] Only later in his career was he required to commute from our home in northern Virginia to NSA headquarters at Fort Meade.

As the years rolled by, Mom and Dad continued to live their lives in the pleasant suburbs of a prosperous America. She taught private lessons to innumerable piano students and played the organ every Sunday at Mass.[2] He was active in church functions and sang in a local barbershop chorus, the Fairfax Jubil-Aires. He also attended my youth baseball games and participated in my brother's Boy Scout activities. As to my sisters, both of

---

signals and diplomatic codes. David Brinkley, *Washington Goes to War* (New York: Alfred A. Knopf, 1988), 116-118.

[1] The U.S. Defense Department closed that facility after the Cold War ended, although its location had proved to be perfect for radio message interception. In late 1943 enemy radio intercepts revealed that the Germans fully expected the D-Day invasion to land on the beaches of Calais, instead of at Normandy. Liza Mundy, *Code Girls* (New York: Hatchette, 2017), Mundy, *Code Girls*, 297-299; *Fauquiernow.com*, Wednesday, Nov. 6, 2013.

[2] Mom was a devout a Roman Catholic; she made sure no meat was served at supper on Friday night and we all attended Mass every Sunday morning. To please her, I became an altar boy in grade school after memorizing the required Latin prayer responses. At the end of each week, Mom made sure we knelt on the hard wood floor beside our beds in order to complete a navigation of the rosary beads before turning in; somehow, my request for a waiver from that activity was granted upon reaching high school age. Pop, on the other hand, was also raised in the Catholic faith, but he seemed to operate at a different level than Mom; he claimed exemption from rosary detail, but to his credit he faithfully served as an usher and assisted with the offertory collection at Mass on Sunday.

our parents had what can best be described as traditional attitudes; like some among their generation, they were less than enthusiastic about female participation in sports. Instead, my sisters were encouraged to learn domestic management skills and the culinary arts.

As we grew older, our family life seemed to settle down and better days ensued until our mother's breast cancer returned after nearly twenty years of remission. Relieved that her long suffering had finally come to an end, we lost our emotional oasis to that dreadful disease in the summer of 1979.

After that family tragedy, it took Dad several years to come to grips with her passing, but eventually he did and he sold the family home, pulled up stakes and left for sunny Myrtle Beach. While residing there, he mellowed somewhat and enjoyed the warm weather, sandy beaches and his favorite Scotch whisky: Dewar's on the rocks. He let his gray hair grow out (previously cut in a flat-top) and played regular rounds of golf with former NSA colleagues, "who happened to live in the area."

With the passage of time, my relations with him became attenuated, as he became more distant and much less interested in family affairs; ultimately that led to disaffection. By that time, he had resuscitated his charming persona and found female companionship, while pursuing the social landscape of South Carolina's Grand Strand.

Not until his deteriorating health required it did the family arrange to bring him home to Virginia to ensure his medical needs were met. Coronary artery disease together with a significant cognitive decline caused his sunset days to be sadly diminished. After only a few short months, his health went into steep decline and his life ended in the autumn of 1996.

Now my parent's mortal remains lie in a shared grave on a grassy hilltop in the rolling Virginia country setting of Culpeper National Cemetery. While they no longer tread this Earth, their memory and spirit remain, and we are grateful for every advantage they provided us in life.

Thus, ends this linear narrative of my father's life, as I came to know it. In accomplishing this task, I endeavored to be as open as possible in setting forth his journey through life, centered on his notes and war diary and my own observations. I leave this quest with a certain amount of sadness and disappointment, knowing that our relationship could have been so much better. Unlike the warm ties I had with my mother, I regret that attempts to understand him in life were elusive and efforts to gain his praise went unnoticed.

Recently, my wife and I had the opportunity to travel to the United Kingdom. There, we made a special effort to visit Scotland, since that was where the 15th Cavalry Regiment (Mechanized) first made European landfall in early 1944. During our visit, I was reminded of my father's dismay that the Republic of Ireland, the nation of much of his ancestry, had remained neutral throughout World War II.

Of course, Dad was well aware of the bitterness between the British and the Irish people. He also recognized that much bloodshed had been spilled to gain her independence, but in spite of all that, he believed Irish neutrality provided advantage to Nazi Germany during the war.

In any case, while touring Edinburgh Castle, we noticed a substantial number of former servicemen with the "Gough" surname, who were listed among the World War II casualties on the Scottish National War Memorial Roll of Honor. There, in the solemn setting of that Gothic shrine to military service and bravery, we encountered a poignant passage that may apply to my father's journey:

"The Souls of the Righteous are in the Hand of God; There Shall No Evil Happen to Them, They are in Peace."

EPILOGUE

Having finished this account of Dad's life, it is now up to others, including his living descendants and those yet unborn, to assess the contribution he and his generation made to our nation during the turbulent twentieth century. In doing so, it may be useful to consider how World War II left its mark on him and all those who fought against the Axis powers.

As an excursion into the realm of psychobiography, the discussion below supports my doubt that my father sustained any chronic nervous or psychological disability as a result of his combat exposure in World War II, while others of his generation were not so fortunate. Based on decades of VA appellate adjudication experience, involving countless neuropsychiatric disability cases, I believe the following analysis has validity.

At the outset, I begin by observing that years after the American Civil War, Gen. William T. Sherman, delivered a speech in which he stated, "There is many a boy here today who looks on war as all glory, but . . . it is all hell." That became known as his "War Is Hell" speech.[1] Earlier, he had made a similar comment: "War is cruelty . . . you cannot refine it."[2] Like me, those who have read about the many wars that have taken place in our history, know the catastrophic effect combat can have on individual soldiers and their families. Through the efforts of skilled professionals and public media, many in America are now aware that combat-related stressors and/or in-service traumatic events can lead to chronic mental disease in some individuals. The term in use today for this is post-traumatic stress disorder (PTSD).

In prior years, the phenomenon was described as "shell shock,"[3] "battle fatigue," or "war neurosis."[1] By any name, it is a genuine mental disorder

---

[1] Michael Fellman, *Citizen Sherman: A Life of William Tecumseh Sherman* (New York: Random House, 1995), 306; James M. McPherson, *The War that Forged a Nation* (New York: Oxford University Press, 2015), 32.
[2] Shelby Foote, *The Civil War: A Narrative, Red River to Appomattox* (New York: Random House, 1974), 602.
[3] Manifested by "cowering, cringing, and gibbering with fright" at the sound of gunfire, shell shock exacted a heavy toll on the men, reaching more than 50,000 cases by the end of World War I. Gilbert, *The Somme:*

and the American Psychiatric Association (APA) sets forth criteria in its *Diagnostic and Statistical Manual of Mental Disorders* (DSM). Periodically, the APA revises the manual; the latest version, the fifth edition, was published in 2013, and is referred to as DSM-V.

More than twenty years ago, when my father passed away, a prior edition of the DSM was in effect and set forth the basic symptoms of PTSD. Although not all-inclusive, the clinical manifestations of the disorder are essentially as follows:

1. Re-experiencing traumatic events (flashbacks, recurrent nightmares of the traumatic event, intrusive recollections, and intensely frightening thoughts);
2. Persistent avoidance of certain events or objects (emotional numbness, detachment, diminished interest in activities, survivor guilt);
3. Marked arousal symptoms (e.g., exaggerated startle response, hyper vigilance, self-destructive behavior, and sleep disturbance).

Heroism and Horror in the First World War (NY: Henry Holt and Co., 2006), 65 and 148.

[1] We have come a long way as a nation concerning our understanding about combat-induced neurosis. Previously, soldiers were evacuated to an "exhaustion" center, injected with a sedative to allow sleep for as long as three days, and "woken up only for food and to carry out their bodily functions. At intervals they were given saline intravenous injections until, hollow-cheeked, bog-eyed, and trembling they were placed in hot showers and shaved. Then perhaps [they were afforded] a little elementary psychoanalysis." Whiting, *Papa Goes to War,* 159-160. If in doubt about the reality of combat-induced PTSD, one need only read a few pages of a recent historical work concerning World War I trench warfare in Flanders. There, the gruesomeness of combat at the Third Battle of Ypres, one soldier declared, "Every man who endured Passchendaele ['treading on old and new dead'] would never be the same again." Groom, *A Storm in Flanders: The Ypres Salient, 1914-1918: Tragedy and Triumph on the Western Front,* 113-114, 22. During World War II, the U.S. Surgeon General noted there was "no such thing as getting used to combat . . . Thus, psychiatric casualties are as inevitable as gunshot and shrapnel wounds in warfare." Gilbert, *The Second World War: A Complete History,* 599.

Initially, a close review of my father's written work leads me to conclude that he welcomed his overseas adventure to fight for his country. However, his nearly one-year exposure to the devastation of combat surely put that thought to rest. Thus, there is no doubt that his contact with death during wartime amounted to a stressor sufficient to cause PTSD.

Like many others of his generation, he was enthusiastic about entering military service. On learning of the Japanese surprise attack at Pearl Harbor, he and most of his fellow draftees fully embraced the idea of taking part in a just and necessary war. They had read about fascist aggression and knew of the brutality perpetrated in Europe and Asia in the 1930s and early '40s. They understood that those in power in Germany, Italy and Japan were carving a path toward world domination. Contemporaneous magazine and newspaper articles, as well as movie newsreel footage made it clear to them that ruthless militarists had to be dealt with overseas.

By early 1940, free world luminaries including FDR and Winston Churchill had assessed the situation and recognized the threat of tyranny. Others like British Prime Minister, Neville Chamberlain, conflict-averse isolationists like Charles Lindbergh,[1] and Ambassador Joe Kennedy,[2] were blinded by wishful thinking and willing to appease Hitler and his Axis allies.

---

[1] Colonel Lindbergh, the transatlantic aviator, was a spokesman for the American First Committee, which disbanded in shame within a few days after the Pearl Harbor attack; FDR compared him unfavorably to "the summer soldier" and "sunshine patriot" in Thomas Paine's 1776 *Crisis* pamphlet. See Davis, *FDR: The War President, 1940-1943*, 172. FDR reportedly told his treasury secretary that he was absolutely sure that Lindbergh was a Nazi. Joseph P. Lash, *Roosevelt and Churchill, 1939-1941* (NY: W.W. Norton, 1976), 141; Kenneth S. Davis, *FDR: Into the Storm* (NY: Random House, 1993), 504.

[2] Ambassador to the Court of St. James in London, Joseph P. Kennedy, Sr. was an outspoken isolationist, who opposed FDR's plan to provide billions of dollars of aid to Great Britain (Lend-Lease) in late 1940 and 1941. His defeatism became evident when he was quoted in the *Boston Globe* on November 10, 1940, declaring that, "Democracy is all finished in England." Only after the attack on Pearl Harbor, did he "throw himself into the war effort." Michael R. Beschloss, *Kennedy and Roosevelt: The Uneasy Alliance* (New York: W.W. Norton, 1980), 224, 232-243. Yet, both of the ambassador's eldest sons served in World War II: Joseph P. Kennedy, Jr., was a USAAF pilot in the ETO, and John F. Kennedy, a future U.S. chief

Those on the home front during the Second World War were constantly made aware of the war's progress; each time they bought gasoline or went to the store they had to use their War Ration Books. Patriotic citizens held War Bond drives and planted Victory gardens in their backyards; they also saved scrap metal, paper, and castoff rubber tires to support the war effort. Rationing consumer goods made adequate quantities of material more plentiful for military use. For example, nylon stockings for women became unavailable, as nylon was needed to make military parachutes. Men's suits came with cuffless trousers and narrow lapels, and women gave up their pleated skirts and one-piece bathing suits to save cloth for the military.[1] Although gasoline was readily available on the home front, rubber was not; thus, gas rationing was the method used to protect the rubber supply. Another method to stem the rubber shortage was to bar the manufacture of girdles, but the uproar from women around the country was such that the government caved and allowed their manufacture, declaring them a vital part of a woman's wardrobe.[2]

Blue Star banners also proudly graced the front windows of homes to show that an immediate family member of that American household was serving in uniform during the war.

The photograph on the next page shows the actual Blue Star banner that honored Dad's World War II service. During the entirety of the Second World War, it hung with pride in the front window of my grandparent's house in Kansas. Back in Ashland, Pennsylvania, the Blue Star banner in the front window of my Grand Pap's residence contained four blue stars, indicating that four members of the Gough family were in active military service during that war.

---

executive, commanded a U.S. Navy patrol torpedo (PT) boat in the Pacific Theater.
[1] Doris Kearns Goodwin, *No Ordinary Time: Franklin and Eleanor Roosevelt: The Home Front in World War II* (New York: Simon & Schuster, 1994), 355, 357.
[2] Olson, *Citizens of London*, 231; Burns, *Roosevelt: The Soldier of Freedom*, 258.

Thankfully, only blue stars and no gold stars[1] were evident on either of those two banners at war's end.

Sacrifice at home along with universal military service (conscription) set that generation apart. In modern times, without the pinch of hardship, many Americans seem to understand little about our nation's armed conflicts and feel even less about the needs of our warriors and their families.[2]

During the 1940s, our political leaders wisely sent our armed forces in harm's way only when necessary to defend our nation's vital interests and to

---

[1] When a family member in uniformed service perished during wartime, a gold star replaced a blue star on that banner.
[2] Even at a distance of more than a thousand miles from our shores, my maternal grandmother, Frances Hula, willingly took time away from her farm chores in Kansas to be a civilian volunteer in the USAAF Ground Observer Corps during the war. I remember leafing through her aircraft identification manual as a youngster and recall how proud she was about contributing to the war effort. As an adult, it amuses me to think of her looking into the clear Kansas sky for Stuka or Heinkel bombers while hanging her wash out on the clothesline to dry.

preserve our freedom. To that point, my father and his comrades never knew the confusion and frustration of later generations of American service men and women.[1] He and his comrades knew they were at war for the duration;[2] their nightmare would come to an end only with death, disability, a "million-dollar" wound,[3] or victory. With each stride forward, they knew that was one step closer to a happy return to their homeland and loved ones.

World War II cartoonist Bill Mauldin, who made famous the fictitious infantrymen, "Willie and Joe," said it best for Dad and his wartime colleagues: "I didn't kid myself. I was a student of World War One by that time [:] the war to save democracy. Our war didn't save the world for anything or from anything. I didn't feel we had accomplished anything positive. We had destroyed something negative: Hitler."[4]

As a consequence, Pop and his cavalry mates returned from war in 1945 filled with pride and satisfaction that they had finished an important job: saving the world from Fascism. They were well aware of their contribution to the success of what General Eisenhower referred to as the "Great Crusade."[5] Also, the enthusiastic reception they received on their return

---

[1] This refers to our recent national enthusiasm to enter conflicts by proxy, using our military to prop up feckless, inept and corrupt regimes, and our regrettable lack of concern for the psychic disturbance accompanying multiple combat deployments overseas for extended periods of time. Ironically, a former U.S. secretary of defense observed recently that military force has limited capacity to assist in the nation-building process: "Military force, by itself, cannot rebuild a 'failed state.'" Robert S. McNamara with Brian VanDeMark, *In Retrospect* (New York: Time Books, 1995), 330.

[2] "DEROS" or Date Eligible for Return from Overseas did not exist in World War II. Every soldier in recent combat has known it.

[3] In World War II, a "million-dollar" wound was one, "which missed vital organs, bone, and nerves, but would give us a long stay in an English hospital, sleeping under clean, white sheets." Slaughter, *Omaha Beach and Beyond,* 136.

[4] Studs Terkel, *The Good War* (New York: Pantheon Books, 1984) 362.

[5] On June 6, 1944, as the men filed onto their transport craft, they were given a sheet of paper containing "the order of the day" from General Eisenhower, which was also broadcast over loudspeakers to all assault troops on D-Day. It began: "Soldiers, Sailors and Airmen of the Allied Expeditionary Force! You are about to embark upon the Great Crusade

surely warmed their hearts. Many no doubt had psychological wounds that had not healed, but they were able to speak with one another, and shared their common experiences on the sea voyage home. By comparison, the relatively short, hours-long flights home from combat today stand in stark contrast to what my father experienced. He and his fellow World War II comrades had a lengthy ocean crossing, allowing them time to decompress; that extra time was likely beneficial for many of those damaged by that war.

Dad faced the enemy's guns, returned their fire, and he experienced deathly fear in wartime service: first, in Brittany, and later, while chasing a desperate foe across Northern Germany. Near the end of the war he realized how close he had come to death by booby trap, as he impulsively snatched a souvenir flag from a Nazi sympathizer's window. As to that event, he told me once that he had experienced "the shakes" for some time afterward as he realized how reckless and potentially lethal his impulsive act had been.

At first many of his squadron mates wanted to trample and burn it, but after they cooled down, there were many others who saw fit to join him in autographing that vulgar scrap of cloth. Those proud Fox Company cavalryman added their names and hometowns to symbolize their pride in contributing toward victory over the malevolent forces of Nazism.

A photograph of that dreadful piece of cloth appears on the next page. (See the Appendix at the end of this work for a complete listing of the signatures added to that flag.)

---

toward which we have striven these many months. The eyes of the world are upon you. The hope and prayers of liberty-loving people everywhere march with you . . ." Ambrose, *D-Day, June 6, 1944*, 171.

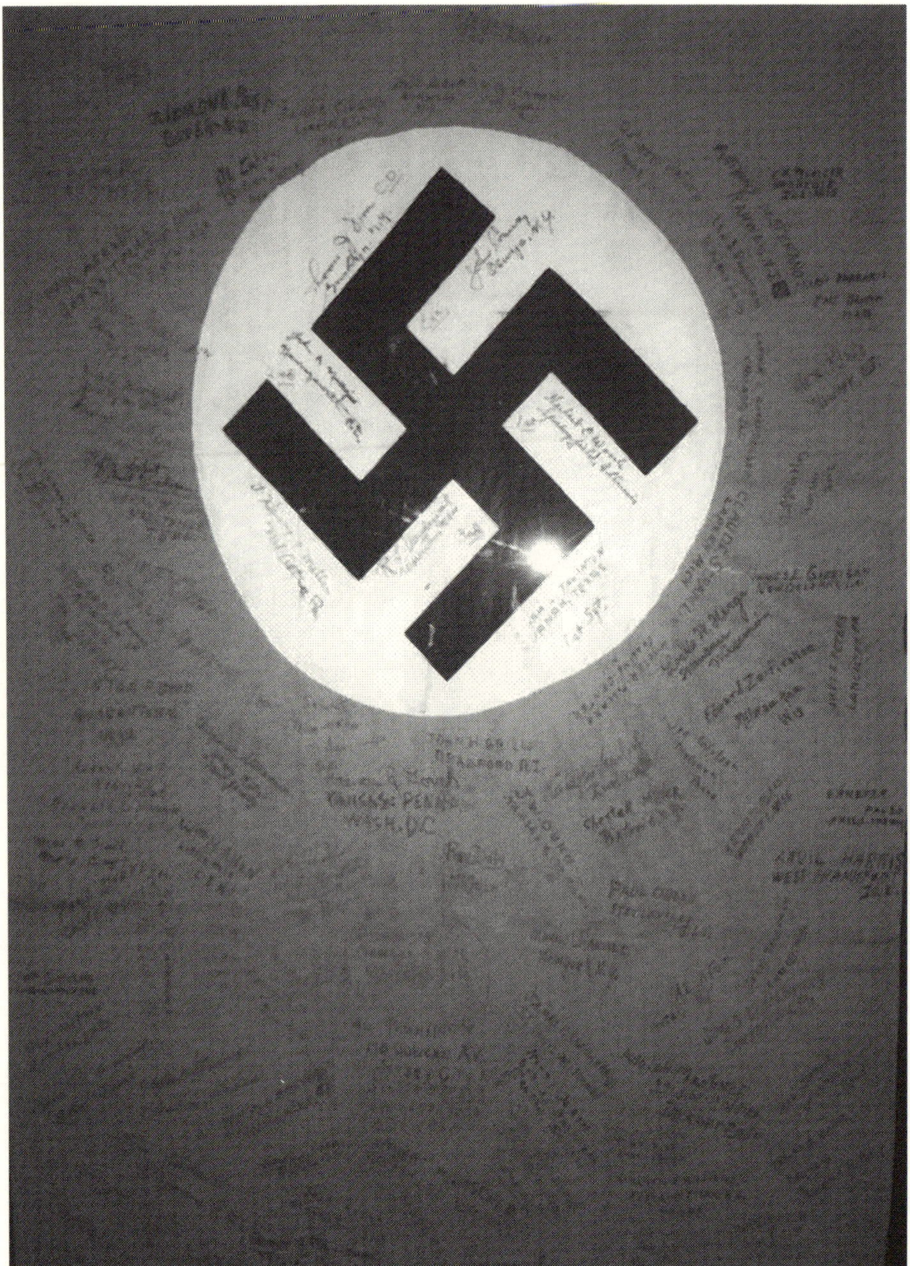

In addition to the troopers of the 17th Cavalry Recce Squadron, it also includes the Cyrillic imprint of a Russian linguist, who apparently accompanied them as they converged on their Soviet allies in Germany; that Russian soldier was likely there as a precaution to communicate over the radio with Soviet Allies, and thus avoid a fratricidal event. (My motivation for including the flag and appendix was solely to pluck from obscurity the names of those brave troopers who served alongside my father in World War II.)

That Nazi flag was delivered by me personally to the curator of the Virginia War Memorial in Richmond, and Dad's notebook diaries have been placed in the hands of the historians at the U.S. Army Heritage and Education Center at Carlisle Barracks, Pennsylvania.

Clearly exposure to combat left its indelible imprint on my father. He learned that which General Sherman had spoken of so many years earlier: war is in fact a hell on Earth and always abominable. He had seen its ugliness for himself, but he had also come to know that some wars are absolutely necessary to fight and win for the benefit of all mankind. The horrible images of death and destruction made it clear that his sacrifice, and that of so many others had not been in vain. Without doubt, he was aware of that when he tramped down the gangway in Boston Harbor in the fall of 1945, and that vivid memory stayed with him for the rest of his life.

As his eldest child, I knew him for more than a half century, and to my knowledge, he never manifested any of the clinical hallmarks of post-traumatic stress. True enough, the family is often the first to recognize the tell-tale signs of that disorder, and as an adult I was on high alert for them. Yet, I can safely say that our family never observed any combat-related survivor guilt, flashbacks, sleeplessness, hyper vigilance, exaggerated startle response or trauma-based nightmares with respect to my father.

To be sure, he was a perplexing individual, and difficult to be around much of the time, but he was never disengaged from his work, nor did he miss any important family activity during our youth. Moreover, he relished the opportunity to engage in postwar social activity, and I have no recollection of a time when his ability to perform productively or function at a high level was ever called into question.

As far as Dad was concerned, he was merely a minor cog in the wheel of America's war machine.[1] To his family, however, he was a hero who had served in defense of his country and somehow beat the odds by returning home without a scratch. Nonetheless, there was never any doubt that he had lost his youthful innocence by war's end, and had become a far more complicated and serious individual.

We know for a fact that some men return from war broken, physically and mentally. Instead, Dad was transformed and energized, aspiring to fold himself back into the fabric of postwar America. To that end, he strove to better himself, losing little time in completing higher education and landed an interesting position with the federal government. Together with his bride Christine, they began a family and had an active social life, which included participation in local church and community affairs. He also found fellowship with friends in his Knights of Columbus chapter and with other veterans at his hometown American Legion hall. Interestingly enough, on several occasions he participated in out-of-town reunions held by members of his World War II cavalry[2] unit, where he enjoyed talking with old army acquaintances about the past. Their wartime service appeared to be the glue that bound them together, and the stories they told could never be adequately shared with others.

The fact that he chose to pursue education and training as a mortician following military service makes clear to me that the sight of a dead human being no longer affected him negatively. In this instance, his in-service combat experience may have had the positive effect of directing him toward the pursuit of a profession that affords the deceased respect and a proper burial. Finally, to my way of thinking, his choice of a lengthy career with a secret U.S. government signals intelligence–gathering agency is dispositive, arguing strongly against the presence of chronic PTSD, based on his military service.

---

[1] One thing was certain to celebrated war correspondent, Ernie Pyle: "In war everybody contributes something, no matter how small or how far removed he may be." Pyle, *Brave Men*, 431.

[2] Nothing annoyed Dad more than hearing someone refer to the cavalry as the "CALVARY"; his negative reaction to that was surely more common than not among his former cavalrymen, but it was no indicator of PTSD.

All the same, as transformed as he was by the time he returned to civilian life, my efforts to please him while growing up were wholly ineffectual. When he was in the mood to be conversant, criticism was his currency of choice, and his skill for assigning blame far exceeded any understanding of the value of words of encouragement. He was an old-school disciplinarian[1] and most of our dialogue was abrupt and one-way by design. While his admonishments were likely well intentioned, sadly scars remain as attempts to win his approval went unfulfilled.

On reflection, I suspect his rigid personality was a byproduct of early adversity, namely the strict upbringing of his youth. Without doubt, the loss of his mother in infancy was an event that profoundly affected him, as rarely can well-meaning care replace a mother's warmth and affection. The pain of that tragedy was likely so significant that he consciously chose to detach himself emotionally from us to avoid its repetition. Ironically, his ability to suppress his emotions may have been the self-preservation mechanism that saved him from chronic PTSD.

For the most part, he seemed burdened by the stoic manner in which he was raised, as his remoteness surely fit the mold of his main role model, our flinty Grand Pap. It is likewise clear that his well-meaning Aunt Mame played a major role in the development of his psyche, as she taught him early to mask his inner feelings and reject the urge to show emotion, since empathy was in short supply during the Depression era.

Also, I am convinced that the work-related rigors of his postwar employment had much to do with his difficult disposition. In his line of work there was no rest, as the Cold War battle was joined daily. However, his irritability seemed situational, escalating in direct proportion to the intensity of world affairs. As a career "cold warrior", his unease centered on the unsettling thought that at any moment mankind might perish in an

---

[1] During childhood, Pop's displeasure normally prompted a smack on the fanny, but in later years, it was nothing more than the usual admonishment to "knock it off". Yet, as the self-willed, firstborn child, it was only natural that I became a target for the bulk of his anger; I don't remember any physical abuse, but my sister Patti recalls that he chased after me once, swinging a "two-by-four." All I remember was skipping out the back door, climbing a tall tree near our home, and staying up there until he cooled down. What prompted that occurrence is unknown, but it most likely had something to do with one of my flippant, smart aleck rejoinders.

all-out thermonuclear exchange triggered by miscalculation, technical failure, or simple carelessness.

AUTHOR'S NOTE

My aim in this narrative was to chronicle the major events of my father's life, especially his military service with the 17th Cavalry Squadron in World War II. As one might imagine, discrepancies in the documentation surfaced on occasion while working with the available record since it is imperfect and does not always match up in every detail. Given the fluid nature of modern warfare, that phenomenon is understandable, since Pop served among the enlisted ranks and was not privy to the overall perspective of the war. In this respect, his diary impressions were recorded mostly at day's end, and their clarity depended on his location within the unit on any given day. Also one must keep in mind the muddle factor in combat and the ever-present fog of war. Thus, when in doubt, official documentation was my touchstone to assure this narrative accurately reflects his participation in the events described.

I submit that it was never my intention here to write at length about the Second World War, as far more capable authors have accomplished that goal. Yet, if somehow my effort stimulates interest in World War II history or adds to the sum of knowledge about that global disaster, it would please me greatly. By adding periodic historical items of interest to the narrative, my purpose was simply to add context, nuance, and perhaps some clarity to assist readers follow my father's wartime odyssey.

While his military service was certainly a defining life event for him, Dad rarely spoke of his wartime experiences. More importantly, I never heard him complain about being a victim of unrewarded sacrifice. Instead, he continued to believe simply in the nobility of service and duty to country. In his mind, he believed firmly that he was nothing more than a lucky survivor of the war.

He was in complete agreement with the legendary war correspondent Ernie Pyle, who dedicated his 1944 book *Brave Men* to the actual heroes of World War II: those thousands of great, brave men [soldiers, sailors, airman, and marines] "for whom there [would] be no homecoming, ever."

In the end, the notes he recorded and his contemporaneous wartime diaries are of importance to my family. Yet, they are of greater value to me because without them, my cathartic journey to come to terms with my father would never have been undertaken. In a way, I suppose my sadness about our lack of a close father-son connection in life made it unavoidable.

APPENDIX

Soldiers from Fox Company, as well as others assigned to the U.S. 17th Cavalry Squadron, 15th Cavalry Group, affixed their signature or mark to my father's war souvenir:

Within the central white circle of that Nazi flag, which contained the black *Hakenkreuz* (the swastika), are the following names:

Thomas J. Fiori, "C.O." (Commanding Officer), Brooklyn, NY
John Conway, "Exc." (Executive Officer), Oswego, NY
Herbert E. Woods, "1st" (Platoon Leader), Springfield, IL
John A. Mulligan, "2nd" (Platoon Leader), Narragansett, RI
R. L. Vandrevil, "3rd" (Platoon Leader), Worcester, MA
Lt. Henry D. Miller, Mt. Aetna, PA,
William L. Thornton, "1st Sgt.", Quanah, TX

Francis R. Gough's signature appears prominently in the middle, directly below the white circle on the flag's red field; subsequently, the following soldiers joined in:

Joe Miller, Buffalo, NY
Zigmund Post, Dover, NJ
James Coughlin, Linden Station, WI
Bill Welch, Norwich, NY
Leonard Stalzer, Marshalltown, IA
Mike Mignemi, Mt. Morris, NY
Octavio Virtuoso, Niagara Falls, NY
Anthony De Stafano, Rahway, NJ
L. H. Moeller, Nashville, IL
Leo J. Panattoni, Niagara Falls, NY
Mario Daddario, E. Boston, MA
Alex Klalo, Newark, NJ
Lowen Rosenberger, Chicago, IL
L. A. Morales, Tucson, AZ
Claude Scramlin, Lapeer, MI
James Garrigan, New Orleans, LA
Al Cohen, Bayonne, NJ

Wilbur E. Reiboldt, Sterling, CO
Hugh McNabb, Detroit, MI
Clarence Bragg, Kinston, AL
Glenn Overlander, Philadelphia, PA
Harold Morrical, Phillips, WI
George R. O' Herrin, Chicago, IL
Walter Sabot, Detroit, MI
Horas H. Oldham, Hartsville, TN
Welcome C. Mullen, Modesto, CA
Eugene F. Custodi, Buffalo, NY
Edward F. Young, Trenton, NJ
Ernest Schwartz, Belgrade, NE
John H. Grills, Bradford, RI
Walter Pollard, Collins Center, NY
Leslie W. Ferge, Wausau, WI
Edward Zeifirakee, Milwaukee, WI
James E. Peters, Lancaster, PA
Joe Wilson, Malvern, PA
Bernard Plasse, Webster, MA
Clifton Sepulvado, Zwolle, LA
Chester Miller, Batavia, NY
J. W. Dunn, Kansas City, KS
Ray Doty, McGraw, NY
August Stoermer, Jersey City, NJ
Clinton P. Good, Morgantown, WV
Albert Edeg, Hebron, ND
Kenneth L. Hanna, Canton, OH
Mac N. Hall, Moro, OR
William H. Allen, Little Neck, Long Island, NY
John Hakim, Wilkes-Barre, PA
Paul Ohlan, Stecleville, IL
Ernest F. Palko, Phillips, WI
Arvil Harris, W. Frankfurt, IL
Jerry Brockman, Kimberly, WI
Al Aten, Vestal, NY
Manuel Rameriz, New York, NY

Veych Stankevich, Leningrad (likely a Russian linguist; his signature on the flag was translated from a Cyrillic signature.)
Anthony S. Schaab, Trenton, NJ
Sam Cappadonia, Mt. Morris, NY
Paul Drake, Cedar Rapids, IA
William Gillespie, Indianapolis, IN
George Hughes, Aurora, IN
W. E. Williams, Electra, TX
America R. Massaro, Rochester, NY
Al Penniplede, Jersey City, NJ
James F. Shepherd, Jr., St. Louis, MO
Adolph Martinez, Denver, CO
James Eckelberry, Corropolis, PA
Glen Schmidt, Indianapolis, IN
James G. Coble, Graham, NC
Nelson Joyal, Barre, VT
William R. Williams, Elkland, PA
Henry Olson, Canton, SD
Eddie Bernard, Wilmington, VT
Miller B. Hall, Philadelphia, MS
Herbert Wierschem, Waterloo, IL
Victor Tuachiarelli, Buffalo, NY
Tony Kozlowski, Albuquerque, NM
Jack Tucker, Winchester, IN
Ralph Cadwell, Crocker, MO
Richard Kinder, Shamokin, PA
Stanley Wollschlager, Baltimore, MD
Earl Doss, Los Angeles, CA
William B. Campbell, Phenix City, AL
Archie P. Underwood, Manchester, NC
Roger G. Rodriguez, San Francisco, CA
Howard Tate, Beckley, WV
Dolph E. Hicks, Troy, TN
Wilfred G. Orland, Summerville, NJ
G. Fincher, Atlanta, GA
Sam Cannaday, Idabel, OK
Joseph S. Jarosz, Detroit, MI

William D. Evans, Hornbeak, TN
Cornelius Lyons, Denver, CO
Al V. Garvin, Los Angeles, CA

SELECT BIBLIOGRAPHY

Gough, Francis R. four pocket dairies (1941-1945), letters, and personal papers, ed. by Jerome F. Gough.

Gough, Christine R. (Hula) wedding album, "Orange Blossoms," including Dad's letters to her both during and after service in the possession of Patricia Gough Wilson and Mary JoAnn Gough Holley.

Company F, 17th CAV RCN SQ Order #4, 16 June 1944, in author's possession.

History of the 17th Cavalry Reconnaissance Squadron for Year 1944, Memorandum to The Adjutant General, Washington, D.C., 1 March 1945; CAVS-17-0.1, Record Group 407, entry 427, National Archives and Records Administration II, College Park, MD.

Caldwell, Kansas High School annual, *The Jayhawker*, 1912.

"The Lion Rampant" *A Brief History of Combat Operations in the European Theater during 1944-45 of the 15th Cavalry Group, Mechanized, 1945*; CAVG-15-0, Record Group 407, Entry 427, National Archives and Records Administration II, College Park, MD.

Marymount College 1941 yearbook, *The Garland*, Salina, Kansas.

Undated mimeographed cavalry reunion handout entitled "History of the 15th Cavalry Group".

Section III, Circular 353, War Department, 31 August 1944.

PUBLISHED WORKS

Alexander, Joseph H. *Storm Landings: Epic Amphibious Battles in the Central Pacific* (Annapolis: Naval Institute Press, 1997.
Ambrose, Stephen E. *The Supreme Commander: The War Years of General Dwight D. Eisenhower.* Garden City, NY: Doubleday, 1970.
———. *D-Day, June 6, 1944: The Climatic Battle of World War II.* New York: Simon & Schuster, 1994.
———. *Citizen Soldiers: The U.S. Army from the Normandy Beaches to the Bulge to the Surrender of Germany, June 7, 1944-May 7, 1945.* New York: Simon & Schuster, 1997.
———. *The Victors: Eisenhower and His Boys: The Men of World War II.* New York: Simon & Schuster, 1998.
Atkinson, Rick. *An Army at Dawn.* New York: Henry Holt, 2002.
———. *The Guns at Last Light: The War in Western Europe, 1944-1945.* New York: Henry Holt, 2013.
Axelrod, Alan. *Patton: A Biography.* NY: Palgrave Macmillan, 2006.
Balkoski, Joseph. *Omaha Beach.* Mechanicsburg, PA: Stackpole, 2004.
———. *Utah Beach.* Mechanicsburg, PA: Stackpole, 2005.
———. *From Brittany to the Reich: The 29th Infantry Division in Germany, September-November, 1944.* Stackpole, 2012.
Barr, Niall. *Eisenhower's Armies: The American-British Alliance during World War II.* New York: Pegasus Books, 2015.
Barr, Niall and Russell Hart. *Panzer.* Osceola, WI: MBI Publishing, 1999.
Beevor, Anthony. *Stalingrad, the Fateful Siege* (NY: Viking, 1998.
The Fall of Berlin 1945. New York: Viking Press, 2002.
———. *D-Day: The Battle for Normandy.* New York: Viking Press, 2009.
———. *Ardennes 1944: Hitler's Last Gamble.* New York: Viking, 2015.
Beschloss, Michael R. *Kennedy and Roosevelt: The Uneasy Alliance.* New York: W.W. Norton, 1980.
———. *MayDay: Eisenhower, Khrushchev and the U-2 Affair.* New York, **Harper & Row, 1986.**
Beschloss, Michael R. ed. *Taking Charge: The Johnson White House*
———. *Tapes, 1963-1964.* New York, Simon & Schuster, 1997.
Blair, Clay. *Ridgway's Paratroopers.* NewYork: Dial Press, 1985.
Blumenson, Martin. *Breakout and Pursuit: U.S. Army in World War II, ETO.* Office of the Chief of Military History, 1961.

———. *Patton: The Man behind the Legend, 1885-1945.* New York: William Morrow, 1985.

Bradham, Randolph. *"To the Last Man": The Battle for Normandy's Cotentin Peninsula and Brittany.* Westport, CT: Praeger Security International, 2008.

Brands, H.W. *T.R.: The Last Romantic.* New York: Basic Books, 1997.

———. *Traitor to His Class: The Privileged Life and Radical Presidency of Franklin Delano Roosevelt.* New York: Doubleday, 2008.

———. *The General vs. the President: MacArthur and Truman at the Brink of Nuclear War*, New York, Doubleday, 2016.

Brinkley, David. *Washington Goes to War.* New York: Knopf, 1988.

Brinkley, Douglas. *Rightful Heritage: Franklin D. Roosevelt and the Land of America.* New York: HarperCollins, 2016.

Burns, James MacGregor. *Roosevelt: The Soldier of Freedom.* New York: Harcourt Brace Jovanovich: 1970.

Caddick-Adams, Peter. *Snow & Steel: The Battle of the Bulge, 1944-45.* New York: Oxford University Press, 2015.

Canfield, Bruce. *The M1 Garand Rifle.* Woonsocket, RI: Andrew Mowbray, 2013.

Carroll, Andrew. *My Fellow Soldiers.* NY: Penguin Press, 2017.

Chang, Iris. *The Rape of Nanking.* New York: BasicBooks, 1997.

Churchill, Winston S. *The Second World War: Triumph and Tragedy.* Boston: Houghton Mifflin, 1953.

Clark, Lloyd. *Crossing the Rhine.* New York: Atlantic Monthly, 2008.

The Battle of the Tanks. New York: Atlantic Monthly Press, 2011.

Close, Bill. *Tank Commander: From the Fall of France to the Defeat of Germany.* South Yorkshire, England: Pen & *Sword* Books, 2013.

Coffman, Edward M. *The Regulars: The American Army, 1898-1941.* Cambridge, Belknap Press of Harvard University Press, 2004.

Cohen, Stan. *The Tree Army.* Missoula, MT: Pictorial Histories Publishing, 2013.

Cooper, Belton Y. *Death Traps.* Novato, CA: Presidio Press, 1998.

Dallek, Robert. *An Unfinished Life: John F. Kennedy, 1917-1963,* Boston: Little, Brown, 2003.

Dario, Mike. *Panzerjäger in Action.* Warren, MI: Squadron/Signal, 1973.

Davidson, Bill. *Cut Off.* New York: Stein & Day, 1972.

Davies, Norman. *No Simple Victory: World War II in Europe, 1939-1945.* New York: Viking, 2007.

Davis, Kenneth S. *FDR: Into the Storm, 1937-1940*. New York: Random House, 1993
———. *FDR: The War President, 1940-1943*. NY: Random House, 2000.
De Bruhl, Marshall. *Firestorm: Allied Airpower and the Destruction of Dresden*. New York: Random House, 2006.
D'Este, Carlo. *Patton: A Genius for War*. New York: HarperCollins, 1995.
———. *Eisenhower: A Soldier's Life*. New York: Henry Holt, 2002.
Delaforce, Patrick. *Smashing the Atlantic Wall*. London: Cassell, 2001.
Dobbs, Michael. *Saboteurs: The Nazi Raid on America*. N.Y.: Knopf, 2004.
———. *One Minute to Midnight: Kennedy, Khrushchev and Castro on the Brink of Nuclear War*. London: Arrow, 2009.
Dupuy, Trevor N. David L. Bongard, and R. C. Anderson. *Hitler's Last Gamble: The Battle of the Bulge, December 1944-January 1945*. New York: HarperCollins, 1994.
Dykstra, Robert R. *The Cattle Towns*. New York: Alfred A. Knopf, 1968.
Earley, Pete. *Family of Spies: Inside the John Walker Spy Ring*. New York: Bantam, 1988.
Edsel, Robert M. et al., *The Monuments Men*. NY: Center Street, 2009.
Eisenhower, David. *Eisenhower: At War, 1943-1945*. New York: Random House, 1986.
Eisenhower, Dwight D. *Crusade in Europe*. New York: Doubleday, 1948.
Eisenhower, John S. D. *The Bitter Woods*. New York: G.P. Putnam, 1969.
Eisenhower, John S. D. with Joanne T. Eisenhower. *Yanks: The Epic Story of the American Army in World War I*. Free Press, 2001.
Ellis, Joseph J. *Revolutionary Summer*. New York: Alfred A. Knopf, 2013.
Ennes, James M. Jr. *Assault on the Liberty*. N.Y.: Random House, 1979.
Esposito, Vincent J. ed. *The West Point Atlas of American Wars, 1900-1953*. Vol. II. New York: Praeger, 1967.
Evans, Richard J. *The Third Reich in Power*. New York: Penguin, 2005.
———. *The Third Reich at War*. New York: Penguin, 2009.
Ewing, Joseph H. *29 Let's Go! A History of the 29th Infantry Division in WWII*. Washington, D.C.: Infantry Journal Press, 1948.
Featherston, Alwyn. *Saving the Breakout*. Novato, CA: Presidio, 1993.
Feifer, George. *Tennozan*. New York: Ticknor & Fields, 1992.
Fellman, Michael. *Citizen Sherman: A Life of William Tecumseh Sherman*. New York: Random House, 1995.
Ferguson, Harvey. *The Last Cavalryman: The Life of General Lucian K.*

Truscott, Jr. Norman: University of Oklahoma Press, 2015.
Foote, Shelby. *The Civil War: (vol. 3) A Narrative, Red River to Appomattox.* New York: Random House, 1974.
Forty, George. *German Infantryman at War, 1939-1945.* Surrey, UK: Ian Allen Publishing, 2002.
Frank, Richard B. *Downfall: The End of the Imperial Japanese Empire.* New York: Random House, 1999.
———. *MacArthur.* New York: Palgrave Macmillan, 2007.
Fraser, David. *Knight's Cross: A Life of Field Marshal Erwin Rommel.* New York: HarperCollins, 1993.
Freeman, Douglas S. *Lee's Lieutenants: (vol. 2) Cedar Mountain to Chancellorsville.* New York: Charles Scribner's Sons, 1943.
Fullilove, Michael. *Rendezvous with Destiny.* New York: Penguin, 2013.
Fussell, Paul. *Thank God for the Atom Bomb and Other Essays.* New York: Summit Books, 1988.
———. *Wartime.* New York: Oxford University Press, 1989.
———. *The Boys' Crusade: The American Infantry in Northwestern Europe, 1944-1945.* New York: Modern Library, 2003.
Gaddis, John Lewis. *The Cold War: A New History.* New York: Penguin Press, 2005.
Gallagher, Gary W. ed., *Fighting for the Confederacy.* Chapel Hill, University of North Carolina Press, 1989.
Gates, Robert M. *From the Shadows: The Ultimate Insider's Story of Five Presidents and How They Won the Cold War.* New York: Simon & Schuster, 1996.
Gellhorn, Martha. *The Face of War.* NY: Atlantic Monthly Press, 1988.
Gilbert, Martin. *The Second World War: A Complete History.* New York: Henry Holt, 1989.
———. *The First World War: A Complete History.* NY: Henry Holt, 1994.
———. *The Somme: Heroism and Horror in the First World War.* New York: Henry Holt, 2006.,
Goodwin, Doris Kearns. *The Bully Pulpit.* New York: Simon & Schuster, 2013.
———. *No Ordinary Time: Franklin and Eleanor Roosevelt: The Home Front in World War II.* New York: Simon & Schuster, 1994.
Green, Michael & Gladys. *Panther: Germany's Quest for Combat Dominance.* Oxford, UK: Osprey, 2012.

Groom, Winston. *A Storm in Flanders: The Ypres Salient, 1914-1918: Tragedy and Triumph on the Western Front.* New York: Atlantic Monthly Press, 2002.

Hanson, Victor D. *The Savior Generals.* NY: Bloomsbury Press, 2013.

Hargreaves, Richard. *The Germans in Normandy,* Barnsley. South Yorkshire, UK: Pen & Sword Military, 2006.

Haskew, Michael E. *Tank: 100 Years of the World's Most Important Armored Military Vehicle.* Minneapolis: Zenith Press, 2015.

Hastings, Max *Overlord: D-Day and the Battle for Normandy.* New York: Simon & Schuster, 1984

———. *Victory in Europe.* New York: Little, Brown, 1985.

———. *Armageddon: The Battle for Germany, 1944-1945.* New York: Alfred A. Knopf, 2004.

———. *Retribution: The Battle for Japan, 1944-45.* NY: Knopf, 2008.

———. *Inferno: The World at War, 1939-1945.* N.Y.: Knopf, 2011.

Hayden, Michael V. *Playing to the Edge: American Intelligence in the Age of Terror,* New York: Penguin Publishing, 2016.

Helferich, Gerard. *An Unlikely Trust: Theodore Roosevelt, J.P. Morgan, and the Improbable Partnership That Remade American Business.* Guilford, CT: Lyons Press, 2017.

Higgins, David R. *The Roer River Battles: Germany's Stand at the Westwall, 1944-45.* Havertown, PA: Casemate, 2010.

Hitchcock, William I. *The Bitter Road to Freedom: A New History of the Liberation of Europe.* New York: Free Press, 2008.

———. *The Age of Eisenhower: America and the World in the 1950s,* New York: Simon & Schuster, 2018.

Hornfischer, James D. *The Last Stand of the Tin Can Sailors.* New York: Bantam Books, 2004.

———. *The Fleet at Flood Tide: America at Total War in the Pacific, 1944-1945.* New York: Bantam Books, 2016.

Huchthausen, Peter A. *October Fury.* Hoboken, NJ: John Wiley, 2002.

Irwin, John P. *Another River, Another Town: A Teenage Tank Gunner Comes of Age in Combat, 1945.* NY: Random House, 2002.

Irwin, Will, Lt. Col. (Ret.). *The Jedburghs.* New York: PublicAffairs, 2005.

Jeffers, H. Paul. *Taking Command.* New York: NAL Caliber, 2009.

Kalugin, Oleg et al. *The First Directorate.* NY: St. Martin's Press, 1994.

Kennedy, Paul. *Engineers of Victory.* New York: Random House, 2013.

Kennedy, Robert F. *Thirteen Days.* New York: W.W. Norton, 1969.
Kennett, Lee. *G.I.: The American Soldier in World War II.* New York: Charles Scribner's, 1987.
Kershaw, Alex. *The Bedford Boys: One American Town's Ultimate D-Day Sacrifice.* Cambridge, MA: Da Capo Press, 2003.
———. *The Longest Winter.* Cambridge, MA: Da Capo, 2004.
Kershaw, Ian. *Hitler, 1889-1936: Hubris.* New York: W.W. Norton, 1999.
———. *Hitler, 1936-1945: Nemesis.* New York: W.W. Norton, 2000.
———. *The End: The Defiance and Destruction of Hitler's Germany, 1944-1945.* New York: Penguin Press, 2011.
———. *To Hell and Back: Europe 1914-1949.* New York: Viking, 2015.
Kindsvatter, Peter S. *American Soldier: Ground Combat in the World Wars, Korea, and Vietnam.* Lawrence: University Press of Kansas, 2003.
Kinnear, Duncan Lyle. *The First 100 Years: A History of Virginia Polytechnic Institute and State University.* Richmond, VA: William Byrd Press, 1972.
Korda, Michael. *Journey to a Revolution: A Personal Memoir and History of the Hungarian Revolution of 1956.* N.Y.: HarperCollins, 2006.
Kotlowitz, Robert. *Before Their Time: A Memoir.* N.Y.: Knopf, 1997.
Kyle, Chris with William Doyle. *American Gun: A History of the U.S. in Ten Firearms*, New York: William Morrow, 2013.
Larrabee, Eric. *Commander in Chief.* New York: Harper & Row, 1987.
Lash, Joseph P. *Roosevelt and Churchill, 1939-1941.* New York: W.W. Norton, 1976.
Lefevre, Eric. *Panzers in Normandy.* London: Plaistow Press, 1990.
Lewis, Adrian R. *Omaha Beach: A Flawed Victory.* Chapel Hill: University of North Carolina Press, 2001.
Lomazow, Steven M.D. and Eric Fettmann. *FDR's Deadly Secret.* New York: PublicAffairs, 2009.
McCullough, David. *Truman.* New York: Simon & Schuster, 1992.
———. *The American Spirit.* New York: Simon & Schuster, 2017.
McDonough, James R. *Platoon Leader.* NY: Ballantine Books, 1985.
McManus, John C. *The Americans at Normandy: The Summer of 1944–*
———. *The American War from the Normandy Beaches to Falaise.* New York: Forge, 2004.
———. *Alamo in the Ardennes.* Hoboken, NJ: John Wiley & Sons, 2007.

———. *The Dead and Those About to Die: D-Day: The Big Red One at Omaha Beach*. New York: NAL Caliber, 2014.

McNamara, Robert S., with Brian VanDeMark. *In Retrospect: The Tragedy and Lessons of Vietnam*. New York: Time Books, 1995.

McPherson, James M. *The War that Forged a Nation*. New York: Oxford University Press, 2015.

MacDonald, Charles B. *The Siegfried Line Campaign: The U.S. Army in World War II, ETO*. Washington, DC: Office of the Chief of Military History, 1963.

———. *The Last Offensive: The U.S. Army in World War II, ETO*. Washington, DC: Office of the Chief of Military History, 1973.

———. *Company Commander*. New York: Bantam, 1979.

———. *A Time for Trumpets*. New York: William Morrow, 1985.

The Mighty Endeavor: American Armed Forces in the European Theater in World War II (NY: Oxford University Press, 1969.

Manchester, William and Paul Reid. *The Last Lion: Defender of the Realm, 1940-1965*. New York: Little, Brown and Co., 2012.

Mauldin, Bill. *Up Front*. New York: W.W. Norton, 1995.

Mazower, Mark. *Hitler's Empire*. New York: Penguin Press, 2008.

Meacham, Jon. *Thomas Jefferson: The Art of Power*. New York: Random House, 2012.

Meyers, Lawrence. *Teacher of the Year: The Mystery and Legacy of Edwin Barlow*. Franklin, TN: H. H. & Sons, 2009.

Miller, Edward G. *A Dark and Bloody Ground*. College Station: Texas A&M University Press, 1995.

Miller, Nathan. *Theodore Roosevelt: A Life*. NY: William Morrow, 1992.

Miscamble, Wilson D. *The Most Controversial Decision: Truman, the Atomic Bombs, and the Defeat of Japan*. New York: Cambridge University Press, 2011.

Misch, Rochus. *Hitler's Last Witness: The Memoirs of Hitler's Bodyguard*. London: Frontline Books, 2014.

Mitcham, Jr., Samuel W. *Retreat to the Reich: The German Defeat in France, 1944*. Mechanicsburg, PA: Stackpole, 2000.

Moe, Richard. *Roosevelt's Second Act: The Election of 1940 and the Politics of War*. Oxford, UK: Oxford University, 2013.

Morison, Samuel Eliot. *The Two-Ocean War: A Short History of the U.S. Navy in the Second World War*. Boston: Little, Brown, 1963.

Morris, Edmund. *Theodore Rex*. New York: Random House, 2001.
Mort, Terry. *Hemingway at War*. New York: Pegasus Books, 2016.
Morton, Matthew D. *Men on Iron Ponies: The Death and Rebirth of the Modern U.S. Cavalry*. DeKalb: No. Illinois University Press, 2009.
Mundy, Liza. *Code Girls: The Untold Story of the American Women Code Breakers of World War II*. New York: Hatchette Books, 2017.
Murray, Williamson and Allan R. Millett. *A War to Be Won: Fighting the Second World War*. Cambridge:Belknap Press of Harvard University Press, 2000.
Mullenheim-Rechberg, Burkard Freiherr von. *Battleship* Bismarck. Annapolis: Naval Institute Press, 1990.
Nagorski, Andrew. *Hitlerland: American Eyewitnesses to the Nazi Rise to Power*. New York: Simon & Schuster, 2012.
Neill, George W. *Infantry Soldier: Holding the Line at the Battle of the Bulge*. Norman: University of Oklahoma Press, 2000.
Neillands, Robin. *The Battle for the Rhine: The Battle of the Bulge and the Ardennes Campaign, 1944*. New York: Overlook Press, 2005.
Omaha Beachhead (6 June-13 June 1944), American Forces in Action Series, Historical Division, War Department. Sept. 1945.
O'Neal, Bill. *Ghost Towns of the American West*. Lincolnwood, IL: Publications International, 1995.
Olson, Lynne. *Citizens of London*. New York, Random House, 2010.
Patton, Jr., George S. *War as I Knew It*. N. Y.: Houghton Mifflin, 1947.
Perret, Geoffrey. *Winged Victory*. New York: Random House, 1993.
———. *Old Soldiers Never Die: The Life of Douglas MacArthur*. New York: Random House, 1996.
———. *There's a War to be Won*. New York: Ballantine, 2013.
Perry, Mark. *Partners in Command: George Marshall and Dwight Eisenhower in War and Peace*. New York: Penguin, 2007.
———. *The Most Dangerous Man in America: The Making of Douglas MacArthur*. New York: Basic Books, 2014.
Pfanz, Harry W. *Gettysburg: The Second Day*. Chapel Hill: University of North Carolina Press, 1987.
Pogue, Forrest C. *The Supreme Command: The U.S. Army in World War II,* . Washington, D.C.: Office of Chief of Military History, 1954.
———. *George C. Marshall: Education of a General*. N.Y.: Viking, 1963.
———. *George C. Marshall: Ordeal and Hope, 1939-1942*. Viking, 1967.

———. *George C. Marshall: Organizer of Victory*. New York: Viking, 1973.
———. *George C. Marshall: Statesman*. New York: Viking Penguin, 1987.
Prados, John. *Normandy Crucible: The Decisive Battle That Shaped World War II in Europe*. New York: New American Library, 2011.
Prange, Gordon W. *Miracle at Midway*. New York: McGraw-Hill, 1982.
Pringle, Heather. *The Master Plan: Himmler's Scholars and the Holocaust*. New York: Hyperion, 2006.
Province, Charles M. *Patton's Third Army*. NY: Hippocrene, 1992.
Pyle, Ernie. *Brave Men*. New York: Henry Holt, 1944.
Rable, George C. *Fredericksburg, Fredericksburg*. Chapel Hill: University of North Carolina Press, 2002.
Reed, W. Craig. *Red November: Inside the Secret U.S.-Soviet Submarine War*. New York: William Morrow, 2010.
Reynolds, Michael. *Men of Steel*. New York: Sarpedon, 1999.
Ricks, Thomas E. *Churchill & Orwell: The Fight for Freedom*. New York: Penguin Press, 2017.
Rooney, Andy. *My War*. Holbrook, MA: Adams Media, 1995.
Rottman, Gordon L. *World War II US Cavalry Groups: European Theater*. Oxford, UK: Osprey, 2012.
Ryan, Cornelius. *The Longest Day: June 6, 1944*. New York: Simon & Schuster, 1959.
Sandburg, Carl. *Abraham Lincoln: The War Years*. Vol. 1. New York: Harcourt, Brace & World, 1939.
Schecter, Jerrold L. and Peter S. Deriabin. *The Spy Who Saved the World: How a Soviet Colonel Changed the Course of the Cold* War. New York: Charles Scribner's Sons, 1992.
Sewell, Kenneth with Clint Richmond. *Red Star Rogue*. New York: Simon & Schuster, 2005.
Shirer, William L. *Berlin Diary: The Journal of a Foreign Correspondent, 1934-1941*. New York: Galahad Books, 1995.
Sides, Hampton. *On Desperate Ground: The Marines at the Reservoir, the Korean War's Greatest* Battle. New York: Doubleday, 2018.
Slaughter, John R. *Omaha Beach and Beyond*. St. Paul, MN: Zenith Press, 2007.
Smith, Dennis Mack. *Mussolini*. New York: Alfred A. Knopf, 1982.
Sontag, Sherry and Christopher Drew with Annette Lawrence Drew. *Blind Man's Bluff*. New York: PublicAffairs, 1998.
Sorley, Lewis. *Thunderbolt*. New York: Simon & Schuster, 1992.
Spector, Ronald H. *Eagle Against the Sun: The American War with Japan*.

New York: Free Press, 1985.
———. *At War at Sea.* New York; Viking Penguin, 2001.
Speer, Albert. *Inside the Third Reich.* New York: Macmillan, 1970.
Stafford, David. *Endgame, 1945.* New York: Little, Brown, 2007.
———. *Ten Days to D-Day: Countdown to the Liberation of Europe.* London: Little, Brown, 2003.
Stanton, Shelby L. *World War II Order of Battle, U.S. Army (Ground Force Units).* Novato, CA: Galahad Books, 1984.
Stargardt, Nicholas. *The German War: A Nation Under Arms, 1939-1945.* New York, Basic Books, 2015.
Stein, George H. *The Waffen SS: Hitler's Elite Guard at War, 1939-1945.* Ithaca: Cornell University Press, 1966.
St-Lo (7 July-19 July 1944) American Forces in Action Series, Historical Division, War Department, Washington, DC: Center of Military History, U.S. Army, facsimile reprint, 1984.
Symonds, Craig L. *The Battle of Midway.* New York: Oxford University Press, 2011.
Taaffe, Stephen R. *Marshall and His Generals: U.S. Army Commanders in World War II.* Lawrence: University Press of Kansas, 2011.
Terkel, Studs. *The Good War.* New York: Pantheon Books, 1984.
Thomas, Evan. *Ike's Bluff: President Eisenhower's Secret Battle to Save the World.* New York: Little, Brown, 2012.
Tooze, Adam. The Wages of Destruction: The Making and Breaking of the Nazi Economy. New York: Viking, 2006.
Trevor-Roper, Hugh R. *The Last Days of Hitler.* NY: Macmillan, 1947.
Turner, Barry. *Countdown to Victory: The Final European Campaigns of World War II.* New York: William Morrow, 2004.
Unger, Debi and Irwin with Stanley Hirshson, *George Marshall: A Biography.* New York: HarperCollins, 2014.
Utah Beach to Cherbourg (6 June-27 June 1944) American Forces in Action Series, Department of the Army, Historical Division, 1947.
Veronico, Nicholas A. *Hidden Warships.* Minneapolis, MN: Zenith, 2015.
Waller, Douglas. *Wild Bill Donovan: The Spymaster Who Created the OSS and Modern American Espionage,* New York: Free Press, 2011.
Weigley, Russell F. *Eisenhower's Lieutenants: The Campaign of France and Germany 1944-1945.* Bloomington: Indiana Univ. Press, 1981.
Weintraub, Stanley. *11 Days in December.* New York: Free Press, 2006.

Wert, Jeffrey D. *Custer: The Controversial Life of George Armstrong Custer.* New York, Simon & Schuster, 1996.

Whiting, Charles. *Papa Goes to War: Ernest Hemingway in Europe, 1944-45.* Wiltshire, UK: Crowood Press, 1990.

Whitlock, Flint. *The Fighting First: The Untold Story of the Big Red One On D-Day.* Cambridge, MA: Westview Press, 2004.

Wilson, James. *Hitler's Alpine Retreat.* Havertown, PA: Casemate, 2005.

Winik, Jay. *1944: FDR and the Year That Changed History.* New York: Simon & Schuster, 2015.

Wukovits, John. *Tin Can Titans.* Boston, MA: Da Capo Press, 2017.

Yeide, Harry. *The Tank Killers.* Havertown, PA: Casemate, 2004.

———. *The Longest Battle.* St. Paul, MN: Zenith Press, 2005.

———. *Steeds of Steel.* Minneapolis, MN: Zenith Press, 2008.

———. *The Infantry's Armor.* Mechanicsburg, PA: Stackpole, 2010.

Zaloga, Steven J. *Stuart U.S. Light Tanks in Action.* Warren, MI: Squadron/Signal, 1979.

———. *Sherman Medium Tank, 1942-1945.* London: Osprey, 1993.

———. *M10 and M36 Tank Destroyers 1942-53.* Botley: Osprey, 2002.

———. *M26/M46 Pershing Tank: 1943-1953.* Botley, UK: Osprey, 2002.

———. *M4 Sherman Medium Tank. 1943-65*, Botley, UK: Osprey, 2003.

Zumbro, Derek S. *Battle for the Ruhr.* Lawrence: University Press of Kansas, 2006.

NEWSPAPERS

Caldwell Messenger

Stars and Stripes

Wall Street Journal

Washington Post

PERIODICALS

"An Ambush in Brittany." *Cavalry Journal.* Vol. LIV, no. 5 (September-October 1945).

Anderson, Eric. "The Dawn of American Armor: The U.S. Army Tank Corps in World War II," *On Point: Journal of Army History,* Army Historical Foundation, Vol. 21 no. 4 (Spring 2016).

Anonymous, "Seizing Strategic Installations." *Cavalry Journal.* Vol. LIV, no. 5 (September-October 1945).

"Battle of Germany". *Army Talks.* Vol. IV, No.2 (May 22, 1945).

2012 Current Medical Diagnosis & Treatment. New York: McGraw-Hill.

Department of the Army Graphic Training Aid 3-2. Government Printing Office, November 1957.

Department of the Army Technical Manual, TM 9-729, *Light Tank M24.* Washington, D.C.: U.S. Government Printing Office, 1944.

Dobbins, Lt. Col. Garret J. "Mopping Up an Enemy Pocket." *Cavalry Journal,* Vol. LIV, no. 6 (November-December 1945).

Dobbins, Lt. Col. G. J. and Capt. Thomas Fiori. "Cavalry and Infantry at St. Malo." *Cavalry Journal.* Vol. LIV, no. 6 (Nov.-Dec. 1945).

Driving Instructions: Light Tank, M5, M5A1, Motor Carriage, M8. Cadillac Motor Car Division, General Motors Corporation, Detroit, Michigan, December 14, 1942.

Feng, Patrick. "M3/M5 Stuart Light Tank," *On Point: Journal of Army History,* Army Historical Foundation. Vol. 20, no. 2 (Fall 2014).

"The M1 Carbine" *On Point: Journal of Army History,* Army Historical Foundation. Vol. 22, no. 4 (Spring 2017).

"M10 Tank Destroyer" *On Point: Journal of Army History,* Army Historical Foundation. Vol. 23, no. 4 (Spring 2018).

"The 8th Tank Battalion" *On Point: Journal of Army History,* Army Historical Foundation. Vol. 25, no. 1 (Summer 2019).

Font, Maj. Glenn E. "Group Supply Problems." *Cavalry Journal.* Vol. LIV, no. 5 (September-October 1945).

Historical and Pictorial Review. Cavalry Replacement Training Center, 3rd Regiment, Fort Riley. Army and Navy Publishing, 1941.

Jones, Maj. Morton McD. "Seizing and Holding a River Line." *Cavalry Journal.* Vol. LIV, no. 6 (November-December 1945).

Kichen, Lee F. "The Death of the Horse Cavalry and the Birth of the Armored Force." *On Point: Journal of Army History,* Army Historical Foundation, Vol. 23 no. 3 (Winter 2018).

Kraft, Maj. William R. "Cavalry in Dismounted Action." *Cavalry Journal.* Vol. LIV, no. 6 (November-December 1945).

Lankford, James. "M4 Sherman" in Mail Call. *On Point: Journal of Army History,* Army Historical Foundation. Vol. 19, no. 4 (Spring 2014).

Larson, Capt. Clark R. and Capt. Frank C. Horton. "Trains Have to Fight Too." *Cavalry Journal.* Vol. LIV, no. 5 (September-October 1945).

McGrath, Nick. "Camp Lucky Strike France." *On Point: Journal of Army History,* Army Historical Foundation. Vol. 20(Winter 2015).

McGuire, Capt. James M. "Reconnoitering An Enemy Position." *Cavalry Journal.* Vol. LIV, no. 6 (November-December 1945).

Marks, Andrew. "The M4 Sherman Medium Tank." *On Point: Journal of Army History,* Army Historical Foundation. Vol. 19 (Winter 2014).

Seelinger, Matthew J. "The M24 Chaffee Light Tank," *On Point: Journal of Army History,* Army Historical Foundation. Vol. 22 (Winter 2017).

War Department Field Manual FM 23-80, *37-MM Gun, Tank, M5.* Washington, DC: U.S. Government Printing Office, 1942.

War Department Field Manual FM 18-5, *Tank Destroyer Field Manual: Organization and Tactics of Tank Destroyer Units,* Washington, D.C.: U.S. Government Printing Office (GPO), 1942.

War Department Field Manual FM 17-12, *Armored Force Field Manual, Tank Gunnery.* Washington, D.C.: U.S. GPO, 1943.

War Department Field Manual FM 2-20, *Cavalry Reconnaissance Squadron, Mechanized.* Washington, D.C.: U.S. GPO, 1944.

Yank magazine, June 15, 1945.

WEBSITES OF INTEREST

https://archives.library.illinois.edu/blog/poor-defense-sherman-tanks-ww2/

http://www.opcdorset.org/WestKnightonFiles/WKnighton.htm

http://en.wikipedia.org/wiki/Limey

https://www.fauquiernow.com/fauquier_news/entry/vint-hill-farms-station-day-planned-for-sunday

http://www.nsarchive2.gwu.edu

LIST OF MAPS

1. The 15th Cavalry Group Across the English Channel

2. The Cotentin Peninsula, July 1944

3. Task Force A in action near St.-Malo, France

4. The 15th Cavalry Group in Brittany

5. Action on the Crozon and Douarnenez Peninsulas

6. Overview of August 1944 advance through Brittany

7. Holland and the Battle to the Roer & Rhine Rivers

8. Path to the Rhine, into and around the Ruhr Region

(Please note: all maps above are oriented to the north.)

ACKNOWLEDGEMENTS

I wish to express special appreciation to several members of my immediate family: my two dear sisters, Patricia Gough Wilson and Mary JoAnn Gough Holley, who provided valuable information about my father's romantic pursuit of our loving mother. In addition, my talented daughter Judith Gough Leishear provided valuable graphic design assistance and prepared superb maps to accompany the narrative. Her involvement was most important as it served to dispel her early childhood notion that her father's heaving shelves of military history books identified him as a "war mongrel."

In addition, I owe a debt of gratitude to my sister-in-law, Lise Swinson Sajewski, who patiently edited my early draft of this work. Likewise, I wish to thank my cousin Teri Gough Seeman, who shared with me her research of our Gough family heritage. I am also grateful for the assistance of my late-Aunt Teresa Olivier Hula and my cousin Kathryn ("Kay") Hula Shrout for their careful compilation of my maternal family history.

Furthermore, my former colleague, Veterans Law Judge George Senyk, deserves thanks for translating from Cyrillic to English the signature of the Soviet radioman who accompanied Dad's unit in Germany near the end of the war.

Also deserving particular thanks are two old friends, Joe Inge and "OT" Crowther, who served on active duty with many other brave warriors, faithfully watching over the East-West German border at the Fulda Gap during the Cold War. They very generously allowed me to pick their brains on occasion as to various U.S. Army armor branch methods and procedures. Both are alumni of the Virginia Tech Corps of Cadets (VTCC) from Company G, 2nd Battalion, and the Classes of 1969 and 1970, respectively.

Likewise, worthy of exceptional notice is another very good friend, my self-appointed literary advisor Roger Spence from Squadron C and the VTCC Class of 1970. While serving on active duty during the Vietnam era, he gallantly defended Davis-Monthan Air Force Base in Arizona from enemy ground attack. His steadfast enthusiasm and occasional badgering played a major role in my completion of this work.

Also warranting my thanks are the excellent public servants at the National Archives and Records Administration in College Park, Maryland, as well as Col. Matthew Dawson, Dr. Arthur Bergeron, the staff at the U.S. Army Heritage and Education Center, historian Rodney Foytik at the U.S. Army Military History Institute at Carlisle Barracks, and Dr. Clay Mountcastle at the Virginia War Memorial in Richmond, who graciously reviewed my work and encouraged its publication.

Finally, I wish to recognize the most important person who shared with me the rigors of this task: my patient, loving wife and best friend, Leslie. Her unfailing support was crucial over the years it took me to complete this project. She tended to my needs and listened patiently as I read her my purple prose. Although efforts to quell my sarcasm were not entirely successful, her gentle encouragement was crucial to the very end. For that and so much more, she has my undying love and affection.

J.F.G., James City County, Virginia

ABOUT THE AUTHOR

Jerry Gough was born in Kansas and raised in Virginia. As a member of the corps of cadets, he graduated from Virginia Tech with a bachelor's degree in economics. Along with many others in the VTCC Class of 1969, he accepted a commission as second lieutenant in the U.S. Army Reserve.

He earned a law degree from the University of Richmond, completed Infantry Officer Basic at Fort Benning, Georgia, and performed reserve training as a rifle platoon leader with infantry units in the Maryland and Virginia Army National Guard. Following a branch transfer to the Judge Advocate General's Corps in the mid-1970s, he became a military lawyer; after completing the Command and General Staff College Officer's Course, Lt. Col. Gough finished his twenty-two years in the army reserve as Deputy Center Judge Advocate at Walter Reed Army Medical Center.

A member of the Virginia State Bar, his civilian legal career included senior attorney positions in the Office of General Counsel, U.S. Department of Veterans Affairs, and at the VA's Board of Veterans' Appeals in Washington, D.C. He completed his thirty-year career as a Veterans Law Judge, retiring in 2003.